Without Democracy
1815–1914

Second Edition

Blackwell Classic Histories of England

This series comprises new editions of seminal histories of England. Written by the leading scholars of their generation, the books represent both major works of historical analysis and interpretation and clear, authoritative overviews of the major periods of English history. All the volumes have been revised for inclusion with the series and include updated material to aid further study. *Blackwell Classic Histories of England* provides a forum in which these key works can continue to be enjoyed by scholars, students and general readers alike.

Published

Roman Britain
Third Edition
Malcolm Todd

England and Its Rulers: 1066–1272
Second Edition
M. T. Clanchy

Church and People: England 1450–1660
Second Edition
Claire Cross

Politics and Nation: England 1450–1660
Fifth Edition
David Loades

Politics Without Democracy: 1815–1914
Second Edition
Michael Bentley

Forthcoming

Crown and Nobility: England 1272–1485
Second Edition
Anthony Tuck

POLITICS WITHOUT DEMOCRACY 1815–1914

Second Edition

Perception and Preoccupation in British Government

Michael Bentley

BLACKWELL
Publishers

The right of Michael Bentley to be identified as author of this work has been asserted in accordance with the Copyright, Designs and Patents Act 1988.

First published by Fontana 1984
Second edition published by Fontana Press 1996
Reissued by Blackwell Publishers Ltd 1999

2 4 6 8 10 9 7 5 3 1

Blackwell Publishers Ltd
108 Cowley Road
Oxford OX4 1JF
UK

Blackwell Publishers Inc.
350 Main Street
Malden, Massachusetts 02148
USA

British Library Cataloguing in Publication Data

A CIP catalogue record for this book is available from the British Library.

Library of Congress Cataloging-in-Publication Data

Bentley, Michael, 1948–
    Politics without democracy, 1815–1914 : perception and preoccupation in British government / Michael Bentley. — 2nd ed.
        p.   cm. — (Blackwell classic histories of England)
    Includes bibliographical references and index.
        ISBN 0–631–21812–2 (alk. paper). — ISBN 0–631–21813–0 (pbk: alk. paper)
        1. Great Britain—Politics and government—19th century.
        2. Great Britain — Politics and government — 20th century.   I. Title.
    II. Series.
    JN216. B46   1999
    320.941'09'034—dc21   99–26095
                                                                      CIP

Typeset in 10.5 pt on 12.5 pt Sabon
by Kolam Information Services Pvt. Ltd, Pondicherry, India

Printed in Great Britain by TJ International Ltd, Padstow, Cornwall

This book is printed on acid-free paper

TO SIR GEOFFREY ELTON
(1921–1994)

Contents

Acknowledgements

Professor Geoffrey Elton asked me to write this book and to him go my first thanks for his kindness and encouragement. Maurice Cowling and my colleagues Clyde Binfield and John Stevenson have read all or part of the book and improved it, though none is responsible for any errors it may still contain. My wife Jane helped me with the task of proof-reading. I must also thank the University Research Fund of my own university for financial help during the preparation of the book.

I have made considerable use of research theses, and benefited immeasurably from the work of other scholars. Locating the authors of completed theses often proves difficult and I should like to apologize here for any inadvertent trespassing on copyright. All material from theses has been acknowledged in the notes and a full list of the studies I have used appears on pages 307–8. When citing other sources, I have tried to avoid clogging the text with references by introducing them only for direct quotations and points of special importance. In order to help the eye traverse a text that includes many references to titles, institutions and legislation, I have also avoided the use of initial capital letters except where doing so seemed ambiguous or eccentric.

MICHAEL BENTLEY
University of Sheffield
January 1984

It is a pleasure to acknowledge the valuable help of Andrea Green-grass in preparing the Second Edition of this book.

M. B.
St Andrews
November 1995

Some Places

Introduction to the First Edition

At no time during the period discussed in this book did Britain experience democracy. At no time, equally, were politicians unconscious of its existence as an inspiration, a dismal inevitability, or a remote and controllable tendency. Yet the implications of this dialogue for nineteenth-century political history frequently disappear in the ironing-out of complication in 'high politics' by historians seeking something more fundamental – an ultimate core of *Realpolitik* that turns out, on inspection, to look very like the history of working-class supremacy. It is as though the explanation of political developments should be seen to rest, beneath the skirts of hierarchy, on the discreet power of the masses (untried but insurmountable) against which the behaviour of politicians must be set in order to be made intelligible. I have chosen to ground this book in a different disposition. For the assumption here will be that the history of Britain's governing classes provides a theme with its own richness and importance; and that political understanding may begin, not only with a knowledge of labour history or a conceptualization of 'class struggle', but also with a view about what politicians believed themselves to be doing and an identification of those perspectives that informed their judgement of objectives and priorities.

Convincing answers to these questions rarely emerge from *Hansard* or the record of any other political institution. Consequently, although the House of Commons, House of Lords, the monarchy, the cabinet, the civil service and the political parties all appear regularly in this book, none comprises its subject. Instead, the centre of attention will be the centre of attention: we shall consider *preoccupation*. Any given moment in cabinet-level politics presented its nineteenth-century practitioners with a handful of perceived problems. They might take the form of 'issues' which had 'come on' or erupted unexpectedly; they might reflect strategic calculations about party policy or electoral difficulties; they might concern more cosmic anxieties about property or agriculture. These problems were rarely perceived to carry equal weight. It therefore says little of the politicians' thought-world if one announces that governments feared revolution

in the cities or Home Rule for Ireland if the material surviving from
the period suggests that only one or two of their members did and
that the rest spent more time worrying about an impending financial
deficit, or the intractability of the Afghans, or the government's
vulnerability in county seats, or the rumours that Gladstone had
become a Roman Catholic. There exists, that is to say, a scale of
political engagement that requires historical calibration. This brief
survey of more than a century's preoccupations can hardly bring to
the task a specialist's fine-tuning; but an overview may lend perspective to those readers seeking a general introduction to the character of
high politics in Britain through the transition from oligarchy to
democracy.

Politicians' lives often amount to one damned thing after another;
and my commission has indeed been to write a narrative history. In
order to prevent a degeneration into mere sequence, therefore, I have
spent some time in each chapter standing back from the flow of
events to try to anchor themes and developments in their wider
setting. Elsewhere the pace quickens of necessity as we follow men
cursed with the responsibility of governing through their problems
and turns of fortune as they saw them. To chart their navigation from
nineteenth-century published documents that tell as much of their
editors as of their subjects may offend purists for whom an immer-
sion in archives remains *de rigueur*, but then the purpose here is a
modest one: to give a reader the flavour of nineteenth-century politics
and a contour-map for his or her understanding of a century's transformation. Modern research in any case supplies its own correctives
and I have made use of them where doing so would not drain the
personality of the book into a bloodless synthesis. A second difficulty
arises in the level of prior knowledge it seems reasonable to assume. I
have attempted to construct a narrative that will attract the serious
student without overwhelming the interested general reader; and one
casualty of this procedure becomes obvious in the number of names
that jostle one another in an account which seeks authenticity but has
not time enough to explain every person it includes. A glossary of
some of those names appears at the end of the book to help remedy
that difficulty and add another dimension to the text. A map of
political place-names has also been included (gross in its mention
of some very well-known towns) to encourage those whose sense of
geography never matched their interest in history.

This book has been written to be read rather than 'used' because its
purpose is cumulative. For within the story told here – and sometimes
between the lines – one can trace an evolution that displays many
facets. And whether one's interest lies in the history of cabinet

government, or the Liberal party, or the churches, or economic pressures, or the empire, or the intelligentsia, or the influence of political personalities, that evolution will best impress itself against an enlarging conception of the period as a whole. Since I have enjoyed communicating my view of Victorian and Edwardian politics, moreover, I hope that some zest will carry over into the minds of those who read it, refresh their image of this richest of centuries and stimulate further curiosity in its mysteries and delights. The years of Canning and Peel, of Gladstone and Asquith, deserve some release from that crippling consciousness of gravity heaped on them by their evangelists.

Introduction to the Second Edition

Revising the ideas and prose of a decade ago has underlined a number of lessons: the transitoriness of historical judgement; the place of intellectual fashion in the writing of books; the imponderability of one's future state of mind; the crux of context in determining how we see the past. So powerful do these constraints appear that I was left often thinking that the only way to 'revise' an overview of a century is to re-write the whole thing and do it in a different way. Sheer impediments of time and inclination in a congested professional life ruled out that possibility. An alternative, and one that would have made very few demands, would have lain in simply updating the bibliography while reissuing the rest. The problem there, of course, is that the reader is left stranded between the sophistication of the apparatus and the barbarity of the text. Perhaps one should avoid either extreme and seek a *via media*; this at least is what I have tried to do. The operation has involved three discernible tasks. First I have read through the whole of the text and reformed or added sentences where the meaning of the original seemed elusive or elliptical. I have taken the opportunity, secondly, to add a few references and quotations where doing so seemed to illustrate better the point under discussion, especially where primary sources have come into print since 1984. And finally I have gone back to the criticisms of reviewers and tried to incorporate their observations, when doing so would not alter the basic character of the book, and to correct mistakes identified by others when doing so would not make the text more erroneous than they had deemed it in the first place.

These are not high-level tasks but I was surprised at the difficulties to which they gave rise and particularly so in two respects. Readers will notice in the original Introduction that the book had been conceived as a narrative: it sets out to tell the unfolding story of nineteenth-century politics by concentrating on the preoccupations of those most centrally concerned. Now 'narrative' has undergone a revolution in its reception and understanding over the last decade, not least through the reflective work of Hayden White and Paul Ricoeur.[1] Professional historians have become more aware of the special opportunities and implications surrounding narrative form and it has certainly occurred to me more than once in thinking about *Politics Without Democracy* that a narrative can be re-told or re-written as an entire story but not re-directed from within while retaining the original shape and plot. It is a simple matter to delete a sentence and substitute a 'better' one. A few pages later, however, it becomes clear that the original sentence had a role to play in the later account whose sentences now in turn require amendment. Yet, in changing those, the mind is carried back to a remark in a previous chapter where the text had been made to anticipate developments, binding events together over time, 'colligating' them, as W. H. Walsh used to say.[2] A single tugged thread can cause the entire fabric to unravel. No matter how misconceived or 'untrue' the story has been made to appear, its interleaved character will always work against pasting in new material or snipping away at the old.

Some reviewers found the particular story presented here misconceived and untrue. Indeed some came close to passion about it. Their close readings have often proved very helpful in attempting this revision: critics identified errors of fact or failures of understanding in certain sections of the account and part of my task has involved me in trying to correct those mistakes for this new edition. But others became aggrieved about 'mistakes' which turned out, when one actually went back to the text, to be contentions that they simply happened to disbelieve. Sometimes they were right to do so: I disbelieved them as well. But they had not read or failed to see the point of the Introduction to the first edition which asserted without ambiguity that this volume had always been intended to be viewed as a study of *perception*, of how contemporary politicians saw their world. *Politics Without Democracy* gives an account of what contemporaries thought was happening around them. It arranges the history around their judgement of priorities and values. It says that the British Empire was boring, not because it was, but because our sources tell us that this is how many senior parliamentarians viewed it. It dwells on Lord Randolph Churchill's private life, not because the author is more interested in it than (say) the dynamics of the British economy, but because the people he is writing about unquestionably were. Critics of the account stand on impeccable ground if they wish to deny that the charting of contemporary perceptions has any historical value and to argue, therefore, that the book should never have been written. They depart from it when they permit the premise and then pepper the project for prosecuting its own self-declared logic.

Travelling around the country I discover that the book is much used in universities and sixth forms and it has been greatly encouraging to see that the death of political history has been exaggerated. One of my initial worries had concerned the allusiveness of the text: I had felt some anxiety for young readers new to the period or for general readers unfamiliar with the nineteenth century. The concern seems to have been unfounded and readers tell me that they find their way around the book without difficulty. Other forms of reception ought to have been easier to predict. The early 1980s perhaps saw the last throes of a rather wooden form of 'class analysis' which the book's thesis did not appease nor its tone conciliate. At any rate, some took offence at an argument that seemed to exclude the working class and women from the discussion and concentrate to a distorting extent on what happened 'at the top'. It was felt that the book looked at the world from the 'top down'; it should have examined it from the 'bottom up'. These responses had dominated political history during the 1960s, especially the 'labour history' variety. People went to the *New Left Review* for improvement from Perry Anderson, E. P. Thompson and Louis Althusser; history had a '1968' level of conviction and inflammation. (I write this in a mood of middle-aged nostalgia rather than cynicism: if only the young of the 1990s could inflame themselves about something.) What that often intelligent discussion frequently left behind it, however, was a soft-centred image of how British politics functioned – one that alleged conviction at the top and 'influence' from below without actually demonstrating it from historical evidence. More than that, its proponents seemed to reject a concentration on cabinet ministers out of an ethical huffiness over great subjects and causes and communities. The fear seemed to be that history would lose its seriousness of purpose and degenerate into the reporting of 'gossip'. Its authors would abandon the wider social and economic picture as they became a sort of retrospective *paparazzi*, turning (as one great observer of historical work was heard to remark) into a fraternity of 'boudoir pimps'.

I thought this view dim-witted in 1984 and I find it just as absurd now. But behind its blandishments one could construct a rather stronger critique than most of its upholders identified. The point that can be made tellingly about this book is that it contributed to the very structuralism whose implications it sought to attack. Few people could see in 1984 – I certainly did not – the degree to which not only marxist analysis but virtually all forms of systematic social science would run into crisis by the end of the decade, far less the collapse of the great tyrannies that had so often used their language of certainty as a form of licence. In the light of a decade's experience, perhaps the book could have been more inclusive in its categories without collapsing into the slush of 'society' so beloved of 1960s and 70s academia. But, again, this says little beyond the truism that all books start from somewhere and that we are not now where this book started. If one were to do it again, then some of the shape and forms of analysis would doubtless take a different turn. Not that the centre of attention would shift very much, because I defend the propositions contained in this book and still find them relevant to understanding how modern British politics works.

For the purpose of this edition I have revised the 'Further Reading' section but have left the primary sources and list of research theses as they stood since the original text was based principally on them. I have not thought it worthwhile to hunt out all those instances in which unpublished work in 1984 has now appeared in books and learned journals, though the Further Reading section contains some important examples of this occurring. Scholars wishing to follow through the work of authors unpublished in 1984 and referred to here should go to a comprehensive bibliographical aid such as the Royal Historical Society's *Bibliography of British History*, volume 5 (1815–1914), edited by John Stevenson and myself and to be published by Oxford University Press.

Through the last months of his life, Geoffrey Elton expressed his pleasure that this book would soon be back in the bookshops in its new form. I cannot now give him a copy as I had hoped to do. This edition is dedicated, therefore, to his memory.

M. B.
January 1995

Part I

Pressure from Without
1815–65

The Transformation of Party

Politicians and the post-war environment

Moscow saved, Prussia liberated, Napoleon surrounded: the European war had reached its end-game by the beginning of 1814. Yet prospects of a final peace gave politicians few grounds for excitement or relief over the next twelve months. Napoleon had become so deep a stain in the current consciousness that the Emperor's miraculous return to fight was somehow less disorienting than his disappearance. Running the war again would prove cripplingly expensive, that seemed clear; but at least it meant doing what politicians had been doing for a period now of more than twenty years – which covered the political apprenticeship and education of most of those in positions of power as the Napoleonic wars drew to their close. It meant a style of leadership which a wartime House of Commons had little option but to tolerate and a control of social mechanisms which had shown their effectiveness since the late 1790s in shackling unrest and rebellion. For all their carnage, the months of Quatre Bras and Waterloo impinged on politicians as a last moment of normality and familiar horizons. Henceforward governments would have to live with expectations and pressures which previously they had suppressed or ignored. Its central practitioners, moreover, would need to recover memories of a political nation which middle-aged men had not seen since they were adolescents.

That these images of the 1780s and 1790s lacked relevance in postwar Britain seems obvious to the modern eye but contemporaries responded to a closer context. There was a natural tendency among the politically experienced to look for a present that resembled a known and successful past: as the 1870s would exhume the dead Palmerston, so Pitt's domination of British politics between 1784 and 1801 offered the best available definition of statesmanship and ordered tranquillity; and though he died in 1806 Pitt left among many of his contemporaries – some of whom were to play major roles in British politics through the 1810s and 1820s – a mental reference-point of luminous importance. This suggested to post-war politicians the smallness of their leaders. 'We want another Pitt,' the Tory peer Lord Redesdale wrote in 1820, 'but where is he to be found?'[1] Even the former Prince Regent, who had become George IV on his father's death in 1820, was prepared to use the man who had thwarted his ambitions in the 1780s as a yardstick for the present prime minister, Lord Liverpool, and his endlessly speechifying colleagues. This looking backwards for successful formulae reappeared in British politics at a number of points, as we shall see. Not least, it helped to form politicians' judgements of how society had changed since 1793.

Some impressions of significant social change unquestionably struck those in power. These politicians had become the first generation of political leaders to possess statistical evidence supporting the hypothesis of an explosive rise in population, together with a recently announced doctrine informing them why they ought to be alarmed about it. The first national censuses, of 1801 and 1811, had provided unassailable proof of a sharp upswing in population; and this at a moment when Thomas Malthus's *Essay on Population* (1798) was no longer seen as economic astrology but rather as a conventional wisdom about the inevitability of famine unless population could be controlled. Fears of this kind had helped the acceleration of agricultural enclosure after 1801 and had prompted the government's interest in pressing farmers to bring marginal land under the plough. Because the power structure was dominated by men who owned and exploited land, agriculture and its problems were all too familiar within political circles. The peacetime danger, indeed, lay in their lending the agricultural interest a disproportionate importance in the economy as a whole.

Yet if landed opinion held a powerful grip on political leadership, there had evolved an impression that 'public opinion' amounted to something more than the farmers' voice. A respectable urban public had been acknowledged and addressed – the use of the term 'middle class' dates from about 1812 – and was broadly identified in the newspaper-readers whose growing number found a reflection in rising sales of stamped newspapers in the first decade of the century. The circulation of newspapers through the post, their availability for the price of a cup of coffee in the London coffee shops or in provincial taverns, made their tuning and exploitation a *sine qua non* for all political managers. Judgements about the limits and operations of public opinion (and of the 'constitution' generally), made by those who believed themselves to be in control of them, often appear, in retrospect, anachronistic, short-sighted and arbitrary. They derived, however, partly from a range of intermeshing assumptions about order, property and religion; and partly from observation of how British institutions functioned. Many questions concerning the stability and permanence of these institutions afforded no simple answer in 1815.

Even after a century and a half it remains difficult to locate changes in Britain's political arrangements in their last thirty years of existence before the structural reforms of 1832. One says 'arrangements' rather than 'system' because, despite the willingness of many historians to discuss what they term 'the unreformed system', that is precisely what it was not. What existed in 1815 must be viewed as historical sediment and not as any schematic design. The combination of King, Lords and Commons had its theorists but no clear origin; the *montage* of constituencies and franchises with their archaic boundaries and qualifications will be traced in no medieval cartulary or Palladian plan; the innumerable points of colour and texture which presented themselves to contemporaries had a cumulative past but only the beginnings of a history. This accumulated precipitate – the 'cake of custom', as Bagehot would later call it – formed the medium in which politicians acted, and informed the perspectives of those outside the political nation. It mattered that politicians carried in their minds an optimistic sense of constitutional progress, just as it mattered that working-class radicals often believed that Britain had enjoyed universal male suffrage until the fifteenth century.[2] But arrangements that lack form require nothing formal to change them. It was not impossible for the political structure of the late eighteenth century to undergo subtle gravitational shifts and to register, in its own time and fashion, new nuances of power and pressure.

The monarchy, for example, hardly occupied after 1815 the same place within the vision of senior politicians that it had done in the days of Pitt. Four years before Waterloo the old King (always a martyr to apparent mental illness) had gone cheerfully but irredeemably mad; and the Prince Regent would never, even when exalted as George IV, attract to himself and his station the personal respect and political authority of his father. Not that George III had ever really acted as the constitutional pirate of Whig propaganda: his slide towards impotence was an absolute one, not a return to relative normality after a reign of tyranny. Carlton House still had its place, to be sure, on the maps of statesmen such as Liverpool, Canning, Goderich and Wellington, but it was clear enough that the power of the King to control cabinets and manipulate electors had receded even before the attack on sinecures and all modes of patronage which a period of economic austerity had made inevitable.[3] George IV would rant as bitterly about the emancipation of Catholics in 1829 as he had about the return of Canning to the cabinet in 1822; and he would be equally ineffective. He would, like his father, advise the House of Lords whom he took to be the King's friends. But 1829 did not echo 1783 and the Duke of Wellington was neither Fox nor North.

The House of Lords had changed too. It had entered a period, which would last until the 1840s, during which its role became indeterminate and therefore dangerous. However, in the folds of its declining power over the next hundred years would be concealed a rich history of influence which administrative historians can easily overlook. It had begun its transition from power to rank, from the pinnacle of the political structure to the apex of social hierarchy. The social composition of the peerage had not, despite the convictions of a battery of Whig dowagers, been muddied by Pitt. Certainly its numbers had greatly expanded; but most of the increase arose through promotions rather than creations. It had become useful to reinvent marquessates – most modern ones date from the 1780s – and multiply dukedoms to fill the void of patronage evacuated by waning sinecures and cash perks. The Salisbury title supplies a case in point and one relevant to our theme in this book because the 3rd Marquess would later become the most celebrated prime minister of his day. The Earls of Salisbury had descended from the second marriage of Robert Cecil, Lord Burghley, whose indispensability to Elizabeth I seemed to presage Queen Victoria's reliance on Salisbury after 1885. Pitt's elevation of the then earl to the marquessate had as much to do with the social power of Salisbury's extraordinary wife, formerly Lady Emily Hill, as with any virtues of the earl himself; but, in the process, a new power was inadvertently created.[4] A peerage now rewarded service as often as it offered a form of career promotion. When the radical Henry Grey Bennet told Creevey in 1816 that the Whig party needed 'a leader with a house and cash', he expressed an exasperation with dignity and sought efficiency.[5] One can see something beyond radical exasperation, moreover, in a decrease in the peerage's control of cabinet places after 1815. The two ministers who were commoners in 1810 had become six by 1818, a number which was to hold steady for the rest of the century.[6] Although three of the four prime ministers to hold office before 1830 sat in the Lords, commentators recognized in the Commons the centre of political ambition and executive preoccupation.

What is striking about the peacetime House of Commons is the degree to which it remained unchanged in its composition. No noticeable influx took place of army officers or merchants – two categories which might have been thought likely to exert pressure. There seems little sign of the 'hardfaced men' or the Tory majors and lieutenant-colonels who were to arrive at Westminster after the next great war a century later. Lawyers catch the eye, but then they had been powerful throughout the eighteenth century and were not to reach their greatest influence until after the reform act.[7] Family connexion remained, of course, a powerful bonding element. Pitt's dismissal of the Commons as 'a parcel of younger brothers' could smart even now: they were still young, a quarter of them twenty-five or younger on first election; they were still, many of them, cadets attached to genera rooted in the early eighteenth century and beyond, with names as familiar as parkland trees: Grenville, Fane, Osborne, Cavendish, Manners, Spencer, Howard, Finch, Lowther. Change seems more manifest, perhaps, in the function of the House of Commons and in its relation to the government of the day.

Increasingly the Commons reverted to the doing of business rather than presenting an arena for oratorical display or the consideration of local and individual complaint. An accelerating rate of executive business, prompted not least by the Union with Ireland in 1800 but also stimulated by the drive for agricultural enclosure, required the government's taking two days of each week during the parliamentary session for its own business. It lay behind the formation of a Private Bill Office in 1810; it prompted the establishment of a working library in the House of Commons in 1818. It found no response, however, in the timing and extent of parliamentary sessions which remained as fixed and circumscribed a component of the parliamentarian's calendar as the Glorious Twelfth and Easter. As one MP explained in 1811, it was 'inconvenient for the Irish members to come till after Christmas, and it was inconvenient for the English members to sit after Midsummer'.[8] A pressure that was growing and a session that was not could promote but one result. By 1830 Croker could report to Wellington's minister Fitzgerald that 137 items of business had been transacted the previous day. 'So great a mass of business I never before saw, and it seems to increase daily.'[9]

For the average parliamentary stalwart the new environment contained much that he had known in, say, the 1790s; he might have an extra committee or two to occupy an afternoon, or notice the late-night sittings which were to become all too familiar, but little else. Cabinet ministers and other leading politicians, on the other hand, had to take note. They began to caucus before the session opened to ensure that they had 'a decided and well-considered opinion'[10] about the issues of the moment. The prevailing style of parliamentary rhetoric became gradually more unfashionable in a chamber which looked to the executive curtness of a Robert Peel rather than to the Olympian periods of George Canning. The latter, indeed, partly explained his continuing political failure during a black period at the beginning of the 1820s by referring to the irrelevance of assets acquired by a fifty-one-year-old man in a different climate: 'what does the reputation of being the First Speaker in the House of Commons do for me? Nothing. It only leads people to believe that *first speaking* is not necessary for carrying on the affairs of the government – that it is very well to have – very delightful to witness – but that business can go on very well without it. And so it can.'[11] This is not to say that parliamentary speaking had ceased to be immense and windy: a recollection of Gladstone's budget or Home Rule speeches in the later part of the century shows how far that road stretched ahead. It was rather a question of style and approach. A politician needed to cultivate, not the manner of Burke and Sheridan, but the more restrained expertise which could do a job succinctly defined by Croker in 1822, one of presenting 'that *flow* of ideas and language which can run on for a couple of hours without, on the one hand, committing the government or, on the other, lowering by commonplaces or inanities the status of a Cabinet Minister'.[12]

The language used by ministers and backbenchers received some invigoration from a sense of party. But it is important to understand that early nineteenth-century political parties were not twentieth-century institutions; indeed they hardly amounted to institutions at all. The Whig and Tory 'parties' consisted, at the parliamentary level at least, of loosely cast confederations of family groups and personal loyalties with an admixture of 'crotchets' and temperamental affinities. Their 'leaders' were not elected by the parties themselves but effectively chosen by the King when he sent for an individual to form a ministry. Once chosen, the leader selected his parliamentary leader for the House in which he, as leader, did not sit; and he appointed a few henchmen to circulate a 'whip' and try to keep the scattered troops together. Yet the division between 'Whig' and 'Tory' did not comprise the only division within parliamentary politics. It could be conflated, especially between 1812 and 1830 when one party exercised so much sway, with pro-administration and anti-administration sentiment. It could be distorted, even overridden, by the presence of skilfully manipulated issues. More profitable than a view of party as a confrontation of coherent groups is, therefore, one which stresses the relevance of party as a floating presence, sometimes central to political action, sometimes bypassed by it. A related conclusion may be that the sensitive historian will seek party in the interstices of change over time. In 1815 party played a different role from that which it assumed after 1821; in 1827 it was completely upstaged; after 1830 it returned afresh in changed costume.

Not that 'Whig' and 'Tory' seemed words without meaning among those who used them. Since 1809 Toryism had developed as a language of Pittite resistance against the enemy within, enriched with a strong flavour of soil, tenantry and aggressive churchmanship. Whiggery, on the other hand, sought cohesion in distance: a series of political disasters since 1789 rendered 1689 that much more attractive. A conviction that the Glorious Revolution had been indeed glorious offered few enough lessons for the present, however. It underpinned the cry for economical reform which appeared with new virulence after the Napoleonic war; but on parliamentary reform Whigs remained silent because they quarrelled among themselves over it. By 1815 Whiggery had become an opposition formula just as Toryism had settled into a governing style.

Enthusiasm for party was noisier and more pervasive at the hustings and in the constituencies.[13] The 658 seats of the unreformed House of Commons accommodated a disproportionately large complement of borough members returned from southern and eastern constituencies; over one half of the 417 representing English constituencies came from coastal counties from the Wash to the Severn.[14] In many of these party feelings ran strong, especially in those whose electorates were large enough to permit substantial corruption without permitting effective control by a patron, though none rivalled Westminster for its size and demotic 'scot and lot' electorate.[15] Unlike the counties, where party continuity was not a marked characteristic because of the sway of individual landed potentates and their heirs, the boroughs tended to maintain a considerable degree of party consistency when choosing new members. Yet such considerations could always pale before local interests and the rule of money. The latter could also force itself on a *soi-disant* radical like Samuel Romilly as a method of countering 'influence'. Having just bought Wareham for £3,000 in 1807, he justified himself in his diary by claiming that only money could keep a man independent of patronage.[16] Even in the counties, each of which in England returned two members before 1821, it was not unknown for an outsider to break in on powerful vested interests, as Henry Brougham did in the celebrated Yorkshire election of 1830.

Violence continued endemically in an environment of condoned corruption and open voting, but it did not leave politicians with the impression that the world was running amuck. When Castlereagh wrote to his brother in 1820 that the recent elections in Down and Derry 'were quite smooth, and cost nothing but a good dinner to friends',[17] he reflected an expectation that electorates existed to be managed and elections to be won. The politician met the people, after all, at a point where the political structure dovetailed into a tangled local hierarchy of social relations: lord lieutenant and justice of the peace, squire and parson, landlord and tenant. Patronage and favours lubricated the mechanism of 'influence' and 'interest', making a disruptive radicalism from *inside* the political structure that much more difficult to launch and sustain. We shall see that this situation had come under challenge by mid-century; but for the moment lineage, land and money put into the heads of politicians an undemanding conception of society which supplied a natural adjunct to their own preoccupations and rhythms. Note the order of appearance, for example, of the *dramatis personae* in this snippet from Lady Georgiana Sheridan's private correspondence in 1830. 'I do not yet know', she wrote to her brother, 'when I am to be married; but after I am, I go abroad for the winter to Italy and up the Rhine; that is to say, if the King does *not* die, which we daily expect he will, poor man! In that case I must go to Devonshire, to a place [her fiancé's father] has there, for he will be elected for some borough there.'[18] The mental furniture of a world like this did not attract attention from those who lived comfortably among it. As with Romilly's anxieties about his borough purchase, the radicals most sensed and resented the degree to which they found politics suffused with priorities and obligations they did not wish to recognize but found it impossible to avoid.

Men at the top of the political pyramid, on the other hand, not only accepted the constraints enforced by their precarious position but often thought them essential to civilized statesmanship. They expected, similarly, that the political landscape would follow the contours of their own year with parliament swelling and retiring with the seasons. Politics was late January or early February when parliament met; it lasted until spring or early summer. 'London is drawing to a close,' Greville recorded in July 1820: what a depth of ritual is contained in such fusions of time and place. The summer was travel (Geneva perhaps, or Paris) and the grouse-shoot in August. Autumn might mean, at a time of crisis such as in 1819, another sitting of Parliament; but usually it involved a round of pre-Christmas country-house visiting among a gallery of relations. Even in 1820, when Lord Granville thought affairs critical, ministers did not reconvene parliament, or, for that matter, remain in the capital. They were 'up, running about in every direction – the Duke of

Wellington to Chester, Bathurst to Longleat and I know not where else, Harrowby at Dawlish, and letting the K[ing] himself go to Brighton, leaving everything at sixes and sevens, and trusting to live through the next month as they can, till the meeting of Parliament brings on the great crisis'.[19] Somehow crises had to hold off till a month or so after Christmas which was usually spent quietly with close family or *en masse* as at Chatsworth. The end of the year allowed a moment's pause before the next wave. It left time also for letter writing. Many of the more reflective and strategic statements in the correspondence of nineteenth-century politicians bear a date between Christmas Eve and New Year's Day.

What did they write about? The question has no historical point as it stands; politicians filled their letters with a dense texture of events and opinions unavoidable among important men caught up in national concerns. Beneath the surface, however, a frequent theme requires comment. For the cumulative impression presented by correspondence is that of a closed world whose criteria for testing relevance and significance often seem odd. A rarefied atmosphere of job-filling and job-seeking could produce, over a long period, an atrophied sense of proportion and a readiness to see a storm in every teacup. Accompanying it in so personalized and competitive an environment was the perception that crucial agencies of change lay in decrepitude, disease and death. Like the closed autocracies of the twentieth century, the early nineteenth-century cabinet shows a bizarre concern with the personal health of its functionaries. There was nothing singular in a general rumour in 1816 that many of the cabinet were unwell; nothing remarkable in the dispersion of the information that the prime minister's pulse 'was forty in March, fifty when he returned from Bath and [was] now forty again'; something predictive rather than trivial in Wellington's report that Louis XVIII's face 'was like a *scab*, all broke out and blotched'.[20] Mr Speaker's erysipelas, the precise number of leeches attached to the temples of the Duke of Clarence during the Catholic crisis of 1829, the bleedings (with weight and volume) of the King and Duke of Wellington: all claimed comment for the changes which they portended. Affliction, unlike so much else in this political world, could not be controlled or even bought. It was indeed damned hard, as Lord Lambton had been heard to mutter, that a man with eighty thousand a year could not sleep.

The perspectives of this compressed community carried across, moreover, into its perception of the body politic. A natural and wholesome condition, free from disease, agitation or (a favourite term) inflammation was the objective. In the political nation as in political man, fear ran at its strongest about what could not be reduced to human control. And in the mind of Robert Banks Jenkinson, second Earl of Liverpool, the section of the body politic most patently inflamed in 1815 was not that part of it that lay within the pale of the constitution but rather the part that lay beyond.

Insurrection, containment and the cabinet (1815–20)

In the three years since Liverpool had become prime minister, following the assassination of his predecessor Spencer Perceval at the hands of a madman in May 1812, he had shown himself heir to an existing style of government rather than a man determined to create a new one. His cabinet exhibited as much as any since 1806 the imprimatur of Pitt: only the names had changed as ennoblement took its course. Henry Addington, prime minister for some three years between Pitt's two terms, was now (as Lord Sidmouth) home secretary in a cabinet led by the man who (as Lord Hawkesbury) had been his foreign secretary. The present foreign minister, Viscount Castlereagh, likewise owed his first advancements in British politics to Sidmouth, as did the new chancellor of the exchequer, Nicholas Vansittart. Some of the more established ministers claimed intimacy with Pitt himself: Bathurst, Harrowby, Mulgrave and Lord Melville. Yet so many years had passed since the late 1790s and 1800s that some of these men had themselves become patrons of a second generation. Thus John Wilson Croker, the ministerial diarist, was very much the protégé of Wellesley-Pole, master of the mint and elder brother of the Duke of Wellington; Frederick Robinson, a future prime minister, was similarly the creature of Castlereagh. These continuities offer more than antiquarian interest, moreover. They help to explain the evolution of politics after 1815 and the responses of government to external stimuli. For then, as now, childhood could prove an influential father.

Apart from comparative newcomers such as Robinson and Croker, most ministers had been born in the early years of the reign of George III, except for a couple who had been born even earlier – the timeless Sidmouth ('so calm, so just, so sage, so fearless')[21] and Lord Chancellor Eldon, sixty-four in 1815, whom the Prince Regent liked to call 'Old Bags'. Though these men owned estates, their acres were not so broad as those of high Whiggery, notwithstanding the presence of magnates like Westmorland, Buckinghamshire and Harrowby. They tended to have matriculated in the staff colleges of political ambition – especially Christ Church, Oxford, and St John's College, Cambridge – and to have congenital connexions with the world of administration through their parents' involvement with the House of Commons, the law, the army, the diplomatic service or the East India Company. If not born to land, they could buy it (as Eldon had done to camouflage a coal background in Newcastle), or more often marry it. Yet in men hoping to direct a still highly localized polity, their experience remained geographically very limited. They had Scottish and Irish trojan horses respectively in Melville and Castlereagh, though neither could inform the cabinet accurately about potential instability in those countries. Mulgrave and Robinson had estates in Yorkshire, but it was the county society of Scarborough, Ripon and Thirsk rather than the grey perspectives of the West Riding that they knew there. For the rest, the home counties, the south-east and the west country filled their horizons; and this at a moment when the axis of working-class unrest and political radicalism had swung sharply north and west towards centres like Manchester and Glasgow. Nor were they aware at first hand of the sufferings of agricultural communities situated in the poor soil areas of East Anglia, those whose 'bread or blood' slogans would have to be answered during the riots of 1816.

The immediate future was dominated, of course, by none of these places nor even London itself, but rather by Vienna and Paris. Castlereagh went off to the French capital in the early autumn of 1815 where he helped establish the Quadruple Alliance of Britain, Russia, Prussia and Austria; and contrived at all costs to avoid entanglements of a more positive kind which might drag Britain into another war on the continent. Danger presented itself in the newly created Holy Alliance of the reactionary monarchs of Russia, Austria and Prussia – a 'piece of sublime mysticism and nonsense', in Castlereagh's memorable phrase – which Britain refused to contemplate joining. When the peace treaties with France were signed in Paris on 20 November, therefore, a treaty of alliance based on the Vienna settlement, and excluding France, was reaffirmed and the idea of reducing international tension through frequent 'congresses' again stressed. So far as France herself was concerned, the settlement suited British interests precisely, as the prime minister assured Bathurst a few weeks earlier; it was 'as *severe upon France* as would in any way be consistent with maintaining Louis XVIII upon the throne'.[22] Keeping the French king in place had been a major preoccupation since Napoleon's abdication in the spring of the previous year; and with its success Liverpool and his cabinet could look forward to a quiet period in foreign affairs and an end to the British military presence in France after the three-year occupation prescribed by the treaties. By then the army might well be needed at home where there was already trouble enough.

Some economic dislocation at the end of a long war, compounded by the effects of the American war recently terminated in the Treaty of Ghent,[23] had been inevitable in a trading nation. The artificial stimulation of agriculture and industry through governmental initiatives could only produce instability when the government terminated them. The creation of paper currency could only produce savage deflation when attempts were made to re-establish parity with gold. The stifling of imports by Napoleon's embargoes and war with the United States between 1812 and 1814 inevitably stimulated fears for an unprotected economy when those constraints ceased to operate. Extra pressure had been exerted on the agricultural sector, moreover, by good harvests in 1813 and 1814. From the government's point of view, the resulting reduction in bread prices helped quiet the Luddite agitation in northern and midland towns; but a disastrous collapse of corn prices – the average price of corn fell by virtually a half between 1813 and 1815 – inspired a simultaneous attack from the rear in a desperate farming lobby pressing for a protective tariff. A conversation had opened between rural producer and urban consumer, neither of whom would be happy unless the other was not. It would form the continuo of Tory politics until 1846.

There was nothing new in the idea of a corn law, for repeated attempts had been made to regulate the export and import of cereals. The law of 1815 was distinctive partly in its high threshold, which brought it into operation when corn prices reached as high as 80 shillings per quarter, and partly in its abandonment of duties and the substitution of total prohibition of imports when the average domestic price crossed the threshold. The bill need not have caused problems in parliament since the opposition there consisted, like the government, of landowners – though some of them offered opposition on behalf of their constituents whose petitions against the bill they duly presented, and some, like Sir Robert Peel, had enough knowledge of industrial areas to oppose on that account.[24] The problem lay rather with the London mobs, fired by the oratory of Sir Francis Burdett and the radicals, and it showed itself during March in a series of attacks on ministers. Castlereagh was chased all the way to his London residence, windows were broken at the House of Commons, while Robinson's house became the scene of a violent siege. 'There is a great clamour out of doors,' the young secretary for Ireland, Robert Peel, wrote on 7 March, 'and last night in the neighbourhood of the House of Commons we were indebted to the military for the preservation of peace. Some members were most vehemently hissed and hooted, and some did not make their escape without the loss of half their coats and a little personal injury.'[25] But far from preventing the government from pressing on with the legislation, the main effect of the disturbances was to make it more difficult for the government to change course and appear to back down in the face of popular lawlessness. Certainly there is little evidence of ministerial nervousness over the agitation; and by the end of the session Liverpool was telling his old Christ Church friend George Canning that the country had been reunited by Napoleon's return. True, the effects of banking collapses that autumn caused some worries for farmers for whom credit remained critical; but some grounds for cheerfulness appeared because sedition had not manifested itself on a broad scale in the towns. In leaving the calling of parliament until 1 February, a later date than usual, the cabinet radiated optimism if not confidence.

Ministers rightly identified finance as their key problem but the difficulties ran deeper than they knew. When they had attempted to continue the property tax into peacetime, despite their original determination to relinquish it, they had succeeded only because Napoleon's 'hundred days' had offered a plausible pretext. Since then a national movement against war taxation had gathered momentum. It was aimed, moreover, not merely at the property tax[26] but also at the malt tax and (after much Whig fanning of the flames) the income tax. In the one session of 1816 Liverpool's government lost divisions in the House of Commons on all these issues as uncommitted Tories deserted him. The Whig opposition, and especially their brilliant rhetorician Brougham, received a timely fillip from Liverpool's embarrassment and pressed him strongly on what had come to be called 'the ground [of] ... Retrenchment – in all ways, with ramifications in the Royal family, property tax, jobs of all sorts, distresses of the landed interest, & c.',[27] and the government was left with little to say. Liverpool did his best to sound trenchant, attacking both the Regent's civil list and the army. But in full view of a country feverishly against what today would be termed public expenditure, little political applause could be gained. His one satisfaction in the first half of the year was a private one; he introduced his friend Canning into the cabinet when the Earl of Buckinghamshire fell from his horse in the spring and vacated the Board of Control. This left Castlereagh, with whom Canning had fought his famous duel in 1809, in low spirits, coming as it did on top of failures to excite the House of Commons with his continental achievements at a moment when they seemed obsessed with economics at home.

In June it rained. And as week after week of wet weather drenched and rotted the corn in the fields, the government reconsidered the response of the towns to soaring corn prices. The thought was not lost on Sidmouth whose Home Office spies had been supplying him with lurid reports of rebellious activity during the previous winter. During August he wrote to his brother:

> The distress in some parts is extreme, but the disposition to disturbance less than might have been expected. There is a general persuasion that the want of demand and employment arises from unavoidable causes, and that no means are neglected to mitigate its effects. But it is to the autumn and winter that I look with anxiety.[28]

The rapid development of Hampden Clubs and similar organizations during the autumn, plus the launching of Cobbett's unstamped *Political Register* in November, apparently justified Sidmouth's fears. Consequently, two meetings at London's Spa Fields on 15 November and 2 December 1816 – especially the second, with its looting of a gunsmith's shop and the (accidental) killing of a man – impinged on a government already concerned about insurrectionary tendencies and actively considering the introduction during the next session of parliament of legislation to curb what Eldon called 'mischief'.

What the government had it in mind to do is unclear. Sidmouth and Eldon knew what they wanted, but historians consistently write about the cabinet politics of these years as though remarks by the home secretary and lord chancellor supply the only primary evidence to be considered when thinking about insurrection as a high-political concern. When the Whig Tom Grenville wrote contemptuously of 'the Sidmouthery',[29] he amused himself with a distortion which retrospectively we need not share. The home secretary was, after all, an authoritarian whose mind took its colour from the reports of his spies and *agents provocateurs*. Eldon was an aged, retributive Anglican with a residue of the sour border Presbyterianism in which he had been brought up: a world in which hanging and flogging lent sinners 'that sense of degradation and regret . . . which is a great security, with men as well as dogs . . .'[30] Others in the cabinet felt less obsessed. Needless to say they worried about insurrection, but they worried about other things as well, especially the continuing problem of governing a country and managing the House of Commons with little money and with virtually no chance of raising any. So when, a fortnight before the 1817 session opened, we find the Whig activist George Tierney telling his friends that the ministers were 'at the wits end' and that 'all the lower followers of Government [were] desperate',[31] it becomes important to remember that it was revenue, and not revolution, that he identified as the cause. Indeed it is noticeable that Whig aspirations in the coming session did not include the exploitation of a supposed revolutionary threat. They looked instead to the manufacture of a parliamentary majority to oust Liverpool and argued about the relative virtue of retrenchment and parliamentary reform as suitable tools for the task.

Seen in this light, it may be that the London mob's attack on the Regent's carriage as he left St Stephen's after opening parliament on 28 January 1817 concentrated ministers' minds. The incident itself was trivial; a scuffle took place in the park behind Carlton House, there was some stone-throwing, and a window was broken in the carriage. Yet a cool-headed man like Peel, who had dismissed the Spa Fields riots as 'trumpery proceedings' and protested against 'magnify[ing] a mob into rebellion', was disturbed when he watched the events of 28 January. It is likely that the government would in any case have established secret committees to inquire into the state of the country. What is plain is that in the train of the Hampden Clubs' petitions, which followed hard on the heels of the stoning incident, it moved very swiftly. Its secret committees were amply supplied with Sidmouth's Home Office evidence (a file marked 'DISTURBANCES' had been opened in the summer of 1816) and an act suspending habeas corpus with a Seditious Meetings Act quickly followed. While Sidmouth hit the ball all around the ground, Liverpool, at the other end of the wicket, stonewalled with legislation on sinecures, doggedly maintaining the second theme in the government's search for solid support.

Unbeknown to either of them, the match was all but won. At the end of the session the Grenville faction within the Whig party seceded and began to look for terms with the government; it was not a massive accretion, to be sure, but it did represent an unpleasant blow for opposition morale. In the country, too, the worst seemed over. The three major disturbances of the spring and summer – the march of the Blanketeers from Manchester and the Pentrich and Huddersfield risings – have about them an atmosphere of helpless despair rather than a presentiment of danger. The Blanketeers, so called because they carried blankets for the long march to London, were mostly turned back at Stockport; the attempt at an armed rising in Derbyshire and the West Riding never got off the ground through the treachery of Oliver the Spy (W. R. Richards) and other paid informers. Each ended in fiasco with, in the case of Pentrich, a savage postscript of execution and transportation. The government had done little to effect the improvements on which they now congratulated themselves: they owed their position to an easing economic situation (partly artificial in that the resumption of payments in gold had been deferred for two years) and to the embarrassment or helplessness of those who wished to oppose them. But Sidmouth would not have been human if he had not cherished letters like this one from Lord Exmouth in September 1817:

> In Devonshire, every article of life is falling, the panic amongst farmers wearing off, and, above all, that hitherto marketable article, discontent, is every where disappearing...In this county all is gladness at the fine prospect of an abundant harvest, and of beautiful weather to save it. I have every reason to unite my voice with my neighbours' to say we owe our present peaceful and happy prospects to your firmness and prompt exertions in keeping down the democrats.[32]

He may have suffered from optimism or stupidity, but his perception does not lose its value as an index of mood and approach. These thoughts have no less relevance to the history of opinion among Britain's elite than those jittery speculations so often quoted by labour historians as proof of a coming revolution.

Even over the winter the story of improvement continued. By the spring Liverpool was regaling the Duke of Wellington with news of strengthening revenue, agricultural recovery and flourishing manufactures. The only shadow, indeed, had been cast by the throne. For when the Regent's daughter, Princess Charlotte, died after an agonizing childbirth in November 1817, a number of ugly possibilities had asserted themselves in political circles about the future of George's already scandalous marriage. Croker had these in mind when he moaned to Peel about 'never [having] looked into a blacker political horizon than is now around us'.[33] But in the spring of 1818 Liverpool not unnaturally chose to think of other things. As he watched the tattered Whigs trying to think of something to say during the 1818 session or enjoyed the silence in the Lords when they did not turn up – according to Lord Folkestone the House was 'regularly empty till 9 or 10 o'clock on the most interesting questions'[34] – his mind must have surveyed the previous year with unalloyed satisfaction. If he had failed to become popular, he could at least hear that it was the Regent's head, and not his, that the Bread or Blood rioters demanded. If his ministers cut poor figures, then the opposition cut nothing at all. If he stood back from his situation he might even be tempted to risk a general election.

Despite the discomfiture of the Whigs and the tactical advantages which had fallen to the government, it was too much to hope that the general election of June and July 1818 would not be hotly contested. The more lively Whigs had entered a phase of democratic activity with an enthusiasm which disgusted Lady Spencer – 'clasping dirty palms', 'smacking greasy chops', and abasing their station in 'toadying our Sovereign the People'.[35] The more populous constituencies such as Westminster witnessed scenes of considerable violence; indeed even the counties were strongly contested, an unusual development in late eighteenth- and early nineteenth-century elections. From the beginning, the current ran against the government and left some ministers nervous of the loyalty of the new House. Assessing the gains and losses, one comes up against the looseness of party labels, but the historian of the election finds something like fifteen gains overall for the opposition.[36] Whigs agreed at the time, however, that they ought to be able to field at least 150 hard-core opponents of government in the new parliament. On the other hand, Liverpool had little cause for alarm. The lesson he learned from the election had nothing to do with insurrection; he simply saw that the retrenchment policy was more necessary than ever in order to avoid defeats in the House. So distant did social instability seem that habeas corpus was revived earlier in the year and the Seditious Meetings Act allowed to lapse in July. From then until the recrudescence of disturbances during the following summer the minds of ministers largely ranged elsewhere.

Much of the collective mind of the cabinet occupied itself in foreign policy in preparation for the conference of allied powers which was to meet at Aix-la-Chapelle in October 1818. For Castlereagh this was a welcome moment of status. He had been miserable since the end of 1815, first of all from his inability to hold the attention of the House (always a problem for him) and then over Canning's admission to the government in the summer of 1816 and his subsequent influence over the prime minister. At Aix, Castlereagh had the company of another political threat, the Duke of Wellington, who was himself to enter the cabinet at the beginning of 1819. So far as policy was concerned, the conference confirmed, in a secret protocol, the continuation of the Quadruple Alliance of 1815, publicly allowing France to feel that she had been included in it, and fixed on 30 November as the date on which the occupying armies would be withdrawn – a significant event, of course, for the future of domestic repression, if the government should wish to impose it. Domestic policy was similarly infolded. During the first parliamentary session of 1819 – for in this crisis year there were to be two – the cabinet thought largely about itself. A predominant difficulty, now that sedition seemed to have been stamped out, lay in whether Sidmouth ought not to be displaced in favour of Peel whom everyone, according to current rumour, believed to be chafing over Canning's inclusion. As one turns over the pages of the diary of the patronage secretary Charles Arbuthnot, this cloud dominates the horizon: one finds little here of dirty palms and greasy chops. In fact, the summer held little for either Canning or Peel. By the end of the following year the former would be out of office and, in all probability, politically finished, while Peel would not enter the cabinet until Sidmouth's resignation in 1821. But Arbuthnot was correct in his belief that the summer would bring change.

Working-class organizations had begun once again to mobilize during the previous autumn at the expiry of repressive legislation. 'Union Societies' and clubs of 'Political Protestants' spread in the north-west, industrial Yorkshire and in London. Yet the government made no response because it located its central problem in parliament and not in the country. For example, in the face of the 'clamor & popular cry' which even the Regent saw would follow the imposition of a malt duty, Liverpool went ahead, on the grounds that malt would be tolerated in the House where a property tax would not.[37] And since the government's perception of prosperity came largely from tax returns – the capacity or willingness of people to pay – they maintained themselves in something of a cocoon through the early summer of 1819. Liverpool remained, it is true, a pessimist by nature; but he now had Canning on whom he would increasingly come to rely for support in his later years. Canning himself had been disturbed by the insurrections of 1816–17 and had supported the repression but he saw better prospects now. 'We have passed the worst,' he wrote in July, 'and if this year passes over without tumult I think we are safe for the time to come.' Sidmouth, typically, knew better. Three days before Canning wrote his letter, the home secretary had issued a circular to all lords lieutenant requiring them to alert their yeomanry against coming violence.[38]

Inevitably, the St Peter's Fields district of Manchester and the bloody events that took place there on 16 August – 'Peterloo', as the battle has become known to history – are associated most readily with '1819'; the attack by yeoman cavalry and hussars on a peaceful crowd of 60,000 assembled that morning to hear Orator Hunt speak about parliamentary reform was, undeniably, an event of major significance. The military killed eleven people, sabred one hundred and forty others and left some four hundred injured. But the importance of Peterloo in the formation of government policy over the next few months can be overstressed. The decision to use force to disperse the meeting had been a local one; the early reports which reached ministers suggested that the meeting had been insurrectionary and the casualties few; there were in any case few ministers for reports to reach since many of them were abroad. Sidmouth publicly congratulated the magistrates on their prudence, and Eldon ranted about the need for legislation and the 'insanity' of everybody, moderates and radicals alike. Neither was listened to by other ministers as they returned from their holidays. The Liverpool/Canning diarchy continued in its confidence that prosperity would soon ease popular pressure. In October, Sidmouth complained bitterly that his colleagues would not heed his call for an autumn session of parliament. Eldon, meanwhile, had cracked – something usually missed by those who quote his hysterical letters as evidence of 'the government's' fears. A man rising seventy had been 'labour [ing] without ceasing from seven in the morning of the 28th October to nine at night of the 31st August'. He had carried the weight of affairs in London during the summer when most of his colleagues sought escape. He was ('I can't bear it longer') at the end of his tether.[39]

Left to themselves the Tory ministers would have muddled on without an autumn session and the repressive legislation that it produced. There seems little doubt that Liverpool would have put his faith in economic recovery and waited for the country to settle down. There is little doubt either that this course would have been dangerous for his government. All the evidence we have about potential popular insurrection points to a massive disruption in the autumn of 1819; and the cabinet was saved from the worst of it by its own ineptitude. The government's decision to remove Earl Fitzwilliam from the lord lieutenancy of Yorkshire as a reprisal for his having written a letter publicly supporting the Manchester meeting turned out to be more significant for politicians than had Peterloo itself. Those who had been cut and trampled in Manchester had no place within the political nation: Lord Fitzwilliam stood as one of its bastions. To attack a landed potentate in this way was guaranteed to draw together what had previously been the threadbare fabric of 'poor lousy whiggery'.[40] Whig unity and aggression, which the government itself had stimulated, made necessary an autumn session of parliament where the Whig attack could be met and the sedition which Whigs seemed bent on encouraging squashed. This was achieved in a series of acts – the so-called 'Six Acts' – which gave the government the powers it needed to bear down hard on the merest symptoms of trouble. By the end of the session ministers had seen off Lansdowne's motion in the Lords on the state of the country, Althorp's in the Commons trying to wangle a Select Committee and a backbench motion on the state of the manufacturing districts. When politicians broke up on 29 December there seemed no reason to reconvene until February.

Politics took a new and severe twist before then, and one which took control from the cabinet and placed it once more in the possession of chance. Not that the death of the old King altered much in itself: he had taken no part in political affairs for almost a decade. Three developments nevertheless became inevitable after 29 January. There had to be a general election because statute required one within six months of a monarch's death. There had to be a new King; and enough was known of the ways of the ex-Regent to make this a wry prospect for Liverpool and his colleagues. Third, and worst, if there were a new King there might also have to be a new Queen. This latter thought brought back the clouds observed by Croker after the death of Princess Charlotte and made 1820 a year of royal politics.

This was not an issue at the general election in February. The recent Cato Street conspiracy, which had just been detected and thwarted, seemed more urgent. Since before Christmas, a veteran of Spa Fields, Arthur Thistlewood, and about fifty supporters had waited for an uprising in the north-west with a view to mounting a *putsch* in London. When that failed to materialize they evolved the plan of assassinating the ministers at the pre-cabinet dinner on 22 February. The uprising turned into a fiasco since the conspiracy had already been penetrated by a government spy, and the authorities dealt quickly with the assault force before it attacked from its base in Cato Street, off the Edgware Road. Perhaps the efficiency of the authorities helped the government a little at the election: certainly the Whigs made only limited gains. But it is hard to see Cato Street as part of any national movement though it may have had an indirect relationship with the rising in western Scotland later in the spring.[41] Its only permanent effect on political society was to deepen the militarism of Lady Harrowby, in whose dining-room members of the cabinet were to have been decapitated. Already the attention of others had moved abroad, amid rumours that the Queen intended coming home to clear her name and claim her throne.

The Princess of Wales had left England in 1815 under the imputation that she had committed adultery – a hypocritical charge, perhaps, in view of the Regent's flexible interpretation of his marital vows, but one which her behaviour abroad, by the side of which Catherine the Great's devouring of men seemed unduly inhibited, had done nothing to quash. A secret investigation of Caroline's personal life on the continent had encouraged the new King in his determination to seek a divorce; but that would require a bill championed in parliament by embarrassed ministers who were already nervous about Caroline's popularity at home. The cabinet quickly realized that its best plan lay in preventing Caroline from coming home at all; and between March and June of 1820 all efforts were bent on furthering that object. A memorandum was concocted offering Caroline £50,000 a year if she would stay away and give up her rights as Queen. The precious document was then entrusted to Brougham and Lord Hutchinson for delivery by hand to Caroline. They lost it somewhere between London and St Omer. Farce, the flaw in so much Georgian politics, again showed through the attempts of ministers to seem in control of their collective destiny. It hardly mattered on this occasion because Caroline told her mortified visitors that she was determined in any case to come immediately to England. She arrived to a warm (and therefore worrying) reception from the populace on 5 June; and from then until the government's abandonment of its subsequent attempt to try Caroline and impose a Bill of Pains and Penalties, the 'Queen' affair became central to political speculation and continued to excite interest even when her cause faded in the new year and during her rowdy funeral in August 1821.

Of course most of the interest was simply salacious, but three aspects of the Queen's appeal made it significant for politicians. In the first place it possessed an obvious class dimension; as Eldon noted in June, the 'Queen's folks' seemed to belong to the lower orders, and a danger consequently existed that popular discontent would attach itself to the Queen's cause. It was also widespread. Although it found its strongest support in London, there developed in the later months of the year considerable provincial support for the Queen. Finally and most importantly, it crucially affected the monarchy at a time when it still exercised very considerable political power. Because of their handling of this issue, rather than because of sedition or retrenchment, the King 'dismissed' his ministers in November, indeed, before having second thoughts. 'Be assured', the Marquess of Buckingham learned from one of his spies in September, 'that the King on this subject is no less *than mad.*'[42] Politicians believed the return of Caroline to threaten them and took seriously her dovetailing into the politics of insurrection. Eldon, it is true, was dismissive in June: armed with his Six Acts he felt that the issue would die away. But others were genuinely disturbed at a development they could not control. Westmorland told Mrs Arbuthnot in August that ministers had come close to panic. Peel found the issue 'formidable' in August. Sidmouth remained anxious about the Queen until her coffin was on its way back to the continent in 1821. Wellesley-Pole fitted her into a pattern of insolence and insubordination which he took to be the ruin of the country.

Yet the minister who suffered most was Canning. Even before the eruption of the Queen affair he had chafed over his juniority at the Board of Control but Caroline's return made even that niche untenable. For his opposition to the government's harassing of Caroline, a woman with whom he had once been on close terms, had only served to confirm in the mind of the King that he must have joined her army of lovers. To this extent even the failure of the Bill of Pains and Penalties did not help Canning. He was still a minister who had earned the loathing of his sovereign and now needed to consider his position. 'I do truly believe', he had written to Huskisson from the continent in October, 'that there never fell upon a Country an evil so gratuitously mischievous, and so entirely without compensation.'[43] Liverpool had consistently refused Canning's attempts to resign since the opening of the Caroline affair. He still hoped that 'a long & thorough talk'[44] would suffice to persuade him to stay. In fact their discussion at Walmer on 7 December was inconclusive but, in view of Canning's resignation from the government a few days later, it seems a reasonable guess that, during the two hours he spent kicking along the beach by himself that morning, Canning had done some important thinking.

Party, policy and Canning (1820–26)

Canning could hardly have come under a cloud at a worse moment. The new parliament had a few more Whigs than had the old, but with insurrection shortly to be buried with the Queen, and policy turning towards that international theatre in which Castlereagh, soon to become second Marquess of Londonderry, continued supreme, the chances of an ex-minister's recovering his position must be slight. Every indication pointed – accurately, as it turned out – to a long parliament in which critics of the government would find their opposition generally ineffective and in which joining the ministry would appear a more profitable *modus operandi* than trying to beat it. Besides, Canning was growing too old for plausible ratting. 'At 51 or thereabouts', he wrote to his wife in the spring following his resignation, 'I cannot afford to hazard new experiments & new combinations... The new step – whatever it be – must be decisive for life.'[45] He had good reason to believe that the King would never have him in high office; the most he could realistically hope for as his next step was a period of distant splendour in an imperial governorship. And yet within two years he had become foreign secretary with a grip on most of the prime minister's strings, and within six he emerged as one of the most feared and despised party leaders in the history of British politics. The explanation lies in these quiet years in the first half of the 1820s, years often ignored by historians seeking to make macro-statements about the 'processes' and 'trends' on which they suppose political causation to rest. The reasons lie in policy to the extent that 'liberal Toryism' was somehow thought germane to Canning's significance. They lie far more in the party realities to which policy remained subordinate.

It seemed unlikely that the opposition would be able to help Canning in the immediate future since the Whigs had proved unable even to help themselves in the post-war years. Of late they had accomplished some sharpening of their image among the electorate. If insurrection had been an awkward issue on which to oppose the government, the opposition had at least made capital out of the administration's penury and improved its position over the government's attack on Fitzwilliam and its botching of the Queen's prosecution. By 1821 signs also existed that Whig policies might harden into a recognizable form. In particular the cause of parliamentary reform had made significant converts in the last few years. It had been, for the most part, a subterranean movement discernible in retrospect in the letters of contemporaries but less openly proclaimed at the time because of the fear that anything resembling a party manifesto on the subject would produce a split. The defection of the Grenvillites to the government in 1821, together with the granting of further seats to the Yorkshire county constituency after the Grampound corruption case in the same year, had meanwhile done much to convince the more radical Whigs that the existing framework of politics too readily helped the powerful and venal.

The Marquess of Buckingham had played no small part in fostering this impression. The idea of splitting off the Grenville faction from the Whigs had not originated with him, and Buckingham had only been won round to it by the thought that it might help him exert more leverage to gain his own precisely defined objective in securing for himself the Paris Embassy. Since then he had oscillated between threatening the government during its parliamentary difficulties in 1818–19 and hoping that Liverpool would not offer him a job during those months in 1820 when the government seemed likely to fall. Negotiations opened seriously in the autumn of 1821 – surprisingly, in view of the government's having experienced little difficulty in the House during that session – at the instigation of Castlereagh (as we shall continue to call him) who seems greatly to have overestimated the political significance of Grenville and his twenty supporters in the House of Commons.[46] By the end of the year a deal had been done:

support for the government in the House in return for a dukedom for
Buckingham and a seat in the cabinet for a Buckingham nominee,
Charles Williams Wynn. 'No small and insignificant party', an obser-
ver remarked, 'was ever bought so dear.'[47] These dealings surely
underlined Canning's sense of exclusion and humiliation; and some
Whigs hoped to exploit his anger during 1822.

Superficially the omens appeared favourable for a sustained parliamentary attack on the government since, although the worries about
insurrection had eased, the worsening economic context had stimulated agricultural (and therefore parliamentary) unrest. Indeed ever
since the boom of 1817–18 the government's economic policy had
gone badly wrong. In 1819 the decision, long deferred, to resume
payments in gold inaugurated a period of deflation just at the time
when the economy had in any case moved into recession; and a
depression which would bottom out only in the autumn of 1822
had since then caused acute hardship in the farming community. In
the four years since 1818 wheat prices had halved. Landed opinion in
parliament had inevitably put pressure on the government to cut
taxation and strengthen the corn laws, though nothing beyond promises and a select committee had resulted. But the feeling was strong
that, despite the anti-protectionist report of its select committee, the
government would be faced in 1822 with a new corn bill and given a
rough ride in the House.

A pervasive seam of opinion among country gentlemen rested on
an assumption that those in power perceived rural distress as they
did: as an evil intolerable to statesmanship whose avoidance was
central to policy. And here they were mistaken. Ministers knew
something about rural hardship, especially during the crisis year of
1821 when Cobbett and protectionist pressure groups were at their
most vociferous; but they saw general improvement where others saw
isolated good fortune. Robinson's reports of enduring prosperity on
the Lincolnshire estate he had recently inherited from his father-in-
law could blot out many dismal figures from radical activists. Sir
Walter Scott's avowals of Scottish prosperity could be spread with all
the avidity that Mrs Arbuthnot could command, supplemented, perhaps, by her own experience riding *à trois* with her husband and the
Duke of Wellington 'over the Vauxhall Bridge, by Brixton & Tooting
round to Wandsworth & home by Chelsea, a beautiful ride [!] thro' a
pretty part of Surrey all looking rich and happy altho' we are told
every day that we are ruined and starving'.[48] For government, the
country continued to be the seaworthy barque that Sidmouth had
always said it was. If the parliamentary pressure could be borne, the
reasoning ran, the wholesomeness of the rural economy would

reassert itself when conditions improved. Already the protectionist cry had been stifled to some extent by the very persistence of distress after the corn laws had closed English ports to imported wheat in 1820. So far as parliament was concerned, Liverpool expressed some worries in the autumn of 1821, but with his purchase of the Grenvillites he stood in a commanding position. The country gentlemen posed a problem during the 1822 session, to be sure, but when Arbuthnot told them that further rebellion would lead to the government's resignation and the substitution of a Whig administration, they were quick to calculate where their best chance of relief lay.

Other areas of policy had also preyed on the minds of the ministers and distracted them from agriculture. Revolutions in Spain and Naples, the passage through the House of Commons of Plunkett's bill to remove Catholic disabilities and the continuing problem of a royal presence in politics not only diverted opposition attacks but also helped to silhouette Castlereagh as the mainstay of government. With Canning gone, he wore his mantle as the sage of foreign policy, the dominant proponent of the 'Catholic' case for civil emancipation and the man whom the King most liked within an administration he had come cordially to detest. Judging from the cheers Castlereagh received at Queen Caroline's funeral in 1821 he had even become, for a moment, popular. 'He is *better* than ever', Croker wrote at the end of the year; 'that is, colder, steadier... and withal more amiable and respected.' It was as though he had gone through some odd transformation in public opinion. 'I am grown as popular in 1821,' he decided, 'as unpopular formerly.'[49] Nor was he a mere figure-head. As an Irish peer, Castlereagh sat in the House of Commons – an accident which increased his power and made it possible, for example, for him to prevent Peel's promotion to the Exchequer in 1821. He was also exalted by the patent decline of the prime minister through that year. For Liverpool had made it his duty during the last six months of 1821 to impose on the King a minister whom he was determined to reject and had incurred for his trouble what Canning called the King's undissembled, unqualified dislike. Liverpool had failed to impose Canning, moreover; and thereafter his career was never to recover. In contracting a second marriage at the age of fifty-seven, Liverpool registered a turning away from the political world which his colleagues had already perceived and remarked upon. The rest of his administration would amount to a struggle for control against tougher men.

King George's reign, on the other hand, had so far been successful, even glorious. His greatest enemy – his wife – was dead. He had been brought the news as he departed from Holyhead for his state visit to Ireland and his mourning had been understandably brief. 'The passage to Dublin', a fellow traveller noted, 'was occupied in eating goose-pie and drinking whiskey in which his Majesty partook most abundantly, singing many joyous songs.'[50] He had been out of the country for her funeral which had been insurrectionary and unpleasant. He had squashed the attempt by Liverpool to force on him the odious Canning. He had in prospect the latter's removal to somewhere far away and his own forthcoming royal visit to Scotland in the summer of 1822. Yet it was just at the point that King George seemed set to turn himself into the English Sir Walter Scott that his luck failed him and Canning's took a remarkable turn for the better. On board the *Royal George* yacht in the Leith Roads on 15 August 1822 the King received an urgent message; and this time there were to be no pies or whiskey or songs. Three days earlier, on the morning of the Glorious Twelfth, the foreign secretary had slit his own throat with a penknife.

Castlereagh had not been himself for some time. The burgeoning dementia, one perhaps associated with blackmail over a sexual awkwardness at just the moment when popular excitement ran high over the Bishop of Clogher's having recently been discovered with a guardsman, had been noticed by colleagues, especially Wellington. The suicide came nevertheless as a cataclysm. Parliament was in recess (the only redeeming feature of the event from Liverpool's point of view) and the shock and scheming of front-rank politicians therefore lie embedded in their correspondence. Until the King came back from Scotland, Liverpool locked himself away and wrote agonized notes in which figured the recurrent term 'crisis'. At the other end of the political spectrum Brougham saw similar colours. 'Put all their other men together in one scale,' he wrote to Creevey on 19 August, 'and poor Castlereagh in the other – single, he plainly weighed them down.' Where the radical judgement diverged from that of the prime minister was in its anticipation of the future. 'As for the question of his successor – who cares one farthing about it?' asked Brougham. Liverpool had a number of answers, none of which encouraged optimism. He had two problems, for Castlereagh had occupied two posts, foreign secretary and leader of the House of Commons. To make Canning leader of the House obviously had its attractions: he stood head and shoulders above everyone else in oratorical range. But then there was Peel, whom Liverpool had brought into the cabinet as home secretary a few months earlier, following Sidmouth's retirement. A two-hour conversation at the beginning of September had left Liverpool with the impression that Peel hoped to lead the House and Peel with the impression that Liverpool would not let him. There was the 'real *blot* and sin'[51] –

Vansittart – whose continuing fiscal incomprehension argued that he be moved from the Exchequer. There was Huskisson who, since 1814, had been masterminding economic policy from the anonymity of the secretaryship of woods and forests, a banishment which Wynn's elevation to the cabinet as Buckingham's puppet had done nothing to sweeten. The prime minister postponed his nuptials with Miss Chester in a mood of acute dejection.

It is difficult at this distance precisely to identify what was 'wrong' with Canning. Grey's famous jibe about the son of an actress seems a poor explanation. Canning had peculiar parents but his grandparents were not odd or outcasts in political society, nor had his education and upbringing been other than respectable. Christ Church, Oxford, hardly counted as an orphanage, and it had been there that he had come into contact with Liverpool. Another explanation feeds on his 'liberal Toryism', but this seems equally stale. He claimed to be a *liberale* as a supporter of Greek independence and colleagues sometimes regretted his doctrines; but his mild sympathy for Catholics and his sniffiness about Russian autocracy have to be put against his stern face over parliamentary reform and his support for Sidmouthery after the war. More frequent than lamentation over his doctrines were in any case suspicions that he did not believe them. Indeed the problem seems to have lain not so much in anything Canning believed or did as in a personal manner which implied, as reports of it ran in and out of Tory society, a certain deviousness and an unacceptable level of ambition. He was too busy; he tried too hard. From Mrs Arbuthnot, the microphone of muttered gossip, one hears of a consistent 'dirty underplot' in which Canning is supposed to be engaged. From Wellington, who paradoxically had urged Canning's appointment as foreign minister, one hears a story over the next two or three years of policy bungles and (more significant, perhaps) a certain lack of 'address'. From most political observers, Tory or Whig, there arise persistent and growing rumours that Canning's inclusion as Commons leader and foreign secretary – the decision to which Liverpool found himself driven – will bring Whigs towards government and blur what should be focused. Recent historians convincingly argue the contention that 1822 presented no watershed between a later, 'liberal' Toryism and an earlier, repressive, unreconstructed one: many of the moves towards liberalization plainly took place before 1821. But the significance for the political elite of those months in the autumn of 1822 cannot be overstressed. A new style of politics was about to begin.

Much of this style derived its patina from responses to events developing rapidly on the continent and in Ireland. In 1823 the crucial theatre was the Spanish one. Since the revolution of 1820 pressure had mounted within the Quintuple Alliance to liberate the captive King Ferdinand, destroy the constitution of 1812 and reinstate monarchist legitimacy. At Verona in October and November 1822 Wellington's resistance to the idea of intervention had been overridden, an agreement made that an ultimatum should be presented to the Spanish government and, in the event of its being rejected, an invasion carried out by the French. The delivery of Villèle's note in January and the invasion of March drove the first wedge between Canning's understanding of foreign policy and Wellington's and inaugurated the latter's profound mistrust of the future prime minister. Wellington's orientation in foreign policy in these years was legitimist and pro-French; he consequently conceived Canning's to be revolutionary and pro-Spanish. Through 1823 – and especially in August when Canning refused to advise sending troops to Portugal to help the king of that country cope with his revolution – Wellington's estimation of Canning declined. Complementing the growing split within the government was one also inside the Whig party over the same issues. 'We do nothing but abuse one another', Lord John Russell wrote to Brougham in March; 'the violent laugh at the moderate and the moderate look grave at the violent.'[52] Some of these polarities appeared also in the Irish context. The country had recovered somewhat from the potato failure of 1822 and the cause of 'Catholic Emancipation' seemed for a time to have rotted with that crop. But during 1823 the Catholic Association had been formed by Daniel O'Connell, and politicians were to hear more of it and him during 1824 as lines of force ran from Dublin to South America, uniting O'Connell with Bolivar.

People and places far from home had come into prominence within the perception of politicians because domestic politics had apparently stabilized. A reshuffle at the beginning of the year had at last brought in Huskisson at the Board of Trade and expelled Vansittart from the Exchequer. Any 'awkwardness' about this latter move had been avoided by substituting Castlereagh's protégé Robinson, thus retaining a balance of power between Canning and the ghost of Londonderry. Economic distress had showed some signs of easing, however, which made it harder for Huskisson to demonstrate his indispensability. In any case he had only got 'what the French call *administrative* experience' which would not help him at a level where 'manner' was everything. So when Wynn examined the 'real and efficient Cabinet' from the outside in the autumn of 1823 he still saw, despite the shuffling of cards, only Liverpool, Bathurst, Wellington and Canning.[53] The prime minister's complaints, often quoted since, about knots of parties in the cabinet date from this time: they form part of a fabric of evidence which shows that the politics of administration had ceased to be agreeable. Parliamentary politics, on the other hand, had become an arena of unwonted friendship. The sessions of 1823 and 1824 were the most placid of the decade. The Whigs stayed subdued, partly because they thought Canning would shortly move towards them, partly because their leader, Earl Grey, had once again become torpid, 'I never remember it so quiet,' Mrs Arbuthnot wrote at the beginning of 1824; 'there is literally nothing to talk of.' By the end of the summer she was musing that the prime minister might as well be dead for all that had been heard of him.[54]

Yet this impression was as misleading as it was general. Far from having received its quietus, political animosity had become more heated in 1824 than at any time since 1815 but its location had shifted. Ever non-popular, the crux of politicians' activity had become non-parliamentary: for a few months it moved upwards into the rarefied atmosphere of ministerial battle where even the King appeared as little more than a disadvantaged spectator. On at least three occasions in 1824, the three most important members of the government – Liverpool, Canning and Wellington – threatened resignation; and they mounted that threat over one issue, the question of whether certain South American ex-colonies should be granted official recognition by the British government. The reason for the fury lay in the positions taken by Wellington and Canning over Spain in 1823. For Spain's imperial past had deposited a rich but anarchic group of ex-colonies in South America. Now that France had invaded the mother country, the question arose: should France be allowed the possibility of reannexing those colonies and benefiting from their wealth and trade? Canning was determined to prevent an undermining of the European balance of power by committing the British government to recognizing the independence of the nascent states of South America. But Wellington saw in such a policy the destruction of the Quintuple Alliance, the encouragement of revolutionary barbarians, and the entangling of British money and arms in states 'which had not a *white* government' and which lacked the means of stability and self-protection.[55] In fact Canning shared the horror of imposing on the King 'a cocoa-nut-coloured minister to receive at his Levée',[56] but he saw humiliation as the price of trade and investment. What he and Liverpool called into existence in 1824–5 was less a New World, therefore, than a speculative explosion which in twelve months would come to rival the South Sea Bubble as an episode of economic imperialism.

The King, for his part, held unambiguous views about jungle fighters and cocoa-nut-coloured ministers. Bolivar's revolution in Peru was for him only one face of a worldwide assault on monarchy: to recognize the legitimacy of such ventures was to encourage O'Connell in Ireland and Hunt and Cobbett in England. Nor had Wellington missed the link between South America and Ireland; he too could not see how it could be thought consistent to legitimize Bolivar and yet resist O'Connell. In 1825, moreover, as the campaign against recognition became very much a one-man show on the part of Wellington, this battle moved into public and political view. Catholics' complaints that, if elected to parliament, they could not in conscience take the oath, threatened to become a popular cry if one of them should win a seat. Granted that the Whigs were desperate for something to say in parliament, that eventuality also promised a set-piece in the House.

In its first year the Catholic Association had made a slow start in mobilizing opinion against continuing proscription of Catholics from public office. O'Connell's brilliant tactic of Catholic Rent – the invention of mass subscription at a penny a month – brought, however, a marked change of pace during 1824, and politicians' understanding of the urgency of the Catholic question underwent a revolution in that year. Opinion in government circles swung sharply against the lord lieutenant, Wellesley, who, despite being Wellington's brother, had pro-Catholic tendencies; and in the session of 1825 the chief secretary, Goulburn, introduced a bill designed to outlaw the Catholic Association which promptly abolished itself and reformed as the New Catholic Association in order to circumvent the legislation. More spectacular was Sir Francis Burdett's attempt to introduce an emancipation bill in return for the disfranchisement of 40-shilling freeholders (a group we shall meet in the next chapter) in Ireland. This produced two important consequences: it demonstrated to the satisfaction of many Whigs that Canning was a temporizing turncoat who had no more intention of forcing emancipation than had Castlereagh; and its rejection in the House of Lords created the possibility of Liverpool's calling an election on a 'Protestant' platform and putting an end to persistent rumours that he had 'changed his politics' and turned Catholic. He certainly did his best during a bracing half-hour while winding up the Lords' debate on Burdett's bill:

> He said, that the Catholics were not entitled to equal rights in a Protestant country, and that opinion he would sustain... The difference was this – it was stated in a moment – the Protestant gave an entire allegiance to his sovereign; the Catholic a divided one... He knew it had been said, that the progress of education, and the march of civilization, had wrought wonders amongst the Catholics... But he would

remind their lordships that the horizon was often clearest and most serene when the tempest was nearest. And here he would appeal to history, and ask their lordships at what period did the established church appear to be in a more flourishing condition than at the Restoration of Charles 2nd? And yet in twenty years afterwards it was that the greatest revolution took place in the condition of that church, and it was next to a miracle that, by machinations of a popish prince, it was not over whelmed in one common ruin with the state and constitution of this country.[57]

Liverpool's own policies in fact rendered this posture artificial. His dependence on Canning made it difficult for him to ignore the latter's pressure for a postponement until the end of the following session when he, Canning, hoped the heat would have been taken out of the Catholic issue. Liverpool's willingness to give Canning his head in foreign policy, moreover, had rushed the government into the South American jungles. As the speculative frenzy which followed recognition began to founder, evidence of coming disaster mounted at the Board of Trade. By September 1825, when the decision was taken to postpone the election, Huskisson was warning of an imminent financial crash which only a tolerable harvest had delayed thus far. The crisis actually came in December when London banks (and the country banks which they controlled) began to fail. A week before Christmas, Peel had to defend Threadneedle Street with troops.[58] It is true that the crisis passed relatively quickly and that the last session of this very long parliament – the longest since the Septennial Act of 1716 – was negotiated without disaster. But the developing distress among the farming community, and the threats from Ireland once O'Connell revivified the Catholic Association, told their own story. Whatever the results of the inevitable general election, issues had been brought into prominence which cut across the grain of 'party' in so far as any recognizable parties now existed. Among 'the People', only the farmers and the Irish had achieved a demonstrable impact on Liverpool's long parliament. However, on the eve of its dissolution, politicians nevertheless saw clearly that their horizons and prospects had become very different from those of 1820.

Emancipation, reform and the Duke (1826–30)

The election of 1826 offered few political lessons. Observers agreed that the 'Protestants' had made a limited number of gains, though they felt unsure how many, and historians have not been able to clarify the issue.[59] It had played some part, however, in underlining the possibility of anti-Catholic politics in a world sullied by Canning; and it had encouraged a startling speculation to which politicians were constantly to be driven in the next three years – that the 'Catholic' question had to be faced by government and that only a 'Protestant' government would be strong enough to face it. Certainly Canning could no longer rely on the efficacy of cultivating a central Toryism with a Whig fringe. In face of an assertive 'old Tory' party he would need to make terms with (rather than love to) the opposition, should he become first minister. Three issues had helped to establish Canning's political identity: the desirability of Catholic emancipation, the growing pressure to redraw the corn laws, and Wellington's delineation of an alternative foreign policy. For the moment, any split à outrance had been averted by a Protestant election. But Robinson's corn bill had been forced on the landed interest in the spring to quieten insurrectionary developments in northern manufacturing towns and the election had greatly strengthened O'Connell in Ireland – especially through the spectacular success of the 'Catholic' movement in returning a Protestant emancipationist at Waterford. Several months before Liverpool's stroke and resignation in February 1827, his Toryism was dead and buried. When Wellington came to the pre-session cabinet dinner at the beginning of November he found that ministers who had not seen one another for six weeks had nothing to say. When Huskisson wrote an optimistic letter to Canning about the political future, he was unaware that the violence seen in the East Retford constituency at the election three months before had already set in motion a chain of events which would intersect with his own future in eighteen months' time.

It was not apparent in the autumn of 1826 that the Duke of Wellington would soon play a crucial role in Tory politics. Though he had been a cabinet minister since 1819, his post (master of the ordnance) hardly offered one from which a great political reputation could be made, and his battles against Canning over South America and Portugal had not been public. Indeed, he had allowed himself to be implicated in Canning's foreign policy by acting as plenipotentiary at St Petersburg when Anglo-Russian mediation between Greece and Turkey had been discussed there in the spring of 1826. Nonetheless he had demonstrated a consistent Protestantism and a defensiveness about agriculture which he used with great effect when he consolidated his grip on the House of Lords in 1827. His assumption of the role of Protestant pillar and mentor to the peerage was aided meanwhile by the death of the Duke of York – the first of a series of spectacularly significant deaths to affect party orientation between 1827 and 1830.

York's removal mattered to 'Catholics' and 'Protestants' alike. As the King's brother and heir to the throne he had commanded great resources of propaganda for his manic opposition to Catholic emancipation: his speech in the Lords during the discussion of Burdett's relief bill of 1825 had been printed in gold leaf and widely circulated. His death advanced the Catholic cause in two ways. It silenced an opponent; and it meant that the Duke of Clarence would become King in the event of George IV's going mad, a serious and canvassed possibility. And although Clarence was noisy and unstable, he did not understand the fanaticism of his elder brother, was not personally so disgusting as his younger one, and seemed embryonically to be 'a very decent King'.[60] From the 'Protestant' point of view, on the other hand, the advantages were arguably greater. In the next twelve months Wellington would attract to himself much of the charisma that York had acquired and would exploit it more effectively. For the moment, York harried his enemies, even in death. At an interminable service in the freezing conditions which attended York's funeral in January 1827 Canning caught the chill which hastened his own death a few months later.

Canning had become de facto prime minister long before Liverpool was seized of his apoplectic fit. His succession to the formal leadership was, however, by no means automatic, and the bewildering activity among politicians between February and April 1827, when Canning's ministry was completed,[61] bears testimony to the plethora of possibilities deemed to be available. Yet the atmosphere was unlike that of August 1822: it is noticeable that the premier's death created far less clamour than had his foreign minister's five years before. The crucial question among politicians now arose not from intra-party balance but rather from their fusion. For it was clear from the outset that Canning would not be able to take Wellington and the 'old party' with him; clear too that he had little chance of taking the Whigs *en bloc*. Two party splits were therefore promised by the likelihood of Canning's receiving a request from Windsor to form a government; and as the plausibility of other candidates faded – Wellington, Bathurst, Peel, Robinson, Wellesley and Harrowby had all been mentioned in 'the Conversation in and out of Parliament'[62] – both promises were fulfilled. Wellington, Peel, Eldon and Bathurst stayed out. Harrowby and (eventually) Bexley adhered; Robinson was bought with a peerage to lead the Lords as Goderich of Nocton, a decision which would shortly cause him untold pain and lead to his becoming the most miserable premier in the history of nineteenth-century politics. From the Whigs, Lansdowne, Tierney and Devonshire were brought into the hybrid cabinet but other powerful Whigs preferred, as Brougham said, 'to live in 1780'. Grey persisted in his loathing of Canning and announced his neutrality; Ellenborough pressed for firm opposition to the new government; the young Whig/radical group around Althorp wanted no part in the deal. Yet for the moment Canning had succeeded in his purpose of destroying party. He had un-Whigged a part of the Whig party, as Lord Londonderry nicely quipped, and un-Toried a part of the Tories.[63]

What was imperative in the new party context was that Canning should control what his colleagues wanted to talk about – and especially in parliament. The most pressing issue of the moment, that of Catholic emancipation – had to be stifled quickly. In the interregnum between Liverpool's illness and Canning's accession, Burdett's second parliamentary attempt at Catholic relief had failed in the Commons, the first motion to do so since 1819 and a signal comment on the effects of the 1826 election. Although the margin of defeat had not been wide enough to threaten Canning's succession, he obviously would do everything possible to avoid 'Ireland' while parliament sat. He would also avoid parliamentary reform, unpalatable both to Canning, who had consistently opposed it, and to his old Tory remnant who would plainly walk out if provoked. Foreign policy remained, of course. Wellington was gone, the Whigs liked Canning's Greek liberalism, and the moment was ripe for the hardening of the St Petersburg protocol of 1826 into the Treaty of London which was signed in the summer. One issue, however, seemed at once unpleasant and unavoidable. Like the Catholic resolution, the threat of a new corn law had emerged during the previous autumn and its presence in parliament in the current session would be bound to strain Canning's relationship with rank-and-file Tories. Dilution of his original measure helped to make the corn bill tolerable to the Commons; but in the Lords Wellington emerged for the first time as a public statesman and destroyed the bill by inserting into it a price 'floor' of 66s below which imports would be prohibited. In the second chamber Goderich had proved no match for him. Over the next few months he was to prove it repeatedly.

Canning's health had patently begun to fail and when his death came in August no one appeared likely to continue the style of management which he had tried to effect since 1822. The King would have no Whig for prime minister; nor would he have Peel and Wellington since he disliked the former and was afraid of the latter. He turned, inevitably, to Goderich. And in the presence of this dithering and tearful Canningite, who had no parliament to stiffen him (it had broken up in June), George IV came into his own and for six months became the King he had always intended being. His beckoning of Goderich inaugurated a period of royal bullying over places and policies: indeed the only constitutional significance of Goderich's pathetic performance lay in the revival of power it afforded the monarchy. The King used that power to force Herries into the Exchequer, rather than Lansdowne, and to keep out other disagreeable Whigs, especially Lord Holland who, as the nephew of Charles James Fox, was congenitally beyond redemption. Exclusion from such a ministry hardly entailed dishonour and the most embarrassed politicians of these months were those who had become associated with it. Wellington made a grave error of judgement in allowing himself to become commander-in-chief, without a seat in the cabinet: some of the more crusty Tories saw his adherence as the beginning of a capitulation to Canningism. Huskisson, on the other hand, squirmed as only an 'administrative' politician could at Goderich's ineptitude. 'Never surely', he wrote to Granville after the regime finally crumbled, 'was there a man at the head of affairs so weak, undecided, and utterly helpless!'[64]

Herries's resignation, following a trivial argument with Huskisson, persuaded Goderich to resign without meeting parliament; but a more fundamental predicament was posed by the prospect of meeting it at the end of January 1828 without more Whig scaffolding. The King needed, in his own judgement, to be saved from all Whigs and those Tories whom he could not control. He sent – it was an index of his desperation – for Lord Harrowby. Now Harrowby's career had peaked a quarter of a century before in 1804 when Pitt had given him the Foreign Office, only to slide into immediate decline after he fell down the stairs there and withdrew in broken health. Since then he had been no more than an aristocratic ingredient in central Tory politics, and he saw at once the hopelessness of the King's request. With Harrowby's refusal the King was driven back towards Wellington and Peel and a return to Tory factionalism. He saw little more of the Whigs. Their purchase on politics had temporarily ceased and would only be recovered when the Catholic problem had been met, when the King himself had been replaced and when Reform had been rediscovered among the Whig virtues which so preoccupied Earl Grey.

Wellington had understood for some years that an exclusively 'Protestant' government could not survive and he did not attempt now to create one. He distinguished, however, between 'Catholic' and 'Whig'. No offer was sent to Grey, nor even to Lansdowne, who had been home secretary under Canning and Goderich. The 'ma-levolents' – those who had opposed fusion with Canning – remained thinkable but, since most of them were unthinkably radical, the choice reduced in practice to Ellenborough who came in to hold the privy seal. In the party, rather than Irish, sense Huskisson was as far left as Wellington intended to go; the ex-Canningites broadly retained the offices they had held under Goderich. Eldon, on the other side, was not asked. The administration boasted more than 'a Government concocted out of the Army List and the ultra-Tories', as one Whig sourly alleged, but it did give rise to comment about its class inade-quacies. Herries and Goulburn were 'of the class of under-secre-taries', after all, in the eyes of a second-generation aristocrat like Ellenborough. Mrs Arbuthnot spoke more tartly of *'rif raf'*.[65]

Peel inevitably returned to the Home Office and took the leader-ship of the Commons though with understandable misgivings. He had cut a poor figure since the break with Canning: always there, always on his feet, always talking about himself, his doctrines and his difficulties. Fellow politicians had rapidly tired of one who needed constantly to purge himself and redefine his relationship with the universe. He had insisted on having Huskisson to help him in the task of managing the House but even so the fight there would plainly be an uphill one which he would have to fight virtually alone. Well-ington faced an even harder task in the Lords with the Catholic question on the horizon and neither Grey nor Lansdowne to help. Still, these difficulties could be magnified. If Grey were Olympian, he was at least remaining on his mountain. If Lansdowne were lost, he was also, in the words of one of his own party, 'admitted by common consent to be the damnedest idiot that ever lived'.[66] Certainly the Whigs would come to put great pressure on, and ultimately defeat, this government. Before they could do so, however, they would need to seek issues on which they could regroup and put behind them the rifts Canning had fostered.

The 'Catholic' issue was a bad one: it aroused passions too closely connected with the squabbles of recent years and it offered poor chances of parliamentary success against an avowedly 'Protestant' administration and electorate. Better prospects appeared in the griev-ances of Nonconformists. Whigs had a long tradition of pressing for repeal of the Test Acts and Corporation Act passed in the reign of Charles II to contain the civil dangers of Dissent. They had not returned seriously to this theme since the 1780s, but if ever they needed a tradition it was now. The rapidly developing numbers and self-confidence of Nonconformity made this a good moment to move; but Lord John Russell's motion for repeal emerged less from popular pressure than the new party configuration.[67] Moreover, the strategy worked: the government was beaten in the House and was compelled to accept a reform which at least Wellington and Bathurst had strongly opposed. The Whigs had found a degree of harmony and had given considerable heartburn to ultras like Eldon and Newcastle who saw repeal as a first step towards emancipation of Catholics. Nor had cabinet unity been helped by an issue over which the Canningite remnant had opposed the prime minister. At the end of the 1828 session the young Whig convert Sir James Graham looked forward to 'Capital blunders' by the government, as a result of which 'there w[ould] arrive the golden opportunity of forming a party in the H. of Commons on some broad and intelligible principle'. In recent years cheerfulness had not been a Whig characteristic, but now there emerged a new mood. 'I really am disposed to believe', Graham went on, 'the road to power is open.'[68]

He was helped in his optimism by Wellington's having lost his left flank two months earlier. The Canningites – Huskisson, Grant, Palmerston and Dudley – had been displeased with Wellington's dictated foreign policy as there drew nearer the war between Russia and Turkey which it had been British policy over the last few years to prevent. Repeal of Tests had done nothing to ease policy tensions, but the argument boiled over at two other points. One was corn, for the Canningite Charles Grant had rendered Wellington's attempts to retain maximum protection for the farmers the subject first of harangues and then of a threatened resignation from the Board of Trade. Grant hardly counted for much, indeed Wellington would have been happy to see him go, but he did not wish to give the impression of dismissing Huskisson, who did matter, by proxy. The necessity did not arise, however, because in May 1828 East Retford finally caught up with Huskisson when economic problems were eclipsed by the question of how to redistribute parliamentary seats disfranchised after the 1826 election. In cabinet, Huskisson declared himself committed to giving the seats of Penryn and East Retford to unrepresented major towns. Between this Canningite position and the ultras' solution of transference to neighbouring rural hundreds, the cabinet chose to compromise and gave Penryn to a town but East Retford to Bassetlaw. For Huskisson this was not good enough, but he probably did not expect his resignation to be accepted. Wellington in fact snatched at it, delighted at a 'clean' opportunity of ridding himself of 'the four' who had acted so consistently in concert against him. It was in the highest degree significant that the Tory government had spilled its blood over parliamentary reform; and as parliament broke up, the lesson was taken away to Holland House, Bowood, Althorp,

Wentworth Woodhouse, above all to Howick, to be digested. Yet the Whig commitment to reform had to wait till the beginning of 1830 because, meanwhile, the departure of the Canningites finally had brought the 'Catholic' question to a head.

In his new mood of confidence Wellington had decided to replace Grant at the Board of Trade by Vesey Fitzgerald, who sat for the Irish constituency of County Clare. On his elevation to office Fitzgerald was required by statute (this one persisted until 1918) to submit himself for re-election. When Daniel O'Connell fought and won that by-election in July 1828, therefore, the government faced the grave prospect of losing its Irish seats to Catholics who were debarred by its Anglican oath from sitting in parliament. The second half of the year saw two urgent developments for politicians as a result of that prospect. Wellington, Peel and Lyndhurst wrote a secret memorandum about the situation and tried (unsuccessfully) to persuade the King to rescind his instruction preventing the cabinet from discussing Catholic emancipation. At the popular level, not only did the activities of the New Catholic Association move up a gear but they attracted opposition in England from a widespread Protestant or 'Brunswick' movement inspired by the Duke of Cumberland and Lord Eldon. That parliament was in recess was, for once, a difficulty for ministers since they had no way of quieting the popular, 'No Popery' cry before it became too loud to prevent emancipatory legislation gaining a hearing. The added secrecy of the negotiations with the King also made it impossible for Wellington to explain his policy to his pro-Catholic lord lieutenant of Ireland, the Marquess of Anglesey, whose insubordination earned his dismissal at the end of the year and started hares about ministers' intransigence which ran precisely counter to their intentions.

Needless to say, much of the festive season was spent in the sharpening of swords in anticipation of the King's speech in the new year. The impossibility of conceding emancipation and the impossibility of resisting it offered both a battleground and a rallying cry; and leading Whigs waited to see how Wellington would cope with the King and Peel, his greatest obstacles if he intended proposing a relief bill. Huskisson had mounted a horse with a head at each end: if the Whigs successfully chastised Wellington for failing to emancipate he would lead his small army towards them; if the ultras successfully rallied Protestantism he would move their way instead. Whigs and Canningites were alike disappointed, nevertheless, between January 1829 and the bill's passing through the Lords in April. Before Wellington met parliament he had already squared Peel who eased the pain by resigning his Oxford seat ('a democratical and

unconstitutional proceeding', as Croker complained), and giving the
Commons a four-hour explanation. The King was stickier. He had
been bundled along with promises of full consultation for the first
few weeks; but when he found out that the oath of supremacy would
have to be modified he refused to be bundled further. Yet he left his
attack on the ministers too late, for when Wellington threw up the
government the King was left, as in January 1828, with no one to
rescue him. Eldon was called and suggested the Duke of Richmond
who was marginally more laughable than Harrowby had been.
Within twenty-four hours the King invited Wellington to return
with the success of his despised bill now assured.

In these months politicians had witnessed the most complete *boule-
versement* of policy and personality. They had listened to Grey's
eloquent panegyric on Peel, of all people, as though it were some
experimental Esperanto. They had watched the government lose all
its support without acquiring any serious opponents. 'At present
there is no party,' Greville wrote on 11 June, capturing a widespread
mood; 'everything is in confusion – party, politics and all.' Amid
shattered confidence it was the hope of the administration that 'the
métier of Tories [was] to support the King's Govt.'.[69] Among Whigs
the hope rather took the form that some new bond might be forged
before Wellington consolidated his position after what was undeniably a great personal achievement. Consolidation could perhaps have
been gained, at a high-political level, by attracting new blood (pre-
ferably old Whig) into government and then seeking a favourable
moment for dissolution while the enemies of the regime were in
disarray. But it would have to be won also at a lower level. Neither
repeal of Tests nor the passage of Catholic emancipation had been
'democratic' in its inspiration; yet the simple fact of pliability in
policy encouraged the sentiment that democratic pressure could tell,
whatever Wellington's private views about it.

Through 1829 and 1830 thoughts about 'the people' and their
relation to politicians' lives recurred frequently in speeches and correspondence and carried a sense of relevance and seriousness which
earlier utterances had not always suggested. Of course one can return
to 1820 and Peel's famous letter to Croker with its celebrated definition of public opinion and its vision of political channels becoming
too small for what must pass through them. That holiday speculation, composed at Bognor and far away from the *mentalité* of cabinet
politics, found little reflection, however, in Peel's subsequent political
behaviour. In the wake of emancipation the mood was different.
Severe economic distress in the autumn of 1829 brought widespread

suffering in both manufacturing and agricultural districts. When parliament reconvened in January 1830, observers commented on the buzz of complaint among members disturbed by Wellington's failure to take the problem seriously. The Duke's success with the Catholic question had certainly left him overcharged: 1829 was a year in which he often mentioned Waterloo in conversation. He was greatly irritated by those who continued to oppose him and began to lose the considerable political judgement he had acquired since 1823. He believed that he need do no more than pick off individual parliamentary critics and attach them to his administration. He believed Grey to be a supporter at a time when Grey was rankling at having received no invitation to join. He believed, misled by sycophantic intimates such as the Arbuthnots, that the country remained sound in its support.

The Whigs, meanwhile, showed new life. Russell's motion in February 1830 to enfranchise Manchester, Leeds and Birmingham helped, despite its failure, to congeal Whig and radical sentiment. More important, it brought Grey out of the shadows by helping him to see the strength of reform feeling at a time when the lower House had found new leadership in Spencer's son, Lord Althorp. There were even rumours that Huskisson and his group might learn to live with Grey. In this situation the Duke's best hope lay in abandoning any plans for an election, scraping through the rest of the session and trying to relieve popular and parliamentary tensions during the autumn. But control was slipping away. From this point onwards Wellington could do little but ride events. Of these, two were crucial: the death of the King in June and the revolution in France a month later.

When George IV's health, long since broken, degenerated into dropsy in April 1830, politicians began to ruminate on the election that his imminent death would be bound to occasion. As in 1820, the vagary of a monarch's health would force an election at a moment unpleasant to government. As in 1826, a summer election would force an autumn session with equally unpleasant forebodings. As if by conspiracy, Charles X's government in France threatened to go up in flames just at the instant when the British government was intent on damping down at home. Since the appointment of Polignac as first minister in 1828, even possibly since Charles X's accession in 1824, the stability of French politics had come into question. Wellington had originally felt too pleased at the arrival of an ally in the struggle against Russian ambitions to be concerned about the backlash which might follow Polignac's ill-judged domestic repressions; but the consequences in Britain of the 'July days' in France were nevertheless to be grave. We now know that the revolution did not impinge on the British general election of 1830. When the news crossed the Channel, only a minority of English seats were undeclared and even in those no acceleration of the reform impetus seems apparent.[70] As autumn approached, the French experience became nonetheless a reference point in political thinking, one whose presence was made the more insistent by Captain Swing's rural riots which set alight much of eastern and southern England.

Despite a low level of contested seats, the election had, without French help, run strongly against government, especially in the counties where Brougham's virtually unopposed return for Yorkshire presented only the most spectacular instance of opposition success. Any salvation plainly must come from a fusion with some party or sizeable group, but in the light of the new balance of power this would be harder to bring about than in the previous year. When Huskisson was run over by the train while opening the Manchester to Liverpool railway in September, his death opened possibilities of an arrangement with the ex-Canningites. But it was a mark of their confidence in an alternative government that Palmerston made difficulties when asked to join in October. Quite simply, it was too late both to suppress 'ye most violent and democratical principles ... daily spreading'[71] *and* maintain political configurations moulded in the very different circumstances of 1823–7. Expectations of a reforming ministry committed to radical change had run beyond the likelihood of Wellington's jaded and misinformed administration proving able to contain them. They had run within the political nation, moreover, not merely without in the underworld of taverns, reform clubs and provincial newspapers. To explain what had happened since 1827 in the language of popular radicalism, as though high politics had responded only to 'the country' and what it demanded, is to miss the point of what those in power thought they were doing and mislocate the reference-points toward which they looked for guidance or warning while doing it. For contemporaries, meanwhile, such subtleties of interpretation could hardly preoccupy politicians even if they had the patience or foresight to contemplate them. Matters had become all too immediate and their corollaries none too clear. As Wellington prepared, in the certainty of defeat, to meet a new parliament, politicians and people alike voiced their anxieties for constitution and property as they faced, in common ignorance, the implications of a Whig future.

2

Renewal and Consolidation

The reform coach (1830–34)

Some Whigs had lived long enough to remember Whiggery as Fox
had known it; most had not. The Marquess of Lansdowne may have
clung to his Whig uniform of buff waistcoat and blue coat with brass
buttons. But for every Lansdowne or Grey or Holland or Devonshire
still 'full of old *genuine Whig* bitterness',[1] there were men like Russell
or Durham or Stanley or Sir James Graham for whom the Whig party
had become a reform vehicle on which to charge at Wellington. Their
understanding of party did not dominate their political action: Graham, a Whig, came from a family of Cumbrian Tories; Stanley, no
less a Whig, was soon to found a dynasty of Lancastrian ones. They
saw their task, assuming a modest reform of the franchise, in much
the same light that many of the 'administrative' Tories saw their duty
too; they sought a government of sense, economy and stability. Yet
Grey's Whigs were distinctive in ways which might affect their conduct in office. Though less obviously creatures of agricultural pressure than the Tories, they owned more acres and were entrenched in
county seats. They had their radical fringe, of course, but a man like
Althorp felt more relaxed in the company of the Pytchley than with
London politicians, while Grey's reluctance to leave Howick was
notorious. An apparent 'outsider' among these tightly knit politicians
like the future Whig minister and speaker of the Commons, James
Abercromby, had spent periods as steward of Devonshire's estates
and in representing Calne, Lansdowne's pocket borough.

Connexion, indeed, was no mere legend for all the new blood after
1830. Edward 'Bear' Ellice had begun his progress from the fur-lands
of Canada to Whig party string-puller by marrying Grey's youngest
sister. When the future Earl of Durham married Grey's daughter in
1816 he thereby acquired a political uncle as well as a powerful
father-in-law. Another Whig factotum of the 1830s, Duncannon,

did not, it is true, marry a Grey but he did, like Palmerston, marry a sister of Melbourne and received supplementary benefit from being Fitzwilliam's cousin. Althorp showed himself as unpolitical in marriage as in everything else. Yet the son of Earl Spencer needed no marriage to underline his political potency and at a time when the second Earl's blood was slowing – it was observed in 1831 that doctors could not raise his pulse above thirty-four – the vast Northamptonshire influence of the Spencers would plainly soon change hands. Cementing these relationships was a *mélange* of doctrines and inherited positions about Anglicanism, free trade and international relations – opinions most pungently announced at Holland House, the greatest of the Whig salons, where the third Lord Holland embodied the immortal name of Fox albeit under the tutelage of his terrible wife. In the autumn of 1830 the radical John Cam Hobhouse went there and found the company 'act[ing] and think[ing] as if they were in the days of the Pelhams and Walpoles, with perfect tranquillity and selfish complacency'.[2]

But then, Whigs had some cause for complacency. In the few weeks since the meeting of parliament they had beaten Wellington, and Grey had formed a government committed to Reform. Perhaps the Duke's removal had become a formality once the election results were known: it is certainly hard in retrospect to construct a scenario in which he could have survived for any length of time. Contemporary observers stressed the damage done by Wellington's uncompromising declaration on 2 November against parliamentary reform, but Wellington himself did not believe that his statement brought on the disaster. Looking back on these weeks at Christmas time he saw Catholic emancipation and the French revolution as the fundamental causes of his downfall; and the formation of a political alliance against him in the summer as the proximate cause.[3] About the significance of the July days he was, as we have seen, wrong but he saw clearly when he rejected the allegation that his reform declaration had been central to the collapse of his government. It had been no more than a political tactic to rally ultra feeling behind him: indeed the failure of the negotiations with the Canningites had left him little option. The new balance of power inside the Commons and the debilitating effects of the continuing agricultural riots outside it forced Wellington into planting his flag on 2 November, only to ensure, by resigning over something else, that it would never be taken.

A Commons defeat on the Civil List was the chosen occasion. Had Wellington not seized it, however, it seems all but certain that he would have been beaten on the following day when Brougham moved a reform motion on behalf of the Whigs and their allies. Towards the latter the Duke had shown himself indisposed to move; for just as Peel's attitude to reform had been determined by his refusal to be thought a rat (as in 1829) so Wellington's had turned into a determination to avoid doing anything that Canning had done. Plainly an end had come, if not to the prospects of *le parti conserva-teur* (for we shall watch that rise again), then at least to Wellington's own political future. This much found universal assent. Wellington was finished, 'except' – an unsettling thought – 'it shall be resolved to run all chances and play the Polignac game here'.[4]

Grey, the inevitable successor to Wellington since throwing his weight behind reform, believed that no such risks could be run and that the reform coach should be accelerated. Not that his government embodied any dangerous radicalism. It contained a strain of old Whig purity in the Marquess of Lansdowne, the Earl of Carlisle and Lord Holland; there were the Canningites who had to be repaid for their loyalty (Goderich, Grant, Melbourne – who took the Home Office – and Palmerston – who landed the Foreign Office after more eligible Whigs had refused it); there was the Duke of Richmond whose Tory past was offset by his being Holland's cousin. Only Durham and Brougham represented radical sentiments in the new cabinet and Brougham's had been diluted by his removal to the Woolsack where 'he may rant, storm and thunder without hurting anybody'.[5] Brougham's rival as a popular demagogue, Daniel O'Connell, was offered the job Brougham had wanted – master of the rolls – but declined it. The Whig most clearly in touch with the reform movement in the country was Lord John Russell, but he had lost Bedford at the recent election and was galled to see himself left out of the cabinet while Sir James Graham was brought in. Russell remained outside until the summer of 1831 by which time he had established himself as a major spokesman on the all-important reform question.

Four men had originally been deputed to consider that issue and report to cabinet with suggestions for a bill in 1831. Grey's choice of Durham as convener for the little group was natural in a father-in-law who wanted to control radicalism, while Durham's of Graham seemed equally natural in a patron wishing to advance a protégé. Russell's inclusion followed from the need for the group to be informed about what the reformers wanted. Duncannon's followed simply from the position of something close to party whip which he had established for himself over the past few years. But their pre-occupation over Christmas and the new year lay in trouble at home and revolution abroad. Belgium's rising against the Netherlands the previous August, Poland's rising against Russia a week after Palmerston entered the Foreign Office, and a threatened revolution in Italy proffered warnings that the July days were not over. O'Connell's arrest in January on thirty-one charges of conspiracy, seditious libel and unlawful assembly, ironic after the government's offer to him of a major judicial post, only emphasized the mood of encirclement. It is worth recalling, however, that in England few took to the streets. The King's visit to the City in November had proved more peaceful than the government had feared; and though the new Political Unions were gaining in strength (the Birmingham Union had about 6,000 members by April 1830) they applied pressure within the constitutional system rather than without it through the traditional device of petitioning. Captain Swing's rural risings continued as a major headache. Yet they had no urban counterpart and affected the political structure in two indirect ways: by unifying ultra sentiment, since they hit below the belt that ran from the Wash to the Severn, and by completing the political education of Melbourne, to whose Home Office desk reports of rebellions ultimately came. Greville's depiction of the current mood as one of 'nervous excitement' was nevertheless a fair one, just as Ellenborough's uninformed judgement that the new bill would have to be made more extreme was an understandable reaction.[6]

In fact Grey was already pulling at the reins to go the other way. When the committee of four reported to cabinet at the end of January 1831, he squashed the idea of recommending a secret ballot and only espoused the enfranchisement of £10 householders when the Office of Taxes showed that £20 households were spread too thinly to make the higher threshold worthwhile. For the rest, the proposals took the form of additions to and subtractions from the existing representation, using the guideline that, in the reformed parliament, no borough was to have less than three hundred voters. The substance of the plan was contained in four lists (or 'schedules') of constituencies: a list of those places which would lose both their seats (schedule A); those which would lose one seat (schedule B); one of places which would gain two seats (schedule C); and one of places which would gain one seat (schedule D). These were the lists which Russell, who had been hurriedly reintroduced into the House as MP for Tavistock, would read to a stunned and derisory House of Commons on 1 March 1831. Since the meeting of parliament, indeed, the government had gained little but derision; its revenue proposals had been torn apart and their author, the new chancellor Althorp, subjected to ridicule. 'He had very nearly killed us, poor fellow', Creevey reported at the end of February. The reform plan at least gave the government a chance of cutting a figure and weakening the opposition's judgement that the Whigs must soon fall.

The scenes that day have become part of a familiar act in parliamentary theatre: the jeers, the gasps, the laughter, the incredulity, Peel 'pale and forlorn...[h]is countenance at times...convulsed'.[7] Between March 1831 and June 1832 parliament was nothing less than a stage. As the demand for 'the Bill' (whatever it contained) grew more clamant so corners of popular opinion for whom Westminster was formerly a distant and unknown mechanism became conscious of the struggle in the Commons, from March to September, and then of the resistance of the Lords and the King himself. That consciousness inevitably expanded when the future of reform was called into doubt, i.e. when the first bill was rejected by the Commons in committee in April 1831 and when the second was thrown out by the Lords in the following October.

First indications suggested that the reform bill would fail in the Commons and leave Grey with the impossible task of persuading the King to dissolve parliament at a moment when Ireland was alight with anger over the prosecution of O'Connell (about which the government had changed its mind too late). Despite the horrors of the first reading, Tories consoled themselves with the thought that the bill could not possibly pass the second one. In the middle of March, however, optimism ceased as head-counts promised a close result; so every nerve was straining as the House filled on 22 March when the vote was to be taken. It was three o'clock in the morning of the 23rd when the House divided 302 to 301 in favour of the bill. (The strategists had been confounded by John Calcraft MP who had changed sides at the last minute. He subsequently earned the contempt of both and committed suicide a few months later.) It was a great victory though hardly a convincing one. Some reformers wanted to dissolve parliament at once; some anti-reformers remained confident that the decision would be reversed as the government lost credibility. The ministers pressed on: there was nowhere else to go. 'Except in the matter of Parliamentary Reform,' Croker had written on the day before the decision, 'they are the weakest, most ridiculed, most despised Ministry that ever was in England.'

Suffering defeat from amendment in committee seemed in many ways worse than losing heroically in the public gaze; but at least Gascoyne's tactical *coup* in defeating the government in April with his motion to prevent any reduction in the numerical representation of England and Wales gave Grey the opportunity to press a dissolution on a reluctant King and Commons. Wellington was appalled, the more so as election results began to dribble in with their story of reform gains. 'The alteration of numbers has been double what it has been in any former election,' he complained, 'and the language on hustings, at election dinners, &c., shows that there is now as much of subversive opinion in Parliament as we can well stagger under.' He exaggerated the swing of opinion but only half a dozen of those who opposed the bill's second reading survived in the more open county seats; and although future by-elections showed that popular Toryism still flourished, the government's new majority, perhaps 130 or 140, would render the passage of a second reform bill all but certain.[8]

Efforts aimed at delaying the new bill or fundamentally altering its provisions were defeated in cabinet, and Russell reintroduced the reform bill on 24 June. Second reading stood in no danger this time; but the committee stage dragged through the summer and into September. One important concession was made to the landed influence when the government accepted the so-called 'Chandos clause' which proposed enfranchising tenants-at-will who owned land to the value of £50 per annum. For the rest the session amounted to a slow trudge through detail which drove Althorp close to a breakdown and Peel out of London at the end of August. As the last moments of the bill's passage came in September, attention shifted to the House of Lords and to the offensive which Wellington would be sure to mount there. Some saw revolution if he succeeded. The Duke himself saw revolution if he failed:

> We are assured that there will be a revolution in the country. Produced by what? By force and violence. I defy those who would use such violence. History shows that a great change has never, since the wars of the Houses of York and Lancaster, been produced in England by any authority but Parliament ... We have instances, even lately, of resistance to the law of the largest masses of men who commenced their resistance under the most advantageous circumstances, but they soon found themselves powerless against the power of the government and of the law united.[9]

Not all Tory peers would shortly feel so confident.

Five nights of debating principle and counter-principle did nothing to deflect the peers, many of whom had previously been written off as 'dormant and done for', from their purpose of resistance; and on the morning of 8 October 1831 the bill went down by a majority of 41 or, as a placard in Bond Street put it, '199 versus 22,000,000!'[10] Popular violence did, indeed, result, with riots at Nottingham and Derby which left ministers nervous about their next move. Althorp thought they could survive if they weathered the next fortnight, while conceding that 'just now the crisis [was] rather awful'; Melbourne, from the reports arriving at the Home Office, thought the crisis not only awful but quite new in its intensity; Peel, on the other side, dashed to Drayton Manor to protect his children from the Birmingham Political Union and the Derby rioters.[11] Moreover, on almost the same day that news of a major disturbance at Bristol reached the capital, news arrived also of an outbreak in Sunderland of the Indian cholera, whose arrival from the continent had long been expected. Yet all these things made remarkably little difference to the behaviour of the government. The decision to prorogue parliament quickly, ban any military organization among the Political Unions and then reconvene before Christmas to introduce the bill yet again may have helped quiet the unrest. Perhaps the unrest can in any case be overstated. Francis Place certainly believed that the crisis had passed by mid-October and dismissed even the Birmingham Union as so much 'moonshine'.[12] The cholera, meanwhile, remained localized, became a problem exclusively for the 'lower orders' and underpinned support for the Whigs through the widely held belief that the authorities were inventing lies about cholera in order to deflect attention from reform.

Balked by the House of Lords, the coach could follow one of three roads. Reform might, in the first place, be abandoned or deferred; second, the Lords might be persuaded by further argument that their position was untenable; or they might, third, be compelled to accept the bill under threat of an avalanche of new Whig creations to swamp the Tory majority in the second chamber. The first ruled itself out by the sheer momentum of reform and the government's public commitment to it. The second was tried half-heartedly by Grey in negotiation with a group of peers known variously as waverers, Harrowbites or moderation men who saw greater disaster in rejecting the next bill than in accepting an amended form of it. Led by Wharncliffe and Harrowby, their chances of persuading either side to trim positions remained slight. Compulsion, on the other hand, had enthusiastic supporters in the cabinet – especially Durham, Brougham and Holland – though it faced the nervousness of Grey, Richmond and Althorp, plus the implacable hostility of the new sailor-monarch, King William IV. Once the bill had, with slight modifications, been passed by the Commons for the third time before Christmas, the last scene was plainly set.

Yet the events of April and May 1832 belied all prediction. With insurrectionary activity easing during the spring (except in Scotland where it remained dangerous), and the Tory waverers doing their best to counsel moderation, it seemed certain that the second reading in the Lords would be allowed through. And so it was, less as a result of argument than out of knowledge that an agreement to create sufficient peers to pass the bill had been extracted from the King by the Whig cabinet. The long nightmare of the committee stage ensued; but again it was cut short by a rogue action, this time from the Tory Lyndhurst in a motion to defer the disfranchising clauses until the enfranchising ones had been passed. Grey's government was beaten in the division and the King seized an opportunity to accept the resignation of Whigs rather than countenance the hateful creation of peers. The coach again stood stationary while the King wasted ten days trying to create an administration led by Wellington which, as we shall see, was doomed from the start. Still, with its failure the future of reform at least seemed assured. The King had nowhere else to turn but to Grey, and the guarantee of creations. Even the diehards came to accept what had become inevitable and the bill came to the Commission of Assent in an all but empty House of Lords on 7 June. A witness records that the Duke of Sussex, the King's eccentric brother and a renegade reformer, appeared in the chamber to announce that the happiest day of his life had dawned. 'An old Tory, standing behind him, lifted up his hands in horror and fervently ejaculated, "O Christ!"'[13]

Reform could not be a terminus: the coach had to be driven on. This urgency derived less from Whig or radical ideology than from the looming party division if ministers should stop in their tracks and return to quietism. Only its identification with the party of 'movement' had saved Whiggery from major embarrassment over finance and foreign policy since 1830. Althorp, the leader of the Commons, had grown daily more overwrought and privately pondered the advantages to the government of his shooting himself. Grey seemed severely weakened, both by the political excitement of the past two years and by a recent bereavement. Two possible directions for the foreseeable future therefore emerged. It might be that Durham could achieve what Graham saw as his ambition, to become 'the head of a *movement* Government';[14] or a more moderate figure such as Stanley, the Whigs' only answer to Peel in the Commons, might drive a slower but more stable course. Neither of these things happened because neither was practicable once Ireland reasserted its primacy as a political problem.

Until after the first election on the new franchise in December 1832 speculation was necessarily vague. Inevitably, reformers fared well at that election and Tories fared badly. But it soon emerged that the '200 & 50 Radicals... of the worst description' feared by contemporary commentators had not materialized and that a figure of a hundred or so probably came closer to the mark.[15] At least equally significant, however, were the Irish returns because O'Connell now had, for all the Protestantism of many Irish MPs, nearly forty supporters dedicated to repealing the Union with Britain. It could not be long before that strength, dovetailed as it was into radical power generally, made itself felt. When Althorp rose, therefore, to introduce the government's Irish Church bill in February 1833, critics could be forgiven their cynicism about its origins. The bill aimed at soothing the Irish fever by reforming the despised and alien Anglican Church of Ireland. 'There never was,' O'Connell told the new parliament, 'in the history of the world, so poor a people with so rich a church.'[16] The new measure reorganized bishoprics, abolished church rates ('cess') and First Fruits and placed the income of the church in the hands of a Royal Commission. What it did not touch was the question of 'appropriation', i.e. whether surplus church income should be deployed for other than ecclesiastical purposes. What it announced, to those with an ear for high politics, was that Stanley was in control and that Durham was not. The latter had hoped to steer the cabinet in a more radical direction; but the church act and the coercion act which quickly followed drove him into resignation in March 1833 (with an earldom to comfort his supposed poor health). One kind of radicalism thus left executive politics for the next few years.

But Stanley had hardly consolidated his position. The central causes of Irish unrest – appropriation and tithe – had been avoided and could hardly be side-stepped for ever as petitions rained on the Commons and O'Connell persisted with his incandescent rhetoric. Stanley had, moreover, made so many enemies in his conduct of Irish affairs that Grey took the opportunity afforded by Durham's departure to shift him to the Colonies. Yet this move itself weakened the government's parliamentary position in a crucial area of policy. By the end of July 1833, Greville saw it as doomed. 'The Government conciliate no attachment, command no esteem and respect, and have no following...'[17] The crash that came during the following year was thus already in preparation. The cabinet fell into disunity at the end of 1833 over the Portuguese question where the hopes of Grey and Palmerston to help Don Pedro establish his daughter Dona Maria in that country had been aborted by a group of dissidents which included Stanley and Althorp; only a personal appeal from the King kept Grey from throwing up the seals. Lord John Russell meanwhile confused the Irish problem further by actually going to Ireland to see conditions for himself. His conviction, based on what he saw, that the government must appropriate the church revenue would finally drive the reform coach into a ditch.

In cabinet Russell's persuasions failed to convince his colleagues and the tithe bill which Stanley introduced in the 1834 session contained no appropriation clause. But when Stanley appeared, during his introduction of the bill on 6 May, to be committing the government against the principle of appropriation, Russell declared his willingness to separate himself from the government in order to do Ireland justice. Amid the cheering, Stanley scribbled his now famous note to Graham: 'John Russell has upset the Coach. We cannot go on after his declaration that "if ever a nation had a right to complain of any grievance it is the people of the Church of Ireland".' The resignations of Stanley, Graham and Richmond came before the end of the month; and they were only the first of a rush. By July even Grey himself – he had been threatening resignation since Easter – had been claimed by Ireland.

The details of these last miserable months of Grey's government need not detain us now, providing that we note the importance of the Irish coercion issue as again the fork on which politicians found themselves impaled. Grey's unwillingness to drop coercion and Althorp's refusal to propose it gave the prime minister his chance to get out. The new Whig leader, Lord Melbourne, embodied the mood that reform was *passé* and that the Whig party was moving elsewhere. Lady Holland had feared that 'Lambton [i.e. Durham] & a parti du mouvement w[ould] be upper most';[18] but the movement was rather a gentle one towards the centre, easing into the space which Stanley, Graham and their supporters (the 'Derby Dilly') had vacated. In one sense it was a retreat, an acknowledgement that the wheels of the coach were now horizontal and idly spinning. In another it was an affirmation that the time had come to fight Peel on his own terms in the mainstream of party, just as Grey ultimately had to do against Liverpool and Wellington before 1830. But this time colours were reversed. Melbourne had all the advantages as the leader of the party of government. It was Peel's turn to try to create a doctrine of credible opposition and to do it within a political structure still largely untried.

The new structure

Asking what the politicians had done in 1832 raises questions to which facts and figures about constituencies and electorates provide only a partial answer. Statistics tell one little of what the originators of reform had intended to do; they are similarly silent about what politicians believed themselves to have done as they converged on that first reformed parliament. And it would be a feeble explanation of politics in the 1830s and 1840s which included no understanding of what its central practitioners intended or believed. In the skeleton of the new framework an overt series of changes seems nevertheless clear: it would be reckless to leave them unremarked.

No alteration was made in the size of the reformed House of Commons which retained its 658 seats; but the composition of the representation reflected the subtractions and additions of the reformers' schedules. Three areas benefited from this reallocation: the 'Celtic fringe' of Ireland, Scotland and Wales (with important implications for O'Connell's status in the late 1830s); the English county seats (at the expense, to some extent, of the closed boroughs of schedule A); and the northern industrial towns, many of which were enfranchised for the first time. That Birmingham, Manchester, Leeds and Sheffield received representation hardly comes as a surprise, but it is easy to miss the arrival, albeit with single-member seats, of towns like Stockport, Sunderland, Bolton and Oldham. The theoretical threshold of 300 electors was broadly represented in the allocations, though over thirty English boroughs remained with smaller electorates.[19] The exception, indeed, offers a reminder that there still existed no rule: almost as little 'system' inhered in the new arrangements as in those they supplanted. Despite the guidelines provided by the £10 household in the towns and the £10 copyholder and leaseholder franchises in the counties, the new electorate resembled the chaos of the old in its extent and deployment. The inexhaustible conditions with which the vote was hedged around, the addition of £50 tenants-at-will to £50 leaseholders under the Chandos clause, the blurredness of a 'freehold' which might enfranchise the part-owner of a railway company as easily as a farmer, the presence in the new framework of voters qualified under the old 40s freehold whose privileges the act allowed them to retain but not bequeath: all these difficulties militate against any generalized description of what Grey and his colleagues had achieved. The picture could in any case be no more than a snapshot. In portraying a single instant it would, in a context of rapidly rising population and wealth, conceal those shifts in the structure over the next two or three decades which made Palmerston's world different from Grey's, and Peel's different from either.

The Whigs said that they were creating a polity which embraced the 'middle classes' whose power and prestige in society had long since outgrown their political standing. This was not seriously attempted in practice. At cabinet level only one minister – Althorp – consistently pressed for a more generous enfranchisement of commercial and manufacturing interests. Indeed Russell's original plan would have imposed a differential franchise in such areas and taken steps to prevent the 'swamping' of county seats by urban voters who enjoyed, in pre-reform days, voting rights in the rural hinterlands around urban centres. Intentions of this kind defy precise interpretation, not least because of the ambiguities of the language in which they often were couched. 'People', for example, is a word which in the 1830s seems to mean something like 'middle classes', whereas 'populace' refers to the 'working classes' or 'lower orders'. The phrase 'landed interest' is equally mined. After half a century of 'amphibious' activity by landowners who frequently so diversified their enterprises as to become both industrial capitalists and farming magnates at the same time, the reverberations of 'landed' in the decade of reform ran beyond those to which Walpole's ear had been accustomed. In 1832, for example, Russell included representatives of London and the large towns in his understanding of the 'landed interest'.[20] Some of these difficulties ease, however, when the problem is viewed from the standpoint of results. For what can be said with confidence is that if the Whigs ever intended calling into being a democracy, then they made a signal mess of it. The total franchise probably expanded by about 300,000 or 80 per cent. This provided for a reformed electorate of just over 650,000 people, most of them still in England, out of a population of over 16 million (excluding Ireland). At the parliamentary level of politics a sociological revolution seems no less elusive. Neither in the reformed parliament of 1833 nor over a longer time-scale can one find there a significant increase in the number of middle-class representatives. An analysis of 1847, indeed, still located 267 MPs connected with the aristocracy by birth or marriage.[21]

The reformed structure nevertheless supported an environment which was thought to be remote from that in which Wellington and Liverpool had thrived. The perceptions which politicians framed about this distance lacked clarity and not infrequently they became attached to symbols unimportant in themselves – the 'coarseness', perhaps, of debate in the new chamber, O'Connell's savagery within it, Cobbett's misplaced ranting at it. They could provoke sword-cuts at some imagined democracy as in Wellington's lunges against shopkeepers, for whom his contempt exceeded Napoleon's, or against 'Socinians and Atheists' and other types of Nonconformist:

A new democratick influence has been introduced into elections, the copy holders and freeholders and leaseholders residing in towns which do not themselves return Members to Parliament. These are all dissenters from the Church; and are every where a formidably active party against all the aristocratical influence of the landed gentry. But this is

not all. There are Dissenters in every village in the country; they are the
blacksmith, the carpenter, the mason, etc, etc. The new influence established in the towns has drawn these to their party.[22]

Evidence from poll books reinforces common sense in declaring this
social analysis a lurid nonsense; but its absurdity matters less than its
appearance and dissemination within the upper echelons of the political structure.

Besides, Wellington was unquestionably pointing his sword in a
significant direction. For the growth of urban Nonconformity, both
in absolute terms and relative to the population as a whole, following
a period of much quieter development in the late 1820s, was hectic
enough to reach the sensibilities of politicians and threaten major
consequences in the 1830s. The phenomenon did not reflect itself
strongly at a parliamentary level: only two Dissenters had been
returned for newly enfranchised seats to the reformed parliament by
1834. Yet one of them, Edward Baines of Leeds, epitomized, in his
provincial power and his connexion with the *Leeds Mercury*, a type
of civic potency which did not require a seat in parliament for its
survival. It was this local power which came to the forefront of
politicians' minds at Westminster as they pondered the politics of
municipal government in 1834–5. Repeal of the Test Acts had been
conceded in 1828, but the Nonconformist agenda contained many
more items. Some areas of radical Dissent anticipated, like *The
Extraordinary Black Book* of 1832, a reformed parliament's abolition of tithes and – who knows? – perhaps of bishops as well.

The bishops, understandably, looked to a different future. For them
the crucial problem consisted in how best to heal the rupture in
relations between church and state of which the events of 1828–9
were seen to be symptomatic. The Whig ministry had left them not
only unsatisfied but freshly challenged by Graham's Irish Church act
which the Bishop of Durham, Van Mildert, perceived as something
more serious than an affront to his high churchmanship; it was
'subversive of every rational view of an *Established Church*' and
likely to prove fatal to any understanding of Anglicanism.[23] Only
the extreme wings of the church scored victories in the face of such
challenges. John Keble's Assize Sermon of 1833 inaugurated a period
of sustained intellectualism among high Anglicans for whom Oxford
became a spiritual centre. (The young William Ewart Gladstone gave
adequate demonstration of how profound and how nasty the consequences might be for its sons.) On the radical wing, meanwhile, the
evangelicals – the 'Saints' – achieved a signal success for moral
suasion in their triumph over colonial slavery which they harassed

the Whigs into abolishing in 1833. In the more central regions of churchmanship, both established and Nonconformist, it was not until the 1840s that important thresholds were crossed in Edward Miall's Anti-State Church Association of 1844, which offered Nonconformists a new perspective of political action, and a language of resistance for Anglicans to stand against those who seemingly wished not merely to disestablish the church but dechristianize the state.

Property, like the churches, created its own forms of resistance inside the new order. Some of them were crass: witness the Marquess of Salisbury's vow to send his family and capital abroad and defend what remained with a gun. Most of the resistance was subtle and registered itself within reformed institutions. Slavery amounted to property for those who believed in it; it was no accident that some sixty owners of colonial land found their way into parliament through the 1830s.[24] In the second chamber, furthermore, a far greater body of resistance to reformed behaviour would need to be overcome before democracy gained an inch. The Lords had made it policy to avoid diluting their number with the Whig creations threatened by the government in 1832. Their powers remained untouched by the events of 1832–5; they may even have been increased. In the magnates' own 'countries' the redrawing of constituency boundaries, often undertaken with a view to minimizing surgery, frequently left local potentates with increased territorial sway. In the chamber they controlled, their ranks were strengthened through the 1830s by the promotion of experienced parliamentarians whose presence gave the lie to any view of the Lords as a collection of ignorant backwoodsmen.[25] Despite Aberdeen's conviction that the House of Lords had been castrated by its failure to halt reform, the decade after 1832 showed it virile still – not least in the sphere of Aberdeen's own expertise, that of foreign policy.

For governments and their parliamentary supporters in the 1830s and 1840s the critical areas of policy lay, it is true, in neither foreign nor colonial affairs. They were rather concerned with the exponential growth of government itself; with the fundamental tension between town and land which had made itself felt since 1815; and with the millstone of Ireland. The first of these – the so-called 'revolution' in government – has given rise among historians to an array of models and counter-models to explain the surge of expansion which characterizes the second quarter of the century. None of the models needs to be recreated here,[26] but it is important to be aware of the extent to which a thickening texture of legislation, from the Poor Law Amendment Act of 1834 and the Municipal Corporations Act of 1835

through bills designed to minister to factory reform, sanitation, railways and emigration, placed politicians in a changed environment.
The traditional term of abuse, a 'government of departments', now
became neutralized by the inevitability of the sin it described. Even
the departments themselves could find their sovereignty in jeopardy
as professional administrators developed such a mastery of the sheer
complication of government as to turn an under-secretary like James
Stephen at the Colonial Office into an 'over-secretary' who bullied his
betters. Abdications of this kind among the governing classes did
nothing to convince politicians that they were retaining control of
decision-making in the post-reform world. Instead suspicions were
fostered that England had been lost to 'theorists without a foot of
land of their own' and especially to a new race of 'political economists' such as David Ricardo and Nassau Senior. It is from men
such as these that one hears optimism in 1835 over the auguries of
the past few years. 'Never, in short, was a country more thoroughly
dug up, trenched and manured.'[27]

Echoes of an intellectualized radicalism returned frequently from a
group of 'philosophic radicals' among whom the economists figured;
and certainly this group had proved its power since 1830. The force
of the radicals did not stem from their imposing some Benthamite
Zeitgeist of social inquiry, still less from their becoming the vanguard
of a nascent democracy. Virtually none of their parliamentary number sat for the northern cities enfranchised in 1832. The radicals
tended to lose, moreover, the seats they did hold as the 1830s wore
on: their widespread defeat at the general election of 1837 underlined
the lesson that radicalism did not require a Parkes or a Grote or a
Roebuck to voice its demands. In the mid-1830s the radicals nevertheless indicated, through their strength, the signs of significant
adjustments in the political structure. They were a cohort of parliamentarians at a moment when radicalism had temporarily moved
indoors. They were writers and journalists during a period which
saw a spectacular rise in the power of the printed word in general and
of newspapers in particular.

On both sides of the argument, reform had stimulated an expansion and sharpening of political journalism. Working-class organs
that together comprised the 'great unstamped (by avoiding the official mail and thus the government's stamp duty) enjoyed a high-point
of influence through their denunciation of the reform bill's 'betrayal'.
The cumulative effect of the *Poor Man's Guardian*, the *Black Dwarf*
and many others on proletarian mentality is beyond quantification
but may have been prodigious. Within the political nation, on the
other hand, reform called for benediction from Whigs and radicals

and concerted attack from the Tory opposition. To this extent political literati were pulled into the centre of high-political discussion
rather than permitted merely to bark around its edges. Newspaper
editors enjoyed a similar promotion when politicians divined the
need to communicate with publics they took to be dangerously
enlarged. Greville reports the sending of Peel's Tamworth manifesto
of 1834 to 'the three great newspapers' – *The Times*, the *Morning
Herald* and the *Morning Post*. On the government side Palmerston
was not above writing editorials for Whig papers; he also subsidized
the *Observer* out of secret service funds.[28] Of all the journals the
most powerful remained, of course, *The Times*, under the editorship
of Robert Barnes. Its change of allegiance from Whig to Tory in 1834
came as a bitter blow to this government as it tried to maintain some
purchase on public opinion when the reform issue subsided. If the
time had not yet come for Disraeli to reassure his leader that public
opinion and *The Times* amounted to the same thing, then the time
equally had passed when Wellington could hope to shock correspondents by alluding to 'our governors, called the "Times" newspaper'.[29]

The importance of formulating a public message was reinforced by
a sense of developing urbanism which the experiences of the 1830s
and 1840s urged on sensitive observers. For though the fact of a
rapidly rising population was plain enough – the censuses of 1821
and 1831 both showed increases of over 2 millions in their respective
decades – the spread of the city seemed still more startling. London
and the 'new' cities of the north and west grew by as much as 40 or
50 per cent through the twenties and thirties: a crucial context for
understanding the bitterness of the fight for political control of the
boroughs in 1835 and beyond. Within the cities new organizations
and pressure groups announced themselves. The mind inevitably
turns to the chartists and the Anti-Corn Law League of the late
thirties and forties, but these only comprise the better known elements of that 'pressure from without' which Peel professed to hate.
Political Unions, now many-centred, remained agencies for agitation
after 1832; the National Union of the Working Classes and the
London Working Men's Association were harbingers of the same
mood; the Grand National Consolidated Trade Union presaged, for
all its failure in the short term, a significant move towards industrial
organization. Nor were these pressures confined to the towns. The
noise made by the Anti-Corn Law League should not be allowed to
drown the propaganda of pro-corn law societies in the agricultural
districts. Eight of these appeared in Essex, for example, in 1833-4,
thirteen in Lincolnshire in the later 1830s – 'affording facility to the
collection and expression of the opinions of the Agriculturists to

Parliament on matters affecting their interest'.[30] Both communities, rural as much as urban, sensed a threat. It seemed unlikely, moreover, that tensions between the two would readily diminish as corn prices slumped after 1832 and industrial depression took hold of the towns after 1836.

Without democracy, politicians assumed that policy should be agricultural before it was industrial, and aristocratic before it was either. The flurry of general elections during the thirties (1830, 1831, 1832, 1835, 1837) gave radical thoughts about the secret ballot a good deal of wind; but nothing came of them. Not until 1872 would voting take place in secret; not until 1883 would corruption be controlled. Meanwhile, the English governing class was not dependent on *force majeure* to secure its ends. As a commuting community spending half the year in London and the other half in provinces which the stagecoach and railway had brought closer, it sustained social cohesion to a degree which rival castes in Europe could not hope to emulate – a thought which goes a considerable way towards explaining what did *not* happen in Britain in 1848. Yet enough digging and trenching had taken place to make politicians think about the electorate they had made and the instrument – party – through which they must harness it. Whigs could hardly hope that the radicals and Irish would allow themselves forever to be treated as adjuncts to Melbourne, nor that electoral support would continue to gravitate towards them now that reform had been achieved. Peel, by the same token, could see no future in reassembling a Church-and-Field party to succour tithe-collectors and ignore crises in manufactures. Sitting on the 1828 corn law to await the return of prosperity did not commend itself as a sensible strategy to win over a new electorate.

'Conservatives' and 'Liberals' (1831–41)

Since the political disasters of 1830, Sir Robert Peel had enjoyed a fresh quality of life with his new wife at the recently built Drayton Manor. A marked alienation from current politics helped move his thinking into channels different from those familiar to Wellington. Peel despised and feared reform, needless to say, and not least because he saw that it could not end with what the Whigs contrived to do in 1832. But he saw equally clearly the futility of the Duke's devotion to the politics of a frontal assault on Grey. Relations between the two Tory leaders cooled, therefore, through 1831 and froze in the following year when Peel refused to serve in Wellington's doomed administration of May 1832. No great nous had been required to perceive the hopelessness of trying to stop the Whigs by putting in their way the Iron Duke and the House of Commons Speaker (Manners Sutton), whom Wellington seemed seriously to believe capable of heading a government. On the contrary, the 'days of May' fiasco confirmed Peel in his conviction that only a strong government could take the Whigs' place. Thenceforward he alternately impressed and infuriated his supporters in the Commons. Plainly he was now the major political talent on the opposition side of the House; yet he appeared unwilling to use his supremacy in any aggressive way. As Drayton Manor became an established house, however, so parties of politicians found themselves invited there to talk strategy. By 1833 Peel was coming out of his shell.

The notion of a 'Conservative' party which he brought with him was not in itself new. Wellington and Croker had used the term through the reform crisis as part of their siege vocabulary of raised drawbridge and lowered portcullis. By 'Conservative' Peel meant, however, to prescribe more than defence of the status quo. He formulated more positive obligations for a ruling class than Wellington deemed desirable or necessary. He built on the insight that reform would provoke reaction and that the reaction could be harnessed to party if the tone was right. He watched the Whigs crumble over Ireland and wondered about the future of men like Stanley and Graham now caught in a vacuum. He responded to an implication of 1832 that high politics should be seen as only one facet of the task of registering Conservative voters on the electoral rolls and winning elections with them. What was new about Peel's Conservatism, indeed, was not simply its rhetorical message but rather its commitment to an enlarged understanding of political method – one in which the foundation of the Carlton Club and the electoral work of F. R. Bonham became significant components. Although the Whig dissidents were not yet collaborators nor the Whig ministry beyond salvage, Peel knew by the time of Grey's retirement in 1834 that a new current had been set in motion.

Melbourne's government, formed in August 1834, ran into immediate difficulties on both of its flanks. From the radicals came a threat of insubordination, not least from Brougham who had been excluded. On the right wing, the rumours persisted over Althorp's uneasy adherence and the probability of his removal to the Upper House. The first threat became reality in September when Durham and Brougham tried publicly to outbid one another as originators of reform; the second materialized in November when Spencer finally died and Althorp succeeded to his father's title – an especially awkward development because Melbourne had formerly stressed to the King the importance of Althorp to the ministry's feasibility in the Commons. When he compounded the error by suggesting the name of Lord John Russell as Althorp's replacement, the King, who had not forgotten Russell's 'whisper of a faction' speech of 1831, amazed everyone by dismissing the government. This was the last time in British history that the monarch would be so bold. London, Greville says, was 'electrified'. Wellington was sent for and the cartoonists had a beanfeast as the Duke drove down from Stratfield Saye to Brighton for his royal consultation. Yet Wellington's advice to the King was for once realistic: he advised him to offer the government to Peel who was quickly recalled from holiday in Italy.

It might be argued that in taking office without a parliamentary majority Peel contradicted the statements he had made about the Conservative party since 1832. His eyes, however, were open. Unless he could prevail on Stanley and Graham to join the government, it could hardly last long; in the meantime it would offer a vantage point from which new doctrines could be announced to the public before a general election. Indeed, placed in this context, Peel's actions between November 1834 and April 1835 seem remarkably consistent. Once Stanley and Graham refused to come in, he formed a virtually unpolluted ministry. The Huskissonians had turned Whig and could be discounted; this left only the Grenvillites whose fusion with true Toryism was celebrated in offices for Wynn and Fremantle though not for the Duke of Buckingham. Indeed the landed presence which Buckingham symbolized was thought by commentators to have receded as they contemplated Goulburn at the Exchequer or Alexander Baring at the Board of Trade. Wellington (who had been reconciled with Peel in 1834) and the Earl of Aberdeen remained as isolated promontories of the old order in the government. 'Not a single old family', ran a joke on the radical side of the Commons. 'How are the Aristocracy fallen!'[31] The dissolution of December and Peel's decision to promote a manifesto of Conservative principles can be seen, similarly, as part of the broader strategy. Tamworth did not need a manifesto – Peel had been unopposed there since 1832 – nor was the manifesto uniquely Peel's. A cabinet dinner at Lyndhurst's (the new lord chancellor's) house sat up till midnight working over the details before it was released to the press. The manifesto and the Mansion House speech which followed it ('we hate the pressure from without') were intended to offer the country a consolidated message for its end of year conversations in anticipation of a January election.

Immediate prospects were not entirely favourable. Peel could reasonably hope for some electoral gains but not for a major shift of allegiance. The Whigs, indeed, saw the dissolution as a tactical error which would allow them to exploit their record on reform and the unfairness of their dismissal. The results, when they came in towards the end of January 1835, were in fact two-faced. It was clear that the Conservatives had made significant advances in the English boroughs; it was less than clear that their overall performance would allow them to continue in power. Yet although the government was vulnerable to a concerted attack by Whigs, Irish and radicals, opposition strategists knew that urgent work would be necessary if such an alliance were to be forged. This situation lent weight to an occasion which would otherwise have been trivial – the election of a Speaker for the 1835 session. The defeat of the Conservative incumbent, Manners Sutton, was a slap in the face for Peel if no more. But the real significance of the affair lay in the meetings at Lichfield House in London which had united the opposition factions into a coherent voting *bloc*. The emergence of this 'liberal' identity commented on the degree to which party lines had been redrawn and sharpened over the past six months.

Peel's 'hundred days' of government came to an end in April 1835 after his minority ministry had failed to make any progress with its legislation and suffered the abrogation of its first ambassadorial appointment – Lord Londonderry, Castlereagh's half-brother, who was rumoured to be off his head. Granted his objectives, however, Peel had little cause for misery and did not feel any. The essential task had been completed: parties had reasserted their identities, each with its distinctive language, electoral geography and (as Greville noticed in 1835) parliamentary presence:

> His [Peel's] party is in great part composed of the rich and fashionable, who are constantly drawn away by one attraction or another, and whose habitual haunts are the clubs and houses at the west end of the town; and it is next to impossible to collect his scattered forces at a moment's notice. The Opposition contains a dense body of fellows who have no vocation out of the walls of the House of Commons; who put up in the vicinity; either do not dine at all, or get their meals at some adjoining chop-house, throng the benches early, and never think of moving until everything is over...[32]

The 'Derby Dilly' stood between the two parties and enjoyed a brief period of influence as the larger bodies vied for its favour; but when it was torn apart by the appropriation issue in March 1835, Stanley and Graham moved towards the Conservatives. Outside parliament the question was already being asked; could Peel achieve in the counties the success he had won in the boroughs? Some evidence existed even at this stage of Whig weakness there. In the recent elections, for example, the Whig Palmerston had lost South Hampshire. He himself blamed landlord influences: 'The squire and the parson never had such a pull before.'[33] By-election losses through the rest of the year suggested the poverty of any local explanation, however. It was observed that Whig ministers submitting themselves for re-election after Peel had left office were not safe in county seats. (Russell lost South Devon, and Morpeth held the West Riding only after beating off a significant challenge from a Wortley.) Promotions to peerages among the Whigs, equally, were becoming occasions for elder sons to show by their failure in by-elections that county seats were no longer personal possessions.

Melbourne's return to power in April 1835 did not, therefore, remove one form of Liberal difficulty and it placed under the limelight several others, of which the most important related to Ireland. Russell had made his acceptance of office conditional on Melbourne's acquiescence in the appropriation of Irish Church revenues. The new prime minister consequently faced the prospect of concocting bills likely to be despised by half his own party and certain to be butchered by the House of Lords. Just as damaging was the power of O'Connell, now that the Lichfield House compact had made him respectable. He had been forced, it is true, into renouncing repeal of the Union with Britain as a *quid pro quo* for Liberal support but he remained a central embarrassment for the Whig section of the party at whom Tory propagandists sneered for most of 1835. These were weaknesses which the government could do little effectively to remedy. A more promising option appeared in combating their electoral slide by taking control of the reform of municipal corporations.

A commission had been examining this problem for several years. Its secretary, Joseph Parkes, was better known as the pillar of the Birmingham Political Union; and he made little secret of his objective in wishing to remodel the corporations, notoriously the most corrupt and impenetrable centres of pre-reform Toryism, in such a way as to destroy the roots of the Conservative party. The latter had, under Peel's guidance, accepted the principle of municipal reform at a time when they hoped to carry it themselves and avoid any extremism. Peel's fall had given the plum back to Melbourne who was unlikely to push it away after the *débâcle* in the boroughs at the beginning of the year. The act of 1835 ensured that both councillors and aldermen would be *elected* to office, an attack on the power of Tory local interests. Making the borough councils elective would not in itself render them Liberal strongholds at parliamentary elections; but many believed that the new councils would 'radicalize' the towns, as

Lyndhurst put it, and permanently damage Conservative prospects. For the radical Lord Ebrington the change was crucial: if the opposition of the Lords to the Liberals made Melbourne's government difficult to conduct, that of the towns to the Conservatives would henceforth make Peel's impossible. Similar considerations doubtless inspired Holland's optimism about the future towards the end of 1835. 'Of internal decomposition there is not the slightest appearance, fear or germ,' he tried to persuade the sceptical Ellice, 'and as for external pressure it seems to assume a shape and nature more likely to consolidate than to shatter.'[34]

1836 did little to shatter either Liberals or Conservatives. Indeed by the end of the parliamentary session commentators were speaking of quietude and boredom in tones reminiscent of 1824. The Liberal victory at the first council elections held under the terms of the Municipal Corporations Act, the tolerance bred of prosperity, and the still unconsummated cooperation of the Stanleyites with Peel, gave the government an easy year with only the House of Lords rising to the task of opposition. Even in these months, however, a worry could be heard among the more political minds of the government side that they had very little to talk about apart from Ireland and Russell's fetish of appropriation. They could dissolve, of course, but incidents such as the surprising Conservative win at Renfrewshire at the beginning of 1837 counselled discretion more than courage. The decision was taken for them, however, when the death of William IV forced an election. The King's developing infirmity in the summer of 1837 gave rise to much anxiety about the future, not least because Princess Victoria was only nineteen years old. His death on 20 June could only increase the Liberals' insecurity.

The government had two cards: the Corporations Act and the Nonconformists. That the two were closely related Melbourne had seen at once. 'They are the classes', he had said of the Dissenters, 'who will really gain by the [Act], not the mob or the theorists; every year their strength will be felt more and more at elections...'[35] The Dissenters' Marriage Act and Tithe Commutation Act of 1836 may be seen as practical applications of the same line of thought. And superficially the Liberals were successful in holding Peel at bay in the 1837 general election, for the Conservatives' gains were limited to about thirteen seats which were partially offset by losses in Scotland and Ireland.[36] But beneath the failure of Peel to dislodge Melbourne's government lay considerable grounds for Conservative satisfaction. The thirteen seats they had won could be added to the eight acquired in by-elections since 1835. (From our longer-term perspective we may wish to add the ten which would be won before 1841.) More important, the gains were concentrated in England which the Liberals had now lost at both borough and county levels. As well as losing electoral ground, moreover, the Liberals had lost their radical wing. Melbourne was left with a majority of thirty to face the coming trial of strength with Peel – hardly enough to underpin a style of government characterized by frictions and defections. Russell pinpointed the Liberal dilemma. 'If they attempt little', he wrote to Melbourne, 'their friends grow slack, and if they attempt much their enemies grow strong.'[37] Much of his party's experience over the next few years displayed variations on that theme.

Melbourne had attempted little since 1834, and after 1837 he attempted still less. The accession of Queen Victoria marked, indeed, a threshold in Melbourne's understanding of his duties. In appointing himself private secretary to the young monarch – a post he took to involve the responsibilities of equerry, bodyguard and father-confessor – Melbourne implied a personal withdrawal from day-to-day administration. Henceforth he would limit his interventions to blocking radical initiatives and preventing any reconstruction of the government until one was forced on him in 1839. This rustication at Windsor altered, moreover, the balance of power at Westminster. It made Russell not only home secretary and leader of the Commons but the Liberals' major strategist of the late 1830s. Yet any pleasure which radicals derived from the change proved short-lived. As one of his first acts in the new parliament Russell announced his belief that the 1832 settlement should be seen as 'final', thus jerking to a halt the 'movement' section of the party and its ambition to attack the House of Lords. Certainly Russell's mood had swung away from the hotheadedness over Ireland which had prevented his becoming an effective politician. But he did not turn into a cardboard Whig like Melbourne: he did not allow himself to become preoccupied by social instability and remained level-headed when confronting the chartists from behind his desk at the Home Office. In the Anti-Corn Law League, similarly, he recognized a potential tool rather than a formidable threat. His new moods extended beyond free trade to colonial power and international affairs. By 1840 Russell had undergone a metamorphosis from noise-maker into manipulator.

The weakened electoral situation of the Liberals and their unimpressive parliamentary majority doubtless contributed to the reorientations reflected in Russell's behaviour. More than this, however, seems significant in retrospect about these years. One is left with a strong impression of widening concerns among politicians, a result partly of an expanding political geography as Canada, America, France and the Middle East forced themselves to the centre of attention and partly because of the reappearance of widespread popular unrest and political agitation in the industrial heartland of Britain. The beginnings of an assault on the tariff system by which some sections of the economy were protected (to the disadvantage of the consumer) also contributed to the concerns of this depressed period; it was in 1837, the first year of severe economic difficulty, that Greville's mind turned to the corn laws and their likely repeal. The lenses through which Liberals saw these problems could be constantly removed and replaced as their own search for an electoral identity continued. All the elements of the situation appeared in focus simultaneously: there was no simple concentration on the chartists or the League but rather a partial consideration on such developments in the light of manoeuvres required by rebellion in Canada, slavery in Jamaica or the depredations of Mehemet Ali in Syria. Conservative objectives and responses also reflected confusion. Peel, closest now to Aberdeen and Goulburn and aided by his local registration wizard Bonham, felt in no hurry to force a crisis. Granted that the next election might be delayed till 1843, such inertia left many followers disturbed and sullen.

Before Christmas of 1837 two events had impinged on party politics. Russell's 'finality' speech of 20 November had convinced radicals that they faced a threat and the Stanleyites (who were now officially Conservatives) that their influence on centre politics lay behind Russell's change of heart. Against this background the news arrived on 22 December of insurrection in Canada. For the historians of radicalism and of Canada these closely consecutive events may be separable; but the political historian of Britain will see them fusing. The rebellion of (French) Lower Canada against British authority provided radicals with a test of the government's liberal credentials at precisely the time that Russell had called them into question. Melbourne's response – to give the most powerful spokesman of radicalism an earldom and send him to Canada on behalf of the government to report on the unrest there – was the discovered check of an otherwise witless defender. In a single move, abetted by Durham's acceptance of the offer, the prime minister sent over the water an individual who had become a mouthpiece for radical disaffection since his resignation from Grey's government in 1833. He also drew attention away from the incompetence of his own colonial minister (Charles Grant, now Lord Glenelg) who need not be dismissed until after the crisis had blown over. Peel, on the Conservative side, came under attack for his silence and Wellington for colonialist splutterings which even the House of Lords found suspect. Though the Durham Report of 1838 was to prove a milestone in Canadian constitutional development, the domestic impact of Durham's removal by, and defiance of, the government showed the weakness of radicalism after 1837. The failure of one of their number, the philosophic radical George Grote, to convince the Commons of the advantages of a secret ballot at general elections became part of that same epilogue.

The tensions which Canada had helped to develop tautened further as the growing power of O'Connell's Irish party made itself felt in parliament. Appropriation, it was clear, offered no way out. It had been effectively resisted by a parliament dominated by Liberals; it seemed hardly likely to succeed in one dominated by Peel. So 'the hinge on which... Irish policy ha[d] turned since the schism in Ld. Grey's cabinet'[38] was allowed to rust. Besides, Liberal needs had altered. After the English losses in the elections of 1835 and 1837 it had become more important to build an electoral bastion in Ireland than to crusade against the Irish Church. A Municipal Corporations Bill for Ireland embodied this new thinking in 1838 together with a hope that Peel might let it through in return for an abandonment of appropriation and a settlement of the tithe question. Peel's quietism, however, did not stretch to conceding a significant electoral advantage (whatever the bribe), and the government was obliged to withdraw its bill and think again.

Colonial affairs under the headings of Canada and Ireland had borne their usual fruit among politicians: they were bored. Attendance fell away in the Commons through 1838 as representatives of both sides failed to see what either was hoping to achieve. Melbourne had been spotted on his horse with the Queen but in few other places. Peel had relied on a policy of implied retribution – not exciting but enough to control Russell. The Irish had been jollied along but remained unappeased. The radicals had been profoundly disquieted by two years of evasion and half-truth. This was not a strong position from which to face the challenges which the chartists and the new Anti-Corn Law League posed.

'Chartism' was a broadly based movement with a national organization, though it drew most of its strength from regional bases in Birmingham, the West Riding, Wales, Tyneside and Clydeside. It has often been claimed to offer a conspicuous illustration of the development of working-class consciousness and the potential of proletarian politics. Yet one may with equal justice point to the diversity of the agitation for a 'People's Charter', its provincialism and its blurredness of purpose. None of the six points of the charter (universal suffrage, annual parliaments, secret ballot, equal representation, payment of MPs, abolition of property qualification for MPs) was to be realized before 1858; and for all its unquestionable long-term significance in the history of British labour, chartism made little impact on ministerial politics before 1842. No special powers were taken by government, as in Sidmouth's day, until after the Bull Ring riots in Birmingham in 1839. Until then the chartists appear comparatively rarely in political correspondence and when they do they provoke in their observers more irritation than fear. The mechanics by which information and rumour travelled within a segment of society that remained as gregarious as it was exclusive perhaps made this inevitable. Lansdowne's son, for example, put about the story in the spring of 1839 that when he went to join his yeomanry to control a chartist meeting at Devizes, he found the agitators themselves under threat from the crowd 'and obliged to apply to the Mayor and civil authorities for protection...against some of the scoffers'.[39] Now the illustration is a travesty: no one believes Devizes to lie in the chartist heartland and the report has all the embroidery of badinage designed to provoke amusement during circulation of the port. Yet from such observations the political attitude of a governing class could be strengthened. Certainly members of that class worried about 'mob' rule and 'alarming' reports of chartist attacks in the provinces.[40] But in cabinet circles the tone was not frantic. The first great chartist petition of 1839 had in fact been upstaged in London circles by the temporary fall of Melbourne's government, as we shall see. On returning to the Home Office, Russell continued to allow chartists to take their course until the violence of July legitimized the leaders' arrest.

Mancunian industrialists were largely responsible for the establishment of the Anti-Corn Law League in 1838. Like the chartists, its supporters tended to be classified by politicians initially as part of the pressure from without rather than (for all the wealth and respectability of the League's cottontots) as a new force inside the walls. True, one of the League's most effective propagandists entered parliament when Richard Cobden won Stockport in 1841 (after narrowly failing to do so in 1837). Cobden's partner against crime, the Quaker John Bright, likewise came in for Durham in 1843. By the 1840s, however, the electoral strategy of the League had imposed on it certain changes of style and approach. For the moment it presented itself as a proselytizing organization capturing a mood rendered widespread by economic depression. *The Times* caught it too for a time and Peel saw the corn laws bulking large in the coming session of 1839.[41] But from a Conservative point of view the corn issue was not ideal for driving a wedge between the radicals and the Whigs on the government side. Philosophic radicals could see the force of Ricardo's denunciation of protection but many radicals now seemed neither philosophic nor industrial. Indeed radical leadership often came from the same houses as did Whig: father and son not uncommonly embodied the extremes of Liberal parliamentarism and both saw themselves ultimately as the defenders of a territorial aristocracy. When Melbourne told fellow peers in 1839 that abolishing the corn laws amounted to the 'maddest scheme that ha[d] ever entered into the imagination of men to conceive',[42] he knew he could obtain a hearing in more radical places too. Protection was a tie that bound. Peel needed something more schismatic and he discovered it in Jamaica.

The West Indies offered Liberal ministers at least two kinds of unpleasantness in the later 1830s: that associated with maintaining executive authority over colonies, and that which followed from needing to ameliorate the position of blacks. In the Jamaican case of 1839 these problems fed on one another. The decision of the cabinet to suspend the Jamaican constitution was taken because resistance had been offered by the planters to British interventions and not least to the acceleration of the abolition of Negro apprenticeship which had begun with the abolition of slavery in 1833 and originally been scheduled to expire in 1840. But the government's position could be construed as a contradiction: a liberation via an autocracy. The dilemma embarrassed Liberals since if they betrayed the blacks they enraged the 'Saints' and if they betrayed the ethics of representative government they outraged the radicals. Peel was, to be sure, no less embarrassed by the task of defending the planters and appearing to constrain the mother country's authority; but he was driven along by followers looking for a humiliation of Melbourne who was plainly rattled by the coming debate in the Commons. For his part, Peel probably did not believe the government would fall; nor was this a useful moment to be called to office. He found himself obliged to think quickly, therefore, when Melbourne's government resigned after the defection of a number of radicals had reduced his majority to five in the Jamaica vote of 6 May 1839.

Peel nevertheless did not form the government he was now invited to form. The young Queen refused to part with her ladies of the bedchamber of whom many were wives, sisters or daughters of Whig ministers. Yet the so-called 'bedchamber crisis' hardly seems worth the gossip and furore which accompanied the news of Victoria's recalcitrance and is better seen as an incident in the developing instability of Liberal high politics. Melbourne found himself recalled to power, of course, when Peel refused to do battle with his monarch, but he returned with a team which reflected the collapse of confidence begun in February when he had first been compelled to adjust the ministry. Glenelg's withdrawal in the train of his Canadian failure had then been the cause of a reshuffle. With Spring-Rice's retirement from the Exchequer in August he was now to lose also Poulett Thomson and Grey's son, Lord Howick, whose radicalism had been offended by Melbourne's 'stationary system'. Russell's move to the Colonies, once the chartists had been given their quietus, proved a strengthener but the patent patching-up of a deal with the radicals on the subjects of ballot and corn laws (both were allowed to become 'open questions') said little for future cohesion.

Such cohesion was made yet more improbable by a crisis in foreign affairs that had been threatening Palmerston since 1833. The treaty of Unkiar Skelessi of that year had embodied a major tactical misjudgement by the British foreign secretary. When the Sultan of Turkey had requested British aid against his erstwhile subordinate Mehemet Ali, Pasha of Egypt, Palmerston had refused and driven Turkey into the arms of her traditional enemy to the north; so the Russo-Turkish alliance of 1833 was one which Palmerston had been hoping ever since to undo. His chance came when Mehemet Ali invaded Syria in 1839 and crushed the Turkish forces sent there to expel him. Palmerston seized an opportunity to press the major powers to respond to the pleas of a bankrupt Russia for assistance against the Pasha. However, propping up the tyrannies of Russia and the Porte hardly helped to propitiate radicals at home, especially when the French government under the Liberal Thiers voiced opposition to the coercion of Ali and even threatened a European war. Nor was domestic opposition confined to a few philosophic remnants. Quite apart from considerable support for the French line in the country, an agitation in which certain chartists prominently figured, pressure built up also at a high-political level from Russell, Holland, Ellice and Spencer, presaging a rift between Palmerston and Russell which was to become a familiar feature of Liberal territory for the next twenty years. Only when Russell himself came to suspect the purity of Thiers's intentions did opposition to Palmerston fade away and leave the second half of 1840 strewn with radical flotsam.

If colonial and foreign policy weakened one joint in the Liberal coalition, the continuing failure to impose a satisfactory electoral framework on Ireland weakened another. Time was running out for Russell in 1840: the octennial voting 'certificates' which granted the vote to successful claimants possessing less than a £50 freeholder qualification, under the Irish section of the 1832 reform act, were due to expire in that year. Unless the government could replace that system by a better one, the Irish electorate would decrease sharply when Conservatives challenged its registration and by decreasing would almost certainly become less Liberal. Indeed Conservative advantage lay in attaining one of two objectives in Ireland. They could either sponsor a bill of their own to make the electorate smaller and more exclusive; or, if that proved impracticable, at least ensure that Russell passed no bill to expand it. Stanley's Municipal Corporations Bill of 1840 was a product of the first line of thought for all its 'reform of abuses' flag of convenience. The government, moreover, was beaten repeatedly in the Commons during its passage as the Conservative party smelled blood and found new zest. 'Nothing keeps them away', O'Connell mused in a sour moment, 'when Ireland is to be injured.'[43] Russell eventually killed the bill on an amendment but only at the cost of promising to introduce a bill of his own, an unhappy portent for 1841.

Already Peel had done enough to render that struggle unnecessary. Russell lost a motion of no confidence on 4 June 1841 by 312 to 311, after defections and by-election defeats over the past session had reduced his majority to a whisker. Liberals desperately needed a message around which to regroup and they chose, partly in the light of the popularity and effectiveness of the Anti-Corn Law League, to commit themselves to an attack on economic protection. A genuine predicament had faced Spring-Rice, and later Baring, at the Exchequer when deficits disfigured the balance sheets in 1838, 1839 and 1840. Like Liverpool twenty years before, Melbourne and his colleagues had been driven to view revenue as a central difficulty. By reducing tariffs Russell might simultaneously encourage revenue from imported materials and offer the prospect of cheaper food. There appeared in any case little else worth trying: it would be foolish to ascribe the policy to some kind of intellectual conversion. Even Thomas Babington Macaulay, then a minister in the government and soon to become a romantic historian, failed to find idealism in the lunge for free trade. 'All the chances of our party depend on [it]', he told a correspondent. 'We shall play double or quits.'[44]

The choking of Peelite politics (1841–6)

In the short term the Liberal gamble failed. The general election went badly and especially so in the county seats where antipathy towards relaxing protection abounded. One humiliation was averted when Russell scraped home in fourth place for the City of London (four seats), but Joseph Parkes and his friends spent a miserable few days among 'the tombs of the County dead' as they worked out the scale of their defeat. Peel had in fact won by about eighty. Yet Conservative delight would soon be tempered by the thought that the victory rested heavily on gains in the English and Welsh county seats. The electorates in these constituencies did not comprise the broad base at which Peel's rhetoric since Tamworth had been directed; and the election overall had not reflected, in any simple way, the urban domination established by the Conservative party in the second half of the 1830s. Office, indeed, had come from the very direction which had then seemed so unpromising, that of county-based resistance politics. And it had come to a man who had built for himself a position which depended for its logic and integrity on the sublimation of horse-and-hound sentiment and a willingness to force Tories to be free. As Peel expressed the situation to Arbuthnot after a year's experience of government, 'the true friend to the astounded and complaining Ultra is the man who would avert the consequences which would inevitably flow if some of them could have their own way'.[45] What would those consequences be? Over the next few years considerable insights were to be offered into what might happen when the *parti conservateur* reasserted itself after a period of uneasy experimentation – not least the lesson, learned by all Peel's successors apart from Austen and Neville Chamberlain, that God himself cannot lead Conservatives where they do not want to go.

When Melbourne met parliament to suffer inevitable defeat at the beginning of September, no such negative notions intruded and Peel set about forming a government which drew on the strengths of surviving ministerial talent from the 1820s but also on newer men whose stars were rising. Two former prime ministers, Goderich (now Lord Ripon) and Wellington, received cabinet places. The first proved uncomfortable both at the Board of Trade and later, when he succeeded Lord Fitzgerald (the Vesey Fitzgerald of 1828) as president of the Board of Control responsible for Indian policy. The Iron Duke had likewise corroded; two strokes in 1840 put the Foreign Office beyond him and he came in without portfolio. Wellington's foreign secretary of 1828, Lord Aberdeen, thus returned to that office. He brought to it hardly any public reputation and little executive ability. The illness which he endured ('continual noise and confusion in the Head')[46] interfered with the instructions he sent to British representatives overseas and lent his direction of foreign policy a frequent ambiguity. On the other hand, Aberdeen was friendly with the French minister Guizot at a time when relations with France were of paramount concern following the war scare of 1840; and he had the ear of J. T. Delane, who had succeeded Barnes as editor of *The Times*, when the government as a whole was often out of favour at Printing House Square. Lord Wharncliffe (the waverer of 1832) and the Duke of Buckingham (the 'Chandos' of 1832) symbolized in their inclusion the voice of moderation and a defence of the soil. Lyndhurst, lord chancellor again, was a hardy annual.

Objects of intense political interest among the newer faces were the Whig defectors Stanley and Graham. In taking the Colonial Office Stanley consigned himself, as he later explained, to a backwater of policy, for colonial affairs played a substantially smaller role in the politics of the 1840s than in the years of Canada and Jamaica. He began, by the same token, a journey away from Peel which would eventually lead him to the Toryism of Bentinck and Disraeli in 1846. Graham, on the other hand, took a great leap forward. The Home Office was an advancement and for all his personal unpleasantness – Graham was always disliked for his icy and sardonic manner – the new minister quickly established himself as second-in-command to Peel. As their correspondence shows, the two men shared a common sense of siege as they worked the inhuman hours required by a style of executive direction which had become inappropriate in the context of ever-expanding government, and developed the community of mind reflected in *Punch's* gibe, 'two persons with one intellect'.[47] It may be recalled that in the later 1830s Peel's listening posts had been Bonham and Goulburn; and undoubtedly the latter suffered from Graham's advancement. Though he was now chancellor of the exchequer, Goulburn fell directly under the sway of Peel's authority in an area of policy where the prime minister's urge to dictate was overwhelming. If anyone could confront Peel on questions of economy and trade it turned out to be the young vice-president of the Board of Trade, William Ewart Gladstone, whose voice would be heard more distinctly after his entry to the cabinet in 1843. Meanwhile he spoke to a wider public through the pages of his *The State in its Relations with the Church* (1838) and *Church Principles Considered in their Results* (1840), two documents soon to weigh on him when Ireland loomed large in 1845.

For the moment it did not. Graham worried about violence and sedition in Ireland, but then he worried about it everywhere once the Home Office environment took effect. Peel, however, preferred to keep Ireland at the edge of the board. 'When a country is tolerably quiet,' he consoled Graham, 'it is better for a Government to be *hard of hearing*.'[48] From the outset Peel was clear that his initial problems were those of revenue and economic protection. He must somehow obliterate the deficits that had dogged the last years of Melbourne's government and he must meet the electoral challenge of the Liberals' pressure for a small fixed duty on corn to replace the 1828 scales. Free trade no more entered his mind at that stage than it entered Russell's: the bad harvests of the late 1830s still preoccupied ministers while the good yields of the early 1840s were yet to come. Political commentators on all sides sensed nonetheless that important changes were imminent. 'I consider the corn laws are done for', one observer wrote privately during the election of 1841. 'It does not signify much whether the Tories or the Liberals bring it about, but I can easily see before 3 sessions are over – the restrictive policy must go by the board.'[49] Peel himself approached the question in a mood dominated by the difficulties of raising revenue; he was prepared to countenance a relaxation of the 1828 scales only if he could pay for it by reviving Pitt's income tax which had lapsed in 1816. The cabinet discussed the problem behind a thick curtain of secrecy through the winter of 1841–2. Only when the Duke of Buckingham resigned in February 1842 could the public feel certain that Peel was about to disappoint the counties.

Certainly Peel had wanted 'to feel the pulse of the agricultural folks', as Gladstone put it;[50] but he and Graham worried about their fiscal difficulties. A party meeting demonstrated that the Conservatives were likely to tolerate a mild interference with the corn scales, while the free trade lobby, on the other side, advertised its impotence in the crushing defeat of Villiers's annual repeal motion by 395 to 92. Indeed some Conservatives could discern political advantage in the corn difficulty. Buckingham's loss amounted to a signal gain in the minds of many, especially when he was replaced by the Duke of Buccleuch who carried in his pocket title deeds to a substantial slice of Scotland. On the back benches the county MPs suffered exposure to the rancour of the farmers at agricultural shows and county meetings. Nor could they gainsay the potential severity of the reductions. With corn standing at 66s per quarter, for example, the proposed protective duty would now stand at only 7s instead of the 20s 8d which the price used to attract under the old scheme. Yet with corn prices running high in recent years the county representatives seemingly swallowed their embarrassment and did little to oppose Peel's scheme. Their sensibilities stirred in May when duties on imported livestock were removed, the more so as the price of meat slumped later in the year. But again, although the cattlemen of Scotland and the east midlands were appalled, the agricultural opposition in parliament refused to grow beyond a hard core of about sixty. Within high politics Peel and Graham were right to judge that revenue would prove more dangerous than meat to the government. Better than anyone, Peel remembered the years after the war when Liverpool's cabinet wrestled with the revenue problem and the parliamentary problems it occasioned. The income tax he now proposed was not swingeing (7d in the pound on incomes over £150 for the next three years) but he knew it would hit the parliamentary class where the flesh was soft.

All of this remained the price, however, that 'property' had to pay for the 'cheap purchase of future security'.[51] Peel knew, of course, that economic depression had sharpened mass misery, fed chartism and sustained the Anti-Corn Law League. In 1842, as in 1819, a number of politicians took seriously the threat of social convulsion, not least during that troubled summer. The second parliamentary rejection of a chartist petition in May 1842 helped prompt the 'plug' riots in the north of England in which the plugs of steam-boilers were confiscated by workmen and factory production was brought to a halt. By the time Graham set in motion a wave of arrests in August, political society showed signs of alarm. But the north seemed still, despite the railways, a long way away, as was South Wales where the 'Rebecca' riots erupted at the end of 1843. And though reports continued to reach the capital of intolerable social conditions in northern industrial areas – 'perfectly appalling', according to Greville as he loafed around his autumn itinerary of Newmarket, Cromer, Broadlands, Canford and Hillingdon – their immediacy receded as other currents closed around London. Even Graham managed to calm himself once troops had entrained to the worst affected districts and the chartist leaders been removed to prison. At the same time Prince Albert enjoyed his warm reception from the chartist mayor of Birmingham, who went out of his way to '*vouch* for the *devoted loyalty* of the whole Chartist Body'.[52]

As Peel's second year of office neared its close he filled up space in a letter to one of his embarrassments, Lord Ellenborough, governor-general of India, with a list of his government's political preoccupations.

> You will see that we have an extraordinary combination of difficulties to deal with at home – Ireland and Repeal agitation; a terrible schism in the Church of Scotland; civil war in Spain; increasing jealousies of the Church on the part of Dissent, leading to formidable and successful organization against our Education scheme; trade still depressed, and revenue not flourishing.[53]

The list is interesting for its exclusions: nothing about chartism, or agitation against the 1834 Poor Law, or Lord Ashley's campaign to reduce hours of working for children in factories, or the section of his party which by now felt queasy over Peel's sense of direction. Foreign policy, the church-and-state problem, the revenue and, above all, Ireland; these are still at the centre of Peel's vision. Two of these difficulties – the Irish and the Anglican – became, moreover, convergent streams.

Ireland's problems had been obscured by England's during 1842 but important changes were afoot there. A mass movement dedicated to the repeal of the Union with Britain had gathered considerable momentum as O'Connell pushed it along. A Repeal Association, modelled on the old Catholic Association, proved the efficacy of tried techniques with its mass meetings and its 'Repeal Rent'. Through 1843 the government grew anxious about the Association's success and the dangerous mobs which Westminster saw as its by-product. 'They will put the State down,' Wellington urged, 'unless the State puts them down.'[54] The banning of a proposed monster-meeting at Clontarf in October, the arrest of O'Connell and his subsequent trial, conviction, imprisonment (and eventual liberation despite it all) reawoke the embarrassments of 1833. If 'an entire people' did not teeter on the edge of rebellion, as Graham was bleating in the summer of 1843, the events of the following winter and spring impressed on Peel more forcibly than ever before the necessity of appeasing the Irish. Yet Conservatives had already shown themselves loath to give offices to Irish Catholics despite the prime minister's entreaties since 1841; while at home Peel faced implacable hostility to concessions from the stiffer Anglicans in his cabinet, not least from Stanley, whom he could not afford to offend, and the new entrant Gladstone, whom he could not pretend to understand.

Since 1841 Gladstone's meticulously kept diary had knotted-up with conscience over the imperative to resist popish muddle and yet preserve the constitution as an ecclesiastical polity. He watched, during 1843, the 'most powerful and menacing' divisions in the Church of Scotland end in the so-called 'Great Disruption', as the church split through its inability to resolve tensions over the role of congregations in appointing ministers. He watched, more painfully still, his sister Helen's head turn towards Rome and John Henry Newman's resignation from St Mary's, Oxford, as he moved the same way. Aches of which the prime minister knew nothing were eating at the president of the Board of Trade long before the cabinet came to discuss 'Maynooth' in 1845. From a different direction Graham was exasperated by Dissent which opposed and thwarted his attempts to kill sedition by enlightenment in the educational provisions of his factory legislation. The climate of opinion in which Edward Miall's Anti-State Church Association (1844) would take root and the Dissenting politics which animated the Liberalism of newly incorporated towns marked shifts in church–state relations which Gladstone had hoped to avert.

That Peel should not have mentioned the Conservative party in his catalogue of problems offers one insight into his deepening predicament. For since coming to power he had shown himself strangely insensitive to the instincts on which his followers depended for their peace of mind. Many, perhaps most of them, were what Peel liked to call 'blockheads'. Tory leadership often turned, however, on giving such men words for their conversations and parables for their political guidance. Liverpool and Wellington knew the importance of encouraging the backward and giving those who thought in pictures a consistent image of rectitude. Peel, on the other hand, despised and dismissed his blockheads. The new mansion he had built at Drayton, his *arriviste* triumph in making the Prince Consort like him, his unquestionable prominence – waist, head and shoulders above his colleagues – all this marooned him. He took comfort from the certainty that only he could save England but was oppressed, as his working day stretched into the night, by the thought that even he might not be enough. By 1843 party sensitivity had been seriously offended. 'Are we to agree to every motion which we think most prejudicial to agriculture because they threaten us with retiring?' Richmond's son wrote when the government proposed to lower duties on Canadian corn.[55] Even more intimate colleagues began to worry about Peel's manner. The formation, after the Smithfield Show in December 1843, of an 'Anti-League' to resist further attacks on the agricultural interest threatened a further offensive against Peel in the 1844 session. Worse, Peel had already decided that the cotton, wool and sugar duties must go whether he were hampered or not.

If this determination became apparent, it would offer Russell (now leader of the Liberals) the prospect of cutting a figure once more. His party had been able to accomplish little heretofore, with even by-elections running against them. The squashing of the chartists and the government's successful treatment of O'Connell (before 1844) had left no purchase for radical critics. In foreign affairs the Webster–Ashburton treaty of 1842 had settled part of the outstanding boundary dispute with America; the 'opium war' with China had been ended and Ellenborough's ill-advised thrust against the Afghans and Sind kept out of parliamentary predominance for the moment. Palmerston laughed and groaned ('What with him [Ellenborough] in the East, and Ashburton in the West...'[56]) but Russell knew full well that domestic policy (and effectively that meant free trade in view of the League's growing threat) had to be the hope for the future. Through 1843 he had therefore striven to jerk his collar off the 'fixed duty' hook he had nailed up for himself in 1841. His landed Whigs, on the other hand, were always likely to hang him up again.

Peel's defeat over his proposal to abolish sugar duties in June 1844 can be seen against this background. Commentators deemed it a serious setback, the more so for its being the second of the session. Ashley had brought retribution on Peel for the latter's studiously civil ignoring of his demands for the government to limit child labour to ten hours a day. By grafting this unwelcome provision on to Graham's 1844 Factory Bill he succeeded in forcing the government into a minority. 'We are just now overrun with philanthropy', was Greville's reflection, quaint when placed against the harrowing material used by Engels in his diatribe *The Condition of the Working Class in England in 1844*. When the parliamentary assault on the sugar duties went down by twenty, with over sixty Conservatives in the majority, Peel began to understand that he had lost his party. He, Graham and Stanley wished to resign at once but were persuaded by other cabinet colleagues to ask the House to reverse the vote. Although it did so, enough had been done to convince Peel that he must soon fall. If he knew this, moreover, historians cannot be allowed to pretend that they do not: Peel's last months were acted out in foreknowledge of doom and must be analysed accordingly. 'Our friends', Graham told Lyndhurst after the sugar vote, 'have at last succeeded in rendering our future progress next to impossible.'[57] Those who looked to the slim hope began to ask with increasing frequency a question much asked within the walls of Windsor Castle and Osborne. Could not Sir Robert and Lord John learn to work *together*?

Whether parties would cohere or fragment must rest, it was plain, on the confidence which they could generate in facing the corn law problem. Events of the past two years had shouted its inevitability as an issue. By ceasing to shout and turning its attention to manipulation, especially in fighting by-elections and buying 40s freeholds for potential electors in the shires, the League had forced matters to a head. John Bright's return for Durham in 1843 had been less disturbing, for example, than a League candidate's victory in the City a few months later. The Anti-League, organized since February 1844 into the Central Association for Agricultural Protection under the leadership of the Duke of Richmond, had also retired to its tent. Peel may have been 'converted' by the arguments of Richard Cobden – it was after a speech of Cobden's in 1845 that Peel muttered his celebrated aside to Sidney Herbert, 'You must answer this for I cannot' – but he was exercised too by the electoral muscle which both sides of the argument were developing. In his budget of 1845 he swept away many remaining duties, renewing the income tax for a further three years to help take up the slack, without touching corn; but when Croker looked into the faces of country gentlemen he saw men 'out of spirits' and looking to the government for something 'comforting and gratifying'.[58] Nothing came; for as Ireland enlarged, so options were closed to the struggling administration.

Disaster in Ireland was impending but not yet known. Fears that the potato crop, which comprised the sole subsistence of the western Irish peasantry, had been destroyed by disease gained no general currency among politicians till September 1845 and remained unconfirmed till October. Before the seed potatoes were even planted, however, Ireland had brought Gladstone's resignation from the government. He had told the prime minister at the beginning of 1844 that he could not acquiesce in Peel's plan to increase and make permanent the government grant to the Maynooth seminary which trained men for the Irish priesthood. At that stage Peel had been anxious, in the light of O'Connell's prosecution and trial, to appease Catholic sentiment; but he pulled back in the face of opposition from Stanley and Gladstone. The former, however, had lost some political weight after his promotion (at his own request) to the House of Lords, so Peel returned to his scheme over Christmas and the new year. In the proposal itself there was little novelty: the grant had been increased twice since the Union. From Orange Peel, on the other hand – the man who had argued in 1829 that Maynooth's charter should be revoked and Irish priests brought under the control of government[59] – it implied another *volte-face* to add to the lengthening list. Gladstone chose to make no capital out of Peel's elastic strategy and left the cabinet quietly in January 1845. But in the Commons there were Conservatives ready to roast the premier for his record of betrayal and one of them especially so. He had evolved a style which combined limp-wristed discourse with a playful eloquence designed to score Peel's cheek with blades of grass. He it was who responded to news of the Maynooth proposal by asking his fellow MPs to turn on this 'dynasty of deception'; to 'tell persons in high places that cunning is not caution, and that habitual perfidy is not high policy of state'.[60] Benjamin Disraeli, a climber disappointed by Peel's refusing him office in 1841 and latterly a spokesman of the jejune and ineffective Young England group, had at last found his vehicle, just as the body of confused mediocrity which populated the Tory benches had discovered an advocate of deadly brilliance.

Fissures revealed themselves also in the Liberal position. The deaths of Grey and Spencer in 1845 removed two moderate voices and called forward the radicalism of Grey's son, Lord Howick, who succeeded to the title as third Earl. Like Russell, he suspected that Peel could not last; but unlike Russell he did not despise Peel and was inclined, in some moods, to make him a present of radical Liberalism should his colleagues ditch him. Among these Aberdeen in particular had become unhappy about what power had done to Peel's personality and about the prime minister's refusal to endorse a pro-Guizot position in foreign policy, a disagreement that had prompted Aberdeen to offer his resignation in September 1845. As early as April he had reminded Russell of the need for Liberals to assure themselves of Peelite support before they destroyed Peel.[61] 'Everybody knows that the Tory party has ceased to exist as a party', a commentator observed later the same month. Funeral orations were being composed even as Peel survived the Maynooth crisis and reached the end of the session intact. His best plan, in retrospect, probably lay in attempting further revision of the corn duties in 1846, though this would offer no easy policy after rain destroyed much of the 1845 crop and heightened agricultural resistance.

Besides, events were now running faster than strategy. When news of the Irish potato blight and prognostications of imminent famine reached London, Peel found himself unable to convince the cabinet of the necessity of suspending the corn laws at once and reconvening parliament. As November ground on with no apparent resolution of the problem, Russell saw his chance to escape commitment to a fixed duty and swing the Liberals behind free trade. He had, however, already left London. The session was over and he had joined his sick wife in Edinburgh where she was receiving treatment. Consequently his behaviour had to be both unilateral and non-parliamentary; he announced his change of heart in a public letter which, when it appeared on 26 November, placed more pressure on Peel to do something and also generated electricity among the Liberals. Still unable to persuade his colleagues to suspend (a move that everyone knew would be tantamount to repealing the corn tariff), Peel resigned on 6 December and left Russell with the uphill task of compiling an administration which could take effective power in a parliamentary minority. That Russell failed to do so after ten days of sour negotiation owed something to personality and a good deal to Grey's refusing to work with Palmerston; but it owed more to the underlying rift within the Liberal leadership that had been opening since the summer. Grey's refusal to serve was certainly the last straw for a leader close to exhaustion and all but broken by fears for his wife's life. Yet that refusal had derived from Grey's continuing ambition to collaborate in the formation of a 'Liberal' ministry under the leadership, not of Lord John Russell, but of Sir Robert Peel – 'a Peel liberal Govt, in which Ld J. shd be offered a place but which on his refusing (as he wd do) a good many of us might join'.[62] Grey was thus acting out his role as the son of a father: his recommendations were those which the 1820s had consecrated. But party had not been then what it was now. By Christmas Peel had returned to office with the old gang (minus Stanley who refused to return) and Gladstone back in the cabinet. No one doubted, least of all Peel himself, what the next step must be.

Between the introduction in January 1846 of Peel's proposal to phase out the corn duties over three years and the Lords' passing of his bill's second reading on 28 May 1846, politics was dominated by the inevitability of repeal and Peel's impending political death. In the field of *policy* – on corn, on India, on Maynooth, on the currency – Peel continued a victor until his very last day. But Peelite *politics*, with its autocratic method and dangerous flexibility, had been given notice to quit by the old Tory party. If there were to be a Peelite party, it would have to operate henceforth outside the boundaries of Conservatism defined by Disraeli and Stanley and Lord George Bentinck. This latter universe expanded, moreover, in the early months of 1846. Two of the by-elections held in the first part of the year were won by protectionist candidates, most glaringly at South and North Nottinghamshire, where Lord Lincoln was beaten first by an anti-Peelite under the direction of Lincoln's estranged father, the Duke of Newcastle, and then by Lord Henry Bentinck, brother of the protectionist enthusiast, in the sister seat. In the Commons the forces of darkness were taken to amount to about 200, plus a veritable regiment in the Lords. A few Whig peers hoped to capitalize on the class-war aspect of the issue by using it as a basis for a Whig/Old Tory alliance – 'a monstrous and discreditable connexion' – until Russell stamped on them. Indeed what is striking about these last months of Peel's effective career as a statesman is the degree to which a major recasting of party did not occur. 1829 and 1830 were not relived in 1845 and 1846. Instead a sense of inevitability hung over the Peelites' future in the central currents of politics after Peel had been defeated on his Irish Crimes Bill on 25 June 1846.

In order to understand this stability a perspective is required of the relationship between party and the various interests which were called into play by the corn law issue. There plainly existed an element of 'town' versus 'land' in the debate but it is one which can mislead. Many protectionists owned land; but so did considerable numbers of those pressing for repeal. Disraeli himself lamented that 'good names' remained with Peel; names such as Fitzwilliam and Spencer, until the latter's death in 1845, had been associated with the cause of the Anti-Corn Law League, despite their vast acres.

Similarly, the townsmen who became involved with chartism often opposed repeal since they believed the League to be a tool of an employer class hoping to use the abolition of the 'bread tax' as an excuse to lower wages still further. No simple analysis of the competing groups along the lines of economic interest can untangle the matted textures of the divisions which the corn issue brought about. Nor will it do to speak (as Croker always did) of the 'country gentlemen' as though they formed the exclusive repository of protectionist opinion. Many of these voted in the House in favour of repeal. A more efficient predictor of positions taken up by parliamentarians over corn turns out to be the division over Maynooth in 1845. That this should be so, moreover, should not be seen as surprising or paradoxical because, although the Irish Church had presented a very different issue, it tested the same range of sensitivities within the conception of *party* that Peel had done so much to foster over the past decade. Lord George Bentinck's impassioned defence of the corn duties in the months before Peel's defeat was a defence of the integrity of party rather than an apologia for landed power; it contributed to an opposition self-consciously marshalled 'for the sake of Political Morals and the character of Publick Men'.[63]

Some, it is true, saw revolution written into the events of 1846. Graham and Croker passed heavy hours in their letters to one another, composing ashen depictions of the future, one of them hoping that this concession over corn might at least deaden 'the din of this odious and endless topic of democratic agitation', the other inconsolable before the prospect of 'an elective government... a nominal monarchy with republican institutions'. On the other side of politics Earl Fitzwilliam saw a future for Peel as 'the champion of the democracy'.[64] Their reactions were disproportionate. Wellington, the Jeremiah of 1830, had the sense to strain at no more gnats. Peel, the supposed vehicle of public opinion, dampened Bright's congratulations by remarking that he had never understood, when prime minister, that the public had any interest in the question.[65] Democracy had in fact been brought no nearer by the events of his ministry, nor had any new world been planned. In rejecting Peelite formulae as an aberration within Conservative development, an old world had reasserted itself. Wondering whether Peelite politics might eventually find a home elsewhere asked a question too remote to answer as Lord John Russell composed his government. What was clear was that in doing so he faced a task distinctly different from the one confronting Grey in 1830. The problem then had concerned the making of a Whig future. It must now be made *Liberal* – an operation that would take more years and talent than Russell had it in him to give.

3

The Mechanics of Stability

A moment of anxiety (1846–52)

Confusion was the legacy of repeal among politicians. One vital component of their thought-world had apparently been undermined, if not destroyed, and a measure of economic experimentation indulged in at the very time when custodians of both rural and urban power felt nervous about the economy. Much of this worry turned out to be needless. Over the next few years, however, politicians showed themselves to be disturbed by economic and party instability. Revolution, it should be stressed, rarely preoccupied ministers except for a brief period when Europe suffered cataclysm in 1848 and the chartists brought their third petition to London. Ireland, for all the desperation of its slide to slow starvation, usurped domestic considerations only when it appeared on Treasury agendas or dovetailed into the chartist threat with Smith O'Brien's abortive rising in 1848. India caught a wind when one of the Peelites agreed to govern it but thereafter made little mark until its explosion a decade later. The continent crept closer because Palmerston was again its ambassador; once more Britain had a foreign secretary prepared to subordinate party, policy and above all Russell's titular leadership to the demands of his highly personal understanding of power. With an election pending, however, politicians talked mostly about the new party context and what it might bring. Most of their calculations and predictions came to nothing but these cannot be separated from the history of Lord John Russell's faltering government. As in a placid game between grandmasters, the richness lies less in recorded moves than in annotations of variations never played.

In many ways, the psychology of the political nation presents the most fascinating aspect of these years. Worries among landed proprietors in the early 1840s had been submerged recently in a series of bumper harvests; but the harvest of 1846 proved a disaster and sent grain prices to the 100s mark even after the release of bonded corn. Imports stimulated by the failure exacerbated the difficulties of a currency and credit system which was already under strain from rampant speculation on the railways on the one hand, and the financial controls of Peel's Bank Charter Act on the other. The impending crash seemed no less obvious than the one of 1825, and when it came in October 1847 it impinged on minds still attuned to the 1820s and 1830s. Lord George Bentinck, the new protectionist leader, had been Canning's private secretary two decades before and he had cut his teeth on Huskisson's version of economic truth. Sir Charles Wood, Russell's chancellor of the exchequer, looked back to Baring's deficits in the last years of Melbourne's government and swore oaths to avoid them during his own tenure. *His* mentor had been Peel and it was to this retired statesman that Wood sometimes took his problems. The sense of threat and depression that hung over Wood's early days lifted in the 1850s when the agricultural improvements of the later 1840s inaugurated that period of 'high' farming which it had been the vaunted aim of Peelite policy to stimulate. Manufacturers, similarly, eventually pulled out of the depression into a more confident environment symbolized in the Great Exhibition held in a specially built 'crystal palace' in 1851. In the short term, however, politicians sought to understand post-repeal politics by accepting the Peelite mythology of what had happened in 1846.

This mythology rested on two propositions: that the Conservative party had divided into two sections, one 'Peelite', the other 'protectionist'; and that the division had been brought about by conflict over economic policy. Neither of these assumptions is helpful. Their psychological function at the time derived from the enhancement they gave to the dignity of the Peelites and the encouragement they offered to those who believed the Conservative party might be reunited if its economic stance were to be altered. Disraeli saw at once the urgency of eradicating such impressions, but he faced a long struggle to convince the bulk of the Tory party that 'protection' had been merely one element in the opposition to Peel and should be considered a dispensable attribute rather than a position whose defence was critical to Conservative identity. Indeed, the abandonment of that identity in favour of something older had much to commend it. In one House of Commons speech in 1850 Disraeli used the phrase 'the Tory party' so many times that his audience could not help noticing it.[1] Yet he proved unable to remove the protectionist plank until it had broken at two general elections. For the moment politicians persuaded themselves that the 110 Peelites held the key to the future amid 'a general confusion of parties, persons and principles'.[2] This concentration of limelight on Peel's shattered band directed attention away from the schismatic Whigs.

The very word 'Whig' feels strange in the presence of the Liberal party; but in 1846 that party was moving backwards. A decade had passed since the Lichfield House compact of 1835, and the strains imposed by repeal on a party which still represented some of the broadest acres in the country became considerable. Personal antipathies intruded, as we have seen, to end Russell's attempt to form a government in December 1845. It is true that the bitchiness subsided sufficiently to allow Russell to succeed in the summer of 1846 where he had failed at the end of 1845. Grey, the bugbear of the winter, agreed in effect to take the Colonial Office and keep his mouth shut. But something had gone wrong with Whig politics when Russell's cabinet could look so much like Melbourne's. A crisis in Whig talent had become obvious to contemporaries: there were no young ones. Back in the 1820s and early 1830s the sons of Whig potentates had supplied a certain verve and sharpened the language of aristocratic responsibility. Indeed, some historians, impressed by this electricity, see a genuine and long-term rejuvenation and reformulation of Whig-Liberal politics as its result.[3] When we review the unhappy years after 1846, however, the temptation grows to regard the young whigs of the reform era as ephemeral elements within a political formation that would find it hard to maintain any style of ideological identity for very long.

Indeed the composition of the Russell government did little to signpost the way to a new Whig purpose. Clarendon circulated to the cabinet a note lamenting the lack of one at the beginning of the government's life. 'For years past,' he wrote, '[Whiggery's] vitality and vigour have been failing...It is considered to be aristocratical in its opinions, exclusive in its personnel, and guided by past historical reminiscences rather than by present public opinion.'[4] Nonetheless, only the introduction of Wood brought a new face to the front-rank offices unless one counts the seduction from the Peelites of Fox Maule (later Lord Dalhousie) in 1851. Graham refused to join, while from the Irish and radicals there came no more than a token display. O'Connell was not brought in and a leading radical like Milner Gibson received a post only outside the cabinet. Cobden and Bright were excluded altogether. If more than mischief lay behind the rumour that Cobden had been offered the consulship at Cairo, something significant was being said about the relationship between the government and its radical wing.

Some of the cabinet nagged one another with the fear that the Conservative party would heal unless an immediate election rubbed salt where it was least wanted. To those who knew Tory language in the summer of 1846, however, this fusion seemed as likely as a coalition between the Methodists and Lucifer; and even the Whigs were constrained to delay an election for a year or so in order to let Peel's followers attach themselves to government or, as Bentinck chose to put it, crawl into parliament under the gabardine of the Whigs. But a dissolution had to come: it was predicted by simple arithmetic. Russell could not hope to stay in power when Bentinck's party held the same number of seats – about 270 – while the Peelites sat in the middle with their hundred-and-odd. To this extent the election of July 1847 helped Russell's cause by giving him a paper majority of perhaps twenty or thirty; precise figures defy reconstruction since party ascriptions were exceptionally fluid. The election nevertheless presented more cause for Whig nail-biting than celebration. The Peelites, in the first place, did not suffer as much as the Whigs and Tories had hoped and expected. Their hard core diminished and left only seventy or so from the men of 1846, but new 'free trade' Conservatives topped them up to three figures again. A second problem for Russell emerged from the character of his own supporters: they proved, too many of them, to be the wrong kind of Liberal. Radicals and Irish dedicated to repeal of the Union with Britain had increased their power within the parliamentary party. The unopposed return of Bright and Milner Gibson provided an emblem for this movement and turned their shared constituency from Manchester into 'Manchester' – a radical phenomenon and catch-cry. Even Russell's topping of the poll at the City of London was drowned by the noise made by the man who came third. For Baron de Rothschild's election to the third seat, which his unwillingness to take the parliamentary oath prohibited him from accepting, promised to transform one of the most respectable constituencies in the land into a Jewish County Clare.

Deeper currents lay beneath the surface of the 1847 election. Eddying against the stream of rhetoric about protection came an underpull from Dissent – a force untested electorally since 1841. Since then events had charged Nonconformity with new life and, in Edward Miall's pressure group of 1844, new organization. A proposal from Russell's government to increase aid to Anglican schools revived the controversies of Graham's Factory Bill and imposed on 1847 a new authenticity for 'Maynooth' as the litmus of party. Politicians in their constituencies tried to coax this sentiment by amplifying their anti-Catholic pronouncements. And when they failed to stem the tide, as did Macaulay, Hobhouse and Roebuck, who lost their seats, they ensured that their colleagues – and not least

Russell – were told of the problem. Perhaps Russell would soon begin ruminating on the sentiments that would inform his Durham letter of 1850. Perhaps he had moved already one step closer to the abandonment of 'finality' which both he and Disraeli broached in 1848 and thereby inaugurated two decades of franchise preoccupation.

If any such thoughts existed they remained in the lower parts of the brain: the seat of primal instinct. In 1847 the consciousness of government was occupied more immediately by Ireland. Combating the continuing famine there and redrawing Irish land legislation had already cut the cabinet into a triangle. The advance position was held by Russell and his (reluctant) chief secretary Clarendon who attacked his colleagues tirelessly for their inability to understand the country they had charged him with controlling, while loathing the Irish party quite as stridently as they.[5] Rearguard actions took place between two further factions: the Treasury, represented by Wood and his cheeseparing assistant undersecretary, Sir Charles Trevelyan; and Anglo-Irish Whiggery of whom Lansdowne and Palmerston were the most voluble in fighting the corner of order and Property. Russell extracted from his colleagues an Irish Poor Law, Clarendon managed a diluted arms act; but neither succeeded in guiding Irish affairs in a new direction (though the prickly problem of landlord–tenant relations occupied the cabinet over the autumn and winter).[6] Only after the rebellion of 1848 did enough political pressure accumulate to allow an attack on the land problem with the Encumbered Estates Act of 1849 which accelerated land transfers and thus applied a few drops of oil to the most grating mechanism within Irish society.

Ireland represented one battle which Palmerston was losing. He was fighting on the second front of foreign policy, however, and losing there as well. Domestic affairs rarely preoccupied him. As an Irish peer sitting in the Commons he had to fight elections, but he ensured after his humiliation at South Hampshire in 1835 that he held a seat – Tiverton in Devon – that would present no further problems. Indeed he encountered opposition there only once between 1847 (when the chartist Harney stood against him and received no votes whatsoever) and his death in 1865. In his foreign policy Palmerston had, like his erstwhile detractor at the Colonial Office, Lord Grey, commenced a programme of reverses. When Grey had made it impossible for Russell to give Palmerston the Foreign Office in December 1845, the lights had gone out all over Europe. ('Nous pouvons dormir dans nos lits', as Metternich put it.) His very name had remained sufficient to instil fear there after Peel's fall. But the man who had run rings round Thiers in 1840 now proved unable to thwart the French determination to secure the likely reversion of the

Spanish throne by marrying Louis-Philippe's son to the Infanta's sister. On the other hand, Palmerston's turning away from France helped British radicals to see in him something to admire – one of the more paradoxical characteristics of left-wing Liberalism in the late 1840s. And in ceasing to be merely an ogre in foreign policy Palmerston became in these years a considerable element in cross-party political conversations at home.

These conversations were not dominated by the need to assume a position about working-class insurrection, despite the convulsions on the continent. Two public disturbances caught the public mind in the spring of 1848: a radical-inspired riot against the continuation of the income tax proposed in Wood's budget; and the gathering of the chartists at Kennington Common on 10 April. The first scarcely counts as an uprising despite some cries of 'vive la République!' 'They plundered a baker's shop,' wrote one observer, 'and broke the lamps at Buckingham Palace'; the home secretary's report to the prime minister betrayed no sense of crisis.[7] Far more serious appeared the prospect of a major chartist demonstration in London. The Duke of Wellington, who had retained his position as commander-in-chief after the change of government, decided to meet the challenge head on; and the turnout of military support and specially enlisted constables (among whom stood Gladstone) suggested much executive determination. The government's refusal to allow the body of chartists near the centre of London placed their solitary MP, Feargus O'Connor (Nottingham), in an awkward logistical position which, together with the driving rain, militated against the event having the propaganda value that had been envisaged. Palmerston's request that muskets be sent to Osborne to protect the Queen, coupled with Gladstone's private prayer on the evening of 10 April that 'our hearts feel profoundly the mercies of this very remarkable day',[8] stand as reminders that the meeting had been taken seriously, especially so by Clarendon and Trevelyan. But it remains clear in retrospect that Kennington Common was not divisive among the ruling classes in the way, for example, that the Queen Caroline affair had been in 1820. Rather, it threw parties together in a common defence of order and constitution.

The humiliation of the chartists and, shortly afterwards, of O'Brien's Irish rebels ('suppressed by fifty policemen!' sneered Malmesbury) gave rise to despairing thoughts among radicals about the impossibility of securing democratic progress through the high-political game. 'We must *oust* the dominant class', raged John Bright a week after Kennington Common, 'or they will destroy us.'[9] Yet these exclamations only serve to silhouette the misunderstanding of

political preoccupations current among those responsible for mar-
shalling the pressure from without. Within the psychology of the
governors, the income tax took on more significance than the chartists; and more important than either was the decision of the radicals
formally to dissociate themselves from Russell's government. Winning them back again, or preventing their fusion with other sectors of
parliamentary opinion, became a more enduring concern than anything O'Connor's crowd and its petition could create.

Peel and his ex-ministers watched from a distance. They still held
together for the most part, despite Herries's defection to Bentinck and
Dalhousie's to Russell. What Peel intended is unclear: his premature
death after his horse threw him in 1850 foreshortens perspective and
leaves a major interpretative problem. He achieved a certain consistency in the most unanswerable fashion possible: he died young. By
leaving the stage before everyone else he gained what Russell's long-
evity denied him – a reputation for rising above party which the
1850s might have called into question. Yet it seemed clear enough
to contemporaries that in the foreseeable future Peel intended to take
no part in politics. Graham made some noises about policy but
refused offers from both Russell and Bentinck. The younger Peelites
(Gladstone, Sidney Herbert, Lord Lincoln, Edward Cardwell) soon
chafed at Peel's abrogation of leadership but saw the futility of fusing
with Disraeli's Tories. They convinced themselves that the angels had
gone to sleep and left parties, 'in the best sense of the term', to die,
not least their own which, as Cardwell complained in 1849, 'has
fallen into forgetfulness of itself, and is naturally forgotten by the
world... That Sir Robert Peel's party saved England from confusion
and has been rewarded by its own annihilation is the simple
fact... The general breaking-up of all parties becomes daily more
decided, and chaos continually advances.'[10] What is most striking
about this imagined fluidity is the paucity of fluid. Russell was
worried about his party's cohesion, certainly, but no very significant
defections had taken place by 1848. Indeed Disraeli's moping during
these months conveys precisely the contrary impression: party lines
had proved too rigid to help him bring about the realignments he
wanted.

Part of Disraeli's problem lay in Bentinck's obsession with the
presentation of trade statistics designed to show the truth of the
protectionist case at a time when he, Disraeli, wanted Tories to talk
about other things. At the beginning of 1848 Bentinck resigned the
leadership in disgust at his party's 'tea-table twaddling'[11] over the
Rothschild case. Disraeli still failed, however, to gain a free hand. An

unlikely directorate of Disraeli, Herries and the Marquess of Granby was deputed to run the party and it proved so constricting that Disraeli returned to novel-writing. Economic circumstance in any case remained unhelpful for the jettisoning of Bentinck's crotchet over protection. An agricultural depression, widely believed to be the product of repealing the corn laws, had provoked growing resentment among the landed interest. 'The agricultural distress is so great', Disraeli told a correspondent in 1849, 'and the general prosperity so doubtful, that, even if we were inclined, fusion under the standard of Peel seems impossible.' When, in the coming years of crisis on the land, Tories worried about revolution, the insurrection of farmers, and not proletarians, preoccupied them – the prospect that, 'if we do not do something... before 4 and 20 months are passed, every farmer will be a republican'.[12] In this context Peel's death could not encourage the *rapprochement* with Toryism that otherwise might have been contemplated. It seemed unlikely that the party of the soil would join forces with the Peelites while Peel's son was being drummed out of the Atherstone hunt by local farmers who despised his name.

Russell saw no point in easing these frictions. Indeed, he made them worse in three policy initiatives aimed at consolidating the Liberal party. Freeing the sea from trading restrictions could be viewed by Liberals as a corollary of freeing the land. And the debates on the government's bills to repeal the navigation acts and the sugar duties awoke the bitterness of 1846 once more. Now, in 1849, the point of these proposals was to enlist radical sympathy again and encourage the Peelites in the wake of Graham's latest refusal to join the government. The Liberal bill nevertheless came close to backfiring. The seventeenth-century navigation acts, which confined many cargoes to specifically British ships, were seen by Tories still smarting from what Peel had done as the last bastion of British mercantilism. The House of Lords debate of 8 May 1849 threatened to reverse the Liberal majority for the bill in the Commons and precipitate the consequences about which Russell had recently been anxious – a dissolution, followed by radical agitation. More to the point, however, Palmerston expressed worries that an election now might trigger issues which the Liberals could well do without, 'Ballot, Extension of Suffrage, and other matters of that kind'. Besides, the farmers would vote protectionist.[13] Preparations were therefore made for a pitched battle in the upper chamber. As many 'proxies' as could be got were hurriedly arranged and 'pairs' were contrived on the evening of 8 May even when, as in one notorious case, a government peer was too drunk to be kept upright. The opposition acted even less scrupulously. We have it on Edward Stanley's authority that Tory whips pushed past the tellers two quite insane peers rushed from their institutions to the House for the purpose, 'the keeper of one of them in attendance in the lobby'.[14] In the event it was the government's astute handling of the proxy voting which gave it a narrow majority of ten.

In anticipating suffrage as a coming problem, Palmerston assimilated a Commons anxiety; for Liberal strategy was moving back towards parliamentary reform as a way of regaining radical confidence. This might also distract Cobden, Bright, Roebuck, Hume and their friends from their sniping at fiscal policy which the government had been enduring since Wood's 1848 budget. Palmerston himself had compounded the situation in his insistence, after the emergence of Louis Napoleon in France, on extending the south coast defences against the possibility of invasion. Cobden whipped up an agitation for a major reduction in defence spending, and a popular dimension to the clamour appeared in mass meetings at Manchester and Liverpool.[15] So powerful, indeed, did the pressure for 'retrenchment' become that Disraeli pondered the chances of the radicals joining the Tories if he adopted it. At the high-political level the radicals found an unlikely ally in Wood himself who was determined to find a surplus from somewhere. Their only ally on the question of parliamentary reform, however, remained Russell; and the story from 1849 to the defeat of the government in the Commons in February 1851 is one of Russell's failure to persuade the cabinet to take up franchise in earnest. It might be noted that his opponents often grounded their resistance on the absence of any mass pressure for extension. Politics *without* democracy created within itself the pressure-point for a reform bill; and that pressure had a rationale which bore little relation to any democratic impetus.

Russell's instincts about 'Liberal' needs after 1846 bore on his thinking about reform. They throw light too on his stance over Protestantism in 1850. Unlike retrenchment or reform, the religious controversies that afflicted Russell's government lay largely beyond his immediate control. His hopes of gaining some ground in Ireland by subsidizing the priesthood had come to nothing. The defeat in 1850 of the Bishop of Exeter's attempts to block the admission of the Reverend G. C. Gorham to a parish in his diocese, after finding the latter's baptismal doctrines eccentric, said something about politicians' leverage of bishops but little about their ability to manipulate popular religious sentiment. Russell's major initiative in this area came in the autumn of 1850 in his response to Pope Pius IX's reestablishment of the Catholic hierarchy in Britain for the first time since the Reformation. This assertion of territorial bishoprics under the control of a Metropolitan (Wiseman), replacing the former system (outside Ireland) of vicars apostolic and missionary priests, had been seen in Rome as a spiritual initiative with no implications for the Anglican Church's relationship with the British State – one so feverishly brooded upon by Gladstone in 1838. Public opinion in Britain, fanned by *The Times*'s sense of outrage, saw it differently and prompted Russell to capitalize on what he depicted as 'a pretension to supremacy over the realm of England, and a claim to sole individual sway, which is inconsistent with the Queen's Supremacy, with the rights of our bishops and clergy, and with the spiritual independence of a nation'.[16] This so-called 'Durham Letter', written to the Bishop of Durham and published on 4 November, was supposed to plant the Whig flag in a field of Protestant upland where it had not been seen for a generation. Russell planted it alone: the letter that went to Durham was no more the fruit of consultation than the one that emanated from Edinburgh exactly five years before. Clarendon, Russell's colleague, remarked on the cleverness of the forgery when he saw the text.[17] The letter also offended radicals and Peelites, a thought that urges the question: why did Russell write it and then persist in its *reductio ad absurdum* in the Ecclesiastical Titles Bill of 1851?[18] Perhaps he felt, as Stanley ruminated, that Lord Derby was about to turn the clock back to 1833 and appear once more as defender of the church unless pre-empted in the role. Perhaps he was hoping to cast a shadow over someone nearer home.

For Palmerston had been making his mark on events since 1848. Radical approval of him had risen in proportion with his unpopularity at Court, which was common knowledge. But what brought his methods to the centre of political controversy was his response to the difficulties of a Gibraltarian Jew – Don Pacifico – who claimed the privilege of British citizenship. Pacifico's grievance against the Greek government was real enough: he had been expropriated. The blockading of Greek ports by British ships struck neutral observers nonetheless as an over-reaction. Indeed the episode might have proved damaging to Palmerston had he not turned his parliamentary defence into a rodomontade celebrating, in effect, the liberalism of British foreign policy since Canning. The peroration, with its 'Civis Romanus Sum' motif, established Palmerston's position in June 1850 as an irreplaceable pillar of Russell's government or – more important – of any government. Disraeli's plans certainly encompassed him in the letter-writing days before the 1851 session; and a chance presented itself sooner than even he anticipated. Russell's apologies for the government's dissembling over franchise did not persuade radicals to support him against a reform motion of P. J. Locke-King (Liberal:

Surrey East) on 20 February 1851, so the prime minister suffered defeat at the hands of his own supporters. To Disraeli's unutterable disgust, however, Derby refused to contemplate forming a minority ministry unless he could secure Peelite help. Since everyone took Graham to be a lost cause, Derby fastened on Gladstone as the key to the situation. As in 1834 the one man who held the key to the situation had left the country and gone to Italy. When Gladstone refused office on his return, however, the Tories abandoned their attempt at a ministry and left Disraeli in a sulk.

Back from the dead, Russell's government held out little hope of life. Its leader found himself trapped between the last generation of senior Whigs at his elbow in cabinet and a strong parliamentary grouping (a hundred MPs had voted for the Locke-King motion) who would back Palmerston if he chose to withdraw from the government. By the autumn of 1851 that possibility had strengthened. Relations between Russell and Palmerston degenerated both publicly and privately against the background, not only of radical grievance at home, but also of Hungary's struggle with Austria. This difficulty had first seriously obtruded in British politics during the previous year when the foreign secretary condoned the rough treatment afforded to 'General Hyena' (Haynau, an Austrian military thug) by the British public on his visit in September 1850. It reappeared now in Palmerston's private acceptance of a vote of thanks prompted by his support for Hungarian and Polish freedom fighters, an issue of great sensitivity because the cabinet had recently prohibited the foreign secretary from receiving in London the Hungarian nationalist Lajos Kossuth. Pique doubtless played some part in Palmerston's insubordination in accepting the vote of thanks, but he was also impressed by its source: it came from the boroughs of Islington and Finsbury, the latter of which was the stronghold of the radicals Tom Duncombe and Thomas Wakley. Nor did it lie beyond Palmerston's grasp that the same mechanism which had encouraged him to sin would also prevent Russell from bringing retribution. If the foreign secretary were to be dismissed, his crime would need, from Russell's point of view, to be less popular. When, therefore, the news of Palmerston's sacking broke in London on Christmas Day and Boxing Day 1851, the public reason became Palmerston's unilateral recognition of Louis Napoleon's self-declaration as Emperor of France – a platform which was not likely to attract radicals.

Russell was finished all the same. Warm letters were hurriedly got off to the great Peelite houses over new year and brought tepid replies. Another dash for the reform haven predictably followed the opening of parliament. But the carrying of Palmerston's amendment to the militia bill – the notorious 'tit for tat' – on 20 February put Derby into power and deprived Russell of any political leadership until after – a fact that speaks volumes – the death of the man he had sacked. 'I do beg you to observe', Russell had written to Wood in the first year of office, 'that my object has been all along to secure a majority of Liberals, without attaching undue importance to the possession of power by the Whigs.'[19] By 1852 he had lost Whigs and Liberals alike. The former disliked his expropriations in Ireland and his persistent prattle about reform at home; the latter thought his reformism skin-deep and believed better things of Palmerston's recent behaviour. Rather than weld the 'Liberal' fragments of 1846 into a cohesive force, the experience of Russell's administration had scattered them wider than ever.

No significance need be read into the Tory ministry that followed: its sole function was to prepare for an election. Most of its personnel were of necessity unknown to the public. They were also unknown to the deaf Duke of Wellington whose roars of 'Who? Who?' as he was told the new names gave Derby's first ministry a sobriquet which posterity has retained. Disraeli had hoped to hook Palmerston in the certain knowledge that he, at least, would not 'give...trouble about principles';[20] but Derby felt uneasy at the prospect of Palmerston's return to the Foreign Office, and Palmerston refused any lesser position. Gladstone, on the other hand, ruled out a fusion with the government on the grounds that the ministry was still theoretically committed to protection. The apparition of 'pure' Toryism gave rise to radical prognostications of social revolution should tariffs be introduced. But in fact the government had no thought of tariffs; indeed it had no thought about anything. On the contrary, Derby intended to ensure that the government did not present itself to the public in any clear way in the general election of July 1852. Protection itself was rhetorically dismantled and rebuilt as the half-way house in which Russell had locked himself in the early 1840s. All commentators agreed that no issue presented itself at the hustings. In some areas Protestantism was still potent as a catch-cry; in farming districts some talk of duties was a *sine qua non*; in the cities the radical recipes were pressed. But the central purpose of all thinking Tories – to annihilate the Peelites – could hardly receive great public stress.

The Peelites were not destroyed in 1852. It seemed clear, however, that even after one of the most confused elections of recent times, they had done badly, and returned with only some thirty or forty MPs plus a few disengaged Liberal Conservatives.[21] The Tories, on the other hand, had also failed in their objective of acquiring an overall majority, though they had improved their parliamentary number, to around three hundred. On the Liberal side of the House, the Whig element had suffered in comparison with urban radicals. These changes of emphasis are not striking; and it is consequently easy to underestimate the long-term significance of the 1852 election for intra-party faction. The results confirmed the party of Derby and Disraeli as heir to the Conservative party which Peel had alienated; they left the Peelites waiting in the centre with a mouthful of melted butter; they gave encouragement to radical ambitions for a re-channelling of Liberal energies; they gave notice to the Whigs that parliamentary reform must be made as urgent an issue as Grey's Whigs had made it in the 1820s. In the decade that followed there were to be many changes of government and much angling for party advantage. But what had happened since 1846 at least demonstrated that within the most prosperous and settled polity of Western Europe, the moment for anxiety was past.

A changing climate: the 1850s and beyond

Had the eldest son of a parliamentary family won a seat at the 1852 election, perhaps immediately after going down from Oxford or Cambridge, he would have entered an environment familiar in many of its details to his father or uncle in the years after 1815. The disfranchisement of St Albans for proven corruption stood as a reminder (just before the election) of what the Great Reform Act had not reformed. The general election itself suggested little improvement. A man coming in for the first time might look back on it as an instance of signal venality and agree with Cavendish's claim that the Commons had been filled 'by bribery and corruption' or echo Wilson Patten's suspicion that 'not one tenth of the entire House was legally elected' in a country whose bribery laws were so generally disregarded.[22] Even among the honest there remained the necessity of canvassing for votes, the 'days and weeks of screwed-up smiles and laboured courtesy, the mock geniality, the hearty shake of the filthy hand, the chuckling reply that must be made to the coarse joke, the loathsome, choking compliment that must be paid to the grimy wife and sluttish daughter, the indispensable flattery of the vilest religious prejudices'.[23]

First impressions of the House would likewise fit comfortably into received wisdoms from an older generation. Rows of empty seats often shocked newcomers. Lord Derby's son, Edward Stanley, made a count of absent and silent members in 1853-4 and discovered that, on average, only about a third of the House was likely to appear for a debate while fully half said nothing at all. As in the days of Arbuthnot, moreover, the Tory members drove their leaders to despair by their absenteeism. Stanley found that the middle-class radicals who represented 'commercial boroughs' attended most regularly, followed by the officeholders, then the Irish, and as a poor fourth the country gentlemen for whom the day ended with dinner if, indeed, they had come to London at all. When Disraeli arrived back at Westminster after spending the dead season in Yorkshire during the winter of 1852–3, his bitterness directed itself at his own ranks:

> He complained loudly of the apathy of the party: they could not be got to attend to business while the hunting season lasted: a sharp frost would make a difference of twenty men. They had good natural ability, he said, taking them as a body, but wanted culture: they never read: their leisure was passed in field sports: the wretched school and university system was in fault: they learnt nothing useful, and did not understand the ideas of their own time.[24]

This world seems one in which Anthony Trollope's Tories would have felt at home. It was the one that the Liberal Trollope himself experienced when he fought Beverley, a cockpit of corruption, in 1868.

The grip exercised by landed power had relaxed a little since 1841. But it remained (and was perceived to be) still of decisive importance. 'We do not possess a constitutional government,' as a radical journalist observed in 1855, 'but a landocracy.'[25] Possibly the security of that dominance even increased as harvests became abundant after 1852 and both prices and rents climbed – especially beyond 1856. One can find representatives of the grand manner, to be sure, though none so majestic as Lord Tankerville who sought counter-revolution even in the weather. ('I like a rainy Sunday. The people can't come out and enjoy themselves. I hate the people.')[26] Hidden within this dominance, for all that, lay tensions which had begun to work themselves out in the political structure.

Consider a cameo in the dukeries of Nottinghamshire: a microcosm of political perception from within park gates. The corn law problem had severed Welbeck from Clumber in the late 1840s when Lord George Bentinck took up his defence of the corn laws and Lord Lincoln, now fifth Duke of Newcastle, became a leading light among the Peelites. Bentinck had died in 1848 but Newcastle, recovering from a broken marriage, established himself as a focus of landed power. His estate was crippled by encumbrances but he contrived nevertheless to play a role similar to that played so insidiously by

Thomas Pelham-Holles, the first Duke of Newcastle, in the eighteenth century. The correspondence of politicians in the first half of the nineteenth century contains many letters with that evocative address, 'Clumber'. Indeed, on one weekend in January 1852, a single bomb could have terminated Peelite politics altogether when Newcastle, Aberdeen, Cardwell, Herbert and Gladstone held a pre-session conclave there amid the limes. In local and regional politics, on the other hand, a different picture emerges. Two by-elections occurred in the county constituency of South Nottinghamshire in 1846 and 1851. The first we have already encountered: it was the occasion of Lincoln's defeat at the hands of a protectionist farmer. The second occasion underlined the warning because Lord Newark, scion of the Manvers family of Thoresby Hall, lost to a farmers' candidate who was not even a farmer.[27] The rebuff offered contemporaries another piece of evidence for their file on deference. Thoresby had been the house towards which Lord George Bentinck had been walking when a coronary attack felled him three years before.

In the towns, too, new moods imposed themselves on sensitive observers. Radicals had learned the importance of orienting themselves differently from the 'philosophic' posture of a previous generation. The defeat of chartism had helped release into urban politics a demotic force seeking outlets. Some of it ran towards corporation politics, fastening on the implications of the Municipal Corporations Act and the incorporation movement of the 1840s to provide, as at Leeds, a radical-Liberal town hall. Some ran towards the mounting temperance agitation of the fifties or national pressure groups such as the Anti-Centralization Union or the Administrative Reform Association. Nor were parliamentary politics immune. Feargus O'Connor, who had won Nottingham's second seat in 1847, bequeathed to his successor, Ernest Jones, an impossible task: even Jones relinquished the chartist cause in 1868 to contest Manchester as a Liberal. More significant than any of these developments, however, was the reawakening of trade union politics. It has become a cliché of labour history that after 1848 a 'new spirit' appeared within British unionism, one characterized by a willingness to work within the existing order and render improvements in wages and conditions of work a prime objective. The militancy of the 1840s died away in a prosperous decade in which 'craft' trade unions, established on the model of the Amalgamated Society of Engineers (1851), offered a new image of industrial progress. Whether this shortening of focus imposed itself on the labour movement through a proletarian 'aristocracy' seeking status for itself, or from the sharing of that movement in the fruits of economic success after mid-century, has intrigued a generation of labour historians anxious to test the marxist conception of capitalist development against the British experience.[28] For politicians this new mood presented a threat. When a moderate leader like William Newton of the engineers could advise his fellows in *The Operative* that in the coming election (1852) 'every Town or Parliamentary Borough should have its Operatives' Election Committee composed of and representing both electors and non-electors',[29] a danger had appeared that would worry Lord John Russell as much as Lord Derby.

Political leaders could feel distanced from proletarian unrest by its very quietude in the 1850s. Some disturbances did occur – the engineers' strike in 1852, the Preston cotton strike in 1853 and riots against Sunday closing of shops in 1855 are perhaps the most obvious instances – but events of this kind remained at the edge of consciousness among men otherwise preoccupied and who lacked any sense of an overwhelming 'public opinion' to goad them. Derby's son only came to hear of the Preston strike 'in an indirect manner' despite its taking place twenty miles or so from Knowsley. Clarendon, similarly, looked on the mobs who threw stones in the West End three years later as frustrated youths depressed about the progress of the war in the Crimea. To the back benches, the shires still sent their message of rural community to confound the claims of class warfare. Sir Edward Lytton (Conservative: Hertfordshire) was amused by those who did not know the temper of the '*village* workmen around us'.[30] In a decade besotted by the glories of the Great Exhibition and the Royal family, insurrection apparently had lost its cutting edge and would remain blunted until events in Europe and America sharpened it in the early 1860s. The nervousness, where it existed, derived rather from the supposed relationship between politicians and their constituencies. There is a noticeable concern in the political correspondence of the forties and fifties with what constituencies might tolerate from government and which type of behaviour in their representatives they might be induced to stomach. 'Constituent-worship', the Peelite Roundell Palmer called it, 'a thing opposed to all real Conservatism'. The American caucus seemed to have come closer, and references to the 'Americanization' of British politics accompanied the preoccupation with parliamentary reform in the late 1850s and beyond.[31] Happily, its most wanton protagonist was as yet barely twenty years old and still concerned himself with the ever more radical marketing of screws in Birmingham.

Conservative pessimism had nonetheless become chic. An imminent English republic attracted the attention of Croker, Graham, Derby and Disraeli in his blacker moods; and it did so at the very moment when one had scarcely been less likely. Queen Victoria had found her prince in Albert of Saxe-Coburg-Gotha and since their marriage in 1840 the monarchy had assumed a popular strength in both its dignified and efficient elements which it had not enjoyed since the reign of George III. Albert had accomplished two tasks: he had obviated the Queen's dependence on elder statesmen of Melbourne's stamp; and he had turned the court into a Peelite salon. Between Peel's removal in 1846 and Albert's death in 1861 royal favour and displeasure reached into the cabinet room in Albert's chilliness about Derby, Victoria's loathing for Palmerston, and their joint horror at the prospect of seeing the country led by a Jew. Of course, the 'influence of the Crown' had ceased to be significant in any formal sense; but the dinner parties at Windsor, obligatory shooting at Balmoral and an inundation of underlined sentences from Osborne could not help establishing some reference-points. Nor did a major war and a colonial mutiny lessen the monarchy's self-assurance.

A further reference-point in the correspondence of politicians impresses by its frequency. No one could read these diaries and letters without sensing the weight accorded to the judgement and influence of *The Times* in the 1850s. This sense can be corroborated, moreover, by circulation statistics. The doubling of *The Times*'s readership in the late thirties and early forties had been significant but far from unique: the period had witnessed a general expansion in newspaper awareness. To have redoubled it between 1842 and 1850 presented, however, a remarkable achievement during a period when other leading journals like the *Morning Chronicle* and *Morning Post* were experiencing recession. Delane's paper enjoyed a high-point of prestige as a scourge of government in the first half of the fifties, culminating in its notorious articles from the pen of W. H. Russell on the mismanagement of the Crimean forces. Through Henry Reeve, Whig and Peelite politicians established close links with an institution which they plainly feared and which radicals identified as an enemy. When government made postage charges for newspapers a function of their weight (*The Times* was far heavier than its rivals) and abolished the old stamp duty in 1855, it expressed a determination to curb an overmighty subject. And though the suppression was temporary, *The Times* never regained its disproportionate control of circulation.

For although the discriminatory postage rates ceased in 1858, the relationship between politicians and the literary intelligentsia had already entered a new phase. The volume of social criticism thrust before the public in the disastrous campaigns in the Crimea during 1854 and 1855 helped stimulate a rash of experimental journals in the late fifties. These did not look like the *Quarterly Review* or the *Edinburgh Review* or *Blackwood's*; they were weeklies such as the

Saturday Review and the *Spectator* (newly revamped), discursive journals like the *Contemporary* and *Fortnightly*, reviews and literary monthlies – *Macmillan's*, for example, or the *Cornhill*. In these organs a generation of men trained in classics or in the Oxford school of *literae humaniores* gained a vantage-point from which to project views about representative government and the national character. They were not philosophic radicals; they were not, for the most part, imperial reformers. Rather, they were recruited for their facility, their reading and their wit. Mark Pattison looked on Oxford's responsibility for such men with characteristic acidity and put the blame on their training. 'Its highest outcome', he wrote in 1868, 'is the "able editor" who instructs the public upon all that concerns the highest interests with a dogmatism and assurance proportional to his utter ignorance of the subject he is assuming to teach.'[32] Nevertheless, those who saw themselves as custodians of the highest interests counted themselves among the taught.

What the clerisy of the 1850s aspired to teach differed little from what Newton, Potter or Applegarth were teaching in the proletarian periodicals, or from what the 'Manchester School' saw as its hard-nosed duty. The lessons concerned class fusion and social harmony – a conscious moving away from stances assumed in the 1840s. When parliamentary radicals threw themselves into the campaign for the repeal of the stamp and paper duties they were hoping to remove barriers to knowledge rather than undermine wealth and status. Cobden's magnanimity extended to providing working men with a newspaper: it did not go much further. When Disraeli said in 1854 that the working man had no political representatives to speak of, he made a statement about the toothlessness of the Manchesterism that had alarmed his colleagues ten years before. Dissent likewise baptized stability when its parliamentary leader, Edward Miall, confined his aggression to church rates and burial grounds and permitted himself an emollient vocabulary on class and suffrage. The Earl of Aberdeen had been something of a trembler as Peel's foreign secretary; but it is revealing that, shortly before he became prime minister in 1852, he could no longer see 'any great reason to fear Democracy'. 'Perhaps', he told Gladstone, 'there is even less than at any former period.'[33] If this consciousness of supremacy becomes an 'age of equipoise' in retrospect, it seemed less obviously so in the experienced perception of politicians of the day, who knew perfectly well which pan was up and which down.

Easing social tensions after 1852 helped make democracy safe for the world: it therefore retreated in the consciousness of politicians. No

single preoccupation took its place and the 1850s may be characterized as a decade of diversity in its political problems and issues. This
was especially so in the House of Commons where 'faddism' pre-
dominated and arcane pressure groups crowded the lobbies and
galleries. It does not follow, of course, that the content of *Hansard*
reflected the content of a governing mentality. Senior politicians did
not fill their more strategic moments with the minutiae of educational
provision and Nonconformist resistance to church rates, though these
items bulked large in the business of the Commons during the decade.
Imperial affairs crept up the voting paper to some extent; between
1859 and 1865 the number of questions asked in the House about
this aspect of policy rose by a half.[34] In the aftermath of the Indian
Mutiny of 1857 and amid awareness of David Livingstone's explora-
tions and Christian missionary activity, the concern was natural. It
found little reflection, however, at the level of high politics. Lord
Durham and the philosophic radicals had created a *cause célèbre* in
Canada during the 1830s but the climate had changed. Radicals were
no longer philosophic; Durham was dead; Edward Gibbon Wake-
field, who had been an incandescent ambassador for all imperial
concerns during his years in Britain, departed for New Zealand in
1853. When Gladstone treated the Commons to an hour and a half
on the Australia Bill early in 1850, he found himself amid 'unwilling
ears' in an 'indifferent and inattentive House'.[35] Yet if MPs were
bored by the empire, its growth and potential brooked no contradiction. The very possession by 1860 of the biggest empire in the
world plainly threatened to prompt significant repercussions in the
coming decades.

For the moment, preoccupations expanded in a less structured way
than such omens might suggest – perhaps also in a less serious way.
By the mid-fifties Edward Stanley had come to the conclusion that
each of the earlier years of the decade had been gripped by 'some
prevailing mania' which had guided the conversations of the politically aware; and his list is suggestive. 'In 1848–9 this favourite topic
was foreign affairs: in 1850 reduction of expenditure, and free trade:
in 1851 the Exhibition: in 1852, hunting down the Derby administration: in '53, spirit-rapping and the Russian quarrel: in '54 and '55,
the war.'[36]

The Crimean war began in February 1854 and lasted two years.
Previously unknown towns in this remote region became symbols of
anxiety and celebration: Balaclava, Inkerman, Sebastopol. But the
weave of foreign entanglement that had given rise to the war
remained thickest closer to home; for it had been Napoleon III's
assumption of the title of Emperor of the French in 1851 which

had disrupted the mechanism of the Quintuple Alliance and disturbed the composure of Nicholas I of Russia, who cleaved still to a vision of the Holy Alliance of 1815 as a bulwark against French expansion. In what contemporaries called the 'Near East', France had been isolated during the Mehemet Ali crisis of 1840 and had since sought equality with her European rivals by bringing pressure to bear on the Near Eastern commitments of Russia and Austria. By bludgeoning the Turks into passing control of the Holy Places to the Catholic Church in 1852, the French intended less to secure sacred relics than to upset the Russians who had controlled those Places heretofore. When the Russians replied, first with diplomatic retribution and then the invasion of the Danubian provinces of Wallachia and Moldavia in the middle of 1853, the threat similarly reached Paris before Constantinople. Much diplomatic and military manoeuvre accompanied unsuccessful British and French efforts to call Austria to heel; but we must leave them off-stage. More central to our purpose is the wave of anti-Russian feeling which these months witnessed inside Britain and the effects of the war itself on British politics and government.

Expectation had been aroused in the public that punishing the Bear would prove glorious, redemptive and brief. Through the summer of 1854, while the British and French tried to decide which part of Russia to attack, the prevailing mood thus developed into one of frustration. The autumn offensive in the Crimea brought some excitement, certainly, with victory on the Alma and the Light Brigade's stirring suicide at Balaclava. Little more was accomplished that year, however; and the seepage of distressing reports of the troops' condition and morale as they sat in siege of Sebastopol augured a more serious encounter than might at first have been envisaged. In the early spring of 1855 the government felt the edge of popular resentment against its maladministration. Anti-war radicals helped bring down the unhappy coalition government headed by Lord Aberdeen by voting for Roebuck's motion in the Commons criticizing the conduct of the war – as we shall see; but more had been set in train than could be stifled by a change of government. The entire machinery of government came under public scrutiny following a series of reverses; government's inability to cope with the pressure of its own business attained new levels of importance among journalists. In fact, only the publicity was new: ministers had known for some years of the bursting dam. Derby's foreign secretary, Lord Malmesbury, had reeled under the weight of dispatch boxes waiting for him every day. He asked his civil servants to estimate the growth in business in recent years and learned that outgoing and incoming dispatches had increased from an annual total of 5,000 in 1828 to 32,000 by

1852. He left office, fortunately, before Palmerston had to face the 48,850 occasioned by the first year of the war. It is worth recalling also that Sir Stafford Northcote and Sir Charles Trevelyan were invited to report on recruitment to the civil service *before* the coming of the Crimean war. Whether their recommendation to throw open the service to competitive examination should be seen as more significant than the refusal of parliament to implement it remains a moot point. Only in the sphere of 'local self-government' did unambiguous legislative initiatives take place, a commentary, perhaps, on the effectiveness of the anti-centralization and vestry movements during the war.[37]

The fall of Sebastopol in September 1855 eased the popular pressure on Palmerston's new government. Yet the failure to press that victory forward into a more comprehensive destruction of the Russian forces paradoxically earned further criticism, since the peace negotiations in Vienna and the Treaty of Paris (signed in March 1856) left unsatisfied many hopes of a major spring offensive and the humiliation of the Tsar. Nevertheless popular politics remained foreign politics, even though the war had ended – a development which Palmerston encouraged by his congenital disposition to meddle and which the actions of foreign powers in any case made obligatory. China and India seemed especially troublesome. Since the beginning of Peel's government China had been held down under the terms of the Treaty of Nanking (1842) which ceded Hong Kong to Britain and compensated British traders for the opium which the Chinese authorities had confiscated from them. The second 'opium war' caught fire in the embers of the Crimea and scorched Palmerston when his late colleague, Gladstone, showed from the opposition benches his power as a moralist in uniting the forces of radicalism against the government's Chinese policy in the 1857 session. The general election into which Palmerston was forced did him little harm, however. The electorate plainly enjoyed a brash policy against the Chinese: it was to approve the harrying of the Chinese over the next few years, culminating in the burning of Peking's Summer Palace, as British military weight was brought to bear in order to press the Chinese into honouring the Treaty of Tientsin (1858) negotiated by the future Whig minister James Bruce, Earl of Elgin.

How to govern India once the East India Company had been made to surrender its trading monopoly there had posed awkward questions for governments since 1833. The Company's political and administrative sway in India stemmed from the East India Company Act of 1784 which had instituted a system of dual control: the Company acting on the ground but under the supervision of a 'Board of Control', chaired by a secretary of state in London, which was to have access to company papers and ultimate responsibility for government. In practice the Company led and the government followed; the presidency in London became a jumping-off point for politicians such as Castlereagh and Canning rather than for Indian specialists. In 1833 the Whig government missed an opportunity to effect a more direct mode of rule and did so quite deliberately, not least under the advice of the Board's secretary, Thomas Babington Macaulay. Recoiling from trying to manage a huge continent from the distance of London, the government's Government of India Act of that year merely renewed the Company's charter until 1854, expanded the Board of Control slightly and insisted that one member of the council in India should not be in the Company's service: all decidedly less than a revolution. But the Sikh war, Ellenborough's removal and Dalhousie's expansionist mood as governor had contributed to a pool of criticism. The mutiny of 1857 impinged, therefore, on an already fragile structure of government. Sebastopol had left the British public with a siege mentality which the Indian mutineers' attacks on hopelessly outnumbered defenders at Cawnpore and Lucknow helped agitate. News of the atrocities carried out on women and children expanded the Englishman's image of himself as an embodiment of Christian self-righteousness and licensed rabid reprisals. 'The whole universe appears more occupied with this monster mutiny than anything since the wars of Napoleon,' wrote Clarendon to his wife in August, 'and no wonder!'[38] Little patience was expended on a man like Canning, son of the former prime minister and governor of India since 1855, who tried to minimize the cruelties which accompanied the regaining of control. As one diarist put it in October 1857, 'Lord Canning may be a very kind man (black man his brother, and so forth) but he ought to know that you cannot quell a savage mutiny and re-conquer half of India by using kid-gloves and rose-water.'[39] These responses were melodramatic (the mutiny never posed the military threat that the public anticipated) but two consequences flowed from them. One involved the removal from high politics for a generation of Indian affairs as a governing preoccupation. The Government of India Act of 1858 placed the country under the control of an India Office and instituted the myth of royal government maintained through a viceroy and council while the Queen's renunciation of further expansion in the subcontinent quietened indigenous fears. A second consequence lay in the confirmation of Palmerston as unquestioned interpreter of public opinion.

More than foreign policy had been responsible for this development. For during the 1850s, as in the 1820s, moments of domestic political significance had passed uncelebrated in parliamentary debates and unremarked in the public mind. Placing them in perspective requires a backward glance at the story of party politics since the muddying of the waters in the general election of 1852.

The Conservative party had then received at the hustings no firm support on which to build an administration. Disraeli's abandonment of protection in the autumn had achieved one party objective; but far from beguiling the Peelites it left them even more bitter and disposed to join Russell – especially after Gladstone's mincing of Disraeli's budget had thrown doubt on the credibility of any Conservative finance policy. The fused forces of Whigs and Peelites under the premiership of Peel's former foreign secretary, the Earl of Aberdeen, enjoyed for a time therefore the stability which attends the inevitable. That the Peelites had profited from this arrangement more than their numbers merited did not go unnoticed; no fewer than six of them entered the cabinet at the end of 1852 in the company of six Whigs and one radical. For one Peelite, Lord Lincoln, the coalition amounted to no more than a confluence of common doctrines:

> The fact is that among men of Liberal opinion the difference is not Whig and Peelite, but the men of forty years of age (more or less) and those of the former generation. *Peelism* – if I must still use the word – is really the more advanced form of Liberal opinion, cleared of that oligarchic tendency of the old Whigs, who, wishing to extend freedom, sought to do it by making use of the people, instead of identifying themselves and their own interests with the people.[40]

But others shrank from such language when they recalled the cuts and bruises of recent years.

Palmerston was one of these. His responsibility for Russell's defeat in the Commons in February 1852 had driven him close to accepting Derby's offer of a place. Yet his wish to avoid isolation had kept him out when the Peelites, except for Hardinge, refused to help the Conservatives. About the Aberdeen coalition his feelings could only be mixed. He did not want to risk taking the Foreign Office where Russell might once more make him a scapegoat; but neither did he want to be 'left in a little agreeable political solitude' by remaining outside.[41] The Home Office represented an ideal compromise: it offered both major status and a place to hide while Gladstone lit up the sky with his 1853 budget and Russell burned out the husk of his career in recrimination. Despite Palmerston's initial self-effacement, however, his perspective of the next few years' high politics repays reconstruction quite as much as the more obvious ones of Gladstone or Russell. Seen from the direction of the Peelites, after all, the Aberdeen coalition becomes in retrospect a significant bridge by which the Peelites, previously conceived as an independent party, crossed over to the Liberals. This perspective is not revealing: it illuminates what was predictable, in the case of Peelites other than Gladstone, and in Gladstone's own case it foreshortens the complexities in his life after 1857. Palmerston's viewpoint demonstrates rather that an important fulcrum in the high politics of the 1850s lies not in the coalition but at a point between its crash in 1855 and Gladstone's final (and by no means predictable) commitment to Palmerston and not Derby in 1859.

'The country generally is highly prosperous, trade increasing, the revenue good.'[42] 1853 certainly proved an untaxing year for the home secretary. Palmerston concentrated on the militia and national defence, a hobby horse since the invasion scares of 1851. He became enthusiastic about sewers and the eradication of cholera. At the centre of his concerns, however, were subjects beyond his departmental purview. The developing wrangle with Russia stimulated his strategic instincts and made him a formidable number two to Clarendon who had been Aberdeen's foreign secretary since Russell threw up the job in a huff at the beginning of the year. Palmerston's thinking about policy seemed to his opponents – and to former radical friends – dangerously pro-Turk: indeed he found himself in a stand-up row with Cobden on the subject. Yet he won respect elsewhere by exposing the fudge in much cabinet discussion. He also made much of a phraseology about war which in later years would become a vital part of his rhetoric. 'Peace is an excellent thing', ran this strain, 'and war is a great misfortune; but there are many things more valuable than peace, and many things much worse than war.'[43] Aberdeen had good cause to feel troubled in hearing such doctrines from a man he deemed indispensable to the survival of his government.

The importance of Palmerston's remaining was tested at the end of 1853 over the issue of parliamentary reform. On taking office Palmerston had declared himself opposed to any tampering with franchise. Russell, on the other hand, could not free himself from the worries of the later years of his erstwhile government: he worried about the radicals more than ever, especially now that Bright had cut a far more formidable figure in the House than during the 1840s. Consequently Russell pressed for a reform bill through the autumn of 1853. Palmerston responded by resigning; and he only allowed himself to be persuaded to return when a supplicant Aberdeen made reform an open question in cabinet. Underlying Palmerston's obduracy to some extent was a position about democracy and the harm which, unchecked, the masses might do to themselves. In his cagey language of 1853 this amounted to a worry about mobs in which 'a thousand can be swayed by 5 or 6 agitators'. In the more confident mood of 1862 there seemed less need to mince words in a lecture to Russell. History shows, he told the proven junior, 'that Power in the Hands of the Masses throws the Scum of the Community to the Surface'.[44] Doubtless these sentiments coloured his behaviour in 1853. Nevertheless, his objections were also tactical: Russell's proposing something by definition set Palmerston against it; he was mindful too of the difficulties which reform would occasion inside a coalition government. As it happened, Russell foundered without Palmerston's help. Though he was allowed to bring in a bill in 1854 to lower the county franchise to £10 and the borough threshold to £6, he discovered no excitement over it in the country and withdrew the proposed bill when the war broke out.

In a sense the war legitimized Palmerston's version of foreign policy since 1853, while Russell's eclipse left the home secretary as the only strong candidate to succeed Aberdeen if the latter should topple. Roebuck's Commons motion to institute an inquiry into the running of the war drove Russell into resignation in January 1855 and brought down the government in February. Palmerston, however, was not immediately approached; the court thought it courteous first to ask Derby and later Russell to form a government. Yet in both attempts to form ministries Palmerston needed to be cast in a key role. He refused to join Derby because Gladstone refused to separate himself from the Peelites who proved unwilling to return to the Conservative party. He acceded to Russell's request to join him on the grounds that Russell would also fail to carry Gladstone and thus retire from the field. Granted the Peelites' determination to cling to the political centre, indeed, it soon became apparent that the only realistic alternative to the Aberdeen coalition was another one wearing different clothes. And Palmerston had the merit of having turned into a popular hero who – Gladstone's very vocabulary indicates the depth of his fury – had made the world drunk. 'I am for the moment *L'inévitable*', wrote the new prime minister.[45] Perhaps even he had not fathomed that his inevitability would last a decade.

For the moment he was preoccupied with the likelihood of a dissolution at the end of the 1855 session. Gladstone, Graham and Herbert had resigned from his government almost as soon as they had joined it because they disapproved of Palmerston's willingness to contemplate a parliamentary inquiry along the lines indicated by Roebuck; thereafter they moved towards fiscal policy as a target for rhetoric. Less pressure developed on the new government, however,

than Palmerston had feared initially. He had important Whig support
in Clarendon, Granville and Lansdowne. Sending Russell, his acutely
unhappy colonial minister, to the peace negotiations in Vienna turned
out to be an inspired move which left Russell bearing the stigma of an
unpopular peace and feeling obliged finally to resign. Only Grey
seemed likely to offer any focus for Whig resistance, and his health
and domestic life argued against its becoming effective. The Tory
party, on the other hand, had virtually run out of money until
Derby bailed it out at the end of the year.[46]

Meanwhile the prime minister's years fell off him: 'a babe of grace'
supplanted the aged statesman.[47] He brought a new asperity to his
public statements which included the war, Chinese opium or the news
from India as hooks for bloody remarks about the English birthright.
In high-political circles these could be deemed no less crude than his
still-remembered dispatches. But their value electorally could hardly
be gainsaid when Palmerston swept aside both radicals and Peelites in
the general election of March 1857 (which Gladstone had occasioned
by bringing down the government over its Chinese policy). The
cabinet view that Palmerston's popularity would hold up in the
constituencies proved true, despite some notable opposition successes
in the boroughs. The ebbing of a radical tide in the north and
especially in Manchester, where Bright and Milner Gibson both lost
their seats, suggested one side of the story. The dissolution of the
Peelite remnant suggested another. For 'Liberals' of all hues the
message was clear: if only the Whigs, Irish and radicals could somehow join forces the realignment would give them a majority of over a
hundred.

How to engineer such an alliance seemed less obvious, of course,
during that flat session of 1857. Few issues threatened to disturb
party complacency. 'There is no check on ministers', Stanley
grumbled from the opposition benches in June. 'Out of doors, entire
apathy; within the House party spirit is dead.'[48] Russell had eventually returned from a prolonged sulk in Italy and Switzerland following the setback in Vienna but he seemed a poor focus for
radicalism. Now that the election had decimated them, there were
few radicals to focus. The most pressing executive problem of the
moment – India – agitated the public and the press, as we have seen.
At the ministerial level, however, it left politicians surprisingly
unruffled, with the exceptions of Argyll and Clarendon whose ruf-
flings were congenital. Having spent several years trying to interest
the cabinet in the Irish, Clarendon knew full well the chances of
persuading his colleagues that the Indians mattered. 'Except poor
Labouchere, who turned up his eyes like a duck in thunder, no one

seem[ed] the least alive to the transcendent gravity of the crisis.' Even Disraeli affected to be 'shocked' at the flippancy of the government's 'Private tone'.[49] So if there were to occur any invigoration of party Liberalism it would probably come from outside itself. It might come from the Conservative party which was showing signs of gestating its own reformist faction dedicated to making the Tories a party of government once more. It might (a related thought) come from Gladstone. Recently, many of his colleagues had given him up for mad as he raged against the Divorce Bill of 1857; but they knew him to have lost faith in Aberdeen's direction of Peelite strategy and to feel frustrated in his administrative ambitions. Indeed Gladstone had already ceased to identify himself with the Peelites in any real sense. His situation had become at once more and less complicated than theirs: he was a redundant chancellor of the exchequer 'losing the best years of [his] life'.[50] The prospect of a Conservative ministry threatened, therefore, to introduce a sub-plot of considerable interest and importance.

The birth of Liberal England (1857–65)

Little encouragement offered itself meanwhile. In the autumn of 1857 parliament had to be recalled to cope with the impact on Britain of serious bank failures in America. The financial panic 'engaged all attention' for a while;[51] Peel's Bank Charter Act, which had pinned note issue to gold reserves, had to be relaxed and the discount rate climbed to 10 per cent, higher than in 1847. But Threadneedle Street did not come under siege, nor did Palmerston quaver in his determination to run the autumn sitting as autocratically as he had the summer's. A chance perhaps existed that the Liberals might cohere around reform; but no government led by Palmerston would move far in that direction, as one of his ministers observed, 'without more popular pressure than [was] likely to be applied to them'.[52] More apparent to Liberals must have been the likelihood of drifting further apart under the pull of issues which could only detach left-of-centre Liberals from their leadership. Between 1857 and 1861 these issues largely concerned fiscal and foreign policy. Russell saw India, finance and reform as central in 1858; Lewis chose reform and Italy in 1859; Derby, on the Conservative side, identified foreign policy and the budget as paramount in 1860; Gladstone, then Palmerston's chancellor, saw the paper duties, defence and reform as the next instalment of rough weather in 1861.[53] That is to say, an environment existed which promised little immediate hope of a realignment within Liberal susceptibilities. It might, on the other hand, encourage a successful graft between the Peelites and the Conservatives.

Accident almost joined hands with duty to bring this about. On 14 January 1858 the Emperor Louis Napoleon and Empress Eugénie found themselves the victims of a bomb attack as their coach made its way down rue Lepelletier in Paris. Neither imperial celebrity was harmed but the affair detonated an international incident when it transpired that the bomber, Orsini, had thickened his plot while living in England and had used British-made explosive. Uncharacteristically, Palmerston bent before French demands that the British conspiracy law be amended to prevent the harbouring of revolutionists; and in doing so he lost touch with a wave of public resentment. In the House, radicals reacted strongly against any recession from Britain's role as a sanctuary for refugees from foreign tyranny. Milner Gibson's amendment to the conspiracy bill indeed proved decisive in rallying most radicals, some Tories and some Whigs into a majority of nineteen over the government. Gladstone, Disraeli and Bright walked through the same lobby and Palmerston's ministry collapsed. Within a year the prime minister had fallen from parliamentary dictator to the position of a man believed by many to be finished; and he had done so by failing to follow visceral instinct.

If Gladstone had now accepted Derby's invitation to join a minority Conservative administration (as did Peel's younger brother) and taken the remainder of the Peelites with him, Palmerston could well have followed suit, as he had been tempted to do in the early 1850s. And if the Liberal party had lost both men in 1858 it would have lost part of its capacity, as yet embryonic, to translate the Liberal message into populist terms. For the foreseeable future it would have contained only the voice of monotonous reformism – Bright its bass, Russell a reedy tenor. Why, then, did Gladstone hold back? Perhaps Derby did not try very hard; and Gladstone plainly felt some allegiance to Peelite friends. Selborne would have gone with him and perhaps Newcastle, plus a couple of minor figures, but Aberdeen remained firm in his disavowal of any *rapprochement* with the party of 1846, and important men like Cardwell and Wortley had moved closer to the Liberals over the past few years. All the same, it seems likely that Gladstone took no pleasure in watching another opportunity slip away. Better Derby than Palmerston.

The refusal of Peelite cooperation helped ensure that Derby's government of 1858–9 remained similar to that of 1852 in its personnel and prospects. The only new blood – Ellenborough's was different but hardly new – circulated outside the cabinet, especially in the solicitor-general, Hugh Cairns, who would later become a significant

Conservative politician. The prospects remained those of a minority administration: to hold office on sufferance until the opposition regrouped. Any hope must lie in driving wedges between the slices of that potential majority by espousing causes and issues which most divided the enemy. The decade of the Conservative party's enthusiasm for parliamentary reform thus began, and it originated in Westminster rather than Manchester. For all its predictability, however, the spectre of a Tory government proposing an extension of democracy occasioned a sense of shock among backbenchers and party cadres. Nor was their disquiet confined to franchise. The Government of India Act of 1858 disturbed some Conservatives, if only because Russell appeared to support the bill's original principle, later abandoned, of making five places on the new Indian Council subject to popular election in certain British city constituencies.[54] Derby's enthusiasm for abolishing the property qualification for MPs raised fears which had firmer grounds: the demand for it had, after all, comprised one of the points of the People's Charter. Then came rumours that Derby and Disraeli were arranging conclaves to discuss the terms of a reform bill – at the very time when few people beyond popular agitators seemed to want one. Small wonder that Conservatives began to wonder what it was their party intended to conserve or that a future Liberal lord chancellor thanked God for his own party. 'Democracy', the latter enjoyed saying during the summer of 1858, 'has made more progress in England during the last three months than during twenty years of Whig rule',[55] a better comment on the history of the Whigs, perhaps, than on anything Derby had in mind.

Of course, not all contemporaries allowed themselves to be deceived in this way by the Conservative *volte-face*. Granville saw at once the nonsense of talking about 'democracy' as though the government were acting on such a principle – or indeed on any principle. Cornewall Lewis, similarly, wondered in his thoughtful fashion whether Derby's strategy might not stem from an urge to lose a Commons vote on a 'strongly democratic measure' so as to 'incorporate' Gladstone by kindness.[56] Political intelligence certainly wasted little time on Derby's populism. No great acumen was needed to see that Derby had countenanced the removal of the property qualification because its assessment, since 1838, on the basis of personal rather than landed wealth rendered it a useless form of resistance to radical plutocracy. His contemplation of an extension of the franchise suffered from similar constraints: the process would only roll forward when it could be made an exercise in Conservative engineering via its voting thresholds and redistribution of constituencies. Ten-pound counties (the idea of introducing the urban franchise qualification in the counties) held no horrors because an expansion of the rural electorate, to the extent that one might result, would tend to strengthen social bonds rather than weaken them in the absence of a secret ballot. He rejected six-pound boroughs (one of the starting-points for Liberal proposals) at the outset since they would scoop up some of the 'residuum', those persons left over when 'the people' had been counted. Redistribution offered parallel opportunities for this line of thought. If there had to be a schedule 'A' of disfranchised constituencies, they could be identified by small populations and thus remain small in number. Further, one could ensure that the reallocation of seats went preponderantly to the counties and not to the industrial towns with their pullulating radicals. How many of these Conservative conspirators remembered East Retford? It hardly matters; thirty years on, its argument endured.

In the party environment of 1859, however, parliamentary reform proved both necessary and impossible. By the end of 1858 Walpole, Peel and Hardwicke had voiced profound anxieties at the radicalism of virtually any measure. Henley and Stanley shared their horror but thought nevertheless that anything moderate would fail to pull radical teeth and that they therefore should go further. Henley and Walpole took their respective grievances to the point of resignation in the new year: secret resignation, for the moment, but threatening all the same. The scheme eventually presented to parliament reflected all this tribulation and said as little as possible. Disraeli, trowel in hand, excelled himself in the Commons where he had the job of sounding stirring. They were living in great times. There had been an enormous rise in population, in the nation's capital, in the general level of public 'intelligence' open to the 'multitude'. 'In such a state of things,' Disraeli began his imaginary history, 'a question in England becomes what is called a public question. Thus Parliamentary Reform became a public question; a public question in due course of time becomes a Parliamentary question; and then, as it were, shedding its last skin, it becomes a Ministerial question. Reform has been for fifteen years a Parliamentary question; for ten years it has been a Ministerial question.'[57] After minutes of sustained justification, the outline of the bill seemed hardly worth the panegyric: no change to the borough qualification (Derby had wanted nothing to do with £6 boroughs which the Liberals had muttered about) and no secret ballot. Instead the Commons heard a number of ingenious, but trivial, provisions to add some fancy franchises based on personal wealth and a mellifluous argument that the time had come to break down the discrepancies between urban and rural franchises. In fact Disraeli intended the reverse. Freeholders in towns who had a vote in the counties were to find themselves confined to the town of their residence for their vote while a boundary commission would suck into the towns many currently excluded from them. He thought that the package would push up the county electorate by perhaps 200,000 – music to the Tory ear. There would be 15 new constituencies and only 15 deletions, therefore, from the list of threatened constituencies. Among Liberal sensibilities, on the other hand, the proposals seemed not only risibly timid but based on a worrying principle. A new Liberal MP for a rural constituency, J. G. Dodson, saw Disraeli's game at once:

> It was remarkable that a Conservative Government should propose to do away with the old constitutional distinction between the county and borough franchises...It appeared to him that the ultimate object of the scheme was to draw a sharp line of distinction between town and country, so as to get as much possible trade and manufactures on one side and agriculture on the other...At present the Members of the House represented localities, but this Bill would convert them into representatives of class interest only.[58]

Quite so. The Bill went down on 31 March by 330–291.

The defeat showed that the Liberals had a clear chance of power if they could find some *modus vivendi* between their various factions. Palmerston had hoped since the beginning of the Derby government that a spell in opposition would bring Russell and Gladstone back in his direction; he did not share the widely current view that both he and his party had turned senile. In the early summer of 1859 he pressed matters forward by going to see Russell at the latter's home, Pembroke Lodge; and they determined to announce their reconciliation at what turned out to be an historic meeting of Liberals at Willis's Rooms in London. As in 1830, the opposition was congealing into a force which no government had a hope of resisting. But Derby did not, unlike Wellington, have an election forced on him: he rather chose one in 1859 as his best plan once he had been defeated in the House of Commons in April and again in June. This decision was made defensible by the French. Their temporary attachment to the cause of Cavour in northern Italy had plunged them into war against Austria; and French victories at Magenta and Solferino straddled Derby's fall and Palmerston's return to power. Electorally, the point was not that Italy presented a rallying issue but rather that its ramifications helped distract attention from reform and permitted Derby a language about strong defences and resistance to imperial designs, though Disraeli pressed him to emphasize 'the broad, great

issue...whether Parliamentary Government is compatible with existing institutions'.[59] The thunder was, of course, Palmerston's but it
brought the Conservatives a gain of thirty seats or so with no little
support from Irish clerical opinion. It also gave them an absolute
majority of seats in Ireland for the first and only time in the nineteenth century. The last outcome wanted by the Irish Catholics was a
Liberal government which might commit itself to supporting the
nationalists in Italy against the sovereignty of the papal states. Indeed
both in this matter and in continuing Conservative obstruction of
Liberal attempts to abolish church rates lay the possibility of creating
an ecclesiastical party – a thought not lost on Disraeli (so few were in
these years) but one which the Tory leadership generally did nothing
to exploit. In any case, Palmerston's victory at the general election of
1857 had left Derby with so great an electoral deficit to redeem in
1859 that such strategies had become academic. Derby would be left,
for all his gains, in a minority in the new parliament.

The Queen and Prince Albert now encountered a dilemma. Grave
objections stood in the way of their asking either Palmerston or
Russell to form a government. The former seemed to glory in insubordination; the latter had established equally well-known and documented tendencies towards pettishness and wild judgement. They
sent for Earl Granville. Since 1846 'Pussy' Granville had built his
career on a reputation for the diplomatic *mot juste*, a clubbable
decency, the ability to write a sensible letter and an effortless sense
of dress and social poise. Nor, as a former foreign secretary, did he
strike commentators as an absurd candidate for the premiership. But
Palmerston and Russell had pledged themselves in their Pembroke
Lodge conversations to serve only under the other: they would tolerate no third party. It was plain enough that any administration must
contain one of them in order to be thinkable; the Queen found herself
with little alternative than to ask Palmerston to return. She would
fare better, paradoxically, many years later in 1894 when she helped
force Rosebery on the Liberal party.

Palmerston's second government lasted from 1859 to the general
election that took place a few months before his death in 1865. An
interesting feature of it lies in the degree to which it side-stepped
radicalism and continued to offer an image of executive Whiggery
rather than one of Cobden-and-Bright crusading. Cobden declined, in
fact, to serve. Bright was not asked. The latter's rhetoric since recovering from his nervous breakdown following the 1857 *débâcle* and
his move to Birmingham had proved particularly potent. From these
years date the much-quoted speeches from Birmingham town hall –
the series which included his description of balance-of-power foreign

policy as 'a gigantic system of outdoor relief for the aristocracy'.[60] Palmerston felt unimpressed by Bright's tantrums: he faced enough difficulty at court without dangling a red flag. Milner Gibson, the radical leader, was included – first at the Poor Law Board and then at the Board of Trade when his former post fell to C. P. Villiers, the Wolverhampton corn law campaigner of the 1830s and 1840s. Russell remained the only other man whom Bright could have believed sound on reform; and he had been driven into accepting the Foreign Office. Still, he had agreed to the reconciliation with Palmerston only on the understanding that he would bring in a reform bill similar to that of 1854. And since that meant a further effort to secure £6 boroughs, as opposed to the £10 threshold postulated in Derby's abortive measure, the bill faced Whigs with more of a threat than a promise. Men of the stamp of Granville, Wood and Cornewall Lewis could not be counted on to feel enthusiastic, far less so the vestiges of Peelite Conservatism represented by Newcastle, Herbert, Cardwell and, back at the Exchequer, Gladstone.

Which considerations lay uppermost in Gladstone's mind when he decided to join his enemy Palmerston poses a major problem. We have seen that his walking across some supposed bridge between the parties since 1852 fails as a thesis in the face of his demonstrable preference for a Conservative style of politics and for Derby's leadership as against Palmerston's. His frustrations since the rupture of 1856–7, on the other hand, left him hungry for responsibility. Perhaps an offer of the Exchequer from any secure prime minister would have sufficed by 1859: certainly he stressed that he would have accepted no other office from Palmerston. The alternative was sterility and attachment to a parliamentary party which held out hopes at best of minority power if the Liberal coalition cracked. To raise the spectre of Disraeli seems unnecessary in this context. He and Gladstone had already found themselves in the same lobby. If Derby's performance in the country had matched that at Westminster the two enemies could have sat at the same cabinet table. Events, rather than class, ideology, upbringing or even self-interested strategy, had evolved a logic which pressed Gladstone into the deflection that was destined to harden into a lifelong commitment.

Early in the experience of the Palmerston government, Gladstone's distancing of himself from the Peelites had been noticed by colleagues. He found himself agreeing mostly with the radical Milner Gibson, less so with the others. For the cause of franchise reform he could at the moment do little; the parliamentary reception of Russell's latest bill in the 1861 session echoed the apathy of the country, and Russell withdrew the measure. The prime minister's determination to make defence a rallying point could, on the other hand, offer a suitable ground for opposition, as did the alliance diplomacy revived by Palmerston and Russell to contain France in her Italian ambitions. Gladstone's energies were siphoned off by a domestic issue, however, at precisely the moment when most eyes had turned abroad. Here were shadows of 1857: it had been divorce then; the new preoccupation centred on Gladstone's fight with the House of Lords following its refusal to accept repeal of the paper duties proposed in the 1860 budget. In a sense the contest proved more important than the issue. 'Taxes on knowledge' had come under fire from radicals for years – and the case for keeping them rested only on the political awkwardness of an alternative device for raising revenue such as a higher income tax. By threatening resignation unless the Lords (and Palmerston) backed down, Gladstone both ran up a flag for Liberalism and established the constitutional precedent of the second chamber's incapacity to reject money bills. It would be this precedent on which another chancellor of the exchequer would stand when he menaced the peers with more drastic medicine in 1909.

Beyond the small circle of men directly involved in these issues, domestic politics offered little to rival the spectacle of Garibaldi's guerrillas as they mounted their challenge in Italy. Compared with the season of reverses at home – reform in the Commons, church rates and paper duties in the Lords – the exploits of the nationalists presented a sense of movement and danger. A famous dispatch from Lord John Russell in October 1860 dissociated Britain from international attacks on the freedom fighters and Cavour responded by publishing it. The danger lay in domestic repercussions. Russell's dispatch could be viewed less as a manifesto of libertarian principle than a final fling from a minister who, as Gladstone observed, sported the youth of old age. Yet despite criticisms of his rashness, Russell made little impact at any other point in British politics before he found himself called back to the first place in 1866. Reform, Russell's other name, likewise faded away. When Locke-King brought in a reform bill from the back benches in 1861 he could not repeat his role as parliamentary *frondeur*. It was squashed between the parties who worked together on the floor of the House of Commons. Confrontation seemed to wither in that session. Politicians registered a mood of quiescence and wait and see. Indeed waves from America, Italy, Poland, Denmark and Germany would ultimately prove the only forces capable of ruffling Palmerston's peace of mind.

Funerals confirmed the heaviness. The Peelites went as if by plague in 1860 and 1861 – first Aberdeen, then Graham and Herbert –

followed by the Prince Consort in late 1861 with immediate effect on royal politics as the Queen retired into seclusion. An atmosphere formed in which few evaded reminiscence and none but Disraeli breathed ozone. 'What deaths!' he wrote to Lady Londonderry in the autumn of that year. 'One cannot believe that Peel, Goulburn, Dalhousie, Herbert, Aberdeen and Graham should all have departed, and that their senior, Palmerston, should remain, playing his tricks with the volatility of inexperience!'[61] But less ephemeral considerations played their tricks also. Possibly the reawakening of Ireland by the Italian campaigns (the Pope recruited in Ireland for his army) and the rain-flattened harvest of 1860 reinforced a sense of hopelessness. Possibly radicals sensed something of Bright's disgust with all politics and believed, as he did, that Milner Gibson had turned into a Whig. Perhaps the continual talk of counties and boroughs since 1854 had engendered thoughts about what an aristocracy was meant to do and complementary worries that it had failed to do it. Stanley's diary carries a hint of this between its lines in the early 1860s as he records Edward Ellice's reflection that 'men of rank' from the great houses seem no longer interested in government; or Sir Charles Wood's view that the upper classes have been 'falling off' over the past thirty years; or when he records his own head-counting in the Lords and laments results so offensive to the cause of political activism. Delane equally caught a mood when he saw in the future a post-Palmerstonian world in which the best men from all parties would join together in patriotic fusion.

So long as Palmerston survived, no liaison was likely. The Conservative party bided its time: it could not face the prospect of another dissolution and another minority government; it left Tory violence to the offensive derangement of Lord Robert Cecil who was wonderful both in speech and in print on all forms of Liberal sin. Those in government could therefore afford to allow their preoccupations to expand into normally remote areas. The election of Abraham Lincoln as president of the United States in 1860 had helped stimulate the American crisis of self-identity that had loomed for many years; and the civil war which broke out in April 1861 both presented British reform movements with an inspiring example and posed the British economy a first-order problem. The appearance of Otto von Bismarck as chancellor of Prussia in 1862 likewise proposed a new perspective of self-interest – one which the Polish rebels of 1863 became the first to appreciate when Prussia gave access to their Russian tyrants. The British cabinet saw more of it in 1864 when war became a serious possibility as the only means of expelling the Germans from Denmark after Bismarck had resolved the dispute over Schleswig-Holstein as only he knew how. Nor had Garibaldi any intention of being forgotten. His visit to Britain in 1863 revived the controversies of 1859–60, dashed Disraeli's hopes for a Catholic Conservative party and reminded London of the violent enthusiasm of its Irish immigrants.[62]

Of all these predicaments, the American one pressed most urgently on politicians. Radicals of the Bright stamp stressed the moral side of the question; those on the front bench suffered more from the diplomatic entanglements surrounding the British declaration of neutrality and fears for the integrity of Canada. Harder than either of these, however, came the economic impact of the northern blockade of southern cotton exports. The inevitable catastrophe for Lancashire's mills did not strike at once: the 1860 crop had been plentiful and supplies still existed. But by the end of 1861 the effect on Lancashire's staple industry had become marked. Cotton prices rose from just under 7d a pound in 1860 to well over 2s a pound by 1864; and the workhouses filled in proportion. At the end of 1862 the Earl of Derby watched distress 'rapidly and fearfully augmenting' in Lancashire and anticipated a workhouse population of a quarter of a million in just twenty-four poor law unions by Christmas.[63] No revolutionary outburst developed out of this misery but paragraphs read in the London clubs gave rise to fears of losing the northern boroughs in the next election. Gladstone did not help. His notorious Newcastle speech of 7 October 1862, in which he complimented Jefferson Davis for having made a nation out of the confederacy, proved a major tactical gaffe. Yet the remark can too easily be dismissed as an aberration. Diarists and correspondents provide convincing evidence that, in high-political circles, sympathy for the American south as an embattled property-owning civilization remained widespread and heartfelt.

Sympathy for the Danes also mounted as their relations with the Germans turned sour at the end of 1863. The new Danish king, Christian IX, had unilaterally incorporated the duchy of Schleswig into his kingdom and altered arrangements governing the neighbouring duchy of Holstein. Coming on top of the fortifications issue and accusations of illiberal defence spending, the development was unhelpful from the British government's point of view; and the predictable occupation of the duchies by Prussian and Austrian forces in early 1864 left the cabinet in a quandary which the invasion of Denmark itself only deepened. Palmerston and Russell tried the known paths of diplomacy through a five-power conference. In the last resort, however, they could not deny that they held no mandate for defending Denmark's claim to the duchies by military means. The prime minister, foreign secretary and the lord chancellor (Westbury) discovered themselves isolated in cabinet by their willingness to countenance war. Among the Tories, similarly, only Cecil, Carnarvon and Manners shared their view.[64] The Commons censure motion on government policy nevertheless failed, albeit narrowly (313 to 295) and historians thereby lost an opportunity to examine a recasting of party dialogue on lines which might have cut across the divisions of recent years.

The Conservative leadership sought no such change of direction in 1864. It was losing, however, its fear of a dissolution; indeed the evidence accruing from by-elections suggested that the Tory message had begun to tell in county seats. At the general election the party had done well enough in rural areas to make Russell anxious about the Liberals' future there. 'If the boroughs surpassed our hopes', he had then confided to a correspondent, 'the counties have exceeded our fears.'[65] The early sixties brought depressed wheat prices – those of 1864 were the worst since 1851 – and the government's pious intentions to discontinue the income tax had compelled it to persist in the malt duty. Consequently the county pendulum had swung sharply away in the early years of the decade. Eight of those seats changed hands in by-elections between 1859 and 1865; and of these the Liberals won only three, two of them unopposed. By 1864 Derby had returned to his parlour game of composing lists of ministers for a new (and this time majority) government. Yet in many ways these indications were unreliable. Conservatives liked making pictures from the limited range of pigments provided by rural experience. And even that experience underwent change as corn prices began their climb again: wheat doubled in price between 1864 and its high-point in 1868. Too much could also be read into Palmerston's imminent withdrawal or death. Since 1859, hopes that the Liberals would fall apart in that eventuality had become less well-founded. This impression strengthened as reform gathered momentum in the changing climate of 1864 and found its champion in a most unlikely quarter.

Gladstone's emergence as a major party phenomenon had attracted notice from all sides of political opinion. It expressed, at one level, the decline of 'our old men'. It embodied, more significantly, Gladstone's new understanding of a Liberal *public* and a shift in the political style and method needed to communicate with it. Gladstone had once been a Peelite and had learned how to be a radical; but he should not be left thus half-baked. He had formed a view of the limitations of Westminster and come to appreciate the moral and electoral potential of a wider political nation. What he sought to bring within the pale of the constitution in 1864 amounted to an area of authority to which he might have recourse in force-feeding a moralized republic. He wanted no more social levelling than that to which he submitted himself at 8.30 every morning: the communion of a kneeling brotherhood. But his language had a life of its own and seemed to run beyond intention. It became the medium through which a fragmented Liberalism found an identity. Without that medium Palmerston was capable of winning the next election, as indeed he did; nor could it be said that Gladstone comprised a precondition of a reforming Liberal party. Yet the figure who emerged between 1864 and 1868 possessed unique properties which would enable him to modulate the tone and content of post-Whig politics.

A new tone could be heard in the provinces even in 1864. The appearance of a Reform Union initiated by northern businessmen seeking to do for industrial democracy what they believed themselves to have done for free trade provided one part of the continuo; the Reform League of trade union activists like Applegarth and Odger supplied another. The first declared itself in favour of an acceptable level of inequality by campaigning for a household suffrage. But the League's tone was more strident in its demand for a manhood threshold and helped encourage a feeling among politicians that party lines had ceased to represent true divisions of sentiment. The real question had ceased to be one of Liberal versus Conservative; the relevant distinction lay between those who wanted to 'increase the power of the mob' and those who did not. It was no longer inconceivable, on one side of the argument, that a conservative churchman like E. B. Pusey might ask his readers to support the Liberals and press for universal suffrage in order to strengthen the church.[66] It became no less apparent that other resistance to democracy merely considered itself more necessary and vigilant than ever before; and some of this resistance had a *Liberal* colour. None, after all, pressed the language of defence so insistently in these years than the albino Liberal Robert Lowe who, since 1859, had steeped himself in a loathing for the Whig understanding of history. He had been on the Liberal benches when Edward Baines (Liberal: Leeds), son of the Dissenting MP of 1832, proposed the reduction of the borough franchise to £6 in his abortive Private Member's Bill of 1865. Lowe told the House:

> If this Democracy be a good thing, let us clasp it to our bosoms; if not, there is, I am sure, spirit and feeling enough in this country to prevent ourselves to be overawed by any vague presage of this kind, in the belief that the matter has already been decided in some dark tribunal in which

they sit together to regulate the future of nations. The destiny of every Englishman is in his own heart.[67]

Palmerston's interest in fates and destinies did not extend far beyond rhetorical uplift. His concerns in asking the Queen to dissolve the 1859 parliament had a shorter range: he wanted to use the radical mood to capture another period of power. He succeeded here as before, but the election decided little beyond his own pre-eminence. In England the party balance remained almost identical to that of the previous parliament; it was the radicalization of Wales and Scotland, plus the reversion of Ireland to its tradition loyalties, that gave the Liberals an extra twenty seats or so. Beneath this surface, however, the centre of gravity of the Liberal parliamentary party had eased leftwards, with interesting implications for Bright's radicals, who now included John Stuart Mill, MP for Westminster – a seat still associated with names like Sir Francis Burdett, John Cam Hobhouse and (a faded memory) Charles James Fox. The questions that such Liberalism posed were ones to which Palmerston had no answer; and it may have been a mercy to his legend that he did not need to find any. A chill turned to fever in October 1865 and the institution simply ceased to exist. Amid falling gilts the nation turned to nostalgia and the rescuing of false certainties from the decades bridged by that one consciousness. He had worked with men who had drunk Pitt's sherry. Half a century later his own world had spawned its own *enfants terribles* and rendered Palmerston himself an index of orthodoxy. He never knew most of them but his life touched theirs and gained a reflected modernity. During that last summer at Brocket, Joseph Chamberlain was poised to expand his ambition beyond the boundaries of Birmingham. In the stone cottage at Llanystumdwy, further still in space and time, Mrs George's two-year-old toddler retained as yet his anonymity beneath the protective eye of Uncle Lloyd.

Part II

Pressure from Within
1865–1914

4

Occupying the Centre

Reversing the logic of reform (1865–7)

Without Palmerston the Liberal party sought to remain Palmerston-ian. Many of its members had already turned elsewhere, however, and discovered inspiration in a different master-plan, one that identified the promising prospects for Liberalism in an advanced, urban radicalism whose recommendations would include a more democratic franchise with legislation to delimit the political influence of landed wealth. For these – the 'Commercial Liberals', as Disraeli labelled them[1] – leadership lay closer to Gibson, Bright, Cobden and (more recently) Gladstone than to the traditional Whig names apart from that of the new party leader, Earl Russell. A right-wing deviation also existed in the minds of a group of back-benchers and Liberal peers. Lords Lansdowne, Grey and Lichfield, in the House of Lords, and Grosvenor, Edward Horsman and Lichfield's son Augustus Anson in the Commons, comprised the crucial members of the 'Cave of Adullam' (a Biblical allusion attributed to Bright) which opposed any drastic franchise extension and reaffirmed the role of Liberalism as an enlightened defender of property. If the group had a parliamentary leader then he was that sour invigilator of cant, Robert Lowe; but its power followed more directly from its wealth and social *cachet*. Between them, these ill-matched blueprints for Liberal advance left little room for a concerted approach to the difficulty which everyone above the gangway seemed bent on confronting: Britain's second lurch towards democracy.

Russell's return to the leadership had been agreed in advance of Palmerston's death and it signalled the certainty of a reform bill once parliament reconvened in February 1866. But the ground-rules of political action had changed and in changing made possible a bizarre sequence of shifts both in the relationship between the masses and Westminster and in the function of reform within the dialogue of parties. Logic required of reform that it should emerge as a demand from the masses and harness itself to the party of progressive change. What happened in the eighteen months after Palmerston's death stood this logic on its head. The party of progress discovered itself incapable of reviving the correspondence with reform that had given it life in the 1820s. The party of reaction not only picked up reform but pressed it forward with a radicalism which drove Disraeli behind Gladstone's back and on to his left. And the masses, for all the knocking down of railings in two large meetings in Hyde Park in 1866–7, served not as players but as spectators in a match between overheated politicians locked in a scrum over Palmerston's mantle. It is the strangest story in the modern history of party politics, and four elements are crucial in explaining it: the views politicians formed about popular seriousness over reform; the width of territory occupied by 'Liberals' in the mid-1860s; the minority status of Conservative representation at all points after the 1865 election; and the depth of tactical genius yet to be exhibited by Benjamin Disraeli.

Ever since the resurgence of reform as a party preoccupation at the end of the fifties, the mood of politicians had suggested little sense of urgency or panic over threats of revolutionary action among the working class. Palmerston's instinct that the need for major construct- ive legislation had passed underlay many judgements on the Whig side of both houses of parliament. Gladstone's future minister Henry Bruce reflected this sense of relaxation in 1863. 'All that Brougham and Grey, and Mackintosh and Horner fought for against Eldon & Co has been carried,' he told his brother, 'and the good work having been done, the country does not much care who administers the State.'[2] The appearance of the Reform League and Reform Union added a dimension to the argument that had not been present in 1863. But the evidence surviving from letters and diaries by no means compels the historian to treat the middle years of the decade as though the men most responsible for the formulation of policy had become conscious of a challenge to social stability. The winter of 1865 certainly brought rebellion of a kind in the insurrection of Irish nationalists; a rash of violent incidents involving men calling them- selves 'Fenians' gave Lord Kimberley, the new lord lieutenant, a difficult few months. In the following year, a succession of 'outrages' among trade unionists culminated in a Sheffield street in October 1866 when a saw-grinder who had ceased paying his union subscrip- tion found a wall of his house blown away by explosives. Both of these agitations precipitated important consequences: the one in bringing Ireland again to the forefront of political preoccupation in the British cabinet where it was to remain, with varying intensity, until 1894; the other in accelerating the appointment of a Royal Commission to inquire into the unions which would set in motion, as we shall see, significant developments in labour history after 1868. Neither of them convinced politicians that the reform issue had altered its status. Popular demonstrations came closer to doing so. Yet by the time they began seriously to impinge on government in the summer of 1866, the Liberal administration of Earl Russell – surely the necessary vehicle for reform – had been defeated in the House of Commons and had resigned.

From the beginning no one in that government had deluded himself over the likely difficulties. Russell needed to hold together the centripetal fragments that his party had become; and his legendary tactlessness argued against much optimism among Liberal commentators. So far as personnel was concerned, little change seemed to have occurred. Russell's former place at the Foreign Office went by reversion to Clarendon (Palmerston's choice in the fifties), Clarendon's at the Duchy of Lancaster fell vacant and remained so for a few months. Sir Charles Wood's elevation to the peerage gave rise to a moment of excitement in February 1866 but his replacement by Earl de Grey soon stifled it. The appearance of young Lord Hartington, heir to the vast estates of the Duke of Devonshire, in de Grey's seat at the War Office caused a ruction, on the other hand, if only because Gladstone did not want him. (The complexities of the new minister's private life – his nickname 'Harty-Tarty' proved persistent – kept Whig society amused for the next half-century.) Shuffling the peerage did little to resolve Russell's problems, of course, and one need only look beneath the surface to see signs of malignancy. It was odd that the appointment of an under-secretary at the Colonial Office should have attracted more attention from pundits than that of the foreign secretary. W. E. Forster had entered the House of Commons only some four years before and, seniority apart, Liberal backbenchers grumbled about granting such rapid promotion to an ex-Quaker radical representing Bradford – a man who by all accounts used the rhetoric of 'a regular universal suffrage man, or something near it'.[3] But Russell had felt obliged to appoint a radical to office. While he could not have Bright (Gladstone would not have him), he was desperate for radical reinforcement before he attempted reform. Forster took office, however, on condition that the franchise problem would be approached directly via the introduction of a bill rather than through the appointment (say) of a leisurely Commission. He thus helped the ministry at the cost of knocking a nail into its coffin. The editor of *The Times*, no supporter of Earl Russell, anticipated in a letter of February 1866 the dilemma likely to face the prime minister when parliament met:

> He can't now resist bringing in a Bill but nobody professes to believe that he can carry one. If it is a single-barrelled one [i.e. one that avoids a redistribution of seats], the common sense of the House and the country will reject it; if it includes disfranchisement, it will have equally little chance. And, if it did, by any species of luck, struggle through the Commons, it would reach the Lords so late and with so small a majority that they would refuse to pass it.[4]

What stood in Russell's way was the nature of the parliament elected in 1865 and his determination to do without the Adullamites. Perhaps because the long recess until February encouraged rumours and the premature fear of 'movement', perhaps because the new members (nearly two hundred of them) struck some traditionalists as lacking connexion with the great parliamentary families of which Liberalism was supposed to consist, perhaps because the removal of the late prime minister left the participants without a focus for their darker apprehensions, the House met in a mood of uncertainty and suspicion. Nothing had been done to conciliate the Cave: if Bright had been snubbed, so had Lowe and Horsman. Filling the vacant Duchy with a brilliant radical banker, George Joachim Goschen, pleased no one since it squandered an opportunity to give the Cave something and increased radical jealousies by promoting a man of Teutonic name who had thus far sounded radical about little apart from the secret ballot (and who was even younger than Forster had been in his queue-jumping a few months before). Given a Conservative party at the nadir of despair and ready to run in any direction that offered an escape from marginality, the session promised a number of crosscurrents within and between parties. This reality lay behind the acrimony raised in debates over the minutiae of franchise reform in 1866. It sustained the febrile tone of political discussion in the summer. 'The political excitement among the upper classes', Stanley wrote in June, 'is greater than it has been for the last seven or eight years: I do not believe it is shared to any considerable extent by the people.'[5]

Insofar as 'the people' impinged on Liberal ministers as they framed their reform bill in January and February 1866, they edged the politicians towards caution. Economic growth over the past fifteen years had placed property within the grasp of persons deemed by the strategists of 1832 unfit (and unlikely) to acquire it – and with property came the vote. As in the years before the first reform act, a shift had taken place within the old political order and threatened its subversion. Indeed, when the government presented to the Commons the electoral statistics from which it had been working, many fears seemed to have been based on an element of fact. Over a quarter of the existing electorate already consisted, it seemed, of persons who could be described as working class; so that, if any sizeable extension downwards of the property thresholds were to take place, the spectre of working-class 'preponderance' in some boroughs would become all too visible. Russell himself proved sensitive to such fears: behind the man of 1860 still stood the more nervous one of 1830. The £6 threshold for boroughs recommended in his last reform bill climbed to £7 in the 1866 version, despite Gibson's attempt to pull it down to £5. Reducing Chandos's £50 tenant qualification in the counties to a threshold as low as £10 – the dream, again, of 1860 – likewise encountered opposition from the Whig sector and £14 appeared in the bill. The cabinet was playing games with the future, Gladstone doing its sums. If they went down to £6 in the towns, the new artisan vote would amount to nearly a quarter of a million – a thought that turned the knees to water; £7, on the other hand, would give 150,000, topped up, perhaps, with a franchise for lodgers which might bring in another 60,000. To make the increase even less than this, two courses might be followed in theory: the cabinet could raise the threshold higher still and renounce radical support; or they could transfer the basis of their calculations from gross annual rent to rateable value.

Rent versus rate seems a tedious controversy in retrospect; but it lay nevertheless at the heart of the party problem in 1866 and ultimately proved responsible for the defeat of the government. By following the 1832 model of basing the property qualification for enfranchisement on a rental footing the government achieved two objectives. It constructed, first, an electoral system that would act more predictably than one subject to the local inconsistencies of rating; and secondly, it provided a means of giving the Adullamites a threshold which sounded reassuringly high. Most MPs, after all, had little comprehension of the implications of rental or rating schemes; but £7 sounded safer than the £5 or £6 which a rating system would have invited in order to produce a similar expansion of the electorate. On the other hand, the word 'rating' did not lack psychological penetration on the Tory back benches. Doubtless the Cave and the counties could have come together and forced the government into making suitable changes in its bill. Disraeli, how-ever, patiently explained to his supporters that this was not the point. 'No matter how you modify the bill, it is still theirs, and not ours, and will give them the control of the boroughs for half-a-dozen years to come.'[6] Lord Dunkellin's purpose in rising during the committee stage of the Liberals' reform bill to propose changing it from a rental into a rating bill lay less in amending it, therefore, than in burying it.[7] The government's decision to resign when he succeeded in his mission probably took him by surprise, as it did most other observers. Even the Queen, it turned out, had shown herself unable to stiffen the resolve of Russell's cabinet to fight on and try again. The Conservative party, more conscious of opportunity than difficulty, had no time to reason why.

Those whom the fourteenth Earl of Derby gathered about him over the next few months seemed unlikely to leap in the dark or, indeed, to leap anywhere at all. A placid continuity with the cabinet of 1858 emerged in the appointments through Edward Stanley (Derby's son) at the Foreign Office, Disraeli's return to the Exchequer, Lord Chelmsford's to the Woolsack and the reappearance of minor office-holders such as Lord Naas and Sir Henry Cairns. Newer names said little for radicalism – the third Duke of Buckingham and Chandos, the Duke of Marlborough, the Earl of Carnarvon, the Duke of Richmond – and suggested a lump which the few commoners in the cabinet (Gathorne Hardy, George Ward Hunt and Sir Stafford Northcote) would not easily leaven. They were not, it is true, an elite of 'county' society: few of them owned the acres to attract mention in John Bateman's highly embarrassing *Great Landowners of Great Britain and Ireland* in 1876. Carnarvon and Marlborough could muster about 60,000 acres between them; but the great Tory vastnesses in Scotland, for example, found only one voice in Richmond. Neither did the cabinet threaten reaction. With the exception of their lieutenant-general (Jonathan Peel, Sir Robert's brainless brother who had bought his way up the army hierarchy by purchasing commissions), the government saw no objection in principle to a moderate extension of the franchise with suitable safeguards for property and intelligence. Apart from their tearful neurotic (Spencer Horatio Walpole whose life had been clouded by the assassination of his father-in-law, Spencer Perceval, by the tyrannical regime of Flogger Keate at Eton and by the side-effects of two doses of the Home Office) it did not tremble at the prospect of confronting the masses. The ministry that would soon turn Toryism upside down began, that is to say, with the inertia that is born of ordinariness.

Possibly the background of some of the ministers hinted at a modest volatility. The familiar environment of the rural south-east, Eton, Christ Church and Trinity stands out as clearly as before. But

Gathorne Hardy's early experience, for example, had been northern and industrial until his father left him enough money to buy Hemsted Park, near Cranbrook in Kent. Northcote's background in Devon calls up an echo of Eldon and Sidmouth. Ireland, the cockpit of British politics after 1868, had its representative in Henry Corry, father of Disraeli's new private secretary and devoted aide, Monty Corry, as it did also in Lord Naas, later Earl of Mayo, and Henry Cairns whose First in classics carried the imprimatur of Trinity College, Dublin. A certain (and destabilizing) intellectuality can be found elsewhere among the leaders of Conservative politics. Oriel College, Oxford, had left a mark on its young men during its great age of Anglican revival in the thirties and forties, and its products began, from the 1860s, to appear in senior party circles. The Balliol College of Benjamin Jowett, equally, had already given more to statesmanship than Stafford Northcote. Besides these general movements in Conservative background, the self-conscious intellectuals Cranborne and Carnarvon provided uncomfortable evidence of difficulty. That by March 1867 these two found themselves in the same frame of mind as General Peel testified both to the pungency of reform and the catholicity of Conservative values.

In the summer of 1866 few Conservatives had felt urgent about reform. Perhaps some shared the distant preoccupations of Sir Henry Bulwer who watched from Paris and gave Lady Salisbury the benefit of his wisdom in a private letter during October:

> As to reform itself there are three considerations for you. First – what is best for your party with a view to retaining office, secondly what is best for returning to it, and lastly what is best for the country generally. I have lived so long out of parties that I am not a good judge as to their tactics, nor feel, except as far as friends are concerned, a deep interest in their fate. But I do feel a deep interest in the public welfare, and I have a leaning amongst our classes for the aristocratic element and the democratic one, the gentry and the masses. My sympathy is not bourgeois – the middle order must be consulted and considered as a support to a Government, but it has neither the energy nor the elevation which can carry on a Government. The best chance for our future would be that the gentry should gain the masses. Not a difficult task. But they would have for that to become Englishmen at large and not merely landed proprietors.[8]

On the other hand, few in the Conservative party had time or inclination to become Englishmen at large. The portended fusion between Adullamites and Conservatives that had preoccupied some

MPs earlier in the year had not come about and the ministry formed by Derby contained no admixture of reformers. When a large demonstration in favour of reform defied, in July 1866, a government prohibition by entering Hyde Park, the response of ministers gave no cause for alarm among anti-democrats except for the pathetic ineptitude of the home secretary, Spencer Walpole, whose weakness caused general anxiety. A sense that the incident suggested 'more mischief than malice' in the demonstrators reinforced their reaction that Walpole's hysteria had been 'quite uncalled for, and almost ludicrous'.[9] Certainly no panic entered into the minds of ministers as a result of the meeting. A Royal Commission, perhaps; some general resolutions, eventually, about extending the franchise; a bill, possibly, in a year or two's time: these leisurely reflections come closer to describing Derby's state of mind than any ascribed need to respond to pressure from without. The pressure meanwhile continued throughout the summer and autumn as reform agitations and meetings appeared in a number of provincial centres – Birmingham, Leeds, Newcastle and in the Scottish capital. But the mood of 1831 is hard to find; it certainly did not exist among politicians. Parliament broke up in August anyway and supporters of government scattered to their seats and moors and farms in some anxiety about their tenants' foaming cattle (for the 'rinderpest' of 1865–6 preoccupied Tory back-benchers more persistently than the most spectacular performances of the Reform League); or about their own impending bankruptcy if the financial crisis surrounding the collapse of bankers Overend and Gurney did not ease soon; or the implications of Bismarck's mangling of the Austrians at the battle of Sadowa a few weeks before (3 July); or the sheer press of business – as much in the fields of education and Irish land reform as in franchise – likely to dominate a session still mercifully six months distant.

No one, not even Disraeli, understood the degree to which these instincts and perceptions ignored the reality of a peculiar party configuration. The Adullamites had not been digested; and though they commanded little influence among respected political leaders (an attempt to rope in Earl Spencer failed in the new year) or in the press, their parliamentary presence remained crucial to the government's survival. Moreover, both they and an articulate public had put reform on the placards: it would not readily die away. By the same token, however, the minority administration could not control the passage of a bill through parliament. Through their combinations and agreements, other groupings would be bound to force changes into whatever Disraeli could be persuaded to introduce. Political logic thus rolled the Conservative party towards an unpleasant conclusion. Not only had reform, once begun, to receive a free rein; it had also to be managed in a fashion that would undermine Gladstone's support and set radicals, former Peelites and Adullamites at one another's throats.

Only a major gesture in the direction of democracy would suffice to detach radical opinion from the enemy; and for that reason Conservative thinking appeared to have moved, when parliament met in February 1867, away from caution and timidity. One possibility presented itself in 'household suffrage', i.e. in giving the vote to all householders subject to a residential qualification and protecting property by inserting into the bill, as in their 1859 effort, a number of 'fancy franchises' to reward with extra votes certain classes of voter for (say) paying £1 per year in direct taxation, or having at least £50 in the savings bank, or passing a test in basic literacy. No amount of fancy decoration impressed General Peel, however. Mention 'household suffrage' to him, Disraeli reported to the prime minister, and 'his eye lights up with insanity'.[10] Other anti-democrats in the cabinet could stomach the idea, providing it were rendered harmless by plural voting and the adoption of a property threshold for the householders at around £5 (rating value). After these constraints had come under attack as Disraeli prepared the new reform resolutions for the House of Commons, and after it had finally dawned on Cranborne just how many artisans his party seemed willing to enfranchise, the crisis came. Carnarvon, Cranborne and Peel threatened resignation unless Disraeli toned down the provisions of the bill. He must have taken them seriously for when he introduced his resolutions on 25 February he made one of the worst speeches of his career in lame support of a £6 rating threshold for the boroughs and a £20 one for the counties with no plural voting.

Now whatever else Conservatives wanted, they did not want this. Their preoccupations and anxieties arose neither from the mob nor General Peel: the worry was Gladstone and the likelihood of his return for another long spell of government by sabotage and hypocrisy. Disraeli learned from their response to his miserable resolutions that horse-and-hound Toryism had finally assimilated the teaching he had repeated since 1846. With relief and new hope he withdrew the resolutions and announced, to the amazement of those around him, that the government would proceed immediately with a reform bill. To stop could only mean defeat. Like Grey in 1831, but down a far steeper incline, Disraeli had to let the coach run and leave his dissident cabinet colleagues to jump. By 18 March he had returned to the Commons with his bill and minus the three rebels. Household suffrage, he made plain, had become government policy, with a residential qualification (two years in the boroughs and one in the counties), a property threshold of £15 for the county constituencies and a number of fancy franchises. By itself the scheme would have produced comparatively modest working-class enfranchisement. But it presented nonetheless a formidable challenge to Gladstone's credibility by inviting him to oppose a more 'democratic' bill than the one he had supported and lost the previous year. And Gladstone soon had the point pressed on him. His own party refrained from killing the reform bill at its second reading in March; the radical section of it refused, in the so-called tea-room revolt in April, to help him insert a property threshold into the borough provisions. Gladstone disappeared, as Disraeli had throughout intended that he should, 'under a cloud'.[11]

Keeping Gladstone there involved throttling every amendment to which he lent prominent support; and that much Disraeli could do. But he could hardly fend off amendments from the rest of the Liberal front and back benches during the committee stage of the bill. The details of those amendments must be treated here more briefly than their importance merits.[12] Central to our purpose is the recognition that during the committee stage of the bill, the enfranchisement proposed by it *trebled*. Lodgers, for example, were brought into the bill (subject to a property qualification of £10) for the first time. An amendment introduced by Grosvenor Hodgkinson (Liberal: Newark) drastically expanded the scope of the bill by giving the vote to 'compound' householders, i.e. those whose rates were paid by their landlord. And as the franchise expanded, the constraints on its subversiveness had to be relinquished. 'Duality', the giving of an extra vote to selected groups in order to conserve the influence of property or education, went without a fight. The residence qualification in boroughs came down from two years to one. The county threshold contracted (ubiquitous Locke-King lurked behind this one) from £15 to £12. But although these and other changes radically altered the character of the bill, the inevitability of major amendment had been clear in March and the major policy shift had come in February. Seen in this light, the narrative does not reinforce the view that the second Hyde Park meeting of May 1867 acted as a critical catalyst in the process of generating radical reform.[13] Haste certainly marked the later stages of the bill's passage. But would it not have done so without the behaviour of the crowd summoned by the Reform League on that blazing hot day in the park? If Disraeli hoped to extract permanent advantage from Gladstone's current failure as a politician, he had to charge on to the crucial party question of redistribution. For he who controlled the reallocation of seats and the mapping of constituency boundaries could redesign nothing less than the electoral geography of Britain.

The reform bill received the royal assent on 19 August 1867. Much remained undone: the highly contentious clauses of the boundary bill, the provisions of the Scottish and Irish reform bills, all of which carried over into the 1868 session. Around him, however, Disraeli could see the effects of six months' frantic footwork. The Liberal party, as Gladstone conceded, had sunk into 'an almost unexampled position – a party of vast strength in the House of Commons paralysed by internal dissensions'.[14] Of course many Tories felt anxious about the future, in the club and tearoom if not on the platform. Yet time would show that the decisions taken in 1867 pointed the Conservative party towards the central position in party politics that it would enjoy for much of the last third of the nineteenth century, one that it had not known since the reign of George IV. In the shorter term they must dig themselves in and try to consolidate the advantage that Disraeli had won for them in 1867. In the dust billowing behind 'the Jew's triumphal car',[15] on the other hand, it was hard to see where to dig.

In the dark

When Derby described the events of the past few months as a leap in the dark, he voiced more than a mood of Tory confusion. Many Liberals seemed no less insecure. The first post-reform general election of 1868 left the Liberal chief whip feeling that all had become 'new & changed & large and I fear I must say in some respects *dark*'.[16] Not that pessimism about democracy had infected the House of Commons, outside the habitual dismay of Lowe and Cranborne; the mood rather reflected the presence of the unknown. Politicians acknowledged that the interests which it was their profession to reconcile had shifted significantly in recent years but they lacked any clear understanding of what the new order required of them.

From the perspective of the twentieth century and its retrospect of Britain's developing economic instability after 1870, it is tempting to see in such uncertainty anticipations of a psychology of inferiority in the face of an upsurge in American and German industrial production and the opening up of the Canadian prairies. Insofar as politicians found themselves implicated in that process, however, their familiar fiscal practices suffered no great change. During the economic crisis at the end of the 1870s, Disraeli, now Earl of Beaconsfield, saw no reason to avoid telling the House of Commons that 'Her Majesty's Government are not prepared – I do not suppose any

Government would be prepared – with any measures which would attempt to alleviate the extensive distress which now prevails.'[17] No equivalent of a *Zollverein* found favour in the home of free trade and *laissez-faire* for a further twenty years; there was no essay in state socialism. The geography of depression in any case presented its patchwork quilt of local variation and counter-rumour usual in the experience of the governing classes. Even the notorious harvest of 1879, for example, left many Scottish landowners wondering what the fuss could be about, while in England Granville, for one, told Gladstone that he saw no reflection of the 'dreadful accounts' from Shropshire and Staffordshire at Walmer Castle: there the crops had turned out 'very fine'.[18] Rents, or rather the lack of them, certainly disturbed landlords in these difficult years but for the more political among them the anxiety perhaps lay less in the adverse conditions faced by agriculture than in the lessening leverage which the landed interest felt itself capable of exerting in the reformed framework.

In part this feeling grew out of the obvious diminution of land-owning in the background of members of parliament and an aware-ness of industrial and financial connexions among the middle-class members. That trend had not yet taken on the character of a danger-ous movement, and its rate of advance before the 1880s should not be exaggerated. An examination of the background of Conservative MPs between 1832 and 1900 shows the pace of change by 1868:[19]

Background of Conservative MPs (Percentages)	1832	1868	1900
Landed interest	58.3	47.3	21.2
Industrial, commercial, financial	22.3	30.9	50.4

But political observers of the 1870s and 1880s did not always ground their politics in sociological research. They felt an intimation of the growing isolation of 'Land' within the depressed economic structure. Their industrial involvement in minerals – coal, for ex-ample – had receded noticeably in recent years though railway com-panies still provided an outlet for managerial energy and capital. Their revenues as ground landlords in the towns dragged them into the rapidly changing relationship between the urban and the rural and reminded them of their vulnerability, if Joseph Arch's Agricul-tural Labourers' Union (1872) had not already done so. Their loss of acknowledged electoral influence when Gladstone's first government introduced the secret ballot in 1872 registered, rather than caused, anxieties over the crumbling of various forms of cohesion within the 'deference communities' from which landed political power had arguably received sustenance.[20]

Whatever its long-term significance would prove to be, the town bulked large in this sense of anxiety. In 1861 the census had eroded the complacency which the experience of the 1840s and 1850s, distorted by the Irish famine and a marked upswing in emigration from Britain, had helped engender. By 1852 the population of 1801 had doubled; and the rate of increase since then between censuses in England and Wales had climbed to over 14 per cent per decade. The distribution of this growth, moreover, gave rise to greater worries than its gradient. 'The English nation,' in the words of the 1861 census report, '...without losing its hold on the country, and still largely diffused over 37 million acres of Territory, has assumed the character of a preponderating city population.' By 1871 the preponderance had become starker still (urban population 62 per cent, rural population 38 per cent) and concealed a rate of growth in the towns running at twice that observed outside them. Through the 1870s the curve rose ever more steeply and recorded a greater proportionate increase in population than in any decade since 1831–41. Malthusians revived their bad dreams and politicians experienced a few new ones. Suppose one took, for example, the ten largest increases in urban population between 1871 and 1881: where had they occurred? If one listed them in descending order of increase, London came out tenth; but the other nine told their own story – Salford, Oldham, Nottingham, Leicester, Hull, Bradford, Leeds, Sheffield, Sunderland. Industrial England north of the Trent was taking on new weight at just the moment when the politicians had, largely for their own purposes, enfranchised many of its working-class inhabitants. A harassed Conservative, picking up the first post-reform census in the House of Commons library, would have learned that the population of parliamentary boroughs – those sending MPs to Westminster – had risen by 50 per cent in the past twenty years. A long-established conception of the 'political nation' had plainly come under challenge.

The 'residuum' still existed, of course: major sectors of the working class remained without a vote after 1867. Violence played its traditional part here, usually in a highly ritualized form at election time. It was during a by-election in 1862 that Grimsby witnessed mob destruction; Nottingham experienced persistent electoral rioting until the 1870s. So long as the disturbances took place outside London, however, their seasonal status allowed the authorities to take a fairly relaxed view of them.[21] Labour's behaviour inside the political structure, on the other hand, posed a threat that would now require constant monitoring. A junta of trade union leaders had successfully presented their case to the Royal Commission inquiring into their status after the outrages. The foundation of the Trades Union Congress in 1868 was one result; and the willingness of both parties to make gestures towards it over the next decade suggested the emergence of a new force. This, moreover, amounted to more than mere muscle: a popular consciousness of trade unionism as a legitimate agency for political action rose markedly during workers' support for the engineers during their strike of 1871, though the unions could not hope to achieve regular front-page appearances until they widened their base and coarsened their strategy in the 1880s. The employers needed no such patience. Since the 1840s they had served their political apprenticeship: in the sixties and seventies their time had come. Ship owners in the ports, the steel masters of the midlands and north, the wool men of the West Riding, the iron men of Cleveland – never had their reach seemed longer. In years to come their sheer weight of money would supply ballast to the bottom end of the Conservative party in safe industrial seats. But for the time being most of them were Liberals and chapel Liberals at that. The Iron Duke's image of Nonconformist grocers and blacksmiths stood in need of updating.

Whatever the 'Nonconformist conscience' meant – the phrase seems first to have been used in 1870 – it comprised at the very least a reaction to three problems: disestablishment, education and beer. Granville reflected bitterly on the first after a dismal attempt at arousing an audience in Bradford in 1877: 'They do not care twopence about the Eastern Question, County Franchise or anything else but Miall and disestablishment.'[22] It mattered that Bradford did not care, not least because the government disliked watching one of its own ministers, W. E. Forster, sharing his constituency with Dissenting MPs who opposed Forster's Education Act of 1870 for its 'sectarian' character. Indeed, Edward Miall and, after his retirement in 1874, the Baptist Alfred Illingworth seemed to see their duty to lie in telling Westminster that Bradford had not been amused by Gladstone's first government. Another piece of legislation, Henry Bruce's Licensing Act of 1871, ran into a similar wave of opposition from the temperance lobby, a powerful force from the 1860s forwards, which again accused Gladstone of walking where he ought to have run. The parliamentary strength of the Nonconformists reflected this provincial thrust in a dramatic increase through the 1870s: by 1880 about a quarter of Liberal MPs were Nonconformists. And in the rhetoric of men like the Welsh Congregationalist Henry Richard (Merthyr Boroughs) a broad range of issues received a Dissenting slant, not least the emergence of Wales itself as a distinct political culture with its own priorities to press.

Closer to home, in their constituencies, parliamentary representatives felt a tug in the more organized 'caucus' politics of the 1870s emanating from John Gorst's National Union of Conservative Associations (1867) and the National Liberal Federation (1877) that was to grow out of Joseph Chamberlain's National Education League. But their continuing uncertainties about what the new electorate wanted would prove the greater preoccupation. It appeared when Disraeli appalled Gladstone by pretending that the Irish Church could not be disestablished without holding an English referendum first, an 'ultra-democratic' proposal which Gladstone, 'the People's William', rejected out of hand. The idea of a government's requiring a 'mandate' for controversial policies nevertheless dates from this period.[23] The same fear registered itself in the interest taken in the by-elections of the 1870s as politicians tried to work out the conclusions to be drawn about their new audience. In mid-term these elections offered a test of major issues, as Buckinghamshire did for Disraeli's Near Eastern policy in 1876. They offered some way of deciding when to dissolve parliament and risk a general election. The Liberals' defeat in 1874 and the Conservative one of 1880 both stemmed from misplaced optimism fostered in by-election successes.[24]

Beyond keeping an ear to the ground there seemed little to be done. Perhaps Disraeli meant it when he told the Queen in 1877 that the Admiralty had to go to W. H. Smith, the book stalls man, because he, the prime minister, needed a 'City or Borough member in the Cabinet'.[25] That Smith was a millionaire and sat for Westminster, on the other hand, hardly made him a tribune for muck and brass; even if the Tories had shown themselves less snobbish than the Whigs by allowing Smith into one of their clubs, the penchant for extending and strengthening the club system suggested a post-reform anthropology tuned to the exclusive more than to the demotic. The Carlton, Junior Carlton, St Stephen's and Constitutional clubs, on the Conservative side, and the Devonshire, Eighty, National Liberal and New Reform, on the Liberal, afforded private milieux and comfortable conversation beyond the reach of public intrusion. Conversely, the significance of public rhetoric increased rather than diminished after 1867. Gladstone was to show how a world could be won from a platform. Granville's assuring his leader in 1875 that Hartington and Forster had been instructed to say nothing beyond the 'merely oracular' pending a private conclave of leaders[26] at once reflects the force of the instrument and defines the conditions of its use.

In the light of retrospect, some of the consequences of these alterations in electoral structure become more readily visible, and modern research has partially revealed the contours that contemporaries as yet struggled to identify.[27] The increase in Britain's electorate in 1867–8 was greater in both relative and absolute terms than that provided for in 1832. The register, on the eve of its extension, amounted to about 1,300,000 voters, a natural increase of half a million over the 1832 figure. Disraeli's reform expanded this total to 2,500,000, but the effects of this expansion by no means distributed themselves equally through the constituencies. 'Household suffrage' had been aimed at in the towns, and the borough electorates consequently enjoyed the largest additions, rising on average by about one and a half times their pre-1867 size. Much depended, of course, on the structure of property-holding in a given community and the extent of 'natural' enfranchisement during the economic expansion of the fifties and sixties. London, for example, saw comparatively little change in 1867, expanding by about 40 per cent, whereas the Leeds electorate quadrupled, that of South Shields rose by almost six times and Merthyr Tydfil's exploded by a factor of ten. The disfranchisement of small boroughs that had survived the axe in 1832 gave Disraeli fifty-eight seats to redistribute in 1868. Of these, forty-five went to England rather than Scotland or Wales. Ireland's counties were left alone: the £12 occupation franchise remained, though the borough threshold was lowered. So far as the English redistribution went, more than half of the available seats went to the counties – a discreet example of changing in order to preserve.

Reform did not stop dead in 1867 any more than it had done in 1832. A backwash of radicalism persisted until the end of Gladstone's first government in 1874. In the flurry of Irish Church disestablishment in 1869 it may be forgotten, for example, that the ministry tried to derive advantage in local government. For Disraeli's reform of central representation invited a local complement, just as Melbourne's had sought one in 1835. The Municipal Franchise Act of 1869 receives little stress among historians; but by giving the local franchise to all compound ratepayers, reducing the residence qualification from two years to one and (in the year of John Stuart Mill's essay, *On the Subjection of Women*) enfranchising married women on the same terms as men, the measure created an important groundwork for late Victorian council politics.[28] Terminating the traditional system of open voting in 1872 likewise laid a milestone for radicalism: it joined the abolition of the property qualification for MPs in 1858 as another provision from the chartists' programme. When, moreover, back-bench and even junior ministerial opinion began to swing after 1873 towards wanting to see a household franchise in the counties, the democratic drift became too violent for some Whigs and ex-

Peelites to tolerate. And among unstable Tory elements the post-reform atmosphere could give rise to a form of hysteria – most memorably in J. S. W. E. Erle Drax, member for Wareham: 'Electors of Wareham! I understand that some evil-disposed person has been circulating a report that I wish my tenants, and other persons depend-ent on me, to vote according to their conscience. This is a dastardly lie; calculated to injure me. I have no wish of the sort. I wish, and I intend, that these persons shall vote for me.'[29]

He need not have worried. Most of the evidence accruing from national and regional studies of the post-reform electorate suggests that the power of patrons had not been abolished in 1867 or 1872. Corruption on a significant scale continued until well into the 1880s and in some places until the First World War; more than thirty corrupt constituencies can be identified as late as 1885. Only when land lost some of its economic attraction after the mid-1870s did the political grip of landlords begin to weaken. In the meantime sixteen of the English county seats continued in the gift of patrons even after the second reform act. Perceptually, much seemed to have altered. But the traditional politics of a territorial aristocracy – Whig politics – could be granted a future by contemporary politicians for all that Disraeli had done. A young Whig, signing himself 'An Old Whig', wrote to *The Times* in 1866 precisely to encourage those

> men whose opinions are generally...derived from the opinions of their forefathers...men whose talents and associations are what some might call aristocratic...men who, though attached to existing institutions, conceive that the best way of maintaining them when attacked is to give way in those points which are weak and indefensible, and...believe that by so doing they are in a better and not a worse position for defending the remainder; who, for instance, in order to resist Democ-racy vote for the Reform Bill, and in order to strengthen the Church advocate the abolition of Church Rates.

There remained a snag, as the author acknowledged. Men such as these belonged to a party that could not plausibly evade the leader-ship of Gladstone; and, as another young Whig put it, Gladstone 'has never understood Whig principles and never will'.[30]

Inventing Gladstonian Liberalism (1867–76)

Ultimately the Liberal party became different for Gladstone's having come to it. The problem lies in deciding when, why and to what extent his contribution amounted to a fundamental shift of purpose and identity. So far as Gladstone himself was concerned, important changes in attitude had plainly taken place since the personal crises of the 1840s. The defections to Rome, the judgement, 'legibly divine', of the Irish famine, his reading of evangelical theology in the writings especially of Bishop Butler and Thomas Chalmers, the impact of Darwinist thought after 1859 and the eruption of liberal nationalism in Italy and America: all of these had softened the tractarian prig of the early years.[31] In that sense, 'Gladstonian Liberalism' had appeared ten, even twenty years before the reform crisis of 1866–7. But in the sense of an identifiable *party* practice it seems rarely visible before 1868 either in Gladstone's behaviour within the Liberal elite or in wider Liberal politics. The economic reforms connected with Gladstone's period at the Exchequer under Palmerston may be explained without reference to some all-embracing Liberal ideology: they acknowledge Peel more than Mill and reinforce Gladstone's description of himself as 'a dead man, one fundamentally a Peel-Cobden man'.[32] That Gladstone allowed himself to remain under Palmerston's wing says something, too, for his lack of urgency. Again, his milk-and-water performance during the reform crisis had done nothing to suggest libertarianism. Only after his nose had been rubbed in the mess of 1867 did Gladstone learn the lesson that radicalism had become both a duty and a party requirement. Never again must he allow the suppleness of Conservatism to leave him isolated as a timid trimmer in the face of democracy. 'Mr Gladstone' – not the sombre spiritualist of the diary but the future People's William emblazoned on banners, fly-sheets and Toby mugs – owed his incarnation to Disraeli.

The appearance of a new political style was neither immediate nor self-conscious. Like most other Liberals, Gladstone brooded in the aftermath of Disraeli's *tour de force*, unsure which way to go, content to wait for his breeze. Russell in any case continued as nominal leader until into the new year of 1868 when he retired to Pembroke Lodge to spend his last days in an unhinged petulance which Gladstone's letters never succeeded in soothing. By then, the breeze had begun to blow. Fenian disturbances had returned to London, spectacularly so in the Clerkenwell bombings of 13 December 1867 when a clumsy attempt to release Fenian prisoners with a barrel of gunpowder had led to several deaths. Derby's government could not afford to meet violence with anything more imaginative than repression. For Liberals, however, the spectre of Ireland suggested both a threat, since some important Whigs owned land there, and an opportunity. If Gladstone could involve all wings of his party in an effective Irish policy it might prove possible to reconstruct Liberalism and throw out Derby and Disraeli. Some historians take umbrage at the thought of Gladstone's acting for a party, as opposed to a moral, purpose in 1868;[33] but his clarified understanding of party politics allowed Gladstone no such distinction. The reform difficulty had shown the importance of approaching politics through a realistic conception of what political parties could achieve; and the man who (unlike Peel) would become prime minister four times over the next thirty years had marked this well. After all, seen from an extra-party standpoint the problems of Irish society required one operation more than any other: an assault on the inequities of landownership and the plight of the Irish tenantry. Yet Gladstone saw at once that the subject, about which he had been reading in 1867, would divide his party even more drastically than reform had done. His attack must rather be aimed at the point where Whiggery met Dissent, and that intersection occurred in the movement to disestablish the Anglican Church in Ireland. Whatever Gladstone's task in Ireland would eventually come to comprise – there is little evidence that he yet knew himself – his mission was to pacify the Liberal party.

This matters a good deal but it matters even more that he succeeded. When Gladstone's resolutions on disestablishment defeated the Conservative government in late April and early May of 1868, Disraeli, the new Conservative leader, did not immediately resign; by hanging on through the summer he doubtless hoped that some of the steam would go out of the issue. But by bringing on the question of disestablishment Gladstone had given the Liberals their first compelling message since the corn laws, one resonant with echoes of the fight against the Test Acts in the 1820s and the Irish Church in the 1830s; they were not about to waste it. From the beginning of the poll, results ran against the Conservatives. In the English seats they finished over thirty behind; in Wales and Scotland they fared abysmally; in Ireland their decline since 1859 continued. Gladstone himself was a casualty at South West Lancashire and came back for Greenwich; but overall he found himself with a majority of 116. Disraeli saw no point in waiting to meet parliament and resigned the premiership, leaving Gladstone to kiss hands on 5 December 1868. Liberals naturally spent a euphoric Christmas. One cannot help but wonder nevertheless whether, in a longer perspective, Gladstone would not have been better off had he lost. His first major initiative as leader had paid off remarkably well, but in a man who celebrated his fifty-ninth birthday on 29 December the lesson could too easily become a rigid guide to future conduct at moments of intra-party animosity. Looking back from 1885–6, for example, when he tried to repeat his success with Home Rule, the triumph of

1868 seems in many ways the beginning of Gladstone's undoing. In the short term, however, the only danger lay in standing still. 'If the Liberal party stick in the mud as in Pam's time,' warned Sir William Harcourt, 'they will go smash, and the Tories will come back.'[34]

The Tories did not come back for six years and Gladstone's first administration of 1868–74 meanwhile earned itself the reputation of providing the most radical legislative programme Britain had so far seen in the nineteenth century. It turned out to be a government of halves: between 1869 and 1871 the volcanoes along the ministerial bench spewed their lava over the Irish Church, Irish land, education, the French, the Germans, the brewers, the universities and the army; thereafter they drifted towards that exhaustion with which Disraeli taunted them in 1872. 'As I sat opposite the Treasury Bench', the Manchester audience were told in Disraeli's best sneering tone, 'the Ministers reminded me of one of those marine landscapes not very uncommon on the coasts of South America. You behold a range of exhausted volcanoes. Not a flame flickers on a single pallid crest. But the situation is still dangerous. There are occasional earthquakes, and ever and anon the dark rumbling of the sea.'[35] Further oddity lay in the near omnipresence of religion as a touchstone of party feeling in these years. Deaths and promotions in the Church of England ('It rains Bishoprics') gave Gladstone many opportunities for making appointments that were sound in both the theological and political senses. They also furnished him with an enduring preoccupation, a 'daily & nightly thought'.[36] But the impact of religion did not end with bishoprics or the Irish Church; it impinged, through the susceptibilities of Nonconformists, on education, on the drink question and on the abolition of religious tests in the universities. It threatened, not only through the susceptibilities of Catholics in Ireland but through those of Whigs in England, to render the establishment of an Irish university an immovable object over which, as some members of the cabinet saw in 1871, the government seemed likely to trip and fall.[37]

The cabinet carried the imprint of a troubled decade in Liberal politics. Lowe's Adullamite career perhaps demanded that he be enticed from his Cave with the offer of a major post. Giving him the Exchequer was a bad idea all the same, as Gladstone soon discovered. Bright, on the other side of the party spectrum, accepted the Board of Trade, his first ministerial post, where he rapidly broke down as executive incompetence compounded the nervous collapse of a few years before. The Whig strand emerged in Clarendon's return to the Foreign Office, despite the Queen's displeasure, and the presence of Granville (Colonies), Argyll (India Office), Kimberley (Privy Seal), Hartington (Post Office) and de Grey as lord president of the council. Cardwell supplied a Peelite aftertaste which would strengthen when Roundell Palmer, now 1st Earl of Selborne, agreed to come in after the Irish Church issue had been settled. Selborne's Anglicanism had prevented his earlier cooperation (indeed, he would remain close to his former neighbour, Cranborne, who had himself moved to the Lords as 3rd Marquess of Salisbury) but that difficulty paled before those offered by Forster's former Quakerism or Bright's present one, or indeed by de Grey's decision to consummate an eccentric career as a Christian Socialist by resigning the lord presidency to become a Roman Catholic in 1873–4. James Stansfeld, a new name in the cabinet in 1871, threatened even worse things since he counted among his resonances a Unitarian upbringing in Halifax, his regarding Mazzini as a personal friend and a vague association with the most arresting s-word in Victorian England. Despite a continuing enthusiasm for repealing the Contagious Diseases Acts and securing further sexual liberation for women, however, Stansfeld had more recently taken over a brewery in Fulham and put behind him his dangerous start in life.

Managing his ministers in this large cabinet placed Gladstone's techniques of leadership under no immediate stress. His bill to disestablish the Irish Church encountered few problems in the Commons and passed its second reading on 23 March 1869 by 368 to 250 ('too good to last', as Gladstone rightly judged).[38] He knew that the House of Lords would exploit Liberal divisions over the measure, especially if Disraeli's plan of 'concurrent endowment' (i.e. of endowing the Catholic Church rather than abolishing the Anglican one) gained currency there. Nightmares including memories of Maynooth, the Ecclesiastical Titles Act which this government was hoping to repeal, and the thought of Bright's inevitable fury at endowing Catholics, weighed on the minds of some ministers. Happily, however, similar ghosts haunted Conservative evangelicals who thought the idea of concurrent endowment precipitate. Precipitancy did not, needless to say, worry Disraeli: he would have advocated the reintroduction of Peter's Pence had it promised to get rid of Gladstone. But party dislocation did worry him, enough to allow Cairns, evangelical leader of the opposition in the Lords since the death of Derby, to work out a deal with Granville in order to obtain better compensation terms for the church. This first legislative fracas had concentrated high-political attention on parliament to a degree unusual since the later days of Peel's government, and it was to remain there until the end of the 1870 session. The very fertility of ministers created problems about the best use of that session. The secret ballot had to be postponed to relieve considerable Whig indigestion about it. De Grey inside the cabinet and Forster outside it tried, without success, to interest the prime minister in the educational reforms they wished to introduce. Henry Bruce, the new man at the Home Office, thought the Fenians a tiresome distraction from his own preoccupation – the licensing bill with which he anticipated rousing Dissent and with which he was entirely failing to rouse Gladstone. Chichester Fortescue, the chief secretary for Ireland, fared better. His concern with the problems of Ireland reflected Gladstone's order of priority; and as press support developed for an initiative to meet the misery of evictions, Gladstone identified the next card to play.

To treat the problems of Irish landowning with consistency and intelligence appeared from the outset a formidable proposition. Gladstone prepared himself in his customary fashion: he read books about it. What was at once clear was that no agreement existed about the status of the tenantry. For the English and Anglo-Irish landlords (and therefore for the bulk of politicians at Westminster) the matter could be settled in a sentence by a competent lawyer. For the Irish tenant, however, the basis of English landownership lay in conquest, usurpation and the creation of legal fictions designed to confute the historic 'rights' of the Celtic people. It thus became possible for the tenant to claim a range of liberties over the improvement and even the sale of his land which ran beyond the letter of English law. And this doctrine of 'tenant-right', claimed contentiously everywhere in Ireland but generally acknowledged as Ulster Custom in the north, could not be satisfied by gestures towards compensating tenants for improvements that they may have made or merely by reducing the grounds for eviction. Nothing would suffice short of 'fixity of tenure' and a recognition that in Ulster Custom lay the only practicable basis for landlord–tenant relations throughout Ireland.

That the Irish Land Act of 1870 came nowhere near meeting these conditions owed something to the intractability of Anglo-Irish politics and more than a little to the character of Gladstonian Liberalism. Privately, Gladstone knew by September 1869 that the breeze was still at his back, that the Irish case for extending tenant-right had become persuasive and powerful, that in an ideal world he would press the cabinet towards radical legislation. But the conviction remained less important than the privacy. In public Gladstone represented himself as a defender of property backing into an unwelcome wind. Rather than spur on radicals like Bright when they made dangerous noises about land, Gladstone slapped them down with reminders that strategy was no subject for speeches, that the cabinet must maintain 'the most absolute secrecy, & not... "light" the path, or track *towards* our intentions'.[39] The proprietorial section of the cabinet – Granville placed in it Lowe, Clarendon, Cardwell, Argyll and Hartington – found a receptive ear for their reacting 'against sitting in perpetual sackcloth and ashes because the Irish are violent and disaffected'. What the prime minister avoided saying to his public he also avoided writing (an alarm bell for historians) to tetchy colleagues since words that could be spoken 'with perfect freedom' somehow 'look[ed] ugly on paper'. Better still, the words could remain unspoken and unwritten in committee. 'A Committee keep a Cabinet quiet.'[40]

Dissimulation over Irish land and the pressure of many Whigs for further coercion in the Irish countryside led Gladstone inevitably towards an unsatisfactory Land Act that merely compensated tenants for improvements, recognized Ulster Custom in the north and restrained arbitrary eviction. Failure to pay rent was still to constitute *prima facie* grounds for eviction. Even the House of Lords did not bother to oppose the bill. Yet the subject had entered Gladstone's soul and on Easter Sunday of 1870 he took it to church with him. 'At the Altar this day', he wrote in his diary that evening, 'it was the Irish Land question that I presented before God more than aught else living or dead.'[41] So searing a preoccupation fostered long-term consequences which the world would not see for fifteen years. It also gave rise to a more immediate one. Through spending most of his time thinking about Ireland, Gladstone had failed to think about education.

Since the report of the Newcastle Commission in 1862, politicians had acknowledged the inadequacy of educational provision in Britain and Ireland. Continued reliance on Church of England 'National' schools, non-denominational 'British' schools and other voluntary organizations no longer held any hope of servicing an expanding urban population and some form of in-filling offered at least a starting-point for policy. But if the state were to accept responsibility for establishing and maintaining schools, their finance and curricula would need to transcend deeply divided views among parents and pressure groups over the religious teaching to be envisaged. Nonconformists had already demonstrated the strength of their manifold aversions in their reaction to Graham's factory bill in 1843 and its tacked-on educational provision. The newly forged alliance between the Whigs and Dissenting interests argued the importance, moreover, of avoiding any simple, Erastian solution in the education bill of 1870. Gladstone, for his part, had come a long way since *The State in its Relations with the Church*, but he held to a view of Anglican duty that left him resistant to any dilution of the church's presence in educating the nation's young. Coming to the subject late, after some of his colleagues had already edged him towards compromise, he moved only far enough in 'an eager and agitated House' to accept the amendment of W. F. Cowper-Temple (Liberal: South Hampshire) to permit in schools 'no catechism or religious formulary which is distinctive of any particular denomination'.[42] Neither he nor Forster, whom he brought into the cabinet at the end of June, came to terms with the central Nonconformist grievance arising from clause 25 of the bill which allowed school boards to pay the fees of indigent children in Anglican schools out of taxes paid partly by Dissenters. In authorizing locally elected school boards to establish 'board schools' in areas neglected or inadequately served by voluntary organizations, the act of 1870 made a significant move in the direction of a national education system. Attendance at schools, however, became neither compulsory nor free; and for the act's sponsors there arose a swelling surge of criticism from the formidable Nonconformist lobby of which Joseph Chamberlain's National Education League (1869) voiced the most effective message. For Forster himself the act became not a beginning but an end: it finished him as a serious contender for the leadership of Dissenting radicalism. It also threw into shadow Gladstone's relations with the man he had spent much of his 'Irish' period trying to appease.

Bright was two years younger than Gladstone but had recently come to seem much older. The breakdown feared by his colleagues seemed all but complete by the summer of 1870. Two great measures in the session had diverged from what he took to represent the central principles of rational Liberalism; indeed, except for the disestablishment of the Irish Church, he had found little to applaud in Gladstone's government. Nor was he alone in his low spirits. Granville remarked to a correspondent in June that many of the cabinet showed signs of incipient collapse.

> It is impossible to be too much alarmed at the state of health of the most eminent of the Cabinet. Poor Bright is gone as far as this Session is concerned. Clarendon was only saved from gout in the stomach by strong stimulants to his feet. Gladstone told Bessborough yesterday that he sometimes feels alarmed for his own head. Cardwell at the last Cabinet sat close into the fire, looking as if he wished to cut his throat.[43]

By the end of the month Clarendon was dead and Granville had moved into the vacant chair which he was to occupy for the rest of this, and Gladstone's next, government. The change of personnel helped the Liberal leader greatly because it placed in charge of foreign affairs a man whom he liked and trusted, just in time to help him, Gladstone, mediate between the demands of Bright and those of Bismarck.

Foreign affairs had attracted little attention in the cabinet or the House since Gladstone took office; indeed the silence became so noticeable that the prime minister remarked on it more than once. Bismarck's crushing of the Austrians in 1866 had disturbed Paris more than London. Disraeli's sending of a British force to subdue King Theodore of Abyssinia in 1868 produced some bad jokes but failed to capture the national mind, despite Disraeli's rhetoric. At one level, the French declaration of war with Germany on 19 July 1870 need have mattered little more. The quarrel, ostensibly the result of a German intervention in the Spanish succession crisis following the deposition of Queen Isabella, brought no British interest under immediate threat. By attacking Germany after Bismarck had mangled the Kaiser's Ems telegram into a rebuff to French pride, the French had forfeited much sympathy in British political circles, though it tended to swing back again once the French army had suffered decisive defeat at Sedan on 2 September. But Gladstone was conscious of two difficulties. He wanted to behave impartially towards the antagonists in public while harbouring a private suspicion that something would have to be done about Bismarck; and he wanted to quieten fears in the party and the press that national defences must be strengthened as a response to events on the continent.

Gladstone marched towards his first objective with the same circumspection that he had shown over the Irish problem. Colleagues received emphatic denials that he envisaged any diplomatic intervention in the dispute: Cardwell in particular, as minister for war, had his feathers stroked and oiled. Yet Gladstone's worries about the nature of the ultimate peace treaty and the penalties that Bismarck seemed likely to impose on France could not easily be held down. Left to himself (or with Forster who thought the party pro-French) he would have sought to establish a public British 'view' of what the treaty might legitimately contain. Since he could not be left to himself, he followed a cabinet line of avoiding commitment and trying to maintain good relations with both sides. Defence, meanwhile, proved harder to control as an issue. A panic reminiscent of that of 1859 took hold of backbenchers and journalists, and Gladstone's initial determination to decline a rearmament programme 'without doing anything else' had to be abandoned in face of the cabinet's pressure for extra men and money.[44] So did his resolve to keep Bright in the cabinet: the defence question drove him out, publicly on grounds of ill-health. Already depressed by the education problem, Gladstone had lost his way in the xenophobia he never understood. He complained about the 'change of temperature', but Whig ministers blamed him more than the environment for the government's recent lack of grip. 'Foreign affairs are uncongenial to Gladstone', Kimberley wrote privately in February 1871. '[He] will never shine, when, as now, they occupy the first place in importance.'[45] The preliminary peace of that month between France and Germany, and the *fait accompli* of Russia's overturning of the Black Sea clauses of the 1856 treaty while European attention was distracted, left the government's radicalism jaded.

Elections began to go wrong. Then, in April, the government was beaten in the Commons. The collapse of the French had destroyed much of the rationale for Lowe's budget which now imposed taxation to meet an emergency which no longer existed – or would have done so had he not been driven into retracting it when his proposed tax on matches ignited opposition in the House. Cardwell's abolition of the right to purchase commissions in the army meanwhile caused such a fury of resentment among backbenchers and peers that it had to be carried out initially by royal warrant rather than an act of parliament – scarcely an advertisement for parliamentary management or representative democracy. It was hard to find a single bright point on the horizon. The Paris Commune had surrendered to the Germans in May but the proclamation of the German empire at Versailles did not promise an end to tension. It did, however, signal the conclusion of a period in which Europe had dominated political discussion. From outside the cabinet Bright pictured Granville in the spring 'always thinking of France and of Paris'.[46] But Granville, like Gladstone, was equally exercised over the problem of identifying the reasons for the government's lack of impetus. Gladstone, like Lloyd George exactly half a century later, felt his nervous breakdown coming on and went away to Whitby on the North Yorkshire coast, partly to rest but also to rescue his eldest son, Willy, from the local Liberals who had conceived a strong aversion to their new Member of Parliament.[47] Over the past three years Gladstone had turned the face of the Liberal party leftwards and pulled it away from the central currents of executive activity in which Palmerston and Russell had spent their working lives. He had taken it out of the clubs of St James's – the boast of Whitby – and made it a focus of provincial civic sentiment. He had developed a libertarian language of his own that received only partial expression at Westminster but which nevertheless created a climate of expectation in the constituencies. There had been retrograde steps. The Criminal Law Amendment Act of 1871, which undermined trade unionists' right to picket, received little attention from politicians distracted by defence and Cardwell's purging of the army, though George Odger's splitting of the progressive vote at the Southwark by-election in the previous year ought to have warned them that Labour could do damage when it chose. Resisting America's ludicrous claims for indirect damages arising out of the building of the Confederate vessel *Alabama* suggested that the government could act intelligently under foreign pressure and manoeuvre a reasonable settlement. Being reasonable, on the other hand, seemed unlikely to revive the Liberal populism of 1869–70. Gladstone judged that he needed a cause and the story of the next three years lay in his search for one. He considered, and rejected, doing something with his punitive war against the Ashantis of the Gold Coast in 1873. He thought pliably about Irish education whereupon his own followers, who did not, voted against him in the House. He turned towards retrenchment as the national economy slipped into recession after 1873 only to discover that Lowe had turned the Treasury into a beargarden of bitchiness, incompetence and indiscretion.

Perhaps the new posture of the party encouraged Gladstone to overestimate the significance of its radicals. Counting them presented problems, as it still does, because much depended on the characteristics deemed suitable for the purposes of definition. A modern calculation reflects the precision that only a computer, a pile of division lists and the refreshment of multiple discriminant analysis can provide; but the suggestion that the 1868–74 parliament contained between 100 and 125 'radicals' seems over-stated, granted the instincts of contemporaries.[48] Gladstone's understanding of the radical mentality derived from contact with Milner Gibson, Bright and Forster – and perhaps from the Lancastrian manufacturers who turned against him in the 1868 election. Chamberlain's Birmingham politics or Harcourt's radical Whig circle lay as yet below his horizon. Rather than see a body of fringe subversives, Gladstone recognized in his radicals the moral centre of gravity of the party. This led him to place undue emphasis on the importance, for example, of Bright's recall to the cabinet in 1873, even if he intended (and for once he wrote down the ugly words) 'making use of [it] as a means of at least temporary reconciliation' with the radicals following their disappointments over English and Irish education. But this preoccupation missed the thrust of those who, like Chamberlain, complained that Gladstone's government 'listens to the cynical criticisms of the upper and well-to-do classes' while continuing 'deaf to the growing desire for radical reform'.[49] It also occluded the extent to which Gladstonian Liberalism had suffered losses on its right.

The Whigs had already taken a good deal from Gladstone. Hartington allowed himself grumpily to be shunted off to Ireland as chief secretary in 1871, with emollient words and reminders that his leader had not forgotten 'the ultimate future' when he would, presumably, appoint a successor. They had stomached the secret ballot when the government finally persuaded the Lords to let it through in 1872. But Chichester Fortescue proposed a greater challenge in his plan for an Irish university. For the bill that the government brought before parliament in 1873 beggared any rational defence beyond the hope, as dangerous as it is pious in Irish affairs, that something may prove better than nothing. Its provisions would have established an Irish university that avoided affronts to the religion of its students by prohibiting the teaching of theology, moral philosophy or modern history. Quite apart from the intellectual nonsense of the plan, the Whigs saw it as supplying further evidence for rumours that Gladstone had gone soft on Catholics or even become one. Again, Whig unease at the internal condition of Ireland had strengthened as Gladstone manifested increasing reluctance to apply coercion there, especially after the appearance of a movement led by Isaac Butt to reconstruct the Irish parliamentary body into a 'Home Rule' party dedicated to the establishment of an Irish parliament. The defeat of the Irish University Bill in the early hours of 12 March 1873 followed, therefore, from a Whig, rather than a radical-Nonconformist reaction to Gladstone's recent directions. That reaction continued, moreover, in the view that the prime minister must not be allowed to dissolve and hand over Ireland to the most serious electoral threat since O'Connell's Repealers.[50]

As an alternative to dissolution, the cabinet resigned in the hope that Disraeli would take minority office; but with the Liberals plainly bent on hara-kiri Disraeli had more sense than to accede. So for nine months, from March 1873 to January 1874, the Liberal party exposed its exhaustion to the public until Gladstone sprang a dissolution on his colleagues during the Christmas recess. Since his flight to Whitby, by-elections had run strongly against the government, embarrassing Henry Bruce (whose licensing act had offended the trade and been held by Gladstone to lie behind the poor showing at the polls).[51] An abortive attempt at extending the county franchise in July only precipitated the resignation of Ripon. By the end of the session most of the Liberal metaphors had turned melancholy: 'our tails between our legs', a 'water-logged and sinking ship'. Gladstone knew precisely what he required: a cry that would 'with reasonable likelihood reanimate some portion of that sentiment in our favour, which carried us in a manner so remarkable through the Election of 1868'.[52] The one that came to mind – cheap government – contradicted, however, the logic of everything that he had done since then. Here was the Gladstone of the paper duties, not the Gladstone of Irish Church and Irish land; and the result need have surprised no one.

London and the manufacturing towns – the Liberal heartland – showed a sharp swing to the Conservatives in the general election of February 1874; the opposition finished with an English majority of over a hundred. Even in the Celtic fringe the Conservative party made some gains. In Ireland both parties lost to Butt's Home Rulers, yet it was the Liberal return of just twelve seats that better reflected the severity of the defeat. With all results in, Disraeli could count on 350 in the House of Commons as against 245 Liberals and the new phalanx of 57 Home Rulers. Within the Liberal ranks a hint of modernity deserves notice. A few weeks before the election Gladstone had told Lowe that he had no fear of the labouring classes; among his supporters in 1874 were two working-class men, the first to enter parliament. Unnoticed until their accents marked them, Thomas Burt (Morpeth) and Alexander Macdonald (Stafford) brought with them the voice of an unheard class.

Gladstone had lost and for twelve months he became a Peelite: he despised everybody. The electorate he hated for its corruption and wallowing in beer. His colleagues, when he saw them, won no respect from him for their failing to become obsessed by Disraeli's Public Worship Regulation Bill. In February 1875, thirty years after his first resignation, Gladstone renounced the Liberal leadership and the party fell to the most squalid of its *idées fixes*, the finding of a new leader. Of the three possibilities (Forster, Hartington and Granville) none had a hope of overmastering opposition from the radical and Whig fringes. A temporary solution found favour: Hartington to lead in the Commons and Granville in the Lords; thus the party left its conductor and courier waiting, without route or map, for the driver to return. And indeed Gladstone had already made a start. His widely read tract on *The Vatican Decrees and their bearing on Civil Allegiance* showed Nonconformity his violence against papal infallibility and erased some of the awkwardness of Ripon's conversion. Moreover, although he absented himself from much intra-party discussion in 1875, Gladstone did not resign his seat or quit the opposition front bench. His point was made. No future could lie in trying to reoccupy the middle ground that Disraeli had now conquered, staked and mined.

For Palmerston read Disraeli (1872–80)

At the beginning of 1872, a group of Conservative notables including Northcote, Hardy, Cairns and Lord John Manners met at Burghley, seat of the Marquess of Exeter, to decide what to do about Disraeli. The ex-premier had written *Lothair*, his penultimate novel, and succumbed to a series of illnesses since 1868; he had accomplished little else. Possibly the activities of this cabal and its determination to replace him by Edward Stanley, now 15th Earl of Derby – the decision reached at Burghley – spurred him towards action. Undoubtedly 1872 became his only good year as opposition leader. Two highly effective speeches at Manchester and the Crystal Palace helped him establish in the public mind the rhetoric of a Conservatism dedicated to the empire and the advancement of social reform at home. The death of Mary Ann, Disraeli's wife, at the end of the year brought on a serious relapse, but by then his image of exhausted volcanoes had begun to work for him. He watched the Liberal party tear itself apart through 1873, having squashed opposition within his own party (except from Carnarvon and Salisbury, the malcontents of 1867). Squaring these two and buying off Derby played a larger part in Disraeli's priorities as he took office again in February 1874 than did the portents of economic crisis and foreign complication that were to catch up with him by 1876.

His primary difficulties resolved themselves with surprising alacrity. Carnarvon agreed to take the Colonies and the Marquess of Salisbury broke, with unutterable distaste, a seven-year silence to accept Disraeli's offer of the India Office which he had resigned in 1867. The 15th Earl of Derby's return to the Foreign Office (which he had occupied as Lord Stanley in 1866–7) promised, meanwhile, to keep quiet one who retained all the acres of his father with little of the judgement or weight. Northcote's promotion from the Board of Trade to the Exchequer recalled that of his spiritual leader Gladstone in the 1840s, but posed no threat. With some ballast from well-tried friends (Cairns, Hardy, Manners) the problem remained merely one of introducing 'representative' men into junior posts. The prime minister defined such persons as 'every one who might be troublesome', especially the farmers' representatives whose constituency had turned restive after two years of bad harvests and dwindling rents. He did not go so far as to heed Forster's ironic suggestion of making Joseph Arch, the labourers' leader, a member of parliament, a proposal which had left the Tory benches in catalepsy with 'derisive laughter and emphatic shouts of "No!, no!" '[53] But he did make a couple of the agricultural spokesmen junior ministers and took a personal interest, over the next twelve months, in the Agricultural Holdings Bill which gave the British tenantry mild compensation for improvements in the case of their eviction. The 'revolt of the field' seemed for the moment to be staying there, however, and Disraeli saw no need for activity at Westminster.

Pressures existed all the same to force the government in the direction of developing a policy. Some of these operated externally: the bishops and the trade unionists bulked large among them. Some were modulated internally by politicians who instinctively disapproved of inactivity. The new appointment to the Home Office, Richard Assheton Cross, presented a case in point. His background as a Lancastrian lawyer and banker gave his politics an executive tinge better suited to the committee room than to the platform, though his defeat of Gladstone at South West Lancashire at the last election had given him a certain public notoriety. He knew Derby from their schooldays at Rugby but he currently took much of his tone from Northcote. Between them, he and the chancellor of the exchequer urged on Disraeli a 'forward' policy – towards Scotland, for example, where the party had just had its best election since 1852, towards labour and licensing and education. Often Cross failed in his persuasion, completely so in the Scottish instance. Sometimes he was simply upstaged. No amount of constructive argument could atone in 1874 for Ward Hunt at the Admiralty who made the government an object of ridicule through his hysterical ranting over Britain's naval defences. Nor was it easy for a sensitive Anglican to control Disraeli's wish to let the bishops have their way in attacking ritualism in the Church of England.

Cross did not stand alone in disapproving of the Public Worship Regulation Bill introduced into the House of Lords by Archbishop Tait in the government's first session. Gathorne Hardy thought the party 'mad' and profoundly ignorant of the issues involved. Carnarvon characteristically saw it as a plot intended to snub himself and Salisbury, and indeed both of them wondered about resigning.[54] But for Disraeli the matter had little to do with conscience: it was a question of easing a fear, made widespread in a number of show-trials, that the established church had become too tolerant of Romish practices, by giving bishops more power to curb them. The resistance in the House to what he took to be common sense left Disraeli with the view that the Commons had turned into 'a chamber reeking with medieval superstition'.[55] Politicians in touch with the mind of the cabinet may have overestimated the impact of the subject in the House; many MPs seem quickly to have tired of the debate. At a high-political level the problem of Anglican ritualism nevertheless blotted out much of the concern that Northcote attempted to foster over his lack of revenue and Cross's attempts to interest colleagues in his proposed labour laws. Nor did the act kill off the agitation, as a furore over Edward King's episcopal practices at Lincoln would show two decades later. But in tandem with the creation of a number of new dioceses over the next few years it did supply a new framework for episcopal authority.

That organized Labour gave the Conservative government less trouble than the Church of England says much about all three interests. In opposition Disraeli had tried to nurse the unions following their disappointment at Liberal legislation and especially the Criminal Law Amendment Act of 1871. The overture had provoked amused contempt from the Liberal front bench and the newspapers; and Disraeli's setting up of a Royal Commission on the Labour Laws on his return to office did not necessarily imply radical intentions. In 1875, however, the government responded to the Commission's report with some boldness in its Conspiracy and Protection of Property Act, which legalized peaceful picketing, and an Employers and Workmen Act which limited unions' payments of damages for breach of contract. On the function of the first of these, Disraeli commented with his usual honesty: it was 'one of those measures, that root and consolidate a party' while helping (a lump of sugar, this, for the Queen) to 'reduce the materials for social agitation'.[56] What materials he had in mind must have seemed as unclear to contemporaries as it does today. In the autumn of that year even *The Times*, surveying the Trades Union Congress meeting at Glasgow, complimented its delegates for speaking 'as if they breathed a larger air' than had their predecessors in the age of chartism and insurrection.[57] True, the cabinet had not so much beckoned Labour through the door as found it standing in the hall; but either way, the workers had come in from the cold and rain of Kennington Common.

So had Ireland. Smith O'Brien's rising of 1848 seemed no less distant than the chartist petitions now that the Home Rule party had made plain its strategy of focusing British attention on the Irish problem by dislocating public business through 'filibustering' – the tactic of keeping members in their seats for most of the night by making speeches of heroic length, irrelevance and tedium. The damage that the Irish threatened to cause legislative schedules certainly brought the government great anxiety: the Irish members would have claimed the credit for Disraeli's 'thinking of my House of Commons difficulties the whole time'.[58] Indeed the presence of a new breed of politician gave the Commons the ambience of street-theatre and concentrated the mind on its activities. As with Glad-stone's government, however, this period did not last long. When Salisbury and Carnarvon acquiesced at the end of 1874 in cabinet plans to return to the educational issues raised by Forster's act of 1870, most of the serious parliamentary problems had been sur-mounted. Through 1875 Disraeli and his colleagues sat impassively on the Treasury bench, watching the Liberals without a leader seek-ing, through the figure of Hartington, 'a first attempt at a Middle party, a recovery of the old Liberal position demolished for the first time, by John Mill, Gladstone and Cobden'.[59] But as the prime minister graciously tossed to the opposition select committees on anything they wanted and raised rhetoric to a new level of vacuity, he knew who was wearing Palmerston's clothes.

By the end of 1875 the image had gained clarity among the more boneheaded Conservatives in the re-emergence of 'Abroad' as a category of concern. The desperation of the Khedive of Egypt to find some money quickly from somewhere gave Disraeli the oppor-tunity to use the Rothschild millions to pull off his celebrated *coup* in buying Khedive Ismail's interest – nearly 50 per cent – in the Suez Canal which had, since its opening in 1869, reoriented the priorities of policy in an imperial state with responsibilities reaching to India, Australasia and the Far East. A flutter of resistance arose in the evangelicals of both parties who found brilliant improvisation some-how disturbing in its morality; but the purchase won a remarkable *succès d'estime* among red-meat Tories and in the press. India's coming to prominence only compounded the message. A visit by the Prince of Wales in 1875 and the Queen's assumption of the title 'Empress of India' in the following year, which provoked more oppo-sition than the Suez purchase, added zest to Disraeli's Palmerstonian role. By the time of Disraeli's decision to go to the Lords in the summer of 1876 as 1st Earl of Beaconsfield, Gladstone himself had noted the resemblance of the government's style to that of his old Whig leader. It had to be said, of course, that even Palmerston had kept himself 'entirely above flattering as these people have done (with great effect) the most vulgar appetites & propensities of the people'.[60]

Imperial enthusiasm has been so readily associated with the Disraeli administration of 1874–80 that one can miss the degree to which that government lacked any coherent imperial policy and approached the problems of the empire in much the same way as had its predecessors. The administration that had become embroiled in wars both in India and Africa during these years bounced from one expedient to another in response to events: neither Disraeli nor his ministers held any ideology about imperial expansion except insofar as they believed history showed it to be a bad and dangerous thing. Members of parliament no more enjoyed discussing the empire than had their fathers; the historian of the subject concludes, indeed, that *Hansard* in these years leaves a modern eye with the impression that the House of Commons almost resented imperial intrusion in its affairs.[61] Between 1876 and 1878 those intrusions intersected, however, with the problems posed by Russia and Turkey. Both mattered to the custodians of empire: Russia because she bordered on and threatened Afghanistan and thus made the north-west frontier of India a crucial defensive zone; Turkey, because her continued independent existence afforded a buffer-state between Russia and British interests in the eastern Mediterranean. Had these facets of the Russo-Turkish difficulty remained in the form cast by the Treaty of Paris in 1856, no anxiety need have arisen at the Foreign Office and policy could have been left in its cool, post-Palmerstonian channel under the guidance of the permanent under-secretary, Lord Tenterden, and his pacific minister, Lord Derby. But in recent years Turkish power had proved fictitious and Russian ambition all too real. As Salisbury put it with typical pungency, all would be well 'if only Turkey could be persuaded to stop crumbling to pieces'.[62]

Shoring it up again offered one line of policy. However, this would cost not only money that the government had little chance of raising but also public sympathy for subsidizing a corrupt and bestial tyranny. The power of that opinion, suitably orchestrated, became apparent in the summer of 1876 when reports mounted that the Turks had massacred Christian subjects in Bulgaria; and, from September of that year until the Congress of Berlin in July 1878, the affairs of the Balkan states, sandwiched between Austria-Hungary and Russia in the north and Turkey in the south-east, dominated high-level political discussion in England. Parliamentary business, the farmers, Lord Sandon's education bill, the revenue: all receded as both front benches acquired new identities as doves and hawks, 'Russians' and 'Turks'.

What gave the Bulgarian atrocities such a potency in England was the extent of the agitation in the constituencies. That agitation did not begin with Gladstone: it grew from the outrage of the intelligentsia, especially Bishop Fraser of Manchester (a Gladstone appointment), the tractarian H. P. Liddon, canon of St Paul's, the historian Edward Freeman and the brilliant northern journalist W. T. Stead (later to achieve fame as radical editor of the *Pall Mall Gazette*). But Gladstone took it over when the power of the agitation as a mass movement had become clear. Reclining, ill, in bed with the writing paper pressed against his knees, Gladstone scribbled urgently at a manuscript that turned into *The Bulgarian Horrors*, a pamphlet that sold 200,000 copies in the first month. Meanwhile, the Conservative prime minister's lack 'even of the slightest sentiment'[63] did the government no good at the Buckinghamshire by-election towards which politicians looked for some guide to the repercussions of Bulgaria and, to a lesser extent, Sandon's introduction of compulsory education. Although the Conservative candidate retained the seat, he did so by a margin of less than two hundred votes in the safest of county constituencies which had supported Disraeli loyally until his peerage had removed him. Salisbury took the message to read, ominously, 'that the traditional Palmerstonian policy is at an end'.[64] This took him, Salisbury, further along his path in developing a doctrine about foreign policy that placed prescience above the emotionalism that he believed bent Disraeli's judgement. But any Tory sense that the country had turned 'Russian' and anti-Turk soon showed itself misplaced. There were still Liberals, for example, like Hugh Childers, who 'would willingly pay an Income Tax of 2s 6d in the £ to keep the Russians out of Constantinople'. There were constituency Liberals in Northants who 'annoyed and horrified' Earl Spencer because they appeared 'simply mad against Gladstone and Russia'. There were by-elections that could be interpreted differently from Bucks, such as South Shropshire at the beginning of November, 'a heavy discouragement', as Gladstone said.[65] Government divided itself between pro-Turks like Disraeli who wished at all costs to resist Russian control of the Balkans, and those like Derby who held war in greater horror than the Turks. Salisbury took neither view but nevertheless felt pessimistic when the cabinet decided to send him to Constantinople at the end of 1876 to prevent the Russo-Turkish war for which Russia was plainly preparing in order to 'liberate' oppressed Christians in the Ottoman empire. He set off in characteristic anticipation of 'seasickness, much French and failure'.[66]

Turkish pride and Russian strategy guaranteed the accuracy of Salisbury's prediction. The negotiations at Constantinople failed in January 1877, and in April the Russo-Turkish war began, supplying a theatre for party calculation for the next year. The fall of Plevna to the Russians in December, their imposition in March 1878 of a vindictive peace treaty at San Stefano (with its engorged Bulgaria that the Russians had hoped to use as a trojan horse in their southward expansion) and the Great Powers' toning down of Russia's proposals at Berlin in July, produced considerable party volatility at Westminster along the way, despite Britain's neutrality. For British politicians, preoccupied with repercussions at home, the significant consequences were threefold. Public and parliamentary attention, in the first place, rapidly waned. Disraeli soon could congratulate himself on his foresight in claiming that the 'general insanity' would not last long; by the spring of 1877 Freddy Leveson, Granville's younger brother in the House of Commons, was reporting 'the greatest apathy' about the war among members.[67] In the senior reaches of the Liberal party, second, the war re-established the Gladstonian style of politics and effectively displaced Hartington. Against the advice of most of his colleagues, Gladstone pressed in May 1877 his parliamentary resolutions calling for European coercion of the Turks and thus completed the resurgence of radical Liberalism that Suez and Bulgaria had begun. Finally, the war removed Derby (permanently) and Carnarvon (temporarily) from Conservative high politics and placed Salisbury in the commanding position he was to enjoy there for the rest of his life.

Derby had felt unhappy for some months. His streak of temperamental liberalism had brought him offers from Gladstone during the last government, and retrospect suggests he would have done better had he taken one of them. So long as he could rely on the support of senior Conservatives in maintaining his pro-Russian position, he could remain in the cabinet. But Salisbury had moved to a 'war' position in the event of the Russians failing to relinquish Constantinople (if they succeeded in taking it) while erstwhile sympathizers such as Cairns, Cross and Richmond wanted a firmer line still. Only 'Twitters' Carnarvon stayed with him to fight in the last ditch against the war party of Disraeli, Hardy, Manners, Hunt and Hicks Beach. Publicly the two pacifists stayed in the cabinet until the spring of 1878; but privately they had resigned in January. Salisbury replaced Derby at the Foreign Office and Hardy (now Lord Cranbrook) took the vacant chair at the India Office from which he proceeded, in the second half of 1878, to destroy the public credit that Beaconsfield and Salisbury created at Berlin.

'Peace with honour' amounted, from the British point of view, to dismembering the vast, Russian-dominated Bulgaria called into being at San Stefano, and hardening off the transfer from Turkey to Britain of the island of Cyprus. Still, to have contained Andrassy, Gortchakov and Bismarck suggested a maturity of statesmanship which rescued the reputation of the government from its disgrace over the atrocities two years before. Yet the very act of tethering the Russians unleashed Beaconsfield's own mad dog in India. If only his friend Lord John Manners had accepted the viceroyalty when Beaconsfield offered it to him in 1876[68] the situation might have proved manageable. But in Lord Lytton the government had appointed a viceroy who would seize the first opportunity to apply pressure to the recalcitrant Amir of Afghanistan, once war with Russia had been ruled out. The second Afghan war broke out in November 1878. Simultaneously, moreover, the new high commissioner of South Africa, Sir Bartle Frere, had slipped his leash in order to worry the insurrectionary Zulus and their remarkable chief, Cetawayo. For Cranbrook and Hicks Beach, the respective ministers in London, events in India and Africa seemed to be conspiring to embarrass them. Beach felt especially alarmed: he did not earn his nickname of 'Black Michael' through unreasoning optimism. He tried to restrain Frere in a letter lacking in Christmas spirit, perhaps because he had to write it on Christmas Day:

> The revenue returns are bad: trade is at a standstill: distress is consider-able: it is difficult to see how next year is to be met without additional taxation: and in the present feeling of the country...any proposal for additional taxation is by no means unlikely to involve the defeat of the Government.[69]

Too late. On 12 January 1879 British soldiers marched into Zululand and to their deaths in the blood-baths at Isandlhwana and Rorke's Drift.

The government struggled on every front. The Zulus held out until June and put a severe strain on the Exchequer and its chancellor. The Afghans reacted against initial military defeats by murdering the British minister in Kabul. The Irish stirred again in a movement to reduce rents under the leadership of a superb orator, Michael Davitt: this stirring took its mature form as the Irish Land League in October 1879. Scottish disaffection was read into the inability of the Earl of Seafield to use his vast territorial sway to prevent the return of a Liberal at the Elgin and Nairn by-election in September. Closer to home Northcote had become obsessed by the national revenue, Beaconsfield with one part of it – the 'agricultural bankruptcy'.[70] The premier turned to the Land for his understanding of political behaviour as naturally as Gladstone had turned to Drink. For his part, Gladstone had accepted at the beginning of the year an invitation to stand as Liberal candidate for Midlothian at the next election and had since carried out a highly successful 'stump' of constituencies, twisting the knife in his probing of the government's failure in foreign policy since the Suez purchase and Bulgaria.

Probably both Beaconsfield and Gladstone expected too much of popular feeling about foreign policy. As late as October 1879, Childers felt that the Liberals would still lose a winter election should

Beaconsfield decide to dissolve. The government nevertheless wished to precipitate an election on something other than foreign affairs or the economy. They picked up Davitt and chose Ireland. Rattled by the chronic prospects for revenue, they seized on their first cheerful by-election results at the beginning of 1880 and rushed into a dissolution on the platform of resisting the rot in Ireland and at all costs preventing Home Rule. It was a weak manifesto but at least it distracted attention from Gladstone's panoramic surveys of disaster from Constantinople to Cape Town. The Whig stalwart Earl Spencer, quite missing the point, was pleased. 'I see that Dizzy dissolves on Home Rule', he wrote to his brother in March 1880. 'It will not be a difficult question for our party for we practically do not differ from the Tories on it. We wish the maintenance of the Imperial Parliament.'[71] No wonder Spencer never wrote his memoirs.

5

Conservative Ascendancy

Crisis in Liberal identity (1880–86)

In one sense the election of 1880 protrudes from the continuum of Victorian Liberal history as a peak in the persuasiveness of Gladstonian rhetoric and appeal. 'Midlothian' language about the wickedness of Beaconsfieldism, compounded by the economic downturn, produced a remarkable result in the total of 414 MPs expected, on paper, to support a new Liberal government. This return superficially seemed greater than any Whig-Liberal result since 1832. But a moment's analysis of the 'Liberals' in 1880 immediately questions any optimistic verdict on their future. At least 60 must be subtracted at once since, as Irish Home Rulers, their commitment to Liberal policy lay in a single direction – towards a road which most potential ministers would wish to see remain untrodden. In England the Liberals had done well in the boroughs, but their complete return for all categories of English seats (borough, county and university) stood at only 53 more than the Conservatives'. Ireland, Wales and Scotland had enlarged that majority to 176. A success so rooted in the 'Celtic fringe' gave rise, however, to considerable comment and anxiety. That Spencer reported one school in Braemar full of pictures of Gladstone, Hartington and Granville, and 'Down with the Established Church' scrawled on the portico of a second, doubtless helped refresh jaded Liberal leaders.[1] But would it be enough?

Besides, around the walls of Westminster, Gladstone, Hartington and Granville cut figures very different from their Scottish portraits. They appeared there not as the vanguard of moral politics but rather as symbols of competing Liberal styles: the Gladstonian and the Whig. True, the Whig leadership had shown itself realistic in overriding the Queen's naive request that Hartington should try to form a government; he and Granville insisted that she should send for Gladstone. But among the better Bloomsbury squares a suspicion persisted that the rationale of Whiggery in a sub-democratic society – 'to separate the real deliberate wishes of the people from their thirst for plunder'[2] – had disappeared in the headiness of Midlothian. Promising to extend the franchise in the counties to the threshold now obtaining in the boroughs had already encouraged the young Whig George Joachim Goschen to refuse office. Fears concerning the government's intentions over land reform in Ireland and Scotland, perhaps even (unthinkably) in England, left landowners like the Duke of Argyll sitting very lightly at the cabinet table and the young Marquess of Lansdowne no less so in junior office. Then one had to reckon with the faces no one, outside Birmingham, hung in schools, those of Joseph Chamberlain (Board of Trade) and the radical lawyer Sir Charles Dilke (Local Government Board from 1882). With over a hundred radicals of various colours behind them they presented to the stability of Gladstonian government as serious a challenge as the resistance of property. Although the prime minister surrounded himself with many of the Whig administrators familiar from his first ministry, and succeeded in bringing back Bright to the Duchy of Lancaster, he and they and their perspectives had altered in ways which made 1868 feel a lifetime away.

Gladstone's second and third administrations (April 1880 to June 1885; January 1886 to June 1886) certainly reflected few of the features of the first, beyond their preoccupation with 'the bane and curse and difficulty' of Ireland.[3] Retrospect suggests three cycles of activity. A period of intense, often parliamentary, politics lasted until Gladstone's customary breakdown at the end of 1882 and convalescence at Cannes. With the problem of Irish parliamentary obstruction to some extent overcome by new procedures in 1882, party activity moved to a more strategic plane in the second half of the government, not least because the death of Beaconsfield in 1881 had placed the direction of Conservative thinking, if we ignore the Grand Old Woman, Sir Stafford Northcote, in the hands of Lord Salisbury, a mastermind of party strategy, and also unleashed in Lord Randolph Churchill a Tory-democrat firebrand whose enthusiasm for subverting all strategies had become his sole innocent pastime. This period of Liberal politics, during which virtually every minister threatened or promised to resign at least once, ended in the withering away of the government in the summer of 1885. The next twelve months present a third cycle: a period of sustained strategic calculation within high politics of a virulence reminiscent of 1827. The preoccupations of politicians during these years may nevertheless reflect a greater consistency than this rhythm implies – partly because ministers concentrated on four critical elements of policy in the revenue, Ireland,

Egypt and franchise, but also through the degree to which those elements fused into the single challenge of finding some way of redefining the character of Liberalism in order to give it a cluster of virtues suitable for a Whig-radical party which had grown too wide to fit into Lichfield House or Willis's Rooms.

A legacy of external problems required immediate attention from the new government of April 1880. The stipulations of the Congress of Berlin in their bearing on Turkey had been abrogated by Turkish dissimulation and evasion: a 'bag and baggage' expulsion of the Turk from Europe seemed, therefore, a likely outcome of Gladstone's return. Beaconsfield's adventures in Afghanistan and the Transvaal bequeathed a similar *damnosa hereditas* to a government intent, theoretically, on withdrawal in both zones. None of these problems was in fact 'solved'. Gladstone's anti-Turk obsession secured a more aggressive stance which encouraged the Ottomans to cede Balkan territory to Montenegro and Greece but achieved little of the surgical neatness that radical backbenchers might have expected. Party realities meanwhile compelled Gladstone to fudge the difficulties in India and South Africa. Whig defensiveness over the possibility of a Russian invasion of Afghanistan prohibited the handing back of the country to the Amir. The Afghans' defeat of a British regiment at Maiwand in July 1880 suggested, on the other hand, the advisability of letting go of some of it. Inevitable compromise ensued; but the return of Kandahar province to the Amir, a question of considerable party and newspaper interest in September, left Britain with a messy dual control which would drag her into crisis when the Russians appeared to threaten the border at Penjdeh in 1885. Even less quietude was imposed on the Transvaalers. Doubtless Gladstone hoped that his recall of Sir Bartle Frere and the feeding of him to radical sharks in the House would help him ride out the storm. But if the Zulus had lost some of their belligerency, the white Transvaalers had not: they were determined to see the restoration of Boer self-government. Their armed rising in December 1880 and the death, at their hands, of the British governor at Majuba Hill in February 1881 made 'that horrid Transvaal business...uppermost in political thoughts' for a few months.[4] And although the Boers gained their immediate constitutional objective in the Convention of Pretoria in August, part of the ground-plan for the Boer war of 1899–1902 had been drawn by a government of men supposed to be 'Little Englanders'.

As these problems receded, so did the wider world. With the great and glaring exception of North African affairs, world events impinged little on British high politics in the first half of the 1880s.

The reconstitution of the *Dreikaiserbund* in 1881 and the Triple Alliance of Germany, Austria-Hungary and Italy in 1882 received a fairly restricted attention in London among the professionals at the Foreign Office and from Gladstone himself. The prime minister's interest in European politics owed something to his messianism about Bismarck, to a habit of meddling that ran back at least to the Schleswig-Holstein question and to a new imperative: his duty to save the country from Granville. Considerations of seniority, friendship, loyalty and experience had led to Granville's reappointment at the Foreign Office in 1880. Almost immediately, however, he had shown signs of breaking down. At the lord mayor's dinner in London in 1881 his speech lacked brevity, shape and intelligibility; and over the next few years his senility grew more apparent, notoriously culminating in his leaving cupboardfuls of unopened documents when he left office in 1885. His desperate financial straits remained private but nevertheless drained him. The failure of his Stoke-on-Trent iron works in the depression drove him to borrow substantial sums from the Earl of Derby and others. When he died in 1891 he owed more than a quarter of a million pounds.[5]

Possibly the embarrassment of Granville encouraged Gladstone to keep foreign affairs largely to himself; he tended to consult the cabinet rarely about them and expected it to rubber-stamp what he and Granville had worked out.[6] By contrast, his preoccupation with revenue between 1880 and 1882 had more public consequences. On taking office Gladstone decided to make himself chancellor of the exchequer as well as prime minister. Granted the predicament into which Lowe had thrust him in 1873, he had a rationale for handling the Treasury himself; but the strain soon became too great even for him and he brought in Childers to relieve him at the end of 1882. For the interim, the problems of revenue and taxation impinged urgently on politicians, not least because Gladstone had, by his seventy-first year, turned reality into a vast solipsism: his colleagues, critics, friends and family had become figments of whatever version of truth Gladstone took to be the case. He believed his own preoccupations ought to be reflected in theirs, and since he used power autocratically the wish could be made self-fulfilling.

As in 1874, he sought retrenchment. 'At present,' he wrote to Granville in May 1880, 'we have not a sixpence to give away.'[7] The depression had plainly left the agricultural sectors badly overstretched, however, and he gave a little help by releasing the farmers from the hated malt tax and transferred the charge to the brewers – a tit for tat for their bearing him down in 1874 – and the income tax. With his Peelite conception of trade and a genuine reverence for

Cobden's commercial treaty with France of 1860, which would shortly come up for renewal, Gladstone had no time for any form of economic tariff. Despite the malt tax, therefore, he found few friends among tenant farmers looking for some sort of state protection; and the performance of Liberal candidates in rural areas, where this rankled, left much to be desired in a series of 'disagreeably significant' by-elections in 1881–2 of which North Yorkshire and Taunton caused most anxiety.[8] 'Tariffs' eased as a pressure-point by the end of 1882 but the continuing drain on the Exchequer had left Gladstone gloomy long before then. New external complications had already increased the strain. By the time the budget cabinets met in the spring of 1882 attention had largely moved to the deepening problem of Ireland, where the difficulties 'seem[ed] to mount like Alp on Alp',[9] and to the deserts of North Africa which, since Disraeli's purchase of the Suez shares, even a Liberal government dared not ignore.

Initial reports from Ireland held out the hope that the nationalists might prove tractable. Forster, the new chief secretary, informed London that the levels of distress had been exaggerated, and the cabinet decided against renewing the coercion act used by the previous government. The nationalists, meanwhile, had found a new leader since his appearance in the Commons for Meath in 1875. And for all his helping with the strategy of parliamentary obstruction during Beaconsfield's ministry, signs existed that Charles Stewart Parnell, an Anglo-Irish landowner from County Wicklow, would work with British politicians and especially with that section of the cabinet sympathetic to radicals of all colours. Both Forster and Parnell changed their minds after Forster's bill to compensate Irish tenants for eviction following non-payment of rent failed in the Lords in June 1880 and precipitated Lansdowne's resignation. From that point onwards, Parnell's Home Rulers returned to the offensive in a programme of parliamentary obstruction, while Forster adopted the role of cabinet hawk in pressing for the renewal of coercion. Since Gladstone himself identified coercion with failure, the problem came to exhibit two facets: the government had to find some way of appeasing the land agitation in Ireland; and they needed to relieve pressure on a parliamentary system whose procedures had not been designed to cope with a Parnell or a Sexton. That Irish land still bulked large in the concerns of politicians announced loudly enough that Gladstone's Irish Land Act of 1870 had not worked. The campaign for what had come to be called the 'three Fs' – fair rents, fixity of tenure, free sale by tenants of improvements they had made – sought objectives which Gladstone had shrunk from granting in 1870 and for which he saw no necessity now.

But there was no gainsaying the currency of speculation among the governing classes about the moral integrity of landownership. Tenant-right had spread to England since the coming of the depression. A Farmers' Alliance had put up candidates at the 1880 election and tried, with no success, to persuade the government to introduce fixity of tenure in England and a version of tenant-right such as existed in Lincolnshire, the English Ulster. Apart from making Disraeli's permissive Agricultural Holdings Act of 1875 into a compulsory measure, the government ignored what was, after all, largely a Tory problem.[10] When the crofters of the Western Isles gave the land movement a Scottish dimension in 1882 through their rebellion against intolerable hardships, they gained nothing in the short term and only a weak Crofters' Act in 1886.[11]

Ireland possessed more muscle which enabled the nationalists to drag another land bill out of the government in 1881. Responding to recent reports from two Commissions, the Land Act granted the three Fs, with a loosened form of fixity of tenure, and established land courts for the consideration of rents. Cracks showed at once in the cabinet: the Duke of Argyll found 'free sale' completely unacceptable and resigned the privy seal. Nevertheless the act went as far as anyone would go in meeting nationalist grievances before the tentative moves towards a new local government system for Ireland in 1883–4. A second line of policy reflected the government's worries about public order. Michael Davitt's arrest at the beginning of 1881 and the suspension of habeas corpus in a new coercion act expressed Whig nervousness (and Forster's pressure) in outward and visible form; they also provoked a wave of obstruction in the Commons which culminated in the Speaker's 'naming' the entire Irish party present in the House and prompting their bodily removal on one celebrated occasion. Coercion remained the path along which politicians approached the Irish question in the second part of the year as European interest slumped. Although the land courts often reduced the rents brought before them, frequently by as much as a quarter, rural disaffection did not diminish while Whig disaffection expanded in resentment against the new rents. Parnell was believed to be actively engaged in sabotaging the working of the act; and when he, Dillon, Sexton and Brennan were arrested in October and sent to Kilmainham Gaol, the forces of legitimate nationalism suffered the same treatment as Davitt's land warriors.

Within English high politics the flexing of muscle in Ireland betokened not so much an exercise in Whig resistance as a last effort from W. E. Forster to acquire credentials as a front-rank statesman. Education, his first vehicle, had run off the road, thanks to Chamberlain and the Education League. Bulgaria had looked promising for a time, especially when he broke from Gladstone in order to champion a central position in the party; but then the agitation had run out of steam while Gladstone had not. The chief secretaryship in 1880 represented a leap backwards for a man who might reasonably have had designs on the Exchequer or the Home Office. In order to jump back again, Forster conceived a Cromwellian *coup* in Ireland beyond which to rally mid-Liberal sentiment and pull along Whiggery by its left hand. And in the later months of 1881 he appeared to be winning. By the spring of 1882, however, the cabinet had chosen to regard the next part of the plan – Forster's appointment to the position of 'lord deputy' of Ireland – with derision, and to compound the offence by releasing Parnell and his colleagues from prison and introducing an amnesty on rent arrears in return for the nationalists' support in suppressing lawlessness. So public a rejection of the policy of 'thorough' left Forster and his confused lord lieutenant, Earl Cowper, no alternative to resignation. Neither would play any significant role in politics again. The new duumvirate of Earl Spencer and (following Lord Frederick Cavendish's brutal murder by nationalists in Phoenix Park, Dublin, in May 1882) George Otto Trevelyan meanwhile placed control of Irish policy in Whig hands with important consequences three years later. A firm Crimes Act in 1882 gave the government the cutting edge it believed itself to need in Ireland without any of the embarrassments associated with surrendering to Forster. For all the horror of Phoenix Park, politicians could relax a little, leave Ireland to Spencer and think about Egypt.

Four ingredients in the Egyptian situation threatened an unstable prognosis. In the first place, since 1878 the French had asserted a dual control with Britain over the unfathomable finances of the Khedive: in the event of any European intervention in Egypt much would therefore depend on what the French would do. Second, it had suited Anglo-French convenience since 1879 to pretend that Turkey exercised a paper suzerainty over Egyptian territory. Indeed, the Sultan had been encouraged to depose the recalcitrant Khedive Ismail and substitute his, the Sultan's, own son Tewfik whose financial tutelage to Paris and London nevertheless remained complete. Third, a nationalist revolt in the north under the leadership of Arabi Pasha had compelled the Khedive to dismiss his ministers at the end of 1881 and seemed likely to attempt the expulsion of Europeans from Egypt altogether. Fourth, a fanatical Islamic cult in the southern area then known as the Sudan had excited the dervishes into mounting a holy war or *jihad* through the inspiration of Mohammed Ahmad, known to his disciples as the 'Mahdi'. North

African affairs had attracted attention at home in 1881 when the French annexation of Tunis, an event often taken in retrospect to mark the first shot of a 'new imperialism' in the late nineteenth century, caused some stir in the middle of the Irish troubles. From the beginning of 1882 until the final suppression of the northern rebellion by the British military at Tel-el-Kebir in September, Egypt gathered momentum among party strategists and came to displace even Ireland as a preoccupation. 'Everything', as Gladstone's secretary Eddie Hamilton put it in July, 'is now Egypt.'[12]

The British bombardment of Alexandria in the same month horrified radicals and disgusted Gladstone. But military action, followed by the occupation of Egypt by British forces, had stemmed from the refusal of the French, reinforced by the fall of Gambetta in Paris, to participate in a joint display of strength while quietly using Turkish forces to eliminate Arabi. Bright predictably resigned and Chamberlain and Dilke gave Gladstone a rough ride in cabinet, eliciting the familiar responses: silence; his feeling old; his impending resignation; the priority of Ireland. The cabinet hawks – Granville, Hartington, Northbrook, Childers – remained cool in the face of Gladstone's huffy letters and insisted on British action.[13] Effectively the intervention put to sleep most of the morals of Midlothian. If Salisbury did not amplify the issue as much as Lord Randolph Churchill would have liked, he knew well enough that the Liberals could be left in their own hole. Egypt had stretched yet further the distance between their radical and Whig fringes: before long the tissue would begin to separate. Pessimists on the Liberal benches could point to Gladstone's determination to introduce local government reforms in Ireland. Were these the thin end of a Home Rule wedge? Even if the prime minister recovered his senses over Ireland, moreover, there remained the question of franchise, promised in 1880 but not yet faced. The Corrupt Practices Act of 1883 did something to reassure radicals that the Liberal party still believed in electoral reform: it removed the grosser electoral practices that had turned many constituencies into havens for corruption even after 1867. But the prospect of altering the county franchise reminded Whigs of 1867 itself and the disaster they had then suffered.

To some extent the problem had diminished. Both parties saw the logic of extending the current household suffrage in the boroughs to the county constituencies and no public 'clamour' threatened to complicate the matter. Yet the very removal of radicalism compromised the radicals and left them with questions to put alongside their Irish ones. Would the agricultural labourers vote Tory, despite the secret ballot, like their farming masters? Would the rural 'radicals' turn out very different from the models envisaged in the caucuses of Birmingham and the National Liberal Federation? Again, one could turn franchise and Ireland into the same question. The second reform act had excluded Ireland from significant change by concentrating on the boroughs; but suppose the new bill included Ireland and thereby lowered the property threshold in the Irish counties. Would the House find itself flooded by the most unregenerate type of Parnellite? But then, think one step further. If Ireland's inclusion enticed the Lords into rejecting the bill, would not their rejection give British radicals the *cause célèbre* of a 'peers versus people' battle which Chamberlain and his friends had been urging for a year or more?[14]

These otiose reflections suited the period when franchise remained the primary preoccupation of an odd backbencher like Arthur Arnold (Liberal: Salford) who picked up Trevelyan's discarded standard. When the discussion entered ministerial correspondence it focused more specifically on Hartington. For the type of bill towards which Gladstone urged his cabinet – one including Ireland but excluding a redistribution of seats – constituted precisely the proposal that Hartington least wanted. He worried that 'we have done very little that we promised and a good deal that we did not'; to run away from the task of redistribution struck him as 'a rather lazy electioneering trick'.[15] About Ireland he reflected the anxieties that troubled all Whigs depressed enough to believe that the bill would survive the second chamber. Though Gladstone held off his resignation and refused to accept that of Chamberlain, Hartington's faith in the government never recovered. The peers, as expected, saw no difficulty in destroying Gladstone's bill: its lack of a redistribution component offered easy game for Cairns in the Lords, and by the summer of 1884 the cabinet had returned to the drawing board. The Lords and Commons were then circumvented by both party leaders. In secret conversations, Britain was partitioned by Salisbury, Gladstone and Dilke. The result, grossly favourable to the Conservative party whose support Gladstone plainly required, gave Gladstone a deal he could sell to the Commons in December – franchise now with a redistribution bill, managed by Dilke, to follow.

Yet even as the cabinet muddled through behind closed doors at Lord Salisbury's house in Arlington Street, its undermining continued at the hands of the Mahdi and his dervishes in the Sudan. Major-General Charles Gordon, whom the government had entrusted in 1884 with the duty of evacuating the Sudan, decided that his duty lay in doing the reverse; he occupied Khartoum, refused to leave and demanded military assistance. On 5 February 1885, news reached Britain that Wolseley's relief-force had arrived too late. Gordon had been murdered, Khartoum lost. A wave of public anger, greater than any since the Indian atrocities of 1857, broke against the government and by doing so encouraged two developments that radicals had hoped to avoid. It revived Gladstone, whose monthly promises to resign were forgotten in the face of this new moral challenge; and it placed further obstacles in the way of evacuating the Sudan, a plan recommended not only by the desperate state of the revenue but also by Russia's audible rubbing of hands over having another bite at the Afghan frontier while the British army chased its tail in the deserts of North Africa. Only Hartington shared the Queen's resolve to hang on to whatever Britain held.

Egypt, Ireland and the revenue had seemingly entered into agreement against the decaying government. When Gladstone relinquished the Exchequer at the end of 1882, revenue had receded as a preoccupation. His appointment of Hugh Childers, however, proved no more successful than that of Robert Lowe fourteen years before. Even the prime minister could not stifle a deep groan as Childers told the pre-budget cabinet in 1885 that he had a deficit of £2 million and wanted the best part of £10 million in additional taxation to redeem it. Egypt took its toll among Whigs by advancing their hysteria when an incident at Penjdeh on the Afghan–Russian frontier convinced them that it foreshadowed a Russian invasion of India. Ireland still seethed: indeed the Land Act seemed to have made the unrest worse. The nationalists caused endless parliamentary difficulty, despite the procedural reforms rushed through by the government in the autumn session of 1882.[16] Gladstone could please no one with his Irish initiatives. When he offered local government he was thanked for proposing Home Rule; when he suggested a land purchase bill in 1885 his own radicals saw it as a feint meant to soften them before another dose of coercion. Every minister, from Northbrook on the right to Dilke on the left, had come to live on his nerves and grown more frail with each boost to Gladstone's self-confidence. The defeat of the government when it came on the budget of 8 June 1885, struck its participants as a belated relief. As the cabinet met for an inquest on the 9th, Lord Rosebery, a recent entrant, caught the mood in his diary. 'All in high spirits,' he discovered, 'except Mr. G. who was depressed.'[17]

A third wave in this cycle of Liberal preoccupations began in the middle of 1885 and lasted until June 1886 when Gladstone's third government collapsed with the defeat in the House of Commons of its Home Rule policy for Ireland. To the historian of high politics it presents a period of exceptional complication which has provoked in recent years considerable reassessment, almost none of it short.[18] Day-by-day, even hour-by-hour reconstructions of ministerial calculation and expectation have lent the events of the period a density that beggars simple summary and blurs any discussion of Gladstone's 'conversion' to Home Rule, Hartington's opposition to it, or the positions taken by more junior Whigs like Harcourt, radicals like Chamberlain, centrists like Goschen or a Tory *enfant terrible* like Lord Randolph Churchill. Students of these months will want to explore the analysis contained in those reconstructions.[19] Here it may prove more helpful to identify events about which historians concur and then to distinguish two types of understanding which the events can be used to sustain.

Between June 1885 and January 1886 a minority Conservative government, headed by the third Marquess of Salisbury, held power because the deferred redistribution bill passed by the Liberals precluded the holding of an election before the compilation of new registers at the end of 1885. During the autumn Gladstone read about the Act of Union of 1800 and privately formulated the view that it had been a calamity which could no longer be defended. Both he and Salisbury communicated with Parnell: Gladstone through Parnell's mistress, Mrs O'Shea, Salisbury through Carnarvon, the Conservative lord lieutenant of Ireland. Shortly before the election, which began on 23 November, Parnell recommended to the Irish electorate that it should vote Conservative. Chamberlain and his aide-de-camp, Jesse Collings, had meanwhile campaigned since January on an 'unauthorized' radical programme. On 17 and 18 December 1885, while polling still continued, the press carried reports leaked by Herbert Gladstone that his father, the Liberal leader, had become a convert to Home Rule. The election gave the Irish party a parliamentary body almost exactly equal in number to the size of the Liberal majority: Parnell thus held the balance of power. When parliament reconvened after the Christmas recess, Salisbury's government was beaten, as expected, in the Commons and Gladstone attempted to form his third administration. Hartington, Henry James and the Earl of Derby refused to serve. Chamberlain and Trevelyan joined the cabinet only to leave it in March 1886 when Gladstone's Home Rule bill was broached. The Liberal opponents of Home Rule established their own London office in April and became known as the Liberal Unionist party. On 8 June, a year almost to the day since the Liberal defeat on the budget, Gladstone's bill to give Ireland a separate parliament failed its second reading in the Commons by 341 to 311. The government resigned immediately and in the ensuing general election found Liberal strength cut by a half from its 1880 figure: 190 Liberal MPs were left to face Hartington's Unionists who numbered 79. In order to threaten the Conservatives' 316, however, both fragments would need to reunite and secure the adhesion of the 85 Irish members.

For another quarter of a century the events of 1885–6 reverberated in British party politics, and participants not unnaturally created for such momentous happenings a portentous history. Gladstone certainly did so when, his career finally over, he composed some auto-biographical fragments in the mid-1890s.[20] In these and his letters, the reader encounters a story-line of Gladstone's consistent concern with Ireland: cloud in the west, object of mission, symbol of national injustice. Home Rule emerges as a predestined conclusion to Glad-stone's missionary work over twenty years of political struggle. Party crises pile around him like shavings beneath the shoes of the carpenter: an inevitable by-product of honest work. Innocence in face of the self-interest of landlords, the boneheadedness of Whiggery, the unscrupulous rhetoric of Salisbury's Conservatives, and Chamber-lain's appetite for conspiracy remains his great political weakness and the ultimate explanation of his failure to achieve Home Rule. John Morley's celebrated *Life of Gladstone* (1903) built on its author's personal empathy with such thoughts and inaugurated an historical tradition which extends to the present.[21] What links the separate works of this genre is not a veneration for Gladstone but a disposition to explain the activities of politicians in 1885–6 through an ideology about Home Rule – each participant reacting to events in accordance with a pre-established framework of belief.

An alternative way of approaching these years highlights a number of difficulties with the 'ideological' schema. In the first place, it turns out to be difficult to find politicians saying anything consistent through the crisis months unless they had blundered, like James and to some extent Hartington, into opening their mouths in public too soon. The Earl of Derby, Beaconsfield's renegade foreign secretary and a minister in Gladstone's late government since the end of 1882, thought ideologically about Ireland but spent much of 1886 depressed at learning that his colleagues did not. Hartington, for example, soon had qualifying thoughts about his early commitment. 'I do not like Home Rule, and never shall,' he told James in July 1886, 'but as things now are, if I oppose Mr. Gladstone and am called upon for an alternative policy, I have not got one, except the bayonet, and I do not think the Liberal party will stand that.'[22] Joseph Cham-berlain's biographer, similarly, finds among his subject's papers 'a tendency to extreme inconsistency'; imperial fervour seems no more convincing a ground for his behaviour than a fear of revolution if the working classes had their reforms delayed by Home Rule.[23] Clinging to Hartington offered a more intelligible imperative for an ambitious man whose hopes for advancement under Gladstone had terminated with the Unauthorized Programme and been buried in his appointment to a mere junior ministry in January. Lord Randolph Churchill, for all his well-known sloganizing against Home Rule ('Ulster will fight and Ulster will be right'), had spent the period since December 1885 blinking orange and green like a traffic light. And among Whigs from Spencer to Harcourt, politicians sought reasons, as they often complained, for doing what they did *not* believe in out of a concern for their party, their career or their loyalty to Gladstone.

Gladstone's own position requires inclusion in the reckoning. Over the Irish Church and the land question he had acted with a degree of ambivalence and political *nous* which we have already noted. His views often took their tone, not only from his reading, but also from the positions taken by those around him; and his divergence from 'normal' wisdom about Ireland can be exaggerated. His mission to pacify Ireland did not demand that he go there: he went once, in effect, for a short visit in 1877 but that was all. Even his devoted lord lieutenant, Earl Spencer, received news of Gladstone's ignorance of what Ireland was actually like. 'I had luncheon with Mr. Gladstone', Spencer's brother wrote in 1882, 'I was much struck by the evident way he thought Ireland was as quiet really as here with only a row or an outrage every now and then.'[24] At no time during the 1880 parliament did Gladstone give any indication that he might move beyond some measure of local government for Ireland. When he did move he had more on his mind than Home Rule. He knew that he was sick beyond words of Northbrook, Carlingford and Childers. Chamberlain and Dilke seemed worse than unpleasant as harbingers of a crude conspiracy to depose him and divert the path of true Liberalism towards a dangerous crypto-socialism. For a man supposed to be trembling on the verge of prophecy, he also lacked 'incandescence'.[25] In turning to Home Rule, indeed, Gladstone showed few symptoms of 1876 and quite a few of 1868.

He had, after all, turned defeat into victory once before. Just as he had then lamented the party's war against itself, so in 1885 he warned a colleague that he could 'neither meddle with a party which is simply a party, nor with a party which is in schism against itself'.[26] No need to wait for a breeze: a gale had been blowing since 1879. The most convinced opponent of Home Rule could not deny the desirability of removing the Irish MPs from Westminster; indeed the thought of sending them home served as a powerful inducement in its own right. A bold stroke of policy aimed at a great moral cause might overcome the preoccupation with property and egalitarianism to which the radicals had become prone and reconvene the forces of progress. If it drove Chamberlain and his crew out of the party, *tant mieux*. If it sent into retirement the set pieces of Whiggery then that, too, could only prove a gain. If it confirmed 'weak-kneed Liberals'[27] like Goschen in their function as muddiers of the water, that of itself would help the Liberal party to reclaim its post-1868 territory and put party dialogue back into the form of which Gladstone and Salisbury were each in their own way masters. To mount an attack on the Union no more implied the depredations of a 'magnificent lunatic', as Dilke liked to call Gladstone, than had the attack on the Irish Church twenty years before. Home Rule, in short, made sense.

But the human judgement of 1868 had gone. Gladstone's antennae no longer told him what he needed to know and he became in Irish policy, as he had never been before, obsessive. He blinded himself to the manifest truth that, without massive and sustained preparation, the second chamber would never pass his bill even if the first could be induced to do so. Herbert Gladstone's deliberate leak of his changed view, designed to marshal Gladstonian sentiment in the party, had in fact achieved the reverse and made the emollience of Gladstone's January conversations harder to contrive. Still, whatever his intentions or tactical shortcomings, Gladstone did shift political preoccupation into a mould of his own making. Nothing approached Ireland in its primacy as an *idée fixe* in 1885–6. The Conservative government's annexation of Upper Burma on 1 January 1886 made no headway among politicians. The disgrace of Sir Charles Dilke's divorce in February and his subsequent political ruin did not attain the prominence it might have received in quieter times. Riots among the unemployed in the spring likewise made little impact when all eyes had focused on parliament for the Home Rule bill. Among the general public even that issue probably provoked little reaction. Derby had been disgusted by the apathy at the end of 1885. He wrote in his diary on Boxing Day:

> Strange to my mind is the slight impression made on the public by events which are nevertheless really important. The conquest, and probable absorption, of the Burmese empire is scarcely noticed: Egypt is as much noticed as though it had never existed: the complication in the Balkans serves to talk about, but nobody seems to care how it ends. Irish affairs do get some attention...but even about this there seems little warmth of feeling.

Gladstone had passed the point – one which Lloyd George would later pass – at which he could understand the force and implications of such observations. Salisbury had not and never did, because his judgement of these matters was not cerebral. Much of the future of party over the next decade lay encapsulated in the Liberal failure to comprehend by rational process what Salisbury absorbed through instinctual habit of mind.

A changing geography

The third reform act had, in the minds of many contemporaries, introduced democracy to Britain. Even educated opinion reflected this misconception with great consistency: the view can be found in constitutional textbooks and the serious journals as much as among the Jeremiahs in St James's clubs. 'Household suffrage' fastened in the mentality of a generation the image of a property-owning society equipped with a new apparatus of legitimacy. It camouflaged the many categories of lodger, tenant, domestic servant and serviceman still excluded from the franchise after 1884; it took no account of continuing anomalies in registering voters. Only recently, indeed, has it become established that perhaps as many as 40 per cent of adult males did *not* have access to the ballot box until the fourth reform act of 1918 – a cautionary note that deserves capital letters in any treatment of the 'rise of Labour' and the status of popular politics in late Victorian and Edwardian England.[28] Not that the 80 per cent increase in Britain's electorate in 1884 should become a footnote. Rather, it needs a geographical perspective. Ireland, where the electorate increased by half a million, and Scotland, where the county electorate doubled, were overwhelmingly the beneficiaries of 1884. The redistribution of seats in 1885 reinforced the power of the Celtic fringe, moreover, by overrepresenting the Irish and Welsh relative to their populations.

Indeed, a case exists for seeing in the redistribution of 1885 the most important single alteration in the political map of Britain during the nineteenth century. It enlarged the House of Commons from 658 to 670 seats. Constituencies containing a population of 15,000 or less were disfranchised – a blow to the Conservative party but one fully expected and for which they had prepared through Gorst's organizational work in the larger towns. Established parliamentary boroughs with populations of between 15,000 and 50,000 retained one MP; those over 50,000 retained two. It did not follow, however, that 'new' boroughs automatically qualified on the same criteria. These rough guidelines in any case contributed less to the final picture than did the manner in which the constituency boundaries were redrawn. Here the Tory party won its *quid pro quo*, for giving up the smaller boroughs. The Burkean notion of 'interests' in the body politic returned, with Salisbury, to the political structure, for he insisted that 'the pursuits of the people' become a central criterion for identifying an homogeneous constituency. Agriculture achieved the separation from industry for which Grey and his Whigs had striven in 1832; middle-class (Conservative) areas in the cities gained cohesion through their being lumped together and roped off from working-class areas.[29] In tandem with the reduction of many borough seats from two MPs to one, this gave Conservatives a good chance of winning urban seats in a straight fight with a Liberal, the more so since 'Liberal' increasingly meant 'radical' now that local Liberals could not run a Whig and a radical in harness with only one seat to fill. Salisbury had thus gained far more than he lost in his Arlington Street conversations; and the consequences were to underpin much of the Conservative success at elections until 1906.

Regardless of their effect on electoral tactics, however, the rationale of the new arrangements ministered to an imagined community that had already disappeared. The dialogue between 'town' and 'country', so insistent a theme in party strategy since 1846, died away when both voices spoke of economic depression from the end of the 1870s. Landed politics, it goes without saying, often found its power undisturbed; research on areas such as Dorset and Wiltshire has shown, for example, that small landowners discovered their power usurped only by larger ones.[30] But urbanism had overwhelmed any conception of a gothic countryside: the strains of medieval revival in Ruskin and William Morris confirmed, as amply as the irrelevance of Collings's plea for everyman's 'three acres and a cow' in the Unauthorized Programme, the passing of one vision of industrial England. Instead of a crude picture of an industrial north and west combating an agricultural south and east, one needed to create a mosaic of regional variation in economic function. Mancunian cottontots, north-eastern coalowners and Birmingham manufacturers no longer supplied the cutting-edge of wealth-creation by 1890. That function had shifted towards the finance capital of the City and its merchant bankers and westward towards the shipowners, engineers and chemical manufacturers of Liverpool, Glasgow and Belfast who underpinned Conservatism, for all the Presbyterianism common in their backgrounds, with the pertinacity that Dissenting Liberalism had brought to mid-century industrialism.[31] Vast personal fortunes affected the political structure at one of its most sensitive points – the marriage market – and gave wealthy women the opportunity to inject their birthright into the plethora of double-barrelled names that originate in this period. In watching the son of Sir William Harcourt marry into the family of John Pierpont Morgan or H. H. Asquith's marriage to Margot Tennant, whose father made £3 million out of chemicals in Glasgow, or Alfred Lyttelton's to Margot's sister, contemporaries saw no more than the iceberg's tip.

The new geography implied a fresh disposition in the make-up of the back benches. To appreciate that at least one half of both parliamentary parties showed commerce or industry in their backgrounds by 1885 doubtless helps the understanding of their behaviour; but it may also mislead if left as an undifferentiated quantum. Those areas of commercial activity that proved especially rewarding in *fin-de-siècle* Britain took on a clear Conservative colouring: indeed the Liberal *Manchester Guardian* complained in 1895 that between them London and Lancashire could put one hundred Tory MPs into the House as a matter of course.[32] Banking and brewing played no small part in Tory backbench society in these years, with names that cast shadows into the next century. Where manufacturing dominated the background, as with Stanley Baldwin's father, Alfred, who entered the House in 1892, or the Glaswegian Bonar Law who came in at the khaki election of 1900, tariff-awareness may have acted as a prime determinant. 'Commercial Liberals', on the other hand, now had two faces. The traditional strength in Nonconformist industrialists could be found in Manchester and the West Riding: one calls to mind Benjamin Armitage (Liberal: Salford, 1880–85), son of Sir Elkanah Armitage, a pillar of Manchester Congregationalism; or Edward Crossley (Liberal: Sowerby, 1886–96) whose carpets outlasted his politics in reputation; or the cigarette millionaire W. H. Wills of Bristol (Liberal: Coventry, 1880–85). But there existed also the pushier radicalism of a new generation modelled on the municipal activism of Chamberlain and Collings – a group which gave rise to a different image of *nouveaux riches* about whom an undercurrent of gossip ran around the clubs concerning their accumulating blackballs and rudeness to the servants. Radicalism was losing the flavour of public school, Foreign Office, high journalism and Inns of Court that it had temporarily acquired from men like Labouchere and Dilke. It had moved out into a third world beyond the City and the centres of urban advance. And there, in an environment of economic decadence, it met the immovable object of organized Labour.

Important developments in the character of trade unionism penetrated the national consciousness during strikes of female match workers, gas workers and above all the dockers, in 1888–9. But the trend reached back to at least the middle years of the decade. Unskilled men and women whose working lives evolved far away from the polished brass and copperplate letterheads of the craft unions formed the rank and file of 'new' unions dedicated to an aggressive assertion of industrial power to win better wages and conditions of work. Their leaders – men like John Burns, Tom Mann and Ben Tillett – used a language sharper than might have found favour with Henry Broadhurst or Joseph Arch; they acted *pour épater les bourgeois*, unlike unionists of the Odger and Applegarth generation. Their participation in the marches and demonstrations of the unemployed signalled a challenge to the ameliorative politics of 'Lib–Lab' unionists who saw themselves as defending working-class rights from within the Liberal party. During the 1890s this mood issued in the conscious move of organized Labour, as trade union membership passed the one and a half million mark, towards the launching of its own political party, the Independent Labour Party (ILP) of 1893, and the emergence of a Labour Representation Committee (LRC) in 1900 to sponsor working-class men for election to parliament. Of course, some working-class men had already become MPs. Since the election of Burt and Macdonald in the 1870s, the Lib–Labs had increased to nine by 1886, a number that did not improve significantly before the breakthrough of 1906. Because three successive secretaries of the TUC could be counted among them – Henry Broadhurst (Stoke-on-Trent, 1880), Charles Fenwick (Northumberland, Wansbeck, 1885) and Sam Woods (Essex, Walthamstow, 1897) – the Lib–Labs nevertheless acted as a point of contact between Labour and the governing classes. Yet the alternative version of what 'labour' meant made its mark even here. William Abraham, soon known to everyone as 'Mabon', found himself passed over by the Liberal caucus for candidature at Rhondda in 1885. He stood as an Independent Lib–Lab – and won: the first of numerous similar examples, especially in Scotland.[33] Joseph Havelock Wilson, the seamen's leader, won Middlesbrough in the general election of 1892 and by so doing became the first candidate to beat a Liberal into second place after standing on an 'Independent-Labour' platform. John Burns won Battersea in the same election. He did not need to beat a Liberal but it aroused notice that he had been sponsored neither by the Liberal party nor by a trade union but by the Social Democratic Federation.

The SDF appeared in 1884 as a mutation of the Democratic Federation of 1881. Its inspiration, Henry M. Hyndman, gained a considerable reputation as a popular writer though he often plagiarized, mangled and bowdlerized Karl Marx's writings. Marx himself – he died in 1883 – had regarded Hyndman as a buffoon; but books such as *England For All* (1881) and *Socialism Made Plain* (1883) contributed to an interest in Marxian socialism which became general in the second half of the 1880s. Another organization that contributed to the discussion was the Fabian Society of 1884. Though never Marxist in orientation it supplied intellectual *brio* in George Bernard Shaw and the partnership of Sidney and Beatrice Webb; the *Fabian Essays* of 1889 echoed, in the year of the great London dock strike, a persistent theme of social criticism. Apart from Burns, these agencies won no parliamentary representation, unless one counts the human extravaganza R. B. Cunninghame Graham (Lanarkshire, North-Western, 1886) who floated around the edge of them. They nevertheless caught a wind that blew, not from Marx's Germany, but from America. Henry George, whose land-tax manifesto *Progress and Poverty* (1879) received a wide readership among the British intelligentsia, widened further by the author's lecture tour in Ireland and Britain in 1881–2, held a considerable appeal for socialists who had come to believe, quite as strongly as cabinet ministers, that the land problem lay at the heart of Britain's economic malaise. Outside socialist circles, however, the problem was framed differently. For here the thinking could address itself less to the question of the land's distribution than to the importance of acquiring more of it from the world's virgin territories.

More than any period of the nineteenth century, the 1880s and 1890s have become associated with a surge of imperialist activity, most notably in the so-called 'scramble for Africa' after 1882. This expansionist mood expressed itself in the determination to further the British trading bridgehead in China, in strengthening the grip on India by annexing Burma in 1886, and in developing a control over first, eastern Africa in the annexation of Uganda (1894), and then, by force of arms as events turned out, the gold-and-diamond cornucopia of the Transvaal between 1895 and 1902. These decades marked the rise to political prominence, as short-lived as it was spectacular, of imperial business managers of whom Cecil Rhodes and his British South Africa Company or Sir George Goldie and the Royal Niger Company supply significant examples. In front of the trade ran missionary churchmen; behind it came the administrators of whom the most luminous was a product of Balliol College, Oxford: Alfred Milner, whose period as governor of the Cape and later governor-general of South Africa offered a nursery to an influential group of civil servants, politicians and journalists who would make their mark when they returned to Britain.[34] The reddening of the atlas could not remain an academic speculation, even if the process took place, as Sir John Seeley alleged in his Cambridge lectures on *The Expansion of England* (1883) during a fit of absence of mind. Three foreign secretaries in the 1890s – Salisbury, Rosebery and Kimberley – discovered that imperial concerns could not be dismissed; in the euphoria of the Queen's golden and diamond jubilees in 1887 and 1897 only a fool would have tried. A distinctively British style of nationalist politics offered the base on which distinctive parties might stand through years of party confusion. Besides, as Rosebery himself pointed out, 'it was desirable the Foreign Secretary should hum "Rule Britannia" while doing his boxes in order that he should not lose heart'.[35]

Perception had its own 'geography': a cluster of reference-points acknowledged by those who governed. These do not obtain a precise fit with the map suggested in retrospect. Imperial affairs, for example, seem to have developed as a preoccupation, not immediately after the Egyptian intervention of 1882, but at some point between 1888 and 1892 and as a response to events in *East* Africa rather than to the bluster of Rhodes's company in the south. Party exigencies at home accounted for the late start. The Home Rule crisis both blocked out wider imperial concerns and stimulated anxieties about the dissolution of the empire which could come into play as the immediacy of the Irish crisis receded. Salisbury's government of 1886–92 relied for its survival, moreover, on Liberal Unionist support; and imperial policy presented an area of intense disagreement between Salisbury's wish to play along with Bismarck in Africa so long as the European consequences did not disturb equilibrium, and the remnant of Liberal ideology in Chamberlain's and Hartington's wish to distance Britain from the machinations of the Triple Alliance. German threats to Zanzibar in 1888–9 pressed, therefore, on sensitive nerves, and when Herbert Bismarck, son of the German chancellor, visited Britain in March 1889 he recorded his surprise at being 'obliged to discuss Zanzibar in detail with Chamberlain, Goschen, Rosebery and Lord Salisbury's two Under-Secretaries of State, each for a good hour'.[36] Rosebery's inclusion among the interviewers may stand as reminder that some Liberals had also begun to see in imperialism a doctrine to cultivate. For them the critical moment came in 1892, partly because they then returned to government with Rosebery as foreign secretary, partly because he committed that government to retaining Uganda. A group of Liberal MPs, among them H. H. Asquith, Edward Grey, R. B. Haldane, Henry Fowler and R. C. Munro-Ferguson, had already begun to work together in the Commons as 'Liberal Imperialists', but in the late 1880s their interests had a domestic focus. Imperialism made its mark as a major political preoccupation only when colonial and foreign policy ran together before the wind of Bismarck's ambition and when domestic politics in the 1890s allowed it the necessary room.

Ireland inevitably loomed large in the interim but again the problem took on a distinctive colour. The 'flowing tide' of election results in favour of the Liberals was taken to represent popular enthusiasm for Home Rule among the British electorate; and when the tide ebbed in 1890 Liberals swam on in the belief that it still flowed, hence Gladstone's well-known disappointment when his majority came out at only forty in the general election of 1892. Attention at the high-political level (and probably in the constituencies as well) had concentrated, not on the justice of the nationalist cause, but rather on two scandals associated with its leader, Charles Stewart Parnell: *The Times*'s forged letter of 18 April 1887 that muddied Parnell for two years with the imputation that he had privately condoned the Phoenix Park murders of 1882; and his citation as co-respondent in the divorce of Captain O'Shea from his wife Katherine, which effectively terminated his influence in British politics. Even Gladstone no longer believed in the practicability of passing Home Rule in 1893. The success story in Ireland after 1886 seemed rather to lie with the Conservative government and the repression practised by Salisbury's nephew and chief secretary, Arthur 'Bloody' Balfour.

If both parties persisted in their jaundiced understanding of Ireland, their visions of Scotland and Wales hardly suggested that they had come to terms with nationalist feelings. The Tory party had won only seven seats in Scotland in 1880 – its worst performance in living memory – which may help explain its readiness to countenance the establishment of a Scottish Office in 1885. Gladstone and the Liberals did nothing, however, to recognize the growing importance of Scotland within the political structure after the redistribution. Disestablishment of the Scottish Church received some half-hearted attention from Gladstone but it seems clear enough that he did not believe in it; the crofters got their bill in 1886. For the rest the rhetoric of Midlothian was deemed enough. No one would have suffered had some advancement come to a man like W. A. Hunter (Liberal: Aberdeen North, 1885–96) in the wake of so signal a Liberal victory in eastern Scotland in 1886; but nothing came. Stuart Rendel, MP for Montgomeryshire, could likewise have reasonably sought more recognition from the Liberals of his importance in Wales; but here, as in Scotland, little effort was made apart from giving junior office to the radical Tom Ellis. Possibly the wheels of patronage could expect no oil when so many social attitudes needed lubrication. Gladstone found it hard enough, after all, to stomach 'an able Wolverhampton solicitor' like Henry Fowler after a lifetime's exposure to 'highly-cultured statesmen of the old stamp'.[37] One wonders what he would have thought of sitting in cabinet with the untamed Portmadoc solicitor who had entered the House for Carnarvon Boroughs in 1890. He spared himself that torment; but Gladstone's successors were to know Lloyd George.

Social commentaries of this kind barely faltered in England. They appeared in a wonderful moment during the deliberations in Gladstone's second cabinet when the Marquess of Hartington dismissed the 15th Earl of Derby as 'the mere owner of Liverpool ground rents'.[38] Joseph Arch's appearance in the House of Commons – the laughable prospect of a few years before – sent sniggers round the House after the 1885 election when he appeared in his round hat and the rural coat that so offended Sir Richard Cross. A parallel prejudice, unknown to Cross, informed Lord Randolph Churchill's description of Smith and Cross as Marshall and Snelgrove. More seriously, such attitudes helped confuse the political parties about where self-interest lay. Rather than feel jubilant about their strong position in the larger towns, some Conservatives looked wistfully to the counties, the seat of their former power. Churchill lamented their loss. Salisbury persisted, more constructively, in his support for free education in the early 1890s, in the face of Nonconformist opposition to it in the towns, partly because 'the agricultural labourers are worth more than the Wesleyan clericals'.[39] Liberals applied the same lesson in reverse: 'Our strength now lies in the counties and we must keep our hold on them.' In fact their 'strength' there lasted only so long as the 'democratic' thrust of policy between the third reform act and the local government reforms of 1888 and 1894 gave them an appropriate image.[40] Their urban machine, on the other hand, all but ground to a halt. The centrality of London and Lancashire was not squarely faced, and the Liberals found themselves nationally unable even to field candidates in many constituencies in 1895 and 1900.

Democratic language in 1884–5 carried the mind towards fears for property and the stability of the state. That 'general cowardice' discerned by Gladstone in Irish landowners had become contagious after 1881: the catalogue lengthened of those who wanted to be up and gone. Lord Pembroke saw for his seat at Wilton no future but 'to be despoiled, cut up and subdivided among the masses'. Nor had Goschen's weak knees become any firmer in the wake of reform. 'Startling propositions of the gravest character,' he wrote in 1886, 'striking at the structure of society altogether, are not laughed out of court, or rejected with indignation, but are played with, and treated as we used to treat the ballot and the six-pound franchise or the Irish Church twenty years ago.' Another decade would leave him little more than an echo of Sir James Graham's later years, sick of everything because everything had indefinably altered – 'methods, tone, subjects, men, principles, appreciations'.[41] Certainly the public had no time for him. Use his name on the platform, as Labouchere did in London in 1885, and you raised groans. Try Hartington and you produced – silence. Eventually 'you have to get up a cheer for the GOM by dwelling upon his noble heart and that sort of trash.'[42]

If some new public struck politicians as having come into existence, new methods of controlling its mood and discovering its mind might also exist. Localism, for example, emerges as a theme after 1885. Just as 1832 and 1867 had encouraged a follow-through in municipal legislation, so 1884 brought on the expectation that local democracy would require attention. The Conservative government of 1885–6 looked balefully at the problem but left it alone. It was C. T. Ritchie's Local Government Act of 1888, which established county councils and divided their functions from the boroughs, and Henry Fowler's Act of 1894, which established parish councils in communities of over three hundred persons, that instigated a keenly felt debate about the virtue of local participation (which the Conservative party opposed) and the continuing needs and status of traditional local centres of power in the landowners and the Anglican Church. Appointments to magistracies present a similar picture of local concern, especially among Liberals conscious of the urgency of changing party balance in the home territory of squire and parson: it is noticeable that new appointments peaked in the years of Liberal accession – 1892 and 1906.[43]

Another mechanism announced itself each evening in the newspapers. Improved communication and newspaper technology helped spur a marked advance in the development of a newspaper readership after 1880. Forster's Education Act and the introduction of compulsory and free education (1876 and 1893) promised further to underwrite a popular journalism which publicists like George Newnes and more especially Alfred Harmsworth, whose *Daily Mail* first appeared in 1896, exploited. Evening newspapers, already well established in London, Lancashire and the West Riding by 1880, spread elsewhere over the next decade, *a fortiori* in the west midlands. This expansion helped redress the imbalance of party support in the provincial press; the Liberal predominance of the 1870s – there were 487 Liberal newspapers in 1878 as against 282 Conservative ones[44] – had been undermined by the turn of the century. Politicians could not avoid taking stock of these changes, if only in appreciating the speed with which a political crisis could now explode. Gladstone's 25,000-word speech on the introduction of his Home Rule bill in 1886 went verbatim into the notebooks of reporters in the gallery. By midnight it had been typeset in Manchester, Leeds and Edinburgh.

The public intruded less obviously in its collective guise as 'society' – an idealized vision of community in which politicians acted as the monitors and servants of a popular sovereign will. Some ingredients of this conception emanated from the universities and a strain of Liberal theory associated with authors such as the Balliol philosopher Thomas Hill Green and a second generation of writers including Bernard Bosanquet, D. G. Ritchie, L. T. Hobhouse, John Hobson and the politician Herbert Samuel. Little of the output directly affected what politicians did but some of the key terms and phraseology found its way into speeches and manifestos by the end of the 1890s. A more imposing presence appeared in the new order of importance granted to social policy. The thought can be overstressed by quoting its enthusiasts, who often bored their cabinet colleagues rigid and went away convinced that their seed had fallen on good soil. Yet the sheer scale of governmental intervention in the lives of the masses had broadened visibly over the past few years and impinged on the consciousness of those who witnessed it. One did not have to cultivate a curiosity for public health, or find Arthur Acland interesting, to become dully aware of the quadrupling of memoranda on 'social' issues presented to cabinet between 1880–84 and 1905–9. Indeed the very language of 'policy' and 'programme', often printed or written in quotation marks, came into common use in this period and gave rise to new demands on party leaders. When activists like Acland or Asquith pressed Liberal leaders to declare their 'policy' they caught some current assumptions. When Esher retorted, 'Why should they?' he reflected a still-strong suspicion.[45] When the National Liberal Federation espoused its 'Newcastle Programme' in 1891 it confirmed the arrival of a word whose unauthorized use had so shocked Liberal opinion in 1885.

With size and speed came impersonality and the momentum of the bureaucratic machine. The 550 letters received in Gladstone's private office during six days in 1882 give, even if 'in excess of the average', some idea of the administrative burden at the centre; in Balfour's private office at the periphery in Dublin, an average of seventy letters a day had to be sent out. In such circumstances civil servants could command much sway. Great careers such as Sir Eyre Crowe's in the Foreign Office, or Sir Robert Morant's at the Board of Education, thrived on them. So did the underworld of the private secretary: Eddie Hamilton and Algy West with Gladstone; George Wyndham, a future Conservative minister, and Jack Sandars with Balfour; Alfred Milner with Goschen. The faceless men behind ministers now seemed to count. It genuinely disturbed Milner, for example, that the Foreign Office and Colonial Office were 'entirely manned *with Whigs*'.[46]

Whatever their politics, new administrators certainly brought with them a changed tone – one much closer to that radiated by the politicians themselves. Men of the stamp of Pauncefote, Currie and Sanderson at the Foreign Office took their place, on occasion, as members of high-political society and slid as easily into political intimacy as any old school friend at a shooting party or the now-fashionable venue of a select golf-links. At the same time, one could no longer expect to place protégés in the civil service, at least near the top: the mandarins had to come up through the university and take their chances in competitive examination. The bureaucracy had developed a life of its own.

People accustomed to opening doors by merely saying their name discovered that the world had become smaller and more hostile. If the monarchy returned to a position of some significance – the Queen prevented the appointment of Labouchere (a republican) to Gladstone's ministry in 1892 and passed over Spencer (a Home Ruler) in favour of Rosebery as her premier in 1894 – the House of Lords came under fire after 1888, as did 'Peer Ministers' whose disproportionate membership of cabinets now attracted criticism.[47] But the rot reached deeper than this. Looking forward, Derby saw 'a worse prospect for the rural aristocracy than has ever been yet in my time', a mood doubtless reinforced by Granville's failure to pay back the money he had borrowed from him. Granville's case had not proved an isolated one: by 1881 Lord John Manners had been driven into securing for himself a state pension while both Northcote and Cross pressed Gladstone for one. The 'leader with a house and cash' sought in the 1810s remained in many ways the object of desire in the 1890s. Professional men seeking to make politics their career contributed to a predicament that even the payment of MPs in 1911 only marginally eased: the twentieth-century phenomenon of the cabinet minister who will not know where to turn if his ministerial salary should unexpectedly cease. The continuing expense of party leadership militated against Asquith's coming to the fore, for example, during the black period for the Liberals after the retirement of Gladstone in 1894. Not that his coming or going would have made much difference in a period dominated by three men for whom money, whether they had any or not, represented the least of their worries.

Chamberlain, Churchill and Salisbury (1886–90)

Joseph Chamberlain resigned from Gladstone's 1886 government a few months before his fiftieth birthday. Little had gone right over the past year. His Unauthorized Programme had failed with the public: the 'urban cow' Labouchere had pressed on him proved hard to find and, having 'put [his] money on free schools', he obtained no great leverage in the cities.[48] He grounded his decision to join Gladstone's second cabinet on the expectation that Hartington would join too and resist Home Rule from within, but coming in soon seemed a tactical error. His main achievement as a minister could be represented by his enemies as nothing more than the undermining of Gladstone's conception of the future. In this function, on the other hand, he had not been alone. On the Tory benches, Lord Randolph Churchill had contrived to give Northcote and Salisbury all the pain that Chamberlain had wished on Gladstone; and though they presented contemporaries with divergent streams of language and strategy, they come together in historical imagination as solvents of the party framework that their leaders had hoped to perpetuate.

As a son of the seventh Duke of Marlborough, Randolph Churchill began life in 1849 with every political advantage. But as a third son he also courted every danger to personal stability encouraged by the English aristocracy in its also-rans. Blenheim's society could not contain his wilfulness. Eton's, which he shared with Arthur Balfour and the future Lord Rosebery, did little to subdue it. At Merton College, Oxford, his behaviour offered, we are told, 'no grounds for the statement that his university career was one of idleness, dissipation and disorder', but the defence seems to protest too much. After university he discovered Parisian night-life and a beautiful American woman, Jenny Jerome, whom he married in 1874, the year of his election to the House of Commons as Conservative MP for the family borough of Woodstock. What his friends called his 'independence' showed itself at once in a readiness to join the company of Whigs and even radicals such as Chamberlain after he entered the House in 1876. Churchill's mark on high politics, however, first appeared in 1880 through the machinations of the so-called 'Fourth Party'. This collection of four politicians – Churchill, Gorst, Henry Drummond Wolff and, in a less committed way, Arthur Balfour – originated in the need to say something offensive about Northcote's incompetence as leader of the Commons. An irresistible opportunity for doing so was provided in 1880 by the electors of Northampton.

Two radicals filled the Northampton seats in the general election. One of them, Henry Labouchere, caused no problem apart from his republicanism, which the Queen thought tasteless. The other, Charles Bradlaugh, presented parliamentarians with a lingering embarrassment which evoked echoes of John Wilkes's challenge to the decencies of procedure in the 1760s. Bradlaugh's notorious views about birth control (the very acme of wickedness, according to the Queen) and his living-in-sin with the redoubtable harridan Annie Besant suggested a lack of tone. His atheism however precipitated the central difficulty for he refused to take the parliamentary oath and asked to attest instead. The uproar and near-farcical scenes in the House and the ensuing protracted wrangling over Bradlaugh's infuriating re-election to parliament terminated only when an exasperated Speaker let him take his seat in 1886 and forbade further discussion.[49] But although the issue never became more than an irritant to government, it brought Churchill into focus as an anchor for Christian orthodoxy and spokesman for an aggressive, anti-squire Toryism.

Thereafter Churchill and his henchmen slapped Northcote daily and won the attention of gallery and press by stinging the men from the counties quite as sharply as did Chamberlain his Whigs. Who could forget Gorst's rising 'to point out that the right hon. Gentleman at the head of the Government had forgotten to answer the Question which the Leader of the Opposition forgot to put'?[50] Churchill's never missing a trick nonetheless left behind a suspicion of sleight-of-hand. The 'Toryism' could be abandoned as quickly as it had been amplified: his attack on Spencer for acting firmly against the murderers of an entire Irish family in the village of Maamtrasna seemed to the law-and-order lobby an instance of opportunism outrunning both policy and prudence. Indeed his Irish vision appeared altogether bifocal. Having a Londonderry for a mother helped him appear Protestant but he could not conceal the degree to which the arch Presbyterianism of Ulster society disgusted him, nor to which his temperamental affinities lay with the professional classes of Dublin. By 1885, when Salisbury appointed him to the India Office, Churchill had gained only one of his objectives in superseding Michael Hicks Beach as the Conservative party's coming man and, moreover, harnessing Beach to his own chariot (as odd a fusion of opposites as that of Bonar Law and Lloyd George thirty years later). He had not displaced Northcote, Cross, Carnarvon and Smith; he had not made himself indispensable to Salisbury.

The eruption of Home Rule into a major preoccupation in the autumn of 1885 did not help Churchill in that it drove Salisbury ultimately to a stance associated with the men Churchill needed to isolate. Rather, it encouraged him to keep his head down until it became plain what Hartington intended to do about Gladstone's new line; and since Hartington did not know himself, Christmas and the new year found many Conservative houses occupied in constructing recherché coalitions of which the most startling placed Salisbury in the Foreign Office in a ministry headed by the Duke of Argyll.

Hartington's eventual intransigence gave rise to a period of violent anti-Home Rule sentiment from Churchill, now that it was clear that no centre movement would work. True, Chamberlain's resignation from the government gave the Conservative leadership 'a very different kind of ally from the lukewarm and slippery Whig, whom it is so difficult to differ from and so impossible to act with' and introduced to centre politics a man completely clear that 'our great object must be to get rid of Gladstone'.[51] Doubtless Churchill hoped that his 'orange card' would help give Chamberlain and Hartington a hand to play in the confused period before Salisbury made plain his position. But of course the Conservative leader had no intention of sitting by while Churchill, Chamberlain, Hartington and Goschen decided how to orchestrate the response to Gladstone. He undertook to squash them in May 1886 with a speech to the party conference – the 'Hottentots' or 'Manicles and Manitoba' speech – which touched every register of Tory violence over the racial inferiority of the Celts and the inevitability of coercion. No sensitive Liberal or Whig could tolerate the language and that was precisely the point. Salisbury had recreated the poles of party dialogue and evacuated the centre. From May 1886 Conservative politics belonged to him.

Robert Arthur Talbot Gascoyne-Cecil, third Marquess of Salisbury (1830–1903), lived his life among aliens. They bullied him at school – his experience of Eton proved as formative for him as it had for Spencer Walpole – and he resolved to curb their confiscations when he and his tormentors grew up. He despised the 'hearties' who milled around the 'honorary fourth class', his own, at Oxford. Any emotional sympathy was reserved for an ever-deepening sense of historicity surrounding his family, whose influence in British government could be traced back to William Cecil, Queen Elizabeth's Lord Burghley, and for the church of Hooker and Laud as it struggled in an industrial society overgrown with covetousness, thick with cant and lies. Though he had made his peace with Disraeli in 1874, he neither forgave nor forgot Conservative complicities in the acceptance of 'progress': the 'transformation scenes' of 1829, 1846 and 1867 remained in his mind as images of what to avoid. From the house that he loved, Hatfield in Hertfordshire, from his London home in Arlington Street or his desk at the Foreign Office, he invited (never instructed) his party to shoulder the burden of resistance to the creeping corruption he saw masquerading as philanthropy:

> We are in a state of bloodless civil war. No common principles, no respect for common institutions or traditions, unite the various groups of politicians who are struggling for power. To loot somebody or

something is the common object under a thick varnish of pious phrases...[52]

In setting clear-headed limits to the looting, Salisbury placed in the way of radicalism at home and nationalism abroad taller obstacles than Disraeli could achieve. And his success in maintaining them underlines both Salisbury's political intelligence and his historical status as the most formidable politician the Conservative party has ever produced.

That Salisbury placed Churchill at the Exchequer when he returned to office in July 1886 may have reflected esteem or a wish to reward Churchill's loyalty since the spring. But the new government of 1886–92 contained little else for the Fourth Party to applaud. Gorst received a junior ministry, but only under the tutelage of Cross, one of the targets of Churchill's criticism, at the India Office. Balfour joined the cabinet in November in a personal capacity rather than as secretary for Scotland, though he went on to create a new stature for himself as chief secretary for Ireland. His sympathy for Churchill declined as his stature increased but, for the moment, Lord Randolph hoped to use him to introduce an emollient tone into Tory democracy and 'play Dilke to Chamberlain, supplying tact and cool judgement'.[53] Churchill scored a further success in pushing his protégé Henry Matthews into the Home Office where Matthews' incapacity made the triumph short-lived. None of these appointments brought closer together the preoccupations and priorities of Churchill and Salisbury. Northcote's appointment (as Earl of Iddesleigh) to the Foreign Office guaranteed that Churchill's pro-German proclivities would find no outlet; and Salisbury's stonewalling over local government reform brought out all the chancellor's impatience. It seemed obvious to Churchill that the Liberal Unionists held the key to stability and that Chamberlain's radical following would demand some initiatives in policy. This concern lay behind his speech at Dartford on 2 October 1886, a performance that attracted much scrutiny in the press. His expectation that Salisbury's government would 'prove to the British people that the Unionist Liberals were right in the course which they took [in leaving Gladstone] and were justified in the great political sacrifices which they made' was seen by many observers to mark an important move towards Birmingham.

In the event it did not matter greatly whether this view had any substance because, within two months of Dartford, Churchill resigned from the government and fell like a stone into darkness. His resignation rested on a number of misconceptions. In the first place, his previous tactical resignation from the chairmanship of the

National Union of Conservative Associations in 1884 had succeeded too well and resulted in his reinstatement: he doubtless believed he could do it again. Second, he overestimated the loyalty of former supporters, such as Hicks Beach and Matthews. Third, Salisbury knew, because his chief whip told him, that the Unionists divided two to one in favour of Hartington by the summer of 1886.[54] Churchill would therefore need to take Hartington with him along any new path he envisaged. Fourth, he chose the wrong path. To resign over the cabinet's refusal to compel Smith to lower his Admiralty estimates seemed to expand what was nothing more than a small-scale disagreement into a contrived challenge to the government's general attitudes. Salisbury had no difficulty in preventing Churchill from representing his action as a fundamental criticism of directions in foreign policy and defence. Fifth, he believed that his objective (a reshuffled government organized around himself with Iddesleigh and the old gang excluded) lay within reach of a unilateral action. For although he consulted Chamberlain about his budgetary strategy in December 1886, he alone took the decision to write the fatal resignation letter from Windsor, where he had just had an audience with the Queen, and release it also to *The Times*. Sixth, he failed to identify anyone *outside* the government who might replace him, claiming, 'I had forgotten Goschen.' Behind all these apprehensions one may trace not only ambition and temper but also the effects of his syphilis and the destabilizing effects of its medication. Churchill was no longer the man of 1884.

Less than a week before his resignation, Churchill had approached Salisbury privately to tell him that Chamberlain would drift back to Gladstone unless a radical local government policy gave him a sign of something hopeful from the government. Even had Churchill not resigned, however, little chance existed of a united local government policy emerging. For Salisbury and Hartington, the brunt of the problem lay in devising a plan for Irish administration that might help moderate the forces of nationalism, whereas Churchill and Chamberlain wanted at all costs to avoid presenting Parnell with what might be seen as the thin end of a Home Rule wedge. Fortified by Churchill's withdrawal, Chamberlain acted according to prediction and turned to the problem of Liberal reunion that had preoccupied the Gladstonian wing of the Liberal party through the previous autumn. In the new year a series of 'round table' meetings took place at Harcourt's house in Grafton Street between Liberals (Harcourt, Morley and the former lord chancellor, Herschell) and Unionists (the ex-ministers Chamberlain and Trevelyan). Despite Trevelyan's eventual return to the fold, for which he earned the contempt of both factions, the conferences failed because the Gladstonians sought to impose terms which seemed to Chamberlain to require his section of the party to dress itself in sackcloth and salute Gladstone as a tribal god. Yet for all their fruitlessness the negotiations had, simply through their being held, damaged Chamberlain's relationship with Churchill, so when Birmingham bounced back to Churchill with a proposal for 'a strong Central Party which may be master of the situation after Mr. Gladstone goes', a cold response followed. Churchill had learned that nothing could be done without Hartington and resolved, from his position of weakness, to 'stick to Lord H. *coûte que coûte*'.[55] By the end of the 1887 session the Chamberlain–Churchill axis no longer existed. Public recrimination between them when Chamberlain successfully resisted Churchill's attempt to fill Bright's Birmingham seat in 1888 merely deepened the rift.

Chamberlainism had arrived at its nadir. Gladstone and Churchill had between them blocked two possible ways forward. To remain in the ditch with Hartington left much to be desired since no one could work out what he wanted. All the resolution and steadiness admired by visitors to Chatsworth and Devonshire House continued to exercise their charm – especially in the latest manifestation of loaded revolvers that Hartington carried about with him in London in case the Fenians attacked him as they had his brother in Phoenix Park. But Hartington gave the impression of lacking any mental process which might issue in a decision; he had rejected Salisbury's offer of the premiership but seemed to see no further than avoiding any kind of commitment. Unionists knew they need go no further for their leader with a house and cash, not to mention the Duchess of Manchester and a string of racehorses. The radicalism of Chamberlain and his friends nevertheless made demands that Hartington could hardly hope to satisfy. An offer from Salisbury to spend a period abroad caught Chamberlain, therefore, in a receptive mood. The prime minister wanted him to lead a Commission expected to resolve a bitter cod war between the Americans and Canadians over fishing and landing rights around Newfoundland. It would at least offer a change of scene and a chance to practise the statesmanship in which he had been frustrated over the past two years. He could not yet know that his success there would do him considerable good at home. Nor could he know that his introduction to Mary Endicott of New England would lead to a third marriage and a revival of *joie de vivre*.

Stability returned to Conservative politics through the early months of 1887. The accession of the Liberal Unionist Goschen not only confirmed the alliance of Tories and Unionists but gave Salisbury a first-rate chancellor of the exchequer. He also received help from personal misfortunes. Iddesleigh died in January 1887 and Salisbury took over the Foreign Office himself, as in 1885. Beach's eyes failed and compelled him to relinquish cabinet office for nearly a year – a godsend for the prime minister since it removed a weak chief secretary for Ireland and allowed him to transfer Balfour who would ignore Ashbourne's whining and wringing of hands over evictions and coercion. The Conservative party controlled the House of Lords. In the Commons its majority of forty-one over the combined Liberal and Irish contingents remained vulnerable to the votes of seventy-nine Unionists, especially when by-elections cut into it during the next few years. But then, Hartington gave no evidence of ambition or animosity. If the path ahead narrowed anywhere, it would do so at those points where vestigial Liberalism impaired the judgement of Hartington's men. Ireland might present one such difficulty if coercion became too crass an enthusiasm. Foreign policy, economic protection and education also suggested themselves as territories requiring circumspection.

In Ireland the land agitation had worsened in the face of a savage *réaction seigneuriale* that expressed itself through widespread eviction of the tenantry. Strengthened coercion (sweetened by yet another land act) seemed to ministers their only possible policy and, with Beach's departure in March 1887, the Crimes Bill acquired more and more teeth through the summer. When it became law in the autumn, it joined the shooting by the authorities of three people at Mitchelstown, County Cork, in September as confirmation of the government's determination to crush the land agitation by force. The nationalists William O'Brien and John Dillon responded in their 'plan of campaign' which called on tenants to organize themselves and resist expropriation; and the human tragedy of the next few years would be written in the files of Balfour's Irish Office in Dublin as he wore down resistance with a pitiless efficiency unmatched since the days of Orange Peel. The killing brought some kindness in a land act which Salisbury loathed for its interference in property-relations and further depression of rents – 'pain and grief to me' – but accepted to appease Chamberlain's need to appear Liberal and sugar the Crimes Bill for Ashbourne.[56] Among public and politicians alike, however, the question had slipped out of attention since April when *The Times* printed the forged letter that it had bought from a rather pathetic crook, Richard Piggott, which smeared Parnell for two years and gave Balfour more room for manoeuvre. In party terms the repression meanwhile cost little: only a handful of Unionists crossed over to Gladstone on the strength of it.

On the other hand, the notion that Ireland had opened up a wound in British society gave Salisbury one justification for avoiding inconvenience in his foreign policy. 'The prospect is very gloomy abroad', he could readily agree with the Queen; yet he soon quietened her sabre-rattling by going on: 'but England cannot brighten it. Torn in two by a controversy which almost threatens her existence, she cannot in the present state of public opinion interfere with any decisive action abroad.'[57] What he wanted from his sovereign, as from his colleagues, was silence. Salisbury saw no point in trying to frame a foreign policy by discussion: democracy, as he once said, is no way to run an empire. Running it remained his central preoccupation for the rest of his career. The cabinet even met at the Foreign Office for much of the time and exchanged views in the shadow of Bismarck. But in Conservative politics Salisbury simultaneously embodied Gladstone and Granville. The considerations reflected in the correspondence of the two Liberals received consideration inside that one mind. Others entered it, of course – he saw senior men at the Office regularly, spoke to Smith almost daily about Commons management, saw Balfour at weekends and wrote frequently to Goschen – but foreign affairs do not emerge from the general political correspondence of this period as a primary subject for discussion, except in the summer of 1888 when fears of the French created a panic, as they always did, over weaknesses in defence.

Salisbury's reticence about diplomacy stood on at least two grounds, one internal, one external. He knew that Unionists would resist forming entanglements with the Triple Alliance; yet in the first of his 'Mediterranean Agreements' (February 1887) he accepted Italy's request to maintain the status quo there in return for Italian support for Britain's continuing occupation of Egypt. In the second Agreement at the end of the year, moreover, he seemed to extend the commitment into recognizing, with Italy and Austria-Hungary, the importance of maintaining (against, in practice, Russian ambitions) the integrity of Bulgaria as established at Berlin in 1878. This commitment subsequently gave Salisbury much anxiety from an external source. Bismarck might use the developing intimacy between Britain and his partners in the Triple Alliance to drag Britain into a second 'Crimea' – a major war to prevent Russia resurrecting by force the big Bulgaria of San Stefano or even going for Constantinople itself. In the meantime Bismarck would attack France: the apprehension of many in Britain during these years. Policy consisted, therefore, in prohibiting either of these disasters while retaining enough German goodwill to secure the British position in Egypt. Goodwill in Africa found expression in the Heligoland–Zanzibar Treaty of 1890 in which

Britain won concessions from the Germans in East Africa in return for the cession of the island of Heligoland in the North Sea. Independence appeared in the sidestepping of Germany's attempts to secure an Anglo-German alliance. Prudence and *politique* in the wake of the defence scare underlay the Naval Defence Act of 1889 with its promise to lay down ten new battleships and thirty-eight cruisers to assert a 'Two-Power standard' of naval supremacy.

Salisbury's global preoccupations put argument over tariffs and county councils in a more diminished perspective than most Conservatives experienced. About economic protection he felt frankly agnostic but his knowledge of the history of tariffs encouraged him to soft-pedal the issue, especially when the prospect of another corn law came into view. Local democracy appalled him no less than national, but he saw no reason to share backwoods' fears of a revolt among the squires whom he rightly deemed inert. So Goschen was given his head in economic management where he performed well, especially in his conversion of the national debt in 1888, until a major error of judgement in his support for Ritchie's local taxation bill of 1890 brought the country's temperance lobby to his door (because the bill contained a proposal to devote revenue from a spirits tax to a fund for compensating publicans when local authorities wished to reduce licences). In the countryside landowners fought a rearguard battle against the transference of responsibility for paying tithes from their tenants to themselves and held out until 1891. Opponents of free education also dug in during the late 1880s; but here Salisbury's Anglicanism and rural understanding of the world fused with considerable backbench support to press forward the introduction of free schools before Liberal Nonconformists, with their fee-paying schools and hostility to subsidized Anglicanism, had their chance to attack the denominational schools.[58] This legislation also had to wait until 1891 but the arguments over it took their toll in discomfiting Liberals who could not decide whether to applaud the theory or decry the tactics. That it did not unduly discomfit Chamberlain, who slipped quietly away when the vote was taken, offers a useful comment on how far he had come since his period as messiah of the National Education League.

'Free schools' in the agenda of the Unauthorized Programme had not implied any extension of subsidies to denominational schools, but by 1889 Chamberlain needed, as the rebuffed Churchill alleged, the smiles of Hatfield. Local government reform 'very much on my lines' had in fact owed little to him; but he at least felt that he had leavened the Tory lump and found a role to play: in Gladstonian politics he plainly had none. 'It is true,' Balfour reflected in November, 'that he will hardly leave us while Gladstone lives, and that after Gladstone dies he will probably leave us anyhow.'[59] But he underestimated the animus between the Unionists and the Liberal party. The revelation of Piggott's forgery of the Parnell letter blighted Chamberlain for a time, since he had wrung every drop of blood out of its imputations. The divorce of Parnell followed closely behind, however, and made the Irish leader more infamous still, especially among the Nonconformists whom Chamberlain had, with allowance for R. W. Dale's loyal Congregationalism, come to despise. In any case, he had returned from America in 1888 with a clear idea that the future must centre not on Ireland but on Africa. 'The whole question of the government of South Africa and of our relations with the native tribes is very interesting and difficult', he wrote to his fiancée during the spring. 'I mean some day to be Colonial Minister and to deal with it, and I should very much like to pay a visit to the Cape.'[60] He was to accomplish the first ambition in seven years; the second took a little longer.

And Churchill? He had rented a house in Egham. The money still ran away like water: horses, high living, speculative investment. Jenny took up with other men. Scandal followed him from Belgravia to Doncaster and Newmarket; it filled his conversation in the darker moments. The year 1889 brought a brief glimpse of the warhorse when he believed that Bright's death would give Chamberlain an opportunity to bring in his old ally for Birmingham Central. Priorities had changed, he soon learned. So had Churchill himself: the after-dinner eyes, glazed with wine and drooping with mercury, no longer frightened their victims across the House or along his own benches. Words began, from 1888, to come in the wrong order or to fuse together. By the early nineties each speech was a black farce of self-parody. Lucidity left him during much of the last period through which Jenny devotedly nursed and defended him. He died in January 1895, owing Rothschilds £66,902.[61]

Disintegration (1890–95)

Although no general election or change of government took place in 1890, the year provides a convenient point of departure for discussing the mood of fragmentation and decadence that characterizes much political language in the first half of the 1890s. Darwinist vocabulary, Marxian socialism and the bitter strikes of recent years fed into a broader consciousness among the politically aware. One sees it in the incidental conversation of politicians past their best.

'N[orthbrook] called', Derby wrote in his diary in February 1891. 'He thought the growth of socialism formidable.' The same sense of a life mounted on wheels comes from a younger correspondent, Sir William Harcourt, whose Whig mind troubled itself over the powers of Queen Victoria's revived court, 'a Court more Tory than Tory with a country becoming daily more democratic'.[62] Perhaps the loss of certain major figures from the centre of the stage emphasized the mood of uncertainty. Salisbury had been glad to see the back of Churchill, but the leader of the Commons, W. H. Smith, had acted as a mainstay to the administration and the deterioration of his health – he had a weak heart – left the prime minister with an obvious difficulty in prospect. Smith died in 1891 on the same day as another principal player, Parnell. Both deaths invited political consequences: the one, in forcing Salisbury to promote his nephew Balfour to, in effect, the position of heir apparent; and the other, in widening the split in the Irish party brought about by the divorce scandal. In the same year, Hartington's father died and the Liberal Unionist leader progressed to the House of Lords as eighth Duke of Devonshire, a subtle shift in the balance of power calling up echoes of Althorp's elevation in 1834.

Not that the House of Lords could remain a backwater after 1886. Once Home Rule became practical politics, the role of the second chamber as a last line of resistance advanced in public attention and Liberal strategy. Labouchere played devil's advocate, indeed, in proposing a series of motions aimed at abolishing it altogether. It was Rosebery's willingness to entertain schemes for mildly redrawing the powers of the Lords that finally turned even the Queen against him during his dreadful government of 1894-5. 'I did not like his talking about revolutions', she said.[63] Though the Liberals failed in the short term to cure themselves of the second chamber, their persistence in attacking the House of Lords was rooted in more than Home Rule. By 1890 that issue had begun to recede in Liberal public argument, not least because the Gladstonians wanted to damp down their internal dissensions over it. During a period when Chamberlain made clear in his speeches that the Unionists would not return to the Liberals even if they repudiated Home Rule, Eddie Hamilton took his usual firm grip on half the truth. It all amounted, he thought, to 'pretty clear proof that it was not Home Rule that really determined them to break away from the Liberal party'.[64] He found it harder to face the fact that Home Rule had not really determined Gladstone to get rid of them in the first place.

Since the defeat of the first Home Rule bill in 1886, the Gladstonians had lowered their voices over most aspects of policy. The conversations about reunion had taken place in the privacy of Harcourt's house. Two discussions about Gladstonian policy took place at Hawarden in 1889 and Althorp in 1891. What emerged from the libraries and dining rooms of these houses was an injunction for everyone to keep quiet and *a fortiori* to keep clear of any details relating to how Home Rule would be implemented. Behind the scenes a battle nevertheless took place between competing strategies. Gladstone himself would speak of nothing but Home Rule; he saw it as a focus for all Liberal sentiment. Closest to him in this judgement stood John Morley, a minister since 1882 and now the man behind the throne. A Liberal intellectual, author and editor, Morley had impressed the political intelligentsia with his book *On Compromise* (1874). Because most people then (and since), did not read beyond the title, an impression gained currency that Morley was in favour of compromise whereas in fact he had argued against it – a forewarning of the countless resignations that Morley would submit to a variety of prime ministers. With inflexibility came also a certain frail pettishness reminiscent of John Russell. Had Morley wanted to supply only what Gladstone needed – an elegant rationale for the Home Rule preoccupation – his career might have turned out happier. But he saw himself as an effective executive politician and nursed an ambition to move out of the Irish back-kitchen, as he called it, and become foreign secretary in the next Liberal government.

The more likely incumbent, Archibald Primrose, fifth Earl of Rosebery, had lost ground in Gladstone's eyes through a thinly veiled dislike of Home Rule as such (he belonged to the imperial wing of the party) and his doubts about the wisdom of concentrating on the single policy. Here was the kernel of an alternative strategy to Gladstone's; but in these years Rosebery concentrated on the politics of the London County Council, with which he was closely associated after 1888, and seemingly lacked the venom necessary to fight Gladstone. For its venom the party went rather to Sir William Harcourt, a formidable constitutional lawyer who had shown himself the only man in the Commons, apart from Gladstone himself, capable of taking on Chamberlain and coming out ahead. In private he savaged opponents, friends and colleagues with the same cheerful bumptiousness; and he pulled no punches with his leader. Harcourt had remained with Gladstone in 1886 for one powerful reason: to succeed him. He disliked Home Rule intensely, not because it contradicted imperialism, because he disliked that as well, but because it offended common sense. The Liberal party lacked two primary resources: supporters and money. To rest the entire Liberal appeal to a 'democratic' electorate on a single Irish policy struck him as more than half mad. If the party needed a wider base, it needed *pari passu* a wider policy, something close to a list of endorsed campaigns – an authorized programme, as it were – to encourage 'faddists' of all colours to support the common cause.

Four years of intra-party haggling after the failure of the round-table discussions produced no resolutions of these differences of approach. Instead they led to an outcome worse than any clear decision might have precipitated; the party agreed to adopt a rag-bag of policy crotchets which embraced Home Rule but also toler-ated every kind of rival to it. Gladstone had lost interest in what the Liberal party did outside Ireland. At a conference of the National Liberal Federation, held in Morley's constituency of Newcastle in September 1891, he acceded to a 'programme' that held everything and nothing like a bottomless net – for the Irish, Home Rule; for the Celtic fringe and the Nonconformists, Scottish and Welsh disestab-lishment; for the unions, an employers' liability bill to compensate workers injured in industrial accidents; for the countryside, new parish councils and land for allotments; for the temperance lobby, local option on whether or not to sell liquor; for the Lib–Labs, payment of MPs; for the democrats, one-man-one-vote and triennial parliaments. Almost no one believed in all of these things. Those who believed in hardly any of them apart from Home Rule joined Morley in believing that the party had run too far and too fast. But Harcourt recalled a lesson now traditional among Liberals. 'In a big storm', he told Morley, 'safety is sometimes to be found only in "cracking on" and we must "run" the ship, she can't "lay to".'[65] Substitute a coach for a ship and the sentence reads like a homily from 1831.

The coming dissolution had preoccupied politicians since the ses-sion of 1891. Salisbury played with the idea of resignation as early as 1890; he had in any case to face the electorate at some point in 1892. Chamberlain pressed for an autumn election in 1892 to give Con-servatives and Unionists time to improve their position in the country. The cabinet, however, chose June. Most Liberals felt by then that they would win: even Harcourt, unconvinced a year before, had come to think so, while Gladstone anticipated a three-figure majority. Some, like Balfour, saw more deeply. The Tory party might lose the election, certainly; but they could hardly remain out for long once the Liberals' antipathies to Home Rule and one another had received reinforcement from the experience of trying to govern. Even if Glad-stone's future ministers confounded such cynicism by discovering a new harmony, the election result, when it came, did not threaten to test Salisbury's patience, for the Liberal majority of forty concealed a return to the neck-and-neck position of the two main parties; the

Liberals won 270 seats in 1892, the Conservatives 268. Unlike the previous occasion, a single extra party did not hold the balance since the Unionists now complicated the picture, though the reduction in their parliamentary strength from 79 to 47 suggested serious erosion in popular support. Within the Liberal figure, the Scottish and Welsh components (31 and 50 respectively) showed more clearly than ever the degree to which Liberalism had shifted its base towards the periphery. From the perspective of these disappointing results, a Home Rule bill could appear only a final gesture from Gladstone before his inevitable retirement.

It is difficult to reconstruct Gladstone's expectations and intentions in 1892–3: possibly they would escape any rational analysis. Widespread rumours that he had lost his reason and become 'half-crazy', an 'old lunatic', a 'dangerous old fanatic', 'the G. O. Madman' may be discounted since they stemmed from imperialists affronted by Home Rule or, more often, the Queen, whose loathing for Gladstone now bordered on the manic. But if the prime minister's mental state was sound, his physical condition had visibly weakened, especially in his hearing and eyesight. Assuming he possessed the stamina to guide a highly contentious bill through the Commons, commentators nevertheless could not see what he hoped to do when the Lords threw it out. He might dissolve, if the Queen let him; but all the electoral evidence of the past few years showed that the Irish question lacked real bite among the British electorate. Perhaps he did not think so far ahead. Certainly he clung to the past in surrounding himself with men of similar stamp. Five of the six Whig ministers who had remained loyal in 1886 received high office: Rosebery (Foreign Office); Spencer (Admiralty); Harcourt (Exchequer); Kimberley (lord president); Ripon (Colonies). The sixth, Granville, had died in 1891. He had a new appointment at the Home Office where Herbert Henry Asquith soon distinguished himself. Some intellectual clothing appeared in the jurist James Bryce, the Unionist renegade G. O. Trevelyan, and A. H. D. Acland who pushed educational priorities with an avidity rarely seen in British high politics and by so doing put on the map a family which was to play a significant role in Liberal politics over the next three generations.

A cabinet committee, centring on Gladstone, Morley and Spencer, worked out the draft of a Home Rule bill: neither Rosebery nor Harcourt had a voice in it. Indeed, circumventing the cabinet became a major preoccupation for Gladstone during this last government. He rarely called one himself and responded to colleagues' requests for a cabinet with hurt weariness.[66] Recrimination and suspicion consequently increased rather than diminished in a 'government of departments' which allowed ministers to plough their own furrows. So far as Home Rule was concerned this remained unimportant because the subject had become academic. In foreign and defence policy, on the other hand, Rosebery and Spencer operated with a free hand in areas of increasing sensitivity whose concerns contributed directly to the collapse of Gladstone's government in 1894 and Rosebery's in 1895.

With one eye on the electorate and another on their promises at Newcastle, the government concerned itself initially with domestic matters through which it hoped to shape an identity. Morley's own base in the north-eastern coalfield left him anxious about a private member's bill proposing an eight-hour day for miners, a sore subject in an area which had already secured shorter hours still. His language about it revealed more than prudence:

> I will have no part in any government that brings in eight hours Bills ...The Labour Party – that is, the most headstrong and unscrupulous and shallow of those who speak for Labour – has captured the Liberal Party. Even worse – the Liberal Party, on our bench at any rate, has surrendered *sans phrase*, without a word of explanation or vindication.[67]

Since he was about to join a government which condoned the shooting of three miners at Featherstone during the strike of 1893, the concern nevertheless requires a sense of perspective. The 'Labour party' existed only as an allegation: it did not come into existence until 1906. And it no more dominated the Liberals in 1892 than did the Women's Liberal Federation which had recently split over the desirability of supporting a women's franchise bill introduced by Sir Albert Rollit (Conservative: South Islington). If fringe politics touched the new government at all, it did so through the rejection for a ministerial place of Henry Labouchere, whose republicanism had not impressed Queen Victoria.

Three elements in the Newcastle Programme looked like practical politics. Home Rule plainly had to come first; employers' liability could be treated alongside it in 1893; and H. H. Fowler, the new president of the Local Government Board, would bring in legislation on parish councils in the following session. The year 1893 would thus offer the House of Lords its greatest moments since the rejection of Gladstone's paper duties in 1860. For although the Home Rule bill struggled through its second reading in the Commons on 21 April with a majority of 43 – a testimony to Gladstone's unique magnetism – the peers swept it away by 419 to 41. Employers' liability died a slower death: the Lords made it useless by surrounding it with amendments and qualifications. In one sense the second chamber's treatment of these and more minor bills played the Liberals' game by giving them a collection of crimes to spread before the electorate in a 'peers versus people' campaign; the Liberal chief whip, Edward Marjoribanks, responded in this way. In the short term, however, it left the government with nothing to tell 'the people', a lesson underlined by its experience at Hereford in August 1893. The sitting member, W. H. Grenfell, later Lord Desborough, resigned his seat in protest against the government's reluctance to move towards bimetallism – a nineties enthusiasm for basing the currency on silver as well as gold in order to cope with a current world dearth of gold deposits. The Liberal candidate then lost the by-election. Harcourt collapsed into one of his sulks and blamed Home Rule. Chamberlain, delighted, blamed the timidity of Asquith's employers' liability bill and told him so. ('He was very cross.')[68] Either way, the augury seemed unpromising for the Liberal message. Hereford stayed Tory for the next twenty years until another economic eccentric, W. A. S. Hewins, won it for the Unionists in 1912.

Even without such indicators of opinion, the cabinet would have resisted Gladstone's instinct to dissolve. Further evidence of the Lords' partisanship – 'filling up the cup', as it was called – seemed the necessary preliminary to asking for a mandate on the second chamber. The hesitancy left Gladstone without direction or purpose. In the second half of 1893 his eyes grew worse and he manifestly could not continue for any long period. Yet he did not resign until an issue arose over which he felt as distant from his colleagues as over Ireland. He chose to make his last stand, like Churchill in 1886, in opposing the estimates of ministers for the armed services; and in order to understand why these had come to attract such attention, we must leave Gladstone searching for his *point d'appui* and turn to Africa, South-east Asia and a changed climate of Anglo-French relations.

At the Foreign Office Rosebery hoped to continue the broad strategy of Salisbury by avoiding entanglements in alliance systems while maximizing amicable sentiment in Germany and France. In the Heligoland–Zanzibar treaty of 1890 the Conservatives had bequeathed to Rosebery a 'solution' to the German difficulty at the expense of the French one. Salisbury had satisfied some German ambition in East Africa and secured the Upper Nile from German penetration via Uganda; but in doing so he had amplified French fears that Britain intended joining the Triple Alliance, which was reaffirmed in 1891, and driven her by August 1891 into the entente with Russia that Bismarck and Salisbury had striven to prevent. This heritage left Rosebery and the more 'imperial' Liberals with three firm feelings:

that Egypt must be retained despite French ambitions to reoccupy the Nile valley; that diplomatic activity, rather than force, would have to suffice to effect that strategy; and that Franco-Russian designs on the empire required the maintenance of the 'Two-Power standard' in capital ships, i.e. that the British force in this respect should match the combined navies of the next two most powerful countries, France and Russia. The foreign secretary's determination to cling on to Uganda despite the worsening financial plight of the Imperial East Africa Company, which had been charged with administering the territory, followed from his decision to delay for the foreseeable future the evacuation of Egypt, despite that policy's forming the cornerstone of Gladstonian thinking about the Middle East and one still aggressively used by Harcourt and Morley. Since Rosebery could extract no money from Harcourt at the Exchequer, he sent out the diplomatist Sir Gerald Portal, ostensibly to report but in fact to implement his own secret instructions to hold Uganda until he, Rosebery, could engineer the declaration of a protectorate – an ambition he accomplished as prime minister in March 1894.

Over the second requirement of a strong naval programme he had little need to plot against Little Englandism because most of his colleagues agreed with him. Gladstone, of course, did not; but almost everyone else had been impressed during the summer of 1893 by what seems in retrospect a moment of farce but which caused serious apprehension among those who lived through it. France's new understanding with Russia had given rise to fears that India might now become the object of a sinister pincer attack from the Russians in the north (the border difficulties had not ended with the Penjdeh incident) and the French striking from their base in Cambodia through Siam and into Burma. Vague descriptions of French naval movements in the Mekong area brought Siam to the centre of political attention in July so that, when a wrongly decoded telegram announced on 31 July that the French had instructed a British gunboat to leave the Mekong river, a twenty-four-hour crisis erupted during which Rosebery gave the French the impression that he was seeking help from the Triple Alliance.[69] Although the mistake soon disclosed itself, the cabinet felt impelled towards maintaining the fleet in good battle order; and Gladstone's one-man campaign of resistance to Spencer's estimates only lasted so long – from December 1893 to his resignation in February 1894 – because ministers worried about the electoral consequences of his removal and tried every ruse to win him round. Yet even those who sent anxious letters and messages to Biarritz, where Gladstone had gone for a rest, saw at once that his alternative – a dissolution – spelled ruination. The preoccupations during these months swung away from Gladstone's demise, therefore, and moved towards the question of the succession.

Gladstone himself saw Spencer as the most appropriate nomination but the Queen, cuttingly, did not ask him for one. Her choice of Rosebery suited her own inclination; he had a patrician background, a facile pen, a charming disposition and a dislike of Home Rule. But it also suited the balance of party feeling. Through that winter of soliciting, the doctrines held by men like Rosebery and Harcourt played little part in determining attitudes.[70] Instead the thinking turned, for all the assiduous canvassing of Harcourt's son 'Loulou', on keeping out of first place a man whose temper would always overpower his judgement. Harcourt had in him more genuine ability and doctrinal conviction than most of his colleagues; but those who had worked with him knew that he bit as hard as he barked. The very contemplation of a Harcourt despotism, for such it must have been, turned even Home Rulers like Morley ultimately towards the easier man. Rosebery soon wished that no one had turned. His fifteen-month ministry of 1894–5 brought humiliation and despair to him personally and a sickening disaster at the polls.

For much of the government's life the prime minister, chancellor of the exchequer and chief secretary for Ireland would not speak to one another. They communicated through intermediaries like estranged parents often do through their children. While Morley brooded in his back-kitchen (Kimberley landed the Foreign Office), Harcourt went his own way with domestic radicalism and Rosebery immersed himself in foreign affairs about which his leading principle had become to keep everything secret from Harcourt. Publicly the government tottered through 1894 without major embarrassment: the local government act put one piece of contentious legislation behind them and by-elections did not run too badly. But in private the correspondence between ministers burned the fingers. When Rosebery expressed to Harcourt, in a weak moment, mild reservations over the death duties that the chancellor proposed to introduce in his 1894 budget, he received an enormous memorandum which contained, amid the abuse, a point of considerable interest to historians examining the relics of one of Britain's last premiers to come from the leisure class.

You desire to avert the 'cleavage of classes' – The hope on your side is natural but you are too late. 'The horizontal division of parties' was certain to come as a consequence of household suffrage. The thin end of the wedge was inserted, and the cleavage is expanding more and more every day. I do not wonder at your casting a longing lingering look on the 'variety and richness and intellectual forces' which have passed away, but these are not the appanage of democracy.[71]

Neither, of course, was Rosebery himself. Even his horses let him down when they won the Derby in this and the following year, compounding the impression of a dilettante politician playing at statesmanship. Rosebery's supposed area of specialism – foreign policy – no longer corrected it. His panicky attempt to keep the French away from the Nile by setting up a treaty with the Belgians in order to block access through the Congo brought an explosion of temper from his colleagues, when they eventually found out about it, and a barrage of criticism from Paris and Berlin that persuaded Rosebery to withdraw his own treaty.

By the end of 1894 a dribble of by-election defeats had reduced the Liberal majority to about thirty. The government stood in acute need of an issue that would pull the party together again. Gladstone could no longer provide one for the cabinet; he was now in retirement and died in 1898. His last speech in the House of Commons had pointed a finger at the Lords. 'The question is whether the work of the House of Lords is not merely to modify, but to annihilate the whole work of the House of Commons.'[72] This offered one strategy; but of course Gladstone's fury at the behaviour of the second chamber had arisen from the peers' rejection of his Home Rule bill. The cabinet wanted to forget Home Rule as soon as practicable, especially after Rosebery had incensed Liberals and nationalists alike by recently referring to England as the 'predominant partner' in the discussion. Another piece of the Newcastle Programme would have to be tried. Yet the issue chosen – the disestablishment of the Welsh Church – hardly summoned up outside Wales the emotion of 1868–9. Its purpose consisted simply in the certainty of its rejection by the Lords. But it seemed especially irrelevant to a public opinion charged with a sense of imperial mission as a war scare swept through the press in the spring of 1895. It remains unclear whether Rosebery instigated the 'Grey declaration' in March. Certainly Edward Grey's statement to the House of Commons that any French approach to the Nile would be considered 'an unfriendly act' by the British government caused in Anglo-French relations a *frisson* that would be felt again during the Fashoda incident of 1898. It revived not only public xenophobia but a serious concern over defence; and in so doing it inadvertently supplied the background for the government's collapse. A snap division in the Commons on 21 June 1895 successfully recommended that the salary of Rosebery's war minister, Sir Henry Campbell-Bannerman, be reduced, to punish his failure to supply sufficient cordite to the army. The 'cordite vote' itself supplied an absurd end to an absurd ministry.[73] Having outfaced Gladstone's refusal to countenance guns, Rosebery tripped over the explosives needed to fire them, just as another Liberal imperialist, Asquith, would stumble twenty years later during the first season of the most terrible war in the history of man.

At least a parliamentary defeat gave the government a chance of escape and its leader the prospect of his first night's sleep for months. Salisbury came back as prime minister but only on the strict understanding that he would dissolve parliament at once. During that election in July 1895 Rosebery prayed for defeat and received it on a scale that devastated his party. Some historians would date the downfall of the great Liberal party of Mill and Gladstone from this moment: certainly, its 177 MPs looked forlorn enough. But then, the party had failed, through lack of money and enthusiasm, even to contest 185 seats; and in that sense the result seems less a defeat than an abdication. Send politics to the devil, Campbell-Bannerman said, and most of the ministers took his advice: they scattered for the summer and autumn. Meanwhile Salisbury added 341 Conservatives to 70 Unionists and discovered that his nephew Arthur Balfour would claim the support of over 400 MPs when parliament reconvened – a very happy prospect. For a time the adhesion of Chamberlain might have looked in doubt, but surely the election would dispel his uncertainties. One wonders whether Devonshire told Salisbury of a letter he had received from Chamberlain earlier in the year when he had been the victim of Tory press attacks. 'I would not give a brass button', he had said 'to fill any office that is likely to be within my reach.'[74] As Chamberlain stormed back into government for his greatest period of imperial responsibility, the eighth Duke perhaps allowed himself just the hint of a smile.

6

Breaking the Mould?

Imperial politics (1895–1905)

Throughout the disruption of Liberalism after 1892, the coalition of
Conservatives and Unionists had itself come under strain. Chamberlain's support for parish councils, death duties and Welsh disestablishment, compounded by the determination of Liberal Unionist peers to
maintain their separate identity in the House of Lords, raised questions over the inclusion of dissident Liberals in the next Tory government.[1] When Rosebery's party so patently came apart, however, the
Unionists found themselves with nowhere to go, short of leaving
political life altogether. Chamberlain and Devonshire's acceptance of
office from Salisbury in 1895 does not, to that extent, demand much
explanation. The posts they chose have given historians more difficulty. Devonshire refused the Foreign Office and took the lord presidency of the council: he presumably saw the absurdity of keeping
Salisbury out of the department he knew better than anyone else. Yet
by so doing he inadvertently brought into his own hands a major party
problem because his office held the responsibility for framing policy
on education, a subject over which he found himself opposing senior
colleagues during the next seven years. Chamberlain's refusal of the
Exchequer and preference for the Colonial Office raises deeper questions. We have already observed Chamberlain's sentiments about
colonial policy in the late 1880s and his expectation that one day he
would take charge of it. But he had also believed it obvious that he
would become prime minister, and the move may have to be set within
a wider strategy. Had he gone to the Exchequer his position would
have required of him some positive thoughts about free trade and
protection; perhaps he did not feel ready to commit himself. After
all, when he did offer his positive thoughts in 1903 he reached a point
of no return in his own career and warped the framework of discussion familiar to Salisbury and Balfour.

All this lay in the future. For the moment Hatfield smiled with a geniality which surprised close observers of the prime minister.

> He is literally in love with Chamberlain. I never heard him talk of any colleague as he does of him, says Chamberlain wants to go to war with every Power in the World and has no thought but Imperialism. The Cabinet so united that he can not get them to deliberate for a decent time, they disperse in half an hour.[2]

Salisbury's honeymoon with Chamberlain and the cabinet soon ended. By 1897 his colonial minister no longer saw eye-to-eye with him over the need to proceed cautiously in the Transvaal or over the related subject of avoiding any overt Anglo-German alliance. At home the schools and the farmers lengthened the cabinets and convinced Devonshire – he had learned what he knew from Gladstone – that Salisbury would do better to avoid holding them.[3] Instead, the prime minister increasingly had recourse to sleep during the longer discussions as the years caught up and his health began to give way. His sense of management weakened; he relied heavily on Balfour and Chamberlain to control the Commons and adopted a posture of benign negativity to the issues raised by colleagues.

Across from him in cabinet sat the Duke of Devonshire, plainly hating every minute of it but conscious of his responsibility, determined to do his best and alert to the onset of 'mischief'. He brought to educational policy a suspicion of his vice-president, Sir John Gorst, and a magnificent despair in face of the subject's complexity. When someone told him of a recent suicide during the crisis of 1901–2, his first thought was to ask whether the deceased had anything to do with the education bill. Sheer incomprehension nonetheless drove Devonshire into achieving, first an acquaintance with, but eventually a mastery of the political and administrative difficulties; and by 1902 he had become a respected spokesman on his specialism. Balfour and Chamberlain, the other key men, stood in fear of no one in the Commons, except perhaps Asquith and the savage little Welshman, David Lloyd George. Yet once these names are acknowledged, it seems difficult to sustain the frequently encountered judgement that Salisbury's third ministry brought together a team of great strength. This thought occurred, if only through a mixture of Liberal reverence and wooden prejudice, to Edward Hamilton as he cast his mind back over the previous administration and compared it with the present one:

> a strong Cabinet no doubt; but I do not know that man for man it is really stronger than the late Cabinet ... The fact is, the late Government was a very successful administrative body. I never knew a better. It was

(essentially) 'a Government by Departments'; but a very strong Government viewed as such. There were some weak members of it – notably G. Trevelyan and S[haw] Lefevre; but there were never more efficient or popular Ministers at the War Office and Admiralty than C[ampbell] Bannerman and Lord Spencer; Fowler was excellent at the India Office...; Asquith was a first-rate Home Secretary; Lord Herschell an excellent Chancellor and man in council; Arnold Morley was a good Postmaster General; Acland did well at the Education Office; and John Morley administered affairs in Ireland with success, disappointing though he was in many other ways. Harcourt has left his mark on Finance, and is admitted to have led the House of Commons with conspicuous dexterity and ability. As to Rosebery, perhaps I may not be impartial. In many quarters he is said to have been a failure and a disappointment as Prime Minister and to have shewn less political nerve than was expected. But I am convinced that, if the difficulties with which he had to contend...are properly appreciated, the wonder is that he managed to carry on with the success he did for over 15 months ...[H]e is more far-seeing than most of his colleagues, and thus has real statesman-like qualities of the highest order.[4]

Even without so glowing a contrast between Rosebery's team and Salisbury's it seemed clear that the latter would have his problems. The Cabinet contained a disproportionate number of Unionists who did little to advance the government's reputation. Alfred Lyttleton's success came early in life when his prowess as a tennis-player and first-class cricketer, which earned him the admiration of W. G. Grace, compensated in Tory circles for his mother's being a sister-in-law of Gladstone. None of those qualities helped him follow Chamberlain in the Colonial Office after 1903. Even the childhood of H. O. Arnold-Forster, Lyttleton's colleague at the War Office, undermined him. He had Thomas Arnold of Rugby as a grandfather, Matthew Arnold (the Liberal essayist) as an uncle, and Mr and Mrs W. E. Forster as guardians after he was orphaned. As a spokesman on army, naval and imperial affairs he made some progress in Tory company and confirmed his Unionism by sitting for West Belfast from 1892. As a minister he seemed to most observers a failure.

Salisbury's own party contributed its share of inert matter. He regretted his experiment with Sir Matthew White Ridley at the Home Office almost at once and was glad to see him retire in 1900. He made a blatant error in promoting Henry Chaplin, squire of Blankney in Lincolnshire, whose 15,000 acres had qualified him for the Board of Agriculture in the second government of 1886–92 but unfitted him for the Local Government Board, where he spoke about bimetallism, protection and the importance of becoming the farmers' friend. In one sense this seemed merely comical in a man who spent more than was prudent on racehorses and the Prince of Wales (a friend from Christ Church days).[5] But it also irritated because Chaplin's language, learned principally from Lord Henry Bentinck – whose by-election disappointments in Nottinghamshire we have already encountered – helped give the government a rural ambience when it had no Marshall or Snelgrove to redeem it. (Smith was dead; Cross had lost his force.) In the last government, northern industry had found an entrée in W. L. Jackson, a Leeds leather merchant and tanner, who had brought into the administration 'middle-class tact and judgement', as Balfour engagingly recalled, 'but good of their kind'.[6] He had begun as Churchill's protégé, however, which started him on the wrong foot, and had failed as chief secretary for Ireland; he did not hold office again. A substitute of sorts appeared at the Board of Trade in the figure of Charles Thomson Ritchie whose experience in his father's jutespinning business in London and Dundee gave him a free trade crotchet that would become important in 1903; but, again, Ritchie's political base remained in three London constituencies which he represented between 1874 and 1905: he brought none of the flavour of northern industrialism. Normally a Tory leader could rely on a 'king of Lancashire' to steady, from his palace at Knowsley, the forces of Conservatism in that all-important area. But Salisbury's king hardly counted as more than a prince in 1895; and if the thirty-year-old Lord Stanley promised great things when he became seventeenth Earl of Derby, for the moment he could go no higher than junior office.

Turning its face towards the past helped the government look in two dangerous directions in its domestic policy. First, it reflected an anxiety over rural depression that encouraged ministers to contemplate subsidizing the farmers. Over the three years of Liberal government wheat prices had fallen lower than at any time during the nineteenth century, and the cabinet responded to what it took to comprise its central constituency with an agricultural land rating bill to reduce the responsibility of landowners for rates, with the Exchequer making up the deficit to local authorities. Party leaders plainly sensed that the squires felt 'still sore and uneasy' about Ritchie's undermining of their local power in the local government act. Chaplin's bill passed only at the expense of an embarrassing revolt on the back benches and the promise of a Royal Commission on urban grievances.[7] A similar sensitivity urged the leadership towards legislating on voluntary schools, whose situation had changed in important respects since 1870. The denominational schools, often the only ones available in rural areas, had become financially disadvantaged compared with the urban 'board' schools. In its new system of county and borough councils, the government possessed ready-made 'local education authorities', should it wish to use them; and no less than three educational commissions had recommended that responsibility for the schools should pass to these bodies. The problems lay in the question of the voluntary schools. If the cabinet proposed their inclusion in a national scheme, it could count on facing concerted opposition from Nonconformists for putting Anglican teaching on the rates. It would also make difficult the position of Chamberlain, whose embarrassments as a former Unitarian already filled a folder. The bill with which the cabinet struggled needed, therefore, to walk many tightropes, and through the session of 1896 it fell off most of them. It did not seek to subsidize voluntary schools from the rates but it did offer to lend them money. It did not compel denominational teaching anywhere but it allowed a school to adopt it at the request of a 'reasonable' number of parents – a proposal that not only rescinded the Cowper-Temple clause of 1870 but presented an obvious hostage to fortune in its vagueness. When the bill staggered out of committee under the weight of more than a thousand amendments the government withdrew it. At the end of the year, one close observer of Tory politics recorded in his diary: 'Politically a damaging session – Education Bill and Mr. Balfour's leadership much attacked...'[8]

Worries of this kind showed a certain lack of perspective, as did the wild dreams of those who believed that the government would see its majority disappear. Few Liberals thought so: they knew that they faced the biggest composite majority since 1832. It was rather on the Tory side that some chafing occurred over the government's misman-agement of legislation and its undeniable lack of panache. At a time of supposed imperial opportunity, few laurels could be won in spending an entire session, as in 1898, talking about an Irish local government bill. In March, one of its more vitriolic back-benchers, shocked by recent reverses in by-elections, reminded the government that 'the God of Battles is no lover of tomorrow. Failure to act...is today the theme of every Radical canvasser in East Berks, as it was in Stepney and Maidstone. It will, if persisted in, dissipate a majority of 150.'[9] This was nonsense: a few by-election reverses gave little cause for alarm and the record of the government over the five years after 1895 – fourteen losses, three gains – hardly compromised its effectiveness. Stepney caused a flurry because, uniquely, it went to a Lib–Lab candidate. But for the most part the government took no cognizance of the ILP or the SDF. Against its disappointments could be ranged certain notable successes, as when the Liberal MP for Great Grimsby joined the Unionists and then held the seat in a by-election with an increased majority. Observers registered their satisfaction, indeed, at the listlessness of the House of Commons and noted that, once education receded in 1897, only in debates on foreign and imperial affairs did the benches stir. This mood reversed, of course, a feeling of boredom we have seen time and again in nineteenth-century politics about foreign policy; and no one reversed it so dramatically as Chamberlain in his new clothes as colonial minister. When Lord Esher dined with him in 1898, he noticed how little Chamberlain's conversation impinged on education, Ireland, agriculture or any of the issues on which the early radicalism had focused. 'He talked of China and West Africa, and of France and Russia, with an amplitude of view and phrase that would have astonished Birmingham ten years ago. He has lately had a strong difference of opinion with Lord S. He believes we are at the parting of the ways, and that we must stand fast for Imperial expansion now or never, whatever the result.'[10]

This global understanding of priorities strengthened markedly after 1895. Its origins may be traced to a pervasive sense of isolation in diplomacy – one reinforced in 1895 when even America became bellicose against Britain over a boundary dispute between Venezuela and British Guiana – and a recognition of the mounting importance of an agreement with Russia. Any sympathy with the Triple Alliance had largely evaporated since Salisbury secured the eastern approaches to the Upper Nile: no atmosphere existed in which a revival of the Mediterranean Agreements might become a priority. Preventing French incursions into the Sudan from the west and ensuring that, if they happened, Russia would not join in, seemed the more pressing considerations. To keep Russia sweet, on the other hand, would involve sacrifice, and the first to be offered was Constantinople, the linchpin of foreign policy since the Crimea. To the horror of Vienna, Salisbury backed away from regarding Russian ambitions in the Balkans as a premier British concern. A second concession appeared in China where a scramble for territory took place in 1897. The German seizure of Kiaochow and Russia's occupation of Port Arthur brought only a mild response from Britain, despite some pressure from public opinion at home. By the same token Salisbury gave the French an easy time in West Africa in order to distract them from designs on the British sphere of influence. Now Chamberlain, and to some extent Balfour, disagreed with this view of priorities. Chamberlain saw more sense in reaching out towards Berlin than in caressing St Petersburg and Paris: he looked, without success, to an Anglo-German alliance that would permit imperial expansion to run forward without concession to any other Great Power. Giving France a

piece of commercial West Africa struck him as too high a price to pay
in a country with the greatest navy in the world. 'We ought –' he told
his under-secretary, *even at the cost of war* – to keep the hinter-
land.'[11] For the moment his centre of attention could hardly be filled
by the problem. 'Preoccupied', as Professor Marsh writes, 'during the
parliamentary session of 1897 with the Jameson raid inquiry, workmen's compensation and the colonial conference, Chamberlain did
not have much time for the despatches about French encroachment
on the territory of the Royal Niger Company.'[12] But the divergence of
view with Salisbury marked their first conflict. The latter's amusement at Chamberlain's readiness to go to war with everybody had
long since turned to irritation. By 1897 Salisbury had grown nervous
of his colonial minister's enthusiasm for confronting either the French
(though he felt it necessary to accede to much of it) or, as seemed ever
more likely, the Boers of the Transvaal.

President Kruger's wealthy republic had not required the emergence of a chauvinist colonial secretary to enter on a dangerous
collision course with Cape Colony and Cecil Rhodes. British settlers
in the Transvaal (known as *Uitlanders*) had followed the scent of gold
and diamonds and stuck to their homesteads despite the Kruger
government's refusal to grant basic civil rights and its imposition of
disproportionate taxation. Urgency entered the situation from a
diplomatic point of view when German capital began to make itself
felt. If Kruger continued in his apparent flirtation with Berlin, the
British government could face a European threat to its most important strategic asset – the Cape – or at the very least economic
debilitation there when Kruger's railway to Delagoa Bay in Mozambique gave him an independent supply line. Rhodes chose to meet this
prospect head-on by contriving to depose Kruger by armed force. His
company agent in Rhodesia, Dr Leander Starr Jameson, was encouraged to launch an invasion of the Transvaal in December 1895 to
coincide with an uprising of the *Uitlanders*. News of the 'Jameson
raid' reached London on the last day of the year and a double crisis
erupted at once. First, a telegram of congratulation from Kaiser
Wilhelm to the Boer leader for his speedy crushing of the insurrection
provoked a mood of Germanophobia in British public opinion; and,
second, as the raid petered into fiasco, questions began to be asked
about the government's complicity.

The degree of Chamberlain's involvement may forever remain
unclear. We know that he had, contrary to his emphatic statements
at the time, been informed that the raid would take place. Earl Grey,
who himself told Chamberlain of the plan, later attested that he,
Chamberlain, 'was led to believe that the inevitable Revolution was

about to take place & he very properly took precautions to ensure its success when it came about'.[13] In public, Chamberlain protested his innocence and dealt with the British problem in South Africa by despatching Milner to become governor of the Cape in 1897. The German side of the difficulty required some diplomatic finesse; but by 1898 Salisbury had won from the Germans a limited treaty to exclude all third parties from Mozambique in case 'it may unfortunately not be found possible to maintain the integrity of the African possessions of Portugal south of the Equator',[14] and to guarantee the security of Delagoa Bay. But Kruger's intransigence, Milner's unremitting imperialism and the enthusiasm of Chamberlain and Selborne at home conspired to keep the Transvaal problem alive and propel it towards a military confrontation.[15] The bludgeoning and intricate negotiations that characterized relations between Britain and the Transvaal in 1898 and 1899 cannot be analysed here; but when Kruger presented his ultimatum demanding the removal of British troops massing on his frontier in October 1899, the opening of the Boer war surprised few people in Britain. The fears held by Beach, Balfour and occasionally Salisbury that aggression would prove a mistake lost their relevance as the nation mobilized for a war that it ought to have won in a matter of months.

On the other hand, the sense of imperial fever that some politicians wished upon the public proved less evident than they might have hoped. Among politicians it could also prove elusive when events of the past year in another part of Africa had lent the recent crisis an ambience of *déjà vu*. For just twelve months before Kruger's ultimatum, the French had put European peace in jeopardy by marching into the Sudan where, at Fashoda, they ran into General Kitchener. For a moment Salisbury himself seemed genuinely nervous, more so than most of his colleagues who saw war with the French as inevitable. And even though the French had backed down, the sense of an impending fight somewhere breaks out of the correspondence of politicians. In the years after 1895 a sizeable proportion of parliamentary time had been spent in the discussion of service estimates which gave rise to bitter exchanges in both the cabinet and the House. Indeed, Lansdowne, the war secretary, came close to leaving the government because of the negative attitude of his colleagues on this issue. Even as war became a real possibility in the autumn of 1899, ministers went away on holiday as usual, untroubled by accusations of 'flippancy'. Their embarrassment when war was declared increased as the campaign turned into a shambles. Under General Sir Redvers Buller the army suffered a series of reverses over the winter which focused attention on the problem of relieving beleaguered garrisons at Kimberley and Ladysmith and a largely civilian population in the town of Mafeking. Only when General 'Bobs' Roberts replaced Buller and the sieges were lifted in the spring of 1900 did some tension leave Westminster and allow the non-service ministers, in anticipation of eventual victory in the field, to turn their minds to more pressing matters at home.

A wave of national thanksgiving washed into cities and towns and left behind street-names such as 'Ladysmith Road' and 'Mafeking Terrace'. At Westminster this manifest joy could mean only one thing in the sixth year of a parliament. Salisbury dissolved in September 1900 and a 'khaki' election in October did everything that the Conservative party desired of it. With 236 constituencies uncontested, Liberal gains amounted to a derisory nine and left the Tory–Unionist coalition facing another five or six years of power. Not so its leader. Speculation had already mounted about Salisbury's capacity to see out the war. His feel for public opinion lacked the immediacy of old; little had been seen of him during a recent severe illness. Some Unionists believed that the succession of the Duke of Devonshire would promote an early fusion between the two sections of the coalition. Among the Balfour supporters, and especially for his influential private secretary Jack Sandars, a disadvantage might soon become evident in the power that a Unionist prime minister would allow to Chamberlain.[16] In fact Chamberlain exerted no great effort to put Devonshire into first place: he felt equally happy with Balfour, perhaps more so in that he at least would not trifle with Rosebery who was showing signs of staging a comeback as an independent imperialist. Nor did Chamberlain share Devonshire's conviction about free trade, a subject of no small importance in 1900 since Beach's budget had introduced a duty on corn to help with the war's expenditure. For the time being these great designs impinged only at moments of leisure or anger. Commentators simply noted significant changes in cabinet personnel – Lansdowne's taking the weight of the Foreign Office from Salisbury's shoulders, Ritchie's appearance at the Home Office, and the rise of an ambitious young man in George Wyndham as the new chief secretary for Ireland.

The surrender of the Boers, daily expected, did not come. Rather, a protracted guerrilla war ensued and consumed the energies of the British War Office for another two humiliating years. Chamberlain's unease developed in proportion with that embarrassment; for the issue on which he had hoped to build a new relationship with his public – the grandeur and potential for peaceful improvement invested in the British empire – had lost much of its force in Britain's seeming inability to curb the pretensions of the Boer farmers. Inevitably his fellow politicians had begun to return to the domestic battles of the late 1890s, especially that of education. They had, indeed, little choice but to do so. On the very eve of the war a government auditor called Cockerton had declared invalid the schools' provision of anything resembling 'secondary' education as a charge on the local rates; and in the wake of that decision the government would have to evolve a policy for this sector and do it quickly. Since the Cockerton decision had national implications, moreover, the cabinet could not easily tackle the problem in a piecemeal fashion as it had tried to do between 1897 and 1899. Consequently it found the perplexity over an education bill a primary call on its attention once it had survived the death of Queen Victoria in January 1901. Devonshire and Balfour clearly wanted a broad-ranging bill to integrate state and voluntary arrangements, notwithstanding the opposition of Nonconformists. Chamberlain's upbringing and the character of his electoral support demanded that he behave more circumspectly; it distressed him to see the spectre of state subventions for denominational schools becoming practical politics once more. A similar echo of past controversy returned from Ireland. This government's land act had done no more to solve the problems of Irish land tenure than had those of previous administrations since 1870. Wyndham's determination to do better, coupled with the readiness of nationalist leaders to join in talks and (a critical element) the appointment to the under-secretaryship in Dublin Castle of a brilliant Catholic, Sir Antony MacDonnell, threatened to bring Gladstone's preoccupation of 1870 back to centre-stage.

Chamberlain saw in these developments a winding-back of the clock, not to the heroism of Gladstone's early radicalism, but rather to the miserable years of the late 1880s and early 1890s with their concentration on intra-party squabbling as opposed to that imperial thinking in which he had hoped to educate his colleagues. He tried to tug them away from these trivialities with his rhetoric in favour of an Anglo-German understanding; and he detected in the war's corn duty a possible ground on which to build. The economic dimension of imperialism had interested him for some years, if not since 1882 as he later claimed. Canada's granting preferential treatment to British manufactures when they entered her tariff system after 1897 had impressed him, especially since he had gained considerable knowledge of the working of the Canadian economy in his Newfoundland trip of 1887–8. In the jubilee year of 1897 he tried to persuade delegates at the colonial conference to come to a general understanding along these lines, but without success. Precedents existed, therefore, for Chamberlain's suggestion to the cabinet that it should persist in the corn duty after the end of the war while waiving it on imports from the empire. Yet time had virtually run out for him. The war ended in the Treaty of Vereeniging of May 1902; and when Salisbury retired in July his departure brought to the Exchequer a violent free trader in C. T. Ritchie. Nothing decisive emerged at once: the cabinet agreed to return to the problem when Ritchie framed his budget for 1903. But when Chamberlain left in the autumn of 1902 for the tour of South Africa that he had promised himself, he probably realized that a major *démarche* would be necessary if his policy and position were to be saved. Even before he set sail, his future had come into question when he suffered a serious cab accident. And the head injuries that he sustained not only contributed to the later collapse of his health but took him out of political circulation at an important moment in the drawing of the education bill.

Originally the cabinet, according to its Anglican critics, had 'funked' the issue, in two senses: it had voted by a narrow majority to apply its new measure only to secondary education; and it had allowed Chamberlain and the Nonconformists a conscience-clause – an educational version of 'local option' which left authorities free to decide whether they would conform to the act in their area of jurisdiction. Both of these limitations now fell away. The first proved unequal to the force of a powerful civil servant, Sir Robert Morant, who bullied the government into retracting its partial approach. The second seemed weaker the instant Chamberlain went into hospital; and Balfour took his chance to drop it. As a rash of by-election defeats underlined the unpopularity of the government, Chamberlain overtly blamed Devonshire for his failing to anticipate, as an ex-Liberal, the popular reaction in the country against what had come to be seen as an attack on Dissent. 'I told you that your Education Bill would ruin your own party... Our best friends are leaving us by the scores and hundreds and they will not come back.'[17] While he wintered in the Cape the bill became law – abolishing the boards of 1870, transferring control to county and borough councils, and bringing all schools in the public sector under a common system of finance. By the time Chamberlain returned in March 1903 a campaign of passive resistance, organized with considerable flair in Wales and more patchily so in England (where the Baptist John Clifford came to prominence following the death of the Welsh leader, Hugh Price Hughes), had given the government a minor embarrassment and irritation. The colonial secretary now determined on giving it a major one.

'Economic retaliation', 'imperial preference', 'tariff reform': his new policy had many names, each with nuances of meaning to be separated and rehearsed *ad nauseam* as the coalition publicly tore itself apart over the next three years. Why Chamberlain decided to launch a unilateral campaign of this kind in May 1903 still presents formidable interpretative problems that are not dissimilar from those that bedevil the understanding of Gladstone's rush towards Home Rule. One may see Chamberlain as a prophet inspired by imperial doctrine, sick of tergiversation, heedless of party complication, intent on throwing everything into one last campaign to rouse the British people into sharing his vision of the empire's future. Seen from another angle, he seems a party maverick, mindful of poor by-election results in the spring of 1903, resentful (the charge of corridor gossip) at Wyndham's rise to prominence with his Irish land bill, depressed at Ritchie's determination to repeal the corn tax, clear that he must reorient the government's priorities if he was to fulfil his destiny and *lead*. To have questioned Salisbury's leadership could only have made him appear absurd; but Salisbury no longer mattered. Balfour's colleagues, by contrast, called the prime minister 'Arthur' and enjoyed the otiose manner which an urban radical might mistake for plasticity. Perhaps we gain some perspective by asking what else Chamberlain could have done. The colonial secretary had had his moment in the war but nothing substantial had come of it. No Conservative premier would offer him the Exchequer again now that his views on the fiscal issue had been clarified through his attacks on Ritchie: to do so would invite the shrill resistance of Tory free traders. The Foreign Office held few attractions after Lansdowne had made closer relations with Russia and France prime desiderata. Besides, who would give it to him? Ahead stretched a period of patent frustration and decline unless he could find an elixir from somewhere.

The speech Chamberlain made to his Birmingham constituents on 15 May 1903 – the first since his return from South Africa – can too easily be read backwards from 1904 or 1905 and portrayed as a breaking-point with Conservatism. In fact he offered a few restrained reflections about 'our children' in the colonies and invited his audience to think about preferential tariffs for the empire. He placed economic considerations last among his reasons for recommending his policy and he distanced himself from 'protection' as a system.[18] Free traders nevertheless saw in Chamberlain's language a threat to party cohesion. Hicks Beach had retired at the same time as Salisbury but he now acted as a convener of anti-tariff Tories along with Salisbury's talented but unbalanced son Hugh Cecil. Inside the cabinet Ritchie and Balfour of Burleigh (no relation to the prime minister) articulated a similar resistance; the Duke of Devonshire did not, at this stage, articulate anything particular, but he mumbled a good deal and obviously frowned on Chamberlain's behaviour. When the colonial secretary continued his theme in the Commons by identifying tariff reform as the sole instrument for financing future welfare provisions, a free trade lobby of about sixty Tories and Unionists launched a Free Food League in July 1903. Their title was sharply pointed: if Chamberlain intended to create a serious tariff structure he would have to envisage placing import duties on food; and every politician could see the consequences of trying to sell that proposal to his constituents. By the summer of 1903 Balfour clearly faced a significant difficulty and he announced to colleagues that the matter would be thrashed out at a cabinet meeting on 14 September.[19] Five days before the critical meeting, Chamberlain sent Balfour a letter of resignation. He could, he said, 'best promote the cause I have at heart from outside', and added that his attitude to the government would remain loyal. Presumably he supposed that Balfour would tremble at the thought of Chamberlain's stumping the country and consequently refuse to accept his resignation. Perhaps he believed that the veiled threat would drive Balfour further along the tariff road than he had heretofore come. Or perhaps he reasoned that, if Balfour let him resign, the cabinet would turn against the prime minister and he, Chamberlain, would return in triumph. What he did not expect from Balfour was virtuosity.

Just before the cabinet on 14 September Balfour saw Chamberlain and gave him the impression that he agreed with Chamberlain's wish to go while promising that he would support Chamberlain's policy from within. He told the cabinet nothing at all about Chamberlain's thinking, leaving the latter to speak in general and ambiguous terms of his determination to resign. He then sacked Ritchie and Balfour of Burleigh with a summary savagery that enabled many colleagues to appreciate for the first time how he had come by his Irish reputation. Fiscal reform could no longer carry the status of an 'open question'; but neither, ministers soon learned, could it be given any other clear status when Balfour surrounded all discussion of it in an impenetrable verbiage designed (successfully) to confuse the Duke of Devonshire into thinking that Balfour was somehow still a free trader.[20] When the bitter victims of the prime minister's axe told Devonshire in monosyllables that Balfour had tricked him into staying in the cabinet, Balfour responded by turning up at Devonshire House with

Chamberlain's resignation letter: proof positive that no free trader need leave a government from which Chamberlain wished to dissociate himself. In sum, the premier had rid himself of his most tetchy protectionist and his most intransigent free traders while keeping hold of the one man whose departure might rock the boat. His tactics had been sordid, disingenuous and quite brilliant. Therein, sadly, lay their sole weakness. Only if everyone acted with Balfour's finesse and rationality would the scheme work; and since it hinged on the future behaviour of the Duke of Devonshire it soon proved its fragility. Devonshire could not sleep; the Duchess nagged him; he received distressing letters from people he respected; he felt, unreasonably but unbearably, that he had let down his friends. In October 1903 he resigned from Balfour's government, never again to hold public office. Even Balfour barely managed to conceal his fury.

Once Devonshire had gone, Chamberlain ceased to represent the most urgent problem on Balfour's horizon. The tariff reformers comprised a clear minority in the parliamentary party. Moreover, he not only had Chamberlain's private and public assurances of loyalty, but also exercised through his promotion of Chamberlain's son, Austen, to the Exchequer a powerful grip over any waywardness from the ex-minister. More significant still, in the wake of Devonshire's returning to the centre of the party spectrum, might be the attempts of Liberals to strike up an understanding with the Unionists; and by the end of the year more than one observer had speculated on the chances of a Devonshire–Rosebery coalition. Education policy would obviously present a major obstacle to such a proposal but negotiations between the two sides did not break down until February 1904 and until then they supplied a cardinal item in the preoccupations of politicians in both major parties. Thereafter, the free trade element became less significant as tariff reformers ran aground on a tide of rising exports – impossible to achieve, according to them, without protection – and a string of poor by-elections at the beginning of 1904. It seemed increasingly to Chamberlain that only one development would give his cause the leverage it needed: the loss of the next general election. 'For our position would be impossible if we won', he told Austen Chamberlain, 'and then found that we were as far off our Imperial policy as ever.'[21] He achieved the ambition – he usually did – in 1906. Until then he could only watch helplessly as Balfour tried to turn discussion elsewhere and eventually recede in his imperial policy to the point at which he could not envisage tariff reform until a colonial conference had agreed to it and a Conservative government had fought a 'second' election specifically on the tariff issue. It appeared to most observers a postponement *sine die*.

In February 1904 the outbreak of war between Russia and Japan gave Balfour some relief by pushing foreign policy to the fore and emphasizing the urgency of a better understanding with the French. Since 1902 policy had consisted of attempting to constrain Russia in the Far East, as in the Anglo-Japanese alliance of that year, while doing everything possible to break the dual alliance between Russia and France. Tariff reform had functioned well inside this framework; an influential pamphlet of 1896, *Made in Germany*, had already implied logical links between economic protection and anti-German sentiment.[22] The rapid expansion of Germany's naval programme suggested in any case that there might be more to fear in German chauvinism than Russian. And if it impressed British politicians in this way, then it more than convinced the French. Consequently the resolution of colonial difficulties with the French government and the announcement in April 1904 of a new *entente cordiale* represented an important move in the recasting of the alliance system, one which the Anglo-Russian Convention of 1907 would complete. But Balfour's government won little acclaim for it. An impression fostered during the spring of 1904 that the government had lost its way and become moribund proved impossible quickly to dispel. An unemployed work-men's bill in 1905, prefiguring in minor key the Liberal legislation of a few years later, perhaps reassured the left wing of the party. A strong Aliens Act in 1905, though it turned out less strong than the failed bill of 1904, commented on fears of immigration from Russian and Polish Jews fleeing the pogroms of the 1890s, but more centrally set out to appease the anti-semitic right in the parliamentary party.[23] Yet the opposition continued to call the tune. Rather than condone a vision of imperial necessity during the Boer war, the Liberals had popularized their aversion to 'methods of barbarism'. In the peace-time reconstruction that followed they had pointed to the use of Chinese slave labour in South Africa. Wyndham's land act had drowned in the uproar produced by its author's tragedy in 1905 as the disclosures came of how MacDonnell had twisted the Irish secretary around his finger when he persuaded the minister to give unthinking sanction to plans for radical devolution. The scandal advanced Wyndham's alcoholism and brought him to resignation in the spring. The licensing bill of 1904 had scarcely fared better: the opposition had derided it as a brewers' whitewash. In the education bill they had discerned an Anglican ramp. As his problems mounted, Balfour did not face the demoralized and pathetic factions his uncle had confronted ten years before. Each passing day secured more agreement that the next government would be a Liberal one and Sir Henry Campbell-Bannerman its improbable master.

Old Liberals – and new (1896–1906)

Humiliation at the polls in 1895 had driven Liberal politicians into a strange frame of mind from which they largely failed to escape until Chamberlain struck his tariff gong in 1903. The preoccupations of recent years – Ireland, the House of Lords, social legislation, Labour – receded after 1898. Liberals entered a period in which they seemed to have lost the ability to think for themselves: they could offer negatives to whatever Salisbury's government said but do little else. Gladstone's shadow still fell, of course, across many areas of policy, and the easiest diagnosis lay in blaming 'Mr. G's general policy since 1880'[24] for everything that had gone wrong over the past two decades. But the malaise arose from a deeper level of anxiety about the very purpose and direction of Liberalism and a number of insecurities over its leadership and direction. Sidney Webb's perceptive remark that Gladstonianism amounted to 'thinking in individuals' certainly explained a good deal of Liberal politics in the seven years after 1895 – a period fixed in Edward Grey's memory as a 'nightmare of futility'.[25] For not only did Liberal politicians continue to analyse social relations in the individualist mood of their schooling, but they also invested certain individuals in their own party such as Rosebery, Grey, Asquith, Spencer and Campbell-Bannerman with absurd powers of magnetism or repulsion. To an overwhelming degree Liberal conversation in the second half of the 1890s turned on personality and its relation to the eternal verities. Except for education, which touched nerves always receptive to Nonconformist irritation, they showed little interest in the problems of the day. The engineers' strike of 1897, the legal offensive against trade unions that culminated in the Taff Vale decision of 1901 (which made union funds vulnerable to distraint by employers in the event of a strike), important new currents in Irish nationalism, the beginning of organized female suffrage agitation: none of these issues penetrated to any significant degree the correspondence of politicians likely to be affected by them. Instead the eye turned inwards.

If either Rosebery or Harcourt had retained the leadership for a few years perhaps the situation might have caused less damage. But they had broken irretrievably with one another after the general election. Rosebery kept the leadership only until October 1896 when Gladstone's irruption over the Armenian massacres convinced the imperialist Rosebery, for no good reason, that he must go. Harcourt of necessity succeeded him and during his two years of leadership created an atmosphere of bitterness such as only he could. He left in a sulk at the end of 1898 after his sympathetic view of Salisbury's handling of the Fashoda crisis struck his colleagues as 'servile'. These resignations hinted at a further difficulty in high politics because both departures had, insofar as they seemed intelligible at all, followed from incidents in foreign policy. We have seen the intensity of ministers' concentration on this aspect of their activities since 1886; and the inflammatory effect of foreign affairs on a party that increasingly could see no accommodation between imperialists and Little Englanders needs no elaboration. Yet Liberals did not readily appreciate the lessons of 1895. Their *débâcle* had shown plainly enough the poverty of Liberal appeal to a public opinion that cared little for the subjects about which politicians seemed exclusively to care. Even within the 'machine' one finds in a man like the secretary of an important Liberal regional federation an amazement that the voters of East Hampshire, during a by-election in 1897, should have known nothing at all about Armenia – a sentiment divined and indeed shared by local Tories. Higher up the structure this sense of unreality strengthens. For the parliamentary party, according to Wemyss Reid, only the return of Rosebery would prevent the foreign policy of Liberals becoming the plaything of 'Dilke, Labouchere, Morley & Co.'. Few had the vision of Haldane: perhaps that is why he was so universally disliked. He realized, unlike Wemyss Reid and his kind, 'that the confidence of the workmen who will turn the next election has to be gained in relation to domestic affairs'; and that here the Liberals had nothing to say. In view of one no-nonsense Liberal employer there could be little point even in looking for anything to say 'until we are reformed and in ordered array'.[26] For others, that order itself depended on a resolution of the party's ambiguities over imperialism; yet during 1898–9 events conspired to increase rather than diminish their confusion.

The question of the leadership provided the first exacerbation. Rosebery had been an imperialist, Harcourt not: would the party now swing back to the Rosebery style in its choice of leader? At the beginning it appeared likely that imperialism would return in the person of H. H. Asquith who had aligned himself, without commitment, with the imperial wing. Everyone saw that Asquith must be regarded as the ablest candidate. By 1898, on the other hand, Asquith had acquired four sons, with their school fees and expenses at university, a second wife whose spending power had become the envy of Mayfair, a stable for her horses, an address in Cavendish Square and fourteen servants. Margot had £5,000 a year from her father which hardly kept her in hats; so, on a barrister's income, these blessings made Asquith's domestic economy volatile. Had he faced the opportunity of taking a cabinet post with a salary he might have accepted the party leadership, but to take the expensive role of opposition leader (and that of a moribund party) did not tempt him. Finding someone else to do it gave the party managers and amateur strategists many headaches. Morley had resigned, undeterred by having nothing from which to resign, at the time of Harcourt's departure. Spencer supplied a trusted and respectable figurehead in the Lords, but a Commons man seemed necessary to control the wayward forces there. Grey and Fowler struck the old guard as too young; Acland's health had collapsed. There remained the cordite minister, Sir Henry Campbell-Bannerman, against whom one might set every kind of objection. He came from the wrong place: Glasgow. He had attended the same school as James Bryce but, unlike the great jurist, had achieved little at university and had gone instead into the family firm of drapers and warehousemen. Here he cultivated his love of idleness and travel. Though he came into the House for Stirling in 1868 he displayed no aptitude for making speeches and found repugnant the effort of doing so. Politics simply did not seem to him so serious a business as his colleagues tried to make it; he always made a point of going to Marienbad each year to rid himself of the tedium and rediscover his perspective. If he had any ambition at all it consisted in a quiet wish that the Commons might one day make him their Speaker. He doted on his wife and deferred, many thought, to her judgement. His ego remained confined; his humour refused constraint. He was, in short, perfect.

Although the accession of 'C-B' eventually brought peace to the opposition front bench, it presented a problem in the early stages since Campbell-Bannerman's sympathies on the crucial 'empire' question had always tended to lie with the Harcourt-Morley side of the party. That he believed himself imperialist enough for any decent man did nothing to mollify the fears of the Roseberyites and Milnerites that foreign policy might go soft. When he made Herbert Gladstone his chief whip in the spring of 1899, following the death of Tom Ellis, the threat seemed more explicit. When the country went to war in October it promised to divide the party as surely as had Gladstone's Bulgarian enthusiasm in 1876. Less than a year before Kruger's ultimatum, Eddie Hamilton had commented on the torpor of party politics. 'Are there any longer two parties of the State?' he had wondered; 'or rather are there any measures of real interest... which one party advocates and the other condemns?'[27] His questions lost their relevance as news reached home of the misdirection of the war. For the next two years, until Balfour's education bill offered an opportunity to regroup, the Liberal factions squabbled over a single issue rather than a multiplicity.

That issue did not take the form of deciding whether to oppose the war as such. A few men on the left of the party did so: Bryce, Channing, H. J. Wilson of Sheffield, the future lord chancellor Bob Reid (later Lord Loreburn), the radical journalist H. W. Massingham and, most notoriously, Lloyd George. The bulk of the party, however, thought the war a regrettable necessity while expressing disgust over Chamberlain's part in fomenting it and, later, over the botching of the campaign. Where the war emerged as a major preoccupation was rather through the question of how far its acceptance and conduct required a recasting of Liberal thinking about imperial society and the role that the state should play within it. For Campbell-Bannerman and the central executors of policy the war comprised an incident in party life – one to be supported or opposed in accordance with long-standing principles and dogmas. Among the imperialists, led in these years by Edward Grey, the often-emotional heir to one of Britain's great Whig families, the war's message demanded a vocabulary of race, destiny and (the vogue phrase) 'National Efficiency'. Much of this language found its first articulation in 1901. In the earlier moments of the war it sufficed to relish 'a sort of stirring all down the backbone' and remind laggards that no future lay in simply attacking the colonial secretary and his cloven foot. 'Anti-Chamberlainism won't do – it is not a policy. There must be something started that will last two or three generations.'[28] Less fevered politicians naturally saw danger in espousing a programme that seemed to take its inspiration from 'Webb-footed' Liberals, as Campbell-Bannerman described them, and gamble the success of Liberalism on making Rosebery prime minister of an 'efficiency' government.

Fears that the khaki election of 1900 would bring this prospect closer by strengthening the imperialist Liberals proved unfounded: indeed, the return of Lloyd George and the passionate Ayrshire miner James Keir Hardie (for the LRC) suggested that anti-war sentiment held considerable appeal. The sea-change in imperial opinion came about rather in June 1901, when Campbell-Bannerman's speech at the National Reform Union contained a rare moment of eloquence primed by first-hand reports given to him by Emily Hobhouse, the Florence Nightingale of the Boer war, of appalling conditions suffered by Boer prisoners in British concentration camps. 'When is a war not a war?' raged the opposition leader. 'When it is carried out by methods of barbarism in South Africa.' In later years Campbell-Bannerman looked back on the phrase as his greatest blunder, rather as Gladstone did on his allusion to the confederacy in 1862. Certainly it brought the imperialists down on him – not least Asquith who had ceased acting as the 'mute' of 1898 and 1899.[29] Rosebery, too, stirred himself in a speech to the Liberals of the City of London. Motifs that would become familiar later in the year made their appearance for the first time: the need to draw Unionists back into the Liberal party, the need for a 'clean slate'. Possibly Rosebery took Asquith's emergence from his tent as a threat to his own supremacy on the Liberal right. At any rate he accepted, with much publicity, an invitation from Chesterfield's Liberal Association to speak in the Derbyshire town at the end of the year. By then his astute dropping of hints in private conversation and the newspapers had whipped up a wave of anticipation over what he would say; and when the time came in December the eyes of Britain's political leaders and advisers focused on the railway sheds in Chesterfield, not one of the more promising locations for a speech intended to provoke a form of cultural revolution.

It lasted two hours and was incomprehensible. Rosebery gave his audience, some of it imported in a specially hired train, a theme and variations on the ideas of 'efficiency' and the 'clean slate' with a bravura passage about 'men who sit still with the fly-blown phylacteries of obsolete policies bound round their foreheads'. His friends frowned over *The Times*'s report of the speech and asked, like their baffled leader, 'What is a fly-blown phylactery?' As a programme on which to sweep the country, Chesterfield had turned out badly; it suggested an undercurrent of argument in favour of a man of push and go, but offered no guidance about what to expect from him. Nevertheless a new organization, the Liberal League, came into being at Rosebery's London house in February 1902 to promote Rosebery's blurred aspirations in the constituencies.[30] Asquith, Grey, Haldane, Fowler, Munro-Ferguson and R. W. Perks comprised the central personnel apart from Rosebery himself, and commentators discovered a significance in the League which seems hard to capture in longer perspective. Of course, any organization containing Rosebery and Asquith merited more than dismissal: Rosebery's magnetism plainly mattered to those who came in contact with him, and Asquith's executive competence and rhetorical strength could not be gainsaid. But perhaps other instincts may also have been aroused.

For the 'Limps' posed a considerable challenge to the direction of post-Gladstonian Liberalism, one stronger than could have emanated from a cave of mere imperial Adullamites. Seen from one standpoint they stood for a Liberalism older than Gladstone's and closer to the centre-politics of Palmerston. In their social exclusiveness and sense

of *de haut en bas* they echoed the manner of early Whigs; indeed
Grey 'and his very superior set' upset Campbell-Bannerman as much
for that reason as for any other, just as Asquith, on the other side,
despised Chamberlain for the stains of his upbringing ('the manners
of a cad & the tongue of a bargee') before he lamented his warmon-
gering.[31] From a different vantage-point, however, the imperialists
appeared to have appropriated some aspects of the Gladstonian
position. Concentrating Liberal energies on one uplifting crusade
for imperial efficiency adopted the Gladstonian method if not his
doctrine. To do so in the language of resonant Nonconformity, not
least through 'Imperial Perks' whose assertive Wesleyanism impreg-
nated the rhetoric of the Liberal League, reminded anti-imperialists
that they held no monopoly of Dissenting sympathies. It also called
up the atmosphere of the Celtic fringe that had become so much the
heartland of Liberal support. Consider, in particular, the Scottishness
of these imperialists. Through Grey they reflected Border strength in
his seat at Falloden and his constituency at Berwick-on-Tweed. As
Grey's train steamed north from York, after one of his NER board
meetings, the landscape would have begun to feel Whig somewhere
beyond Newcastle: it still does. If one continued up the east coast to
Midlothian, then Rosebery's Scottish home, Dalmeny, approached on
the southern bank of the Forth. Further still, Haldane and Munro-
Ferguson lived virtually as neighbours in the hills south of Perth.
Even in the towns, the Liberal League gained more of a hearing in
Edinburgh and Glasgow than anywhere in England.

Whatever its authenticity, however, the Liberalism of the League
ultimately ran into self-contradiction. Only Rosebery saw any point
in acting outside the boundary of party. Asquith had no intention of
jeopardizing his place in the hierarchy, nor would Perks allow his
Nonconformity to play second fiddle to 'efficiency'. And both kinds
of hesitancy marked the imperialists' response to the education bill of
1902. From an 'efficiency' point of view, the League ought to have
applauded the bill's impetus towards centralization and rationaliza-
tion. From a party perspective it needed to oppose any interference
with the 'rights' of Nonconformists.[32] By coming into line with their
colleagues over education, the imperialists implicitly agreed to stop
pressing what they agreed about and to resume the quotidian concerns over which they disagreed as intensely as everyone else in the
Liberal party. They kept their status and, no less objectionably to
Campbell-Bannerman, their money – especially Perks's which seemed
endless. 'Defeated in the open,' the Liberal leader growled, 'they are
intriguing and using their money-bags on the sly.' The underground
work did nothing for the imperialists' image among party workers

and the cumulative result in 1902 came across as boredom, a 'general slackness of politics', as Bryce complained, 'and absence of all topics fit to rouse the flagging interest of electors'.[33] But then, when Bryce wrote his remark in the new year of 1903, Chamberlain had still to make the move that would relegate imperialism to a Boer war memory, revive the urgency of Cobdenism and call to the fore a variety of Liberal doctrines with which neither Rosebery nor Campbell-Bannerman felt comfortable.

Free trade gave Liberals an immediate public harmony: their discord over other matters regained its confidentiality in private correspondence. The imperialists, for example, did not oppose the party line over Chinese labour in the Transvaal, whereas two years earlier the issue might have provided a case study in the politics of racial superiority. Equally, the left wing abandoned its sectionalism and did not press its fads over second chamber reform and disestablishment. In private the feuds continued as much because of Chamberlain as despite him. When he resigned from Balfour's cabinet in October 1903, after all, the collapse of the government became a real possibility. The anti-Campbell-Bannerman faction contemplated a conspiracy in favour of making Spencer prime minister if Balfour fell – musings that recommended themselves to Lloyd George as well as Edward Grey; and although the party continued to recognize its present leader as Downing Street's next occupant, the Leaguers did not end their plotting for his removal.[34] Rosebery himself remained distant. He had changed, however, in hardening his attitude to Home Rule. In his post-Chesterfield mood he saw Irish nationalism as running counter to the theme he had chosen for his recent message: he became Chamberlain to C-B's Gladstone. Happy to swallow education, Chinese labour and temperance, he would not willingly enter again the Home Rule trap Gladstone had sprung on the party. When Ireland became a central party preoccupation in the spring of 1905, Rosebery's final divorce from the Liberal leadership could, therefore, not be long delayed.

Attacking the chief secretary for Ireland, George Wyndham, did not of itself demand any revival of Home Rule sentiment. His Irish Land Purchase Act of 1903 had offered few vulnerable points to Liberals since, through its provision of financial aid from the state for land purchases, it moved towards the objective of a peasant proprietorship that Liberals had claimed to promote since 1870. And when parliament learned that Wyndham had been privy, despite his denials, to Sir Antony MacDonnell's plan to devolve further powers on the Irish executive, the gunfire naturally came from

Balfour's rabid Ulstermen rather than from Liberals committed to devolution. Yet the Conservative crisis over Wyndham's mismanagement, and the prime minister's refusal to save his career, could only bring back to high-political discussion that part of the Liberal programme which promised to eradicate such problems for good by giving Ireland her parliament. By March 1905 it had become apparent that Rosebery would refuse to act with Liberals in furthering that objective. More precisely, he would refuse to join a government committed to it unless Spencer led it or, at the very least, Campbell-Bannerman went to the Lords. His resolution remained untested because, to the surprise of both parties, Balfour survived the 1905 session. During the recess, however, the imperialists concocted their final conspiracy against their leader at Grey's fishing villa in Scotland. The decision of Asquith, Grey and Haldane, who met there, to refuse office in the next Liberal government unless Campbell-Bannerman agreed to go to the Lords – the 'Relugas compact' – doubtless seemed desirable in face of Rosebery's isolation, which the 'Limps' wanted to end, and Balfour's imminent defeat, which they wanted to exploit. If they still held hopes of Rosebery's return they reckoned without his paranoia. Despite Spencer's removal from the scene by serious illness in October 1905, Rosebery persisted in his run at Campbell-Bannerman. His speech at Bodmin on 25 November registered 'high constitutional objections' against Home Rule and protested at the Liberals' willingness to see social reform blocked by an impracticable Irish policy. 'I will say no more on this subject except to say emphatically and explicitly and once for all that I cannot serve under that banner.'[35]

He never did. Until his death in 1929 Rosebery remained on the margin of British politics, at once enjoying and resenting his lack of a role. His outburst at Bodmin had one tangible result and not the one he had expected. It persuaded Balfour that the depth of the rift between Campbell-Bannerman and Rosebery over Ireland would sabotage the formation of any Liberal government. Handing the leader of the opposition so poisoned a chalice presented too great a temptation to resist, especially when Balfour's government had already been beaten in the Commons and looked likely to meet its fatal challenge before long. On 4 December 1905 the prime minister tendered his resignation to King Edward VII. He did not dissolve parliament because he wanted to watch Campbell-Bannerman flounder in full view of the electorate before the inevitable winter election. And had the Relugas men persisted in their plan Balfour might indeed have enjoyed the next few weeks. Asquith, however, turned out more human than anyone expected, to the detriment of the imperialists; Campbell-Bannerman, conversely, showed that he had grown considerably in stature and political nous over the past few years. The new premier compromised the conspirators by promoting them. He made Asquith an offer he could not afford to refuse – the Exchequer – and won round Haldane and then Grey with the War Office and Foreign Office. Despite all Balfour's sense of timing, a Liberal government began to materialize and, once formed, it immediately rushed for the hustings in an election which everyone took to mark a likely turning-point in the modern history of political parties.

Away from the overheated imagination of the imperialists, this coming electoral test had preoccupied the party managers since 1903. It had preyed with particular consistency on the mind of Herbert Gladstone, the chief whip, and R. A. Hudson, secretary to the two major party agencies, the National Liberal Federation and the Liberal Central Association. Hudson's problem, like that of his better known predecessor, Francis Schnadhorst, consisted in holding together coteries of Liberals who delighted in the vocabulary of 'influence' and 'capture', not least the radicals who entrenched themselves in the NLF in the late 1890s. But Gladstone in many ways lacked Schnadhorst's acumen. The Grand Old Man's son had proved a disappointment politically. He owed his first constituency, Leeds, to his father, who was returned there as well as at Midlothian in 1880. In the House, however, the young Gladstone made little mark. He flew the 'Hawarden kite' of 1885 in a misconceived attempt to keep his father in control of the party; he reduced his golf handicap to three. Muscular Christianity proved no substitute for party experience when he reluctantly took on the burden of the whip's office – an introduction to the burdens of party organization which he was to carry for the rest of his political career. Money became an immediate concern: partly because the lack of it caused great anxiety to electoral managers, partly because Herbert's own finances remained chaotic and constantly required the ministrations of the family financier, his brother Henry. But in the critical years after the Boer war two subjects gave Gladstone headaches from which more senior politicians spared themselves. Labour provided one of them, the Nonconformists another.

The LRC had returned two of its candidates at the 1900 election, one of whom, Keir Hardie, secured instant notoriety for his anti-war stance and his dress and manner at Westminster. At a parliamentary level this hardly posed a serious threat. In the constituencies, however, an insidious spread of 'labour' influence had developed because Liberal caucuses shied away from working-class candidates, less out of the class snobbery for which socialists berated them than because elections still cost a considerable sum of money to fight effectively – a thousand, even fifteen hundred pounds. Unless a constituency party could raise the cash (and Gladstone's information suggested that increasingly they could not) it had little option but to select a local employer or businessman with a ready wallet. Problems developed in Liberal–'Labour' relations when local trade unionists and trade council activists no longer backed off when Liberal Associations competed for the smiles of their local bourgeoisie. The LRC secretary, an able socialist intellectual called James Ramsay MacDonald, saw no point in being bloody: he understood the fragility of Labour's new electoral machine. But when Liberals repeatedly annoyed local Labour men by their attitude, local decisions to fight by-elections inevitably increased national frictions. Clitheroe in Lancashire became the setting for the first major eruption of animosity when, in a by-election of 1902, local cotton weavers refused to withdraw their candidate, David Shackleton, in favour of a Lib–Lab approved by the Liberal party. Gladstone had to use central pressure to ease his own man out of the contest and allow Shackleton an unopposed return. For a journal like the incendiary *New Age* the victory opened fresh horizons: 'We can recall nothing more significant than this in modern political history. We have not heard the last of this we may be sure. Suppose the same tactics are followed in one hundred or two hundred constituencies?'[36] Liberal headquarters, while less incandescent, doubtless asked similar questions. The result emerged in 1903 when Gladstone and MacDonald concluded a secret pact designed to avoid splitting the progressive vote in selected constituencies at the next general election – an understanding that would play no small part in helping into the House of Commons twenty-nine LRC candidates, who decided to call themselves the 'Labour party'.

Within months of Clitheroe and its confirmation at Barnard Castle, stolen from the Liberals in 1903 by another LRC man with a future, Arthur Henderson, a disturbing challenge to Liberal stability came from within. If Gladstone had played one of his frequent rounds of golf with the Rev. Silvester Horne, Congregationalist minister at Whitefield's Tabernacle in London and editor of the *Crusader*, he might have been asked the appalling question: 'Don't you think the Free Churches ought to put up a hundred candidates at the next election?' It hardly mattered that he did not, because Horne's partner on the links that day immediately ran to Gladstone with the proposal. He found the chief whip 'not enthusiastic'.[37] In the wake of a declining agitation against the education bill Gladstone seemed prepared to give the Dissenters a few unwinnable seats; but in hoping that the problem would go away he underestimated the confidence of the churches and, in particular, failed to anticipate the strength of the

Welsh revival of 1904–5 – as intense, many believed, as the great evangelical outburst of 1859. He also failed to recognize the inroads that 'Labour' thinking had made into radical Dissent and *a fortiori* into Primitive Methodism. The emotion of these years gave the election of 1906 a special significance in the eyes of Nonconformists. It increased their optimism about the congruence of Liberal and Dissenting strategies; it deepened their determination to abrogate Balfour's interference in education and bring back to the agenda the only word anyone dared use in Wales: disestablishment.

Another development in Liberal politics took on a more subterranean character because it affected the more 'progressive' areas of Liberalism and therefore appeared largely outside parliament. A thoughtful politician like Haldane picked up an occasional tremor. We find him writing an article on 'The New Liberalism' in the *Progressive Review* in 1896 and noting that 'a growing number of the younger Liberals' have begun to employ 'the language of the social good' in their speeches.[38] To see this 'New Liberalism' in any worked-out form before 1906, however, one needs to go to publicists and intellectuals. The editor of the *Manchester Guardian*, C. P. Scott, embodied many of the new doctrines as did the important intellectual Leonard Hobhouse who worked on Scott's staff for a time. Scott had told Hobhouse in the 1890s of his belief that 'the relation of Liberalism and Labour must govern the future of politics, and that the problem was to find the lines on which Liberals could be brought to see that the old tradition must be expanded to yield a fuller measure of social justice, a more real equality, and industrial as well as political liberty.'[39] This wider Liberalism, grounded in the judgement that the maximization of individual freedom in an organic society required for its sustenance an expansion of the power of the state and not the contraction prescribed by classical theorists, informed the writings and rhetoric of a generation of radicals, many of whom would make their mark on the back benches or in editorial office after 1906. Their existence did not trouble politicians whose attention had fixed itself on tariffs or education or Rosebery. But their concerns persisted inside the party structure because they reflected new patterns in the perception by educated people of poverty, class and social need.

The condition of England

Charles Masterman's book of this title appeared in 1909. In it the Liberal MP for West Ham attempted a synoptic survey of British society during a period of self-conscious turbulence; and it reads like a covert manifesto for the minority report of the Poor Law Commission published in the same year, or for William Beveridge's epochal study of *Unemployment* – indeed for the tendency of what Masterman took to characterize New Liberal thought generally. These texts of 1909 do not stand alone: one might refer to Leo Chiozza Money, another backbench London MP (Liberal: Paddington North), whose *Riches and Poverty* (1905) effectively depicted misery in columns of statistics; or to John Hobson's various attacks on the maldistribution of wealth in a capitalist society and its ramifications in colonial and industrial policy; or to William Hurrell Mallock's ingenious rearguard action against those attacks; or to W. A. S. Hewins's attempts to pull the argument back to tariffs and the empire; or to the leavening results of Shaw's plays or the strange parodies of G. K. Chesterton and Hilaire Belloc. Social texts, in short, surrounded the Edwardian intelligentsia, raised their consciousness and encouraged them to discuss their environment with a renewed positivism. The mood expressed itself in a lust for FACTS. No one can read Beatrice Webb's diaries and letters in this period without sensing that, for her, the gathering of social facts – clinical and unassailable – had become a form of sustenance, replacing most of her meals and supplying an inner warmth. For Edwardian social radicals, investigation of their society's dynamics took on the nature of a laboratory experiment, as though the observer had lifted himself clear of what he had chosen to study. After seventy years of metaphysics that had concealed the accessibility of the world in the language of Kant and Hegel, British intellectuals saw themselves suddenly to have entered an exciting phase of liberation. Lord John Russell's grandson felt it acutely during his early years at Cambridge: the new mood, he said, brought him out of a greenhouse on to a windswept headland.[40]

Those new winds carried Masterman's generation beyond the patient empiricism of the 1880s and 1890s associated with men like Booth and Rowntree. The new 'sociology', now a fashionable term, gave rise to recommendations with a social-democratic flavour for acknowledging the interdependence of individuals within the social organism and indeed redefining more sensitively the very meaning of words such as 'individual' and 'society'. Military recruitment during the Boer war had brought to light the physical inadequacy of working-class males and had confirmed the implications of Rowntree's first study of York (1901), which had suggested that 28 per cent of the city's population subsisted below a 'poverty line'. Similarly, the patent inability of early Victorian poor law arrangements to cope with the rapidly expanding urban population documented in the censuses of 1901 and 1911 argued the urgency of reforming the system to remove the current contradictory assumptions that poverty either followed from sloth or that it threatened everyone equally like storm or flood. From government reports, such as that of Sir Almeric FitzRoy's Physical Deterioration Committee or the reports of the Poor Law Commission, from newspapers and magazines, from the university extension movement and the new London School of Economics established by the Webbs, pressure came for radical state initiatives to soften class division and raise the living standards of the masses. Recovering from the loss of conventional religious faith, many of those associated with this movement discovered a surrogate spirituality: indeed, churchmen played no small part in its propaganda through their educational activities and the university settlements in working-class districts of cities.[41] Understanding why the Liberal governments of 1905–15 undertook welfare programmes that included the introduction of legislation on old age pensions (1908), employment exchanges (1909) and national insurance (1911) plainly requires a recognition of these developments.

Different laboratories, on the other hand, produced different results. From the mid-1890s the views of the German biologist August Weismann coloured British discussion of Darwinism in its relation to social theory. A vague hope, implicit in Darwin's own writings, that the acquired characteristics of human beings (those owed to 'nurture' rather than 'nature') could descend to offspring as part of their genetic imprint had helped underpin one conception of 'progress' by supplying a mechanism for social improvement via simple inheritance. Weismann destroyed that hope. The 'hyper-Darwinism' that achieved wide currency in the twenty years after Benjamin Kidd's *Social Evolution* (1894) took as its starting-point the denial of all such 'use-inheritance'; and just as progress had fed on the previous doctrine, so 'degeneration' fed on its successor. This application of science took its positivism quite as seriously as the social-democrats took theirs. Instead of pointing towards liberalism, however, it suggested the importance of radical action to halt the decomposition noticed by those for whom 'race', 'empire' and 'aristocracy' fused together as forces for good. Here the attention moved away from the parliamentary system with its mediocrity, corruption and small-mindedness. The future lay rather with the eugenics programmes of Karl Pearson and Francis Galton, in the countless crackpot applications of 'racial' theory and, above all, in youth – the custodians of tomorrow's imperial culture.[42] No less a responsibility rested on the shoulders of Baden-Powell's boy scouts: they had a supposed military function as a fifth column in the event of a German invasion; but for the Earl of Meath, who presided over several of the leagues and societies that typify Edwardian patriotic politics, the point of becoming a boy scout remained an educative one. 'It arrives in the nick of time...to make of a lad a hardy, virile, truth-speaking, duty-loving Briton, worthy to bear the heavy but honourable burdens attached to membership of the mightiest Empire the world has ever known.'[43]

Imperial instincts of this kind endured because they validated an array of judgements on social questions and political parties. Insofar as they allowed the possibility of any mass politics worthy of the name, they helped stimulate the Germanophobia of later Edwardian England. An enthusiasm for 'invasion novels', detectable since the Franco-Prussian war, became general with Erskine Childers' *The Riddle of the Sands* (1902); and the more mystical moments in the poetry of W. E. Henley and Rudyard Kipling found a mass complement in Harmsworth's *Daily Mail* which serialized stories implying the subjugation of all things English. Yet doctrines announcing that The Race stood in danger of degeneration came awkwardly from agitators and tub-thumpers who seemed to prefer a Celtic medium for their Teutonic message. Fellow-travellers felt more at home in the select groups and societies among the company of like-minded males. Women had their place, an elevated one, in the political process; but they could hardly become citizens when imperial requirements made the ability to carry a rifle a precondition of that privilege. It went without saying that the suffragettes affronted common decency; but what did not go without saying probably played the more important role in fashioning attitudes – a series of intermeshing views about matriarchy redolent of American slave-owning society in the ante-bellum south. Proceeding from girlhood to womanhood constituted at once too serious and too hallowed a business for the sordid environment of political affairs. Even men had their limitations. The 'tommy', admirable from behind the lines as an epitome of wholesomeness and grit, remained unfit to consider those matters of state better left, not to the faceless samurai envisaged by H. G. Wells, but rather to individuals whose history and upbringing had injected statesmanship into their blood.

For an observer convinced that only in the physique of the landed aristocrat could one find 'a small synopsis, a diminutive digest of full, flourishing and fortunate life', it came as a body blow in 1909 to discover in a library catalogue only nine entries under 'aristocracy' when 'democracy' rated eighty-five.[44] Certainly the upper classes' sense of embattlement strengthened during the reign of King Edward. He himself contributed to it, largely despite himself, through his association with the prejudice that the aristocracy had lost its will to govern in a whirl of banquets, bridge-parties, regattas, wine and worse. Liberal attacks on the House of Lords also culminated in this period as the peers struggled in the last ditch through 1910 and 1911 to prevent Asquith's government from legislating them into impotence. In 1907 Lady Monkswell had smiled at the prospect but much would happen over the next few years to make the smiles more nervous.[45] Death duties had already arrived; and when Lloyd George, Asquith's chancellor of the exchequer, proposed in his 'People's Budget' of 1909 a valuation of land and a charge on the landowners of Britain, the stream of tendency had become too wide to miss. Between them, the political and economic offensives threatened a last crisis of feudalism. It did not come at once: 1919 and not 1909 focuses in retrospect as the 'year when Britain changed hands' and estates came under the hammer, turning country houses into hospitals and hotels or leaving indigent owners living à la Brideshead under dustsheets. All the same, enough writing had appeared on the wall by 1911 to make Lady Sackville wonder whether a Welsh solicitor with a chip on his shoulder about landowners had the remotest idea of how costly had become the upkeep of 356 rooms, 52 staircases and 545 windows.[46]

Villadom faced fewer difficulties. Indeed, the middle classes discovered a broadened scope for advancement and mobility, especially among its lower echelons which supplied an army of black-coated salary-earners whose influence in British life remains largely unassessed.[47] They had their own headquarters in the suburbs, especially in expanding London where dormitory lifestyles supplanted an older model of contiguity between employment and home.[48] They had, in their higher reaches, enough money to contribute to the demand for domestic furniture – buying it from Tottenham Court Road became a form of class allegation from those who did not need to do so – or domestic technology such as a vacuum cleaner from one of the great department stores, or perhaps even to think of buying a motor car. After all, the 140,000 cars on British roads by the beginning of the First World War cannot have belonged exclusively to aristocrats and millionaires. Their class-consciousness attained new heights in a period so dominated in its popular psychology by attacks on property by suffragettes or striking workmen. Their dedicated philistinism helped turn to fiasco the first post-impressionist exhibition and the first London performances of *The Rite of Spring*. They had a literature written about them in the plays of Galsworthy and the novels of E. M. Forster, and one written for them in the middlebrow newspapers whose articles and advertisements emphasized the security of their aspirations. These concerned the well-being and 'efficiency' of the nation with special emphasis on moral fibre of the kind encountered early in life at a thousand Greyfriars and Elchesters. Commercial survival in a world of fierce competition acquired the patina of the sports-field and a similar vocabulary – 'bracing', 'vigorous', 'free', 'fair' – with few words of sympathy for the inept. International affairs, once wrested from the control of secretive foreign secretaries and arms dealers, would display the same inner wholesomeness and render war an absurdity. The striking interest in many countries generated by Norman Angell's *The Great Illusion* (1910), which attempted on the eve of the First World War to demonstrate the unthinkability of conflict between nations in their modern state of commercial interdependence, testified to the readiness of a vast readership to see this world view reduced to the tidiness of tabular form. It confirmed no less surely the fear among those who had property to lose that the next bloodshed would come from a war not between nations but between classes.

'We are dealing with a condition of Civil War', Edward Grey said during a cabinet in 1912.[49] He had in mind the coal strike of that spring, the latest and most serious of a string of labour disputes which, taken together, have given the period between 1911 and 1914 the title of the 'Great Unrest'. A change had undoubtedly come over trade unionism since its cornering by the 'legal offensive' of the 1890s that culminated in Taff Vale. A downturn in real wages after 1907 added a spur to protest even though the Liberal government reversed the Taff Vale judgement in the previous year. More significant shifts soon followed: the affiliation of the powerful miners' union to the Labour party in 1908, a marked expansion in the number of trade unionists affiliated to the TUC after 1911 and the use by their leaders of doctrines that suggested a near-continental excitability. Marxism made little headway in any organized form; but two other doctrines caught a strong breeze after 1910. One of them, 'syndicalism', had French origins in the writings of Proudhon and, more recently, of Georges Sorel whose *Réflexions sur la Violence* (1906) found some English converts prepared to use rhetoric that ran far beyond the traditional unionist message in its call for a general strike. 'Gild socialism' enjoyed currency for a few years under the impetus of Arthur Penty and a young Oxford don, Douglas Cole. Its inspiration came from medieval England: indeed to some extent it revived that gothic socialism encouraged by William Morris and Robert Blatchford in the 1890s, seeking a more rational organization of industrial power in the adoption of an individualist guild structure. Although nothing resembling a revolutionary situation developed during the Unrest, Lord Ribblesdale's son spoke for more than his own class when he judged that the workers had got 'shockingly out of hand'.[50] Their aggression and willingness to resort to non-parliamentary politics added zest to a long-standing argument about the nature of democracy in the twentieth century.

Critics of that 'democracy' came largely from outside Britain: indeed it seems odd that this generation did not produce a Carlyle or a Fitzjames Stephen or a Robert Lowe to attack the assumption of democratic progress. In fact a Russian scholar, Mosei Ostrogorski, most contributed to a mistrust among the intelligentsia of democratic mechanisms in America and Britain through his study of *Democracy and the Organization of Political Parties* (1902). Ostrogorski's anxieties over the development of the 'caucus' and its implications for the possibility of genuine democracy anticipated in some degree the formidable indictment of the German political scientist Robert Michels whose theory of the 'iron law of oligarchy', published in 1915, carried the argument towards a fundamental denial of the feasibility of democratic practice while political parties and their leaders persisted in their present *modus operandi*. British theorists tended to find such arguments implausible when they related them to the British experience: the Anglo-American understanding of representative democracy turned out to be more flexible than the Russian or German. A. L. Lowell, an acute American observer of British government, agreed in 1908 that 'all the prophecies of the levelling effects of democracy in Great Britain have so far proved fallacious' in so 'centralized and powerfully organized' a society; but English commentators often found this resistance a virtue. Sir Sidney Low, for example, saw no death struggle taking place between property and the masses, despite the advent of a 'democratic' political structure:

> The great peril, so constantly present to the minds of the philosophical opponents of Democracy, in ancient and modern times, has been averted; and even under a wide popular franchise we have not as yet found ourselves in the presence of two political parties, the one including all those who own property, and the other made up chiefly of those who possess little but their hands and their votes.[51]

We have already had cause to comment on their votes, or lack of them; but their hands – the hard hands that had given Gladstone pause a generation before – certainly seemed more formidable after 1906. Arthur Balfour's language after the election of that year has often attracted comment. In a bitter period following his defeat at East Manchester, he spoke of Britain adrift on a socialist tide and of the Liberal win at the polls as heralding more than the usual swing of a pendulum. 'I do not think the full significance of the drama can be understood without reference to the Labour and Socialistic movements on the Continent', he declared. And the prospect of watching 'the mob of ignorant voters who now elect our parliament' overwhelming the constitution certainly helped direct thinking at the capacity of the reformed framework to hold back the floodwaters. The Liberal assault on the second chamber; the revolt of the Women's Social and Political Union (WSPU) into overt violence in support of their campaign for female suffrage; the willingness of the Conservative party seemingly to countenance a referendum on tariff reform – 'democracy run mad' – the sense among imperialists that democracy, 'that form of Govt that prevails in one form or another in the decay of a State',[52] had eaten into the entrails of the body politic: all these developments insisted that discussion of universal suffrage take place within a changed climate. One catches a glimpse of it in Lady Monkswell who had heretofore regarded democracy as a gloss on legalized theft and therefore a subject of little challenge for her. But one day in 1909 she writes a diary entry which carries its burden of surprise too well to permit of paraphrase:

Sat., 22 May. I had taken some trouble to go to a lecture on 'Democracy', one of a series delivered by Professor Masterman [Charles's brother] in the Royal Gallery in the House of Lords. Albert Mansbridge, a clever young man, gets up these lectures in connection with the University Extension movement.

The thermometer stood above 80°, the great hall was filled by an eager crowd of 1,000 people – as Mansbridge told me the next day – men & women, all somewhat young. I should put them at £20 householders, those that read & think...Among others there were Mr. Harvey of Toynbee Hall, Will Crooks, M.P. [Labour: Woolwich], the Archbishop's son 'Billy' Temple, & Miss Haldane. But first and foremost was Mr. Haldane the Secretary for War in the Chair. Whenever Mr. Haldane speaks in public the suffragettes go & interrupt him, & this p.m. I witnessed the *shocking sight* for the first time. [She describes an interruption and the ejection from the hall of a dozen suffragettes.] This perhaps took half an hour. We then proceeded to business and settled down to listen to Professor Masterman.

His idea of 'democracy' was a very high, noble & religious idea. He is a plain, skinny little man of 40 with *not too good a* pronunciation, but he knew how to lay hold of his audience...I could see from my excellent position the faces of the audience, the interest never flagged, no one fidgeted or went to sleep, in spite of the heat & close packing...I had expected the lecture would be some variety of the usual socialistic cry – Take from the 'idle rich' & give to the 'poor', & could hardly believe my ears to hear the spiritual put above the material, & to be told that religion must lie at the bottom of it all.[53]

'So what?' one might ask. Even if the suggestion of a changed atmosphere for discussion seems persuasive, its effect within the half-closed society at Westminster requires demonstration and often receives none: politicians are viewed as members of the wider community and expected to reflect its concerns and preoccupations. Their bills and speeches do duty as evidence for their aspirations and intentions; and an astute selection of individuals and documents will bring social theory leaping from the archives. At the beginning of successive Liberal governments in 1906 and 1908 the mood seems especially exuberant as a young idealist like Herbert Samuel tried to convince Sidney Webb that Campbell-Bannerman's new administration 'was to be a Government of Social Reform', or as Churchill urges Asquith to lead his new cabinet in 1908 towards 'a tremendous policy in Social Organization' and 'thrust a big slice of Bismarckianism over the whole side of our industrial system'.[54] Once stand back from these exhortations, however, their significance soon diminishes. Neither Samuel nor Churchill held senior posts at the time of their remarks; and as Churchill rose so his preoccupations moved away from social radicalism towards defence and the maintenance of a large navy. Among ministers only he and Lloyd George showed signs of absorbing the radiation of Liberal intellectuals; 'Old' Liberals like Bryce felt, for example, that a cardinal duty of the government would consist in countering the growing supposition that the state had a duty to provide work.[55] Among cabinet ministers who remained quietly agnostic over such issues, their perspective often turned, not on the doctrinal desirability of state intervention, but rather on a crisis in state finance which left governments with little choice but to intervene. Subterranean shifts evident from the distance of half a century left undisturbed many contemporaries whose profession obliged them to think about events on the surface when it required them to think at all.

Two surface developments – the revolt of Labour and the revolution among women – made waves enough for every politician to mark their arrival. Yet the framework within which a politician might place these happenings could differ markedly from that familiar to the leader-writer or don. Labour now presented a double apparition: as a pressure-point within the party framework posing challenges to existing notions of electoral management; and as a revived pressure from without in the strident doctrines of 1910 and beyond. But neither of them excited as much concern from government as their spokesmen hoped and believed. Campbell-Bannerman saw from the beginning that the Liberal government should avoid doing anything to convince Labour that Liberals acted in response to their pressure; nor did anyone see the need to respond in a House of Commons containing nearly four hundred Liberals. When the balance of power between the two major parties resumed its equilibrium in the two elections of 1910, Labour MPs won more concessions – payment of members, for example, in 1911 and the reversal, in 1913, of the Osborne judgement of the House of Lords which had undermined over the past four years the finances of the Labour party by insisting on the right of trade unionists to escape the payment of a political levy as part of their subscriptions unless they contracted into paying one. But the electoral performance of the Labour party in the pre-war years gave Liberals comparatively few qualms. In the mining areas crucial to future Labour power, the Liberals still won seats despite the union's change of allegiance. In three-cornered contests elsewhere the Labour party fared badly. Behind the depressing record lay a number of important organizational advances that suggested to those aware of them the potential of Labour's electoral machine. Those who did not know about them had good grounds meanwhile for believing that the enemy within had been muzzled.[56]

The pressure from without caused some ructions; for men like Lloyd George when he ran the Board of Trade in 1906–8, and the government's industrial troubleshooter, Sir George Askwith, strikes and their suppression became frequent preoccupations. When placed alongside Ireland, the House of Lords, disestablishment, national insurance, tariffs, land reform and a host of minor complexities, they helped engender the sense of harassment that impressed itself on most ministers after 1906. But one can overstress the weight and permanence of the preoccupation. Lloyd George's eyes opened to Labour when he failed to control an audience of workers by simply speaking to them; but that moment came on the Clyde in 1915, not during the period when, for the most part, flexibility and rhetorical skill carried the day. Indeed, the serious disputes of 1911–13 did little to distract him from his object of destroying the feudal system of landholding – hardly the response of an urban puppet. Winston Churchill, Lloyd George's partner in pressing 'progressive' politics at cabinet level, showed in a letter to his wife Clementine how easily the labour troubles could lose themselves beneath the 'in' tray of a busy minister. In the month when Grey saw impending civil war during the 1912 coal strike, the first lord of the admiralty saw a different prospect during a visit to Portland:

The strike seems vy. remote from Portland with its well-disciplined fleet & mountains of coal. It will be a great relief to learn that it is settled. We have so many difficulties to contend with. Still, I think we shall surmount them. Governments are vy. tough organizations. They stand wear & tear & are made to stand it.[57]

Resilience of this kind had strengthened through the internalization of popular pressure within parliamentary politics since the 1860s. The socialism of Robert Smillie or Tom Mann, like the efficiency of Rosebery before and the fascism of Mosley to come, foundered in face of it.

Suffragette militancy shared the same fate. The 'woman question' had a parliamentary history stretching back over half a century and its early activists had operated from inside the constitutional structure; their tactics had included private bills, pressure on MPs by lobbying and the education of public opinion through female participation in local government, the bench, school boards and through breaking down proscriptions against their entering the universities and professions. Little more than this had been expected initially from the Women's Social and Political Union (1903): the Pankhursts and the Pethick-Lawrences came from a class that did not betoken revolution. The 'constitutional' strategy cut no ice, however, with the new Liberal governments. Antagonists in the House talked out three bills in 1906–7; and the seeming impossibility of achieving results through parliamentary action spurred the WSPU to a programme of civil disobedience culminating in the notorious arson campaign of 1913 and the government's persecution, by its 'Cat and Mouse Act', of female prisoners too weak to tolerate further force-feeding. Christabel Pankhurst's adoption of violence possessed, to that extent, a clear logic. 'What is the good of a constitutional policy', she demanded in her *Votes for Women* in 1911, 'to those who have no constitutional weapon?' And if Annie Kenney could only see in the politicians who defied her sense of natural justice 'such hypocracy [sic], such insincerety [sic], such lying and such a lot of humbug', they had provided some evidence for her view.[58] For all that, the shifting of strategy towards an attack on property proved an error because, rather than increase the politicians' embarrassment, it merely eased their difficulty. Public opinion swung behind the 'antis', as the opponents of female suffrage had become labelled; the funds of all feminist bodies (constitutionalist as much as militant) ran into decline as the violence escalated. Among the Liberal cabinet, meanwhile, strong feelings rarely came to the surface except in Grey, who supported the women, and Harcourt who detested them. Lloyd George hedged his bets by supporting only a 'democratic' enfranchisement in order to avoid creating a new constituency of propertied (i.e. Tory) women who might disturb the electoral balance. Asquith himself took the main force of suffragette verbal abuse after 1908 and, though he never achieved the machiavellianism attributed to him by the WSPU, he undoubtedly believed emancipation to be a folly and continued to think it so when he said he had changed his mind during the First World War. But the subject did not greatly interest him and its proponents did not greatly frighten him. Only two of the cabinet showed weak nerves over female suffrage. That the home secretary became shaky will surprise no one familiar with the mechanics of insurrectionary politics through the nineteenth century, but Reginald McKenna did not respond solely to the ambience of his office. He took personally, as he was meant to, the suffragette propaganda that depicted him as the ogre behind the Cat and Mouse Act and it reinforced the sense of political isolation after his removal from the Admiralty. The chief secretary for Ireland, Augustine Birrell, had a less complicated reason for taking fright. A mob of women attacked him as he walked down a London street in 1911 and dislocated his left knee.[59] Dublin did not often strike a chief secretary as safer than the English capital.

Perhaps any non-constitutional politics would fail in a culture so wedded to the primacy of Law. Lawyers still exercised some influence in the House of Commons – they and other professions such as medicine accounted for about 23 per cent of Liberal MPs in 1910 – but the power came rather from a reverence for law as a fundamental reference-point of all civilized life and peaceful change. German legal theory made a deep impression on the generation of Alfred Venn Dicey, Ernest Barker, Sir Frederick Pollock and the incomparable legal historian F. W. Maitland. True, the impact of legal doctrine inevitably remained greatest within the intelligentsia rather than among politicians. A distinction may be drawn, however, between the back benches of the House of Commons, where the march of business seems more obvious than the presence of lawyers after 1906,[60] and the personnel in higher office. Above the level of junior minister, for example, the case for a new understanding of social background weakens considerably: in these regions the story continues its familiar tale of land, lineage and the higher professions in an elite that more closely reflected the social structure of 1890 than of 1910. Even on the Tory benches, where the business element had strengthened noticeably since the arrival of tariff politics, nearly 30 per cent of Conservative members could claim connexion of one sort or another with the aristocracy in the decade 1900–10. Over 95 per cent of them belonged to a London club.[61] Such men still established the tone, if they did not dominate the activities, of the lower chamber. No matter how pervasive urban problems had become in political thinking, the *Zeitgeist* of the Liberal parliaments might have set Palmerston at his ease. 'No other nation in the world transacts business in August and idles in December', Lord Esher wrote to his son in the middle of a difficult summer in 1907. 'The old hunting craze of our forefathers still rules the customs of an assembly not 10 per cent of which can sit upon a horse.'

Its most prestigious MPs drove, instead, in chauffeur-driven motor cars, especially when visiting in the country or going to golf. Walton Heath golf club in Surrey became a surrogate parliament in the pre-war years, always offering a chance of running into Lloyd George or Bonar Law on the adjacent fairway. Through 1910 and 1911 Lord Riddell made a habit of playing there twice a week with Winston Churchill and, re-entering the city after a game one day in 1911, Riddell heard from his partner a remark which intrigued him. 'As we were driving home from Walton Heath, Winston pointed to the teeming population in the streets and said, "I wonder what they are mostly interested in?" I said, "Earning their living and football".'[62] Churchill, like most of his ministerial colleagues, simply had no direct way of knowing. Constituencies did not provide the social forum of later years: high-flying politicians used them as 'seats' and local men saw little of the representatives from one election to the next except, perhaps, when the local town hall seemed a good place for a major speech. All the tendencies of the class structure and its educational arrangements conspired to prevent political leaders from meeting the ordinary people for whose lives they legislated. What they did know they picked up by mediation from working-class MPs such as John Burns or the LRC men, from studying (at a distance) trade union leaders, from listening to men of their own caste who seemed to have the gift of divining the popular will. Chief whips often became super-men in this respect, as though their correspondence with party activists equipped them with special powers. Other categories of mediation came to prominence in this period, however, and of these two seem especially significant.

Churchill's golfing companion offers a clue. Riddell moved easily in the political world of London clubs and society amusement. His great wealth made it possible for him to participate; but politicians sought him out, not for his money (though his offer to build Lloyd George a house near the golf course had been very gratifying) but rather for his public influence. For Riddell possessed more than property: he owned the *News of the World*. In making that newspaper a new force in popular Sunday journalism, Riddell had caught a tide of great power, one that had begun with Harmsworth in the nineties. In 1908 Alfred Harmsworth, later Lord Northcliffe, acquired *The Times* from the Walter family and rapidly turned Fleet Street's greatest institution into the servant of a single, many thought half-deranged, personality. He and his brother, the future Lord Rothermere, would come to dominate the press world during and after the First World War but even now the new press had arrived as a reality. If newspaper editors did not achieve cabinet office, as they did when Lloyd George reached the top of the greasy pole in the middle of the war, they nevertheless became objects of attention from politicians. Traditional journalism survived still: men of the stamp of J. A. Spender of the *Westminster Gazette*, J. L. Garvin of the *Observer* and A. G. Gardiner of the *Daily News* maintained the tone and standards of the late Victorian high period of journalism.[63] For Harmsworth, Riddell or, on the Liberal benches, Sir Henry Dalziel of *Reynolds' News*, however, their new approach gave them fresh access to authenticity in their social knowledge. Most politicians, even Balfour, who affected not to read newspapers, or the obscure son of Alfred Baldwin, who had come into the House in 1908 and who would later discover his own reasons for hating them, knew what the press said about their activities. If Asquith retained his contempt for the Liberal press ('written by Boobies for Boobies'), he could see across a crowded room that Spender wore the same Balliol tie. If Lloyd George found C. P. Scott's concern for the chancellor's soul a little irritating, he nevertheless thought it worthwhile to press Scott to begin a London edition of the *Manchester Guardian* so that the sermons could reach a wider audience. If Walter Long identified a weakness in modern Tory democracy, it lay in its failure to capitalize on this new force in popular and local journalism. Since the quality press acted, meanwhile, as a vehicle for the social criticism of the New Liberals (recall Hobhouse's connexion with Scott or Beveridge's period on the *Morning Post*) it ensured that the communication with government would have a two-way character.

Robertson Nicoll, editor of the *British Weekly*, won for himself a special position in this environment. Riddell, a rival after all, conceded in 1908 that Nicoll was 'much sought after by Liberal ministers';[64] and for a good reason. That Nicoll edited a weekly newspaper gave him little leverage in itself. But he spoke, like his journal, for organized Dissent – the power of the Nonconformist churches that Liberal leaders still tended to see as the litmus paper for their policies and the second mediatory instrument which any sensitive historian will need to confront. Nicoll was no Miall; the government had no Forster. The link between politics and Dissent in Edwardian England never escapes the blurredness created by power when it shades away into influence or mere dialogue. Yet common observation confirmed that the Christian churches, Catholic and Anglican no less than Dissenting, had led or spawned the agencies which took seriously the 'Condition of England question' since the early days of missions to the urban Irish or university settlements in the East End. Their presence still amounted to little more than that – a presence; but it could help build a mood of resistance or a sense of expectation. As with the attendance list for Professor Masterman's lecture, the churches' contribution took the minor key of participation and encouragement. On occasion it became more strident. Silvester Horne, Gladstone's tormentor during the years of Liberal opposition, made a nuisance of himself also after 1906. He surfaces in the historical record, for example, in 1911 when Asquith made a statement, largely unremarked, that his mind had moved towards the granting of universal suffrage. According to the chief whip, Alick Murray, 'the matter had been much discussed', but 'Mr. A. had not really made up his mind until he heard the arguments of Silvester Horne, leader of the Parliamentary deputation'.[65]

All these considerations invest Edwardian politics, loosely understood to run from the end of the Boer war to the beginning of the Great War, with a tantalizing elusiveness. Almost everyone within the parliamentary world seems to have sensed some acceleration in the rate of social change; but few politicians overcame their disadvantages in divining its nature and implications. High politics, seen as a mode of traditional political behaviour, did not die with the birth of democratic conviction. Its character underwent subtle shifts reflected more faithfully in dinner-invitations than statutes, in country-house visitors' books than speeches on the stump; but the assumptions of Harcourt and Rosebery had not lost their relevance in the cabinet rooms of Campbell-Bannerman and Asquith, nor had preoccupations undergone some kaleidoscopic rearrangement. Men brought up on Ireland and revenue, drink and the farmers, the church and the balance of power saw no reason to write themselves off as the detritus of a wrecked generation. When H. H. Fowler, now Lord Wolverhampton, 'took a very gloomy view of the financial situation' but located his 'principal misgivings' in Ireland, he said something sensible about the politics of the moment for all its echoes of twenty years before. Jack Pease's father spat blood over Lloyd George's bastardization of Liberal doctrine after 1909; but in opposing it he meant to stop, with a sizeable band of sympathizers, a dangerous movement in state finance rather than simply resurrect a shibboleth. But more important than either perception remained the assumption, common to virtually everyone who operated the political system, that a tiny oligarchy still possessed the power to start and stop, to accelerate or retard. 'Newspapers, politicians, mobs, all these are useful enough. But the support of the half dozen men or so – who count – is vital.'[66]

'The corner will be turned...' (1906–14)

Of the many difficulties encountered by historians studying the last years of peace, the most persistent possibly lies in overcoming the certainty, unknown and implausible to contemporaries, that the period constitutes a terminus. In front of Edwardian politicians 1915, 1920 and 1925 stretched out as legitimate marker-posts for a foreseeable future, one fashioned from the same continuum of expectation that had informed their vision of the coming election before 1906. Those men had no reason beyond prudence and short-term calculation for 'solving' all their problems before the chiming of some midnight hour in August 1914. It therefore behoves historians to resist rejecting the validity of their politics because they failed to do so: they deserve as optimistic and distanced a future as their modern observers unfailingly accord to themselves. A second cautionary tale comes to mind, moreover, when considering that prospect. For the inevitable taking of stock invited by the eruption of the world's first total war will only make sense when seen in broad perspective; yet much of the history of the period fastens on the internal history of the Liberals, whether in decline or renewal, on the Conservative party 'revival' or on the Labour party's role as harbinger of class politics. In this way the compelling turns of fortune that characterize the period become accessories to a bland historical 'process' and a form of Whig history (all too fresh in the contemporary record) revives in the texts of writers determined to have the Liberals die before Sarajevo or to see Labour's 'rise' implicit in evidence all too short on yeast. Many forget about the Conservative party altogether, out of some unspoken belief that its history provides a neutral wallpaper in front of which real events are acted out. None of these temptations has much to be said for it. The last seems especially foolish when the central problem in our century's politics frequently turns on understanding not so much socialist emergence as Tory persistence.

With their 399 men spilling over the government benches, the Liberals of 1906 believed themselves no one's accessory, certainly not the Labour party's which they outnumbered ten to one, nor the crippled Tory party which the election had reduced to 157 MPs. John Redmond's 83 nationalists stood, as ever, in the wings, waiting for a day when they might again hold the balance of power between the parties as in 1885. In these circumstances, political attention moved away from the opposition benches and towards the government ranks for signs of disaffection and rebellion. There the eye tended to fall only on what gave it most pleasure. For Arthur Ponsonby to have claimed, for example, that the new government had behind it a House of Commons '3/4 strongly radical', he must have seen only what he wanted to see. Herbert Gladstone, one of the men whom Ponsonby would have to convince, saw 'no sign of any *violent* forward movement' and estimated the 'dangerous element' at less than a dozen. Perhaps he, too, was whistling for courage; but a modern estimate of 'social radical' strength in this parliament puts their number at about forty – a tenth rather than three-quarters of Liberal support.[67] Redmond's speculations had their own colour and also suggested grounds for optimism. Take but the 'Whigs' away, Redmond thought, and the new government would commit itself to Home Rule. He plainly did not include the chancellor of the exchequer in his thinking. Shortly before taking office in 1905 Asquith had warned Gladstone of the 'incalculable and fatal mischief' that Home Rule would bring to the Liberal party if they brought it back to the centre of politics. The experience of a landslide victory would hardly have helped him change his mind.[68]

Conservative hopes that the Liberals might weaken from within received small sustenance during the first few months of the Liberal government. Their own internal divisions had diminished, publicly at least, in the 'Valentine letters' exchanged between Balfour and Chamberlain in February; and the final collapse of Chamberlain's health later in the year – he remained, with some periods of remission, an incoherent paralytic until his death in 1914 – removed one threat to Balfour's supremacy. Yet the Tory leadership had few grounds for rejoicing. A new voice of great power had come into the House in F. E. Smith (Conservative: Liverpool, Walton), whose maiden speech so stunned those who heard it that it would prove a common memory in the political memoirs of the 1940s and 1950s and whose personal notoriety as 1st Earl of Birkenhead lent such spice to 1920s society. But a single sparkle could hardly brighten the Commons, and Balfour's mind turned inevitably from the green benches to the red. Plainly the House of Lords must play a major part in Conservative strategy as it had between 1892 and 1895. Which strategy to adopt

posed a problem of some delicacy, and Balfour took pains to keep
Lansdowne's forces on a sensible course:

> It is, of course, impossible to foresee how each particular case is to be
> dealt with, but I incline to advise that we should fight all points of
> importance very stiffly in the Commons, and should make the House of
> Lords the theatre of compromise. It is evident that you can never fight
> for a position which we have surrendered; while, on the other hand, the
> fact that we have strenuously fought for the position and been severely
> beaten may afford adequate ground for your making a graceful con-
> cession to the Representative Chamber.[69]

Few of the Unionist activists in the Lords shared Balfour's
perspective. Over the next few years they attempted to do precisely
what the ex-premier had warned them against doing; and until
1911 much of British domestic politics would become a concealed
argument over the future, even the existence, of the House of
Lords.

Campbell-Bannerman's suppression of the Relugas conspiracy left
him strong in the Commons, especially when to the trio's inclusion
were added the promotion of Gladstone to the Home Office and
Lloyd George to the Board of Trade. In the Lords the government
had only the lord chancellor, Loreburn, and the Earl of Crewe, apart
from old-school Whigs like Ripon and Elgin. Their parliamentary
performance through 1906 and 1907 attracted some admiration,
especially recalled during the dark days of the Great War when
'C-B' became a model of clean Liberal politics. Lloyd George's legislation on patents and merchant shipping, Haldane's attempts to drag
army organization into the twentieth century, Asquith's budgets of
1907 and (in effect) 1908, the abortive education bills of Birrell and
Runciman: this activity, for all the crippling negation of the Lords,
suggested energy and direction. From within, the perspective had a
darker colour. Liberal ministers worried from the start about Campbell-Bannerman who seemed to be breaking down almost as soon as
he took office. His wife, Charlotte, had suffered a stroke in 1902 and
never showed signs of recovery. When she died on 30 August 1906
the prime minister lost much of his own interest in the world and
certainly had no stomach for the fight against the Lords invited by
their treatment of the education bill. Two heart attacks over the next
eighteen months drove Campbell-Bannerman out of office and into
an early grave. Meanwhile the administration separated out into the
usual government of departments.

One of those departments, the Foreign Office, contained a similar
but more dangerous tragedy. For Edward Grey's highly emotional

nature had suffered two blows just at the moment when his career peaked. The death of his mother in the summer of 1905 contributed to his lack of resolution in the negotiations with the other imperialists. But when his odd, shy wife fractured her skull in a carriage accident near Falloden within weeks of his taking office, the alteration in Grey became overwhelming. Rather than become softer and more vulnerable as Campbell-Bannerman had done, Grey acquired the armour of a man who believes himself already dead. He could contemplate political life only by spiritualizing it; his letters through the period breathe a personal religion and consciousness of Right. Two consequences of Grey's cosmology soon became clear. His refusal to assert himself over detail in the 'Office' against powerful personalities such as the Germanophobe, Eyre Crowe, whose famous memorandum of 1907 identified Germany as Britain's next enemy, and his principal private secretary, William (later Lord) Tyrell, allowed minor sectors of policy to be worked out by others; while, second, he showed total unconcern at attacks from his party unless they impugned his standing with God. Had his friend Haldane become foreign secretary in 1906 then many of the party's sensitivities over policy might have communicated themselves to Whitehall. That a majority even of Grey's own cabinet colleagues did not know what he was doing before 1911 suggested, by contrast, that the foreign secretary recognized only one authority. 'Secret diplomacy' had a history detectable in the working of cabinets chaired by Gladstone, Salisbury and Rosebery; but Grey's relationship with his Maker gave it a firmer validation and made policy more brittle than circumstances demanded.

Undoubtedly secrecy brought its own ironies. In November 1905 Asquith had reassured the German ambassador that 'an English government which promised armed assistance to France against Germany would be thrown out of office within a week'. Yet when Grey received news of his wife's accident he had just moved significantly closer to that promise in his conversations with the French ambassador, Paul Cambon.[70] Asquith may have discovered the truth sooner than the five years it took to come out in full cabinet: the evidence seems ambivalent. Meanwhile foreign affairs bit deeply into the awareness of politicians, partly as a result of developing fears of invasion and subversion. The anxiety had its absurd facets of bluster and rumour, as in the derision that greeted the Kaiser's protestation, during an interview printed in the *Daily Telegraph* in 1907, of the innocence and friendliness of the German naval programme, or in the stories appearing in the popular dailies in 1908 of how reporters had identified members of the German general staff surveying the Essex seaboard for points of disembarkation. It also occupied, however, the thoughts of senior Foreign Office personnel and the Committee of Imperial Defence (CID), a body formed during Balfour's government to coordinate military and political thinking. Crowe's memorandum of 1 January 1907, compelling in retrospect for its prescience in identifying the threat from Germany, set the tone for much official speculation. Esher, closely connected with both the Court of Edward VII and the CID, showed a similar foresight in the distinctive language of the period:

> The *great fear* is that war may come before we are ready... It will take five years to get our people screwed up to compulsory service. Perhaps longer... The laws of historical and ethnographical evolution... require that we shall fight one of the most powerful military empires that has ever lived.[71]

Within Liberal circles such speculation had a small and private circulation: its public promotion remained the monopoly of Tory publicists of the 'radical right'. The great fear for the cabinet centred, indeed, not so much on fighting a war with Germany as in paying for the means of preventing one.

A radical reconstruction of fiscal arrangements confronted any government seeking to avoid bankruptcy in post-Boer war Britain. Raising revenue from the masses hardly presented a new problem: we have seen the preoccupation running through the entire period since the Napoleonic wars. But the background against which taxation demanded consideration had changed materially over the past two decades. One classical expedient for calling in money – the imposition of duties on articles bought by the people (corn, sugar, tea, paper, malt) – had withered before Liberal free trade strategy after 1846. Buoyant trade and a supremacy in international finance had helped to compensate; but that position had likewise crumbled in the very different economic climate experienced by post-Gladstonian chancellors. Nor did the predicament stop there. The sharp rise in indigenous and immigrant population, most of it concentrated in the towns and cities where philanthropic mechanisms operated least effectively, placed extra strain on the resources of government – more so now than ever before because decisions to devote finance to education, the maintenance of a high defensive profile and the fighting of a major war had also fallen on a beleaguered Treasury.[72] Doors thus closed behind the Liberal ministers of 1906 before they spoke to a secretary or opened a document; and for men committed to promoting Liberal doctrine, their options had narrowed. Doctrinal considerations stood in the way of following Salisbury's path of reversing the drift towards collectivism; indeed had Salisbury been alive and governing in 1906 he could hardly have avoided some restrained plunder. They could not follow Chamberlain in reviving the indirect system of taxation by announcing a new scheme of tariffs. The way forward had to lie along the road trodden by Beach during the war – to shift some of the burden from indirect to direct taxation and offer, in return as it were, a language of 'contribution' for the purpose of 'benefit'. Everybody knew that further taxation would have to come to finance old age pensions and the Dreadnoughts whose commissioning the government had proved unable to resist. Not everyone realized that it had to come anyway.

Under the Liberal governments, the proportion of direct to indirect taxation increased from 51.4 per cent to over 60 per cent.[73] Credit for the rethinking belongs in part to Asquith whose years at the Exchequer have too readily fallen into shadow beside those of Lloyd George. But despite Asquith's introduction of old age pensions (5s per week or 7s 6d for a married couple) in 1908, Lloyd George's People's Budget inevitably attracted more attention. The new chancellor had inherited from Asquith an important distinction between earned and unearned income: he resolved to use it with great psychological effect on owners of land. In themselves the proposals did not comprise a fiscal revolution: an increase in death duties, a licensing tax to claw back money lost when the Lords threw out the 1908 licensing bill; a new 'super-tax'; a 20 per cent duty on land values payable when estates changed hands; the usual condiments of additions to income tax, tobacco and spirits. The land proposals, however, hit an exposed nerve, not least in the valuation that Lloyd George later claimed had provided his central motivation in advocating the duties. And the debate on the budget quickly dovetailed into doubts over the durability of the constitution. From the beginning Lloyd George had believed that the Lords would pass the bill: he scouted as ridiculous suggestions that they would dare to reject it.[74] Yet once it became evident that Balfour and Lansdowne could not control their more militant peers, he grasped the opportunity to reinvigorate Liberal support with a 'cry' against the Lords on behalf of democracy. Party preoccupations focused on this strategy from the spring of 1909 to the end of 1910. In November 1909 the budget at last completed its passage through the Commons after a massive campaign of opposition and public discussion. 'It seems incredible', Grey wrote to Margot Asquith, 'that the Budget should be over...I haven't an idea what will follow.'[75] The Lords did not keep him in suspense for long. They rejected the finance bill at the end of the month by 350 to 75. Foreign affairs slipped out of consciousness in the face of a coming constitutional rift that brought echoes of 1640 to those near to the Court.

King Edward had played no insignificant part in confusing Asquith's sense of direction in recent months. His formidable grasp of dress and medals extended in many ways to an understanding of fundamental constitutional procedure and a determination to maintain its proprieties. Behind all the gossip about Alice Keppel and the wall of obsequiousness defended by Knollys and Esher, Edward took kingship seriously and felt no compunction over denouncing lax administration and incompetence. The developing constitutional impasse troubled him, and his nervousness and anxiety communicated themselves to ministers or, in the case of Asquith, their wives. The government's boldness departed for a moment; they seemed not to know what to do next. One lesson, however, seemed plain enough. The Lords would have to be coerced in one of two ways: by the moral pressure of a fresh mandate from a general election; or by the creation of enough Liberal peers to swamp the Tory majority. The King granted the first in the hope that it might prevent the second and 1910 became a year of general elections – one in January, one in December.

January's election confirmed a return to Conservative allegiance among seats that the Liberals had wrested from their traditional loyalty in 1906. Popular interest expressed itself in a turnout of 86.6 per cent, higher even than that of the previous election, but the Liberals nevertheless struggled to remain half a head in front against Tory gains. Their final total of 275 left them just two seats in front of the Conservatives and thus entirely dependent on the 82 nationalists and the Labour party which had benefited from a renewal of the Gladstone–MacDonald pact and increased its parliamentary number to 40. Asquith now had no cushion against dissidents within his own party. His radicals wanted a bold stroke against the Lords; the nationalists had already made one a precondition for retaining their support. Perhaps the peers hoped that by passing the People's Budget in April 1910 the fuss would die down. But by then the prime minister had already brought forward his bill to restrict their capacity to obstruct major legislation and, when the royal surgeons failed to save the King from an attack of bronchitis in May, the second chamber's prospects decidedly worsened. Cries of 'murderer' directed at Asquith during the funeral could not be taken to imply that democracy would rally to the defence of privilege if Asquith persisted.

Mass excitement aroused by first observations of the new monarch, George V, soon gave way to a concentration on parliament and the government's bill. That it ought to pass the Commons went without saying since the Irish and the Labour party gave it unqualified support; but no one knew whether the Lords would decide to go down fighting in a battle that could prove damaging to all concerned. Open debate turned to private conclave in June when a collection of party leaders, calling themselves a 'constitutional conference', tried to reach a settlement out of court. Eight men did their best for five months – Asquith, Lloyd George, Crewe and Birrell for the Liberals; Balfour, Chamberlain, Lansdowne and Lord Cawdor for the other side – but with no hope of success. One interesting sub-plot emerged in August when Lloyd George composed a memorandum at his Welsh home in Criccieth and argued for a high-political coalition of 'half a dozen first-rate men'[76] from each party who could frame a policy containing the best elements of each manifesto (Home Rule, in effect, in return for a big navy and a commission on tariffs). Historically the intrigue has importance as the first demonstration of Lloyd George's willingness to think in a cross-party way and operate, when necessary, behind Asquith's back. But 1910 was not 1916, and for the moment Asquith's laughter, when he discovered that Lloyd George had held conversations with leading Conservatives through F. E. Smith, seems justified. Balfour had no intention of further compromising himself in the eyes of his party by joining a coalition rooted in nothing. On the other hand, the breakdown of the conference in November left all its participants anxious for the winter.

The Lords threw out the parliament bill in November 1910 but it seemed trivial by then whether they passed it or not. For Asquith had already obtained the King's authority for a dissolution and, more than that, he had secured from a very unwilling George V a guarantee that the King would create the necessary number of peers should the Lords again reject the parliament bill. That guarantee remained, for the moment, secret. It went into Asquith's pocket for deployment at an appropriate opportunity. In the meantime the election showed nothing beyond the boredom of the electorate. It replicated the result of January with only minor alterations: the two main parties came out exactly level at 272 and the two minor ones each won an additional couple of seats. If Winston Churchill's anticipation during the summer of 1910 of another five years of power had then seemed heroic, it now made sense. Ireland would doubtless make itself felt and the passage of the parliament bill might yet prove an embarrassment. Granted that the key to victory lay safe in Asquith's pocket, however, one prediction seemed sure: a Liberal government would remain in place until Asquith sought a dissolution, under the five-year rule required by his new parliament bill, in the autumn of 1915.

Less distant prospects admittedly threatened further volatility. Under Campbell-Bannerman few offices had changed hands. Asquith had now occupied first place for nearly three years and already a pattern of shuffling had become apparent. In the list of ministers for the whole period from 1908 to 1915 only Grey, Lloyd George and Birrell finished where they began. Even the prime minister altered his brief by taking on the War Office when Seely resigned from it in 1914. Conservative high politics tell the same story. That Balfour's leadership had never attained the authority of his uncle's we have already seen; but the trials of the constitutional crisis, and the party's unwillingness to follow the conciliatory line he had advised in meeting it, brought a campaign against him from within his own party that even he felt he could not tolerate. His resignation from the party leadership in 1911 caused a stir less for itself than for the strangeness of the succession. Andrew Bonar Law's ascent to prominence threw into relief the inadequacy of his rivals – Walter Long, who combined bone-headedness with hypersensitivity, and Austen Chamberlain, whose associations with the Birmingham past that everyone wanted to forget sunk him as readily as his hollow grandeur. Law had a rhetoric evocatively compared to the hammering of rivets. His presence suggested a new aggression; it also argued the likelihood of bitter fighting over Ulster if and when the Liberal government made their move over Ireland. The Labour party of Keir Hardie and Ramsay MacDonald likewise suffered strain in its leadership because of its willingness to continue the electoral alliance with the Liberals and to repress constituency enthusiasts calling for a less timid approach to the fighting of by-elections.[77]

Won or lost, by-elections preoccupied politicians after 1910 with an intensity rarely found in the previous parliament. Isolated results could now make a significant difference to events, perhaps by encouraging the Lords to more determined resistance in the belief that the people supported them, more often by testing hypotheses about the popularity of individual measures or the note taken by the public of issues outside Westminster. Once the constitutional question ended in the defeat of those diehards who wanted to fight in the last ditch against Asquith and his ministers, these issues multiplied quickly in the imaginations of politicians if not of their electors. Though dwarfed by the strikes of 1912, industrial turbulence in 1911 wrenched attention away from the parliament bill as Britain began its dialogue between unionism and corporatism that grew in volume and seriousness after the war. Germany's revival of ambition against the French in Morocco and Russia's against the Turks similarly widened the subject-matter of conversation and correspondence in 1911–12. The House of Commons and the upper chamber contributed to their own irrelevance by losing much of their *gravitas* in hints of ministerial corruption and Lord Willoughby de Broke's holding back of the sea during the Lords debates on the parliament bill. When Sir Edward Carson, F. E. Smith and Bonar Law announced their determination to maintain the Union with Ireland by force, if necessary, they broadcast a view of parliament's irrelevance to which the suffragettes and syndicalists had already contributed. Whoever deserved the laurels for the 1910 elections, the loser had seemingly become one concept of representative democracy.

The Liberal cabinet confronted these events from a perspective peculiar to itself. In the opinion of the more uncomfortable of its members – Loreburn, out of residual Cobdenism, and Morley, out of habit – discussion had degenerated into a perpetual requiem for the Liberal League through the government's toleration of the Dreadnoughts and its 'efficient' attitude to property. McKenna's experiences as first lord gave him a very different impression since, to him, it seemed that a clique of progressives with Lloyd George at their head had set themselves the objective of destroying the naval programme McKenna had urged on behalf of his admirals. This inner tension, rather than the parliament bill, threatened the peace of the cabinet in 1911. Publicly, the constitutional crisis kept it out of sight as the peers regrouped to denounce the parliament bill in ignorance of the royal guarantee. Only when Asquith produced the news of the pledge in that stifling July, when the very heat of London's streets enhanced the fever of the peers and complemented the shouting down of the prime minister by the opposition on 24 July, did Lansdowne and Curzon win converts to their moderate view against the diehards led by Salisbury, Selborne and Halsbury; and the parliament bill, which ended the peers' tampering with 'money bills', imposed a limit of two years on the delaying of other measures and reduced the maximum length of parliaments from seven years to five, moved towards its acceptance on 10 August by 131 votes to 114. But already the government's problem over defence had begun its exposure because foreign affairs had returned to the centre of the stage.

On the day after Asquith wrote to Balfour to inform him of the King's guarantee to create peers, Lloyd George spoke to an audience of City bankers at London's Mansion House. His speech of 21 July responded to a German initiative: the sending of a gunboat to Agadir to convince the French that their 'forward' Moroccan policy had offended Berlin. With the approval of Asquith and Grey, Lloyd George announced to both Germany and France that Britain could not stand by while those two countries bickered between themselves over an area of the world in which Britain had interests. An insistence on consultation seemed to Berlin something more serious: a throwing down of the gauntlet. In the wave of outrage that followed from Germany, Grey felt sufficiently nervous to tell McKenna to prepare the fleet against attack. The excitement soon passed; but the issue had shown that the cabinet's fears over McKenna's running of the Admiralty had some substance. In particular his failure to establish a naval war staff along lines recommended by the Committee of Imperial Defence disturbed colleagues anxious to prepare against surprise attacks. Asquith's embarrassment deepened. He had seen his patronage go wrong before, not least when his lord president of the council fell prey to flagrant insanity in 1908. To replace McKenna, who was not mad and did not want to go, he would need to contemplate a major reshuffle of posts, especially if he wanted to substitute Churchill whose passion for 'these warlike matters...in the inner life of a Liberal Cabinet'[78] had mounted through dull days at the Board of Trade and an unsuccessful spell at the Home Office. But the problem would not go away; he moved McKenna to the Home Office and sent Churchill to the Admiralty, with momentous consequences a few years later. The change at least cleared the air and ministers met the 1912 session in a more galvanized state of mind than they had known during the previous year.

They had, after all, overcome an important legislative hurdle in the autumn session of 1911. To find an appropriate slot in the programme for Lloyd George's national insurance scheme had proved troublesome, for it seemed likely to arouse opposition and unpopularity whenever it appeared. That a measure so obviously aimed at improving the security of working-class people against sickness should have provoked animosity from the very people it purported to protect surprises later generations brought up in a climate of 'welfare'. Yet the history of state intervention in the lives of ordinary people had given few grounds for gratitude since the 1890s, something which ministers probably did not comprehend. One recalls Lord Stanley – Disraeli's future foreign secretary – feeling in the 1860s that the working men would *prefer* 'a master called "the State" who shall interfere in and regulate everything. Modern democracy loves such a master, and seeks to strengthen his position since he represents the universal equality of the citizen, and if you must be governed, they argue, better be governed by a minister or a central authority whom you do not see than by one or many of your richer neighbours.'[79] This says more about a rich man's pessimism than about working-class psychology. In fact trade unionists had come to feel by the turn of century that 'the State' meant legal repression on the part of institutions dominated by their employers; so that, if the national insurance scheme now made it possible to offer the workers that resonant '9d for 4d' of which Lloyd George boasted, then the certain 4d going out of the wage packet seemed larger than the improbable 9d coming back. Still, the act passed through parliament and the government did not fall. By-elections swelled in significance for a few months as politicians tried to estimate the impact of the measure. A couple of defeats in Scotland at the end of the year convinced Asquith, for example, that national insurance had become an electoral albatross. On the other hand, a new session might undo its effects, especially once the initial resentment from trade unionists, doctors and duchesses had died down. The government could turn to its main programme which the controversy with the Lords had placed in abeyance. Two items plainly bulked large within it. The third Home Rule bill had to appear at the top of the agenda if the support of the Irish were to be retained; and a scheme for Welsh disestablishment seemed hardly less necessary to placate Dissent which had shown patience since 1906. Both measures came before the Commons in April 1912.

The severe industrial dislocations of the spring in the coal and dock strikes caused headaches. They also frustrated the radical wing of the Liberal party which chafed at watching their leaders shy away from granting to Vernon Hartshorn's miners the national minimum wage on which the strike had centred. But evidence from the past suggested that the cloud would pass. Although Charles Masterman knew, for example, that the national insurance scheme, with which he had been associated, would make waves, he believed that the Labour party would not benefit from the government's temporary unpopularity, nor even from its repressive techniques during disputes. 'He instanced Llanelly, where two men were shot during the strike riots last August, but where a Liberal Member has just been elected in a by-election.'[80] To some extent the example supported Masterman's claim: the Independent Labour man received only 149 votes in that election. What Masterman forgot to mention was the Conservative vote at Llanelly which reached its highest point for twenty-five years. From this direction, rather than from the nascent Labour party, would come the challenge throughout Britain's constituencies; and those who had identified it as such worried over the tendency of the Liberal party to compose overtures for the weak when it needed to drown the voices of the strong. For Churchill, his New Liberalism lost at sea, the problem for the Liberals could be simply stated as one of keeping the party together and avoiding divisive policies. He plainly worried about the implications of Lloyd George's ideas for land reform which the chancellor had mooted privately. Far better to stick to what they already had:

> I see no reason why we shd not surmount the winter session. A break-down now would be absolutely fatal. Home Rule, the Welsh Church, the Franchise, the Insurance Act, the Parlt. Act itself, we all founder together. On the other hand, once our 3 bills have been sent to the Lds the corner will be turned. We can do this if we don't quarrel among ourselves, if we don't play the fool over the women [by giving them the vote] & if we don't come to bloodshed in Ulster.[81]

His conditions must have impressed the chancellor as stringent, not to say naive.

Franchise and playing the fool with women had already fused into a single problem. Little likelihood existed of this cabinet adopting female suffrage *tout court*; but any franchise bill, even one relating solely to expanding the male franchise in a limited way or ending the plural voting that benefited the Unionists, would have to run the gauntlet of the committee stage and face the possibility of amendment to include females. Until 1911 the government's essays in franchise reform had consequently proved timid, trivial and futile; and as their courage grew so had the intransigence of the Lords increased. With the parliament bill now through, however, Asquith and his colleagues had an opportunity to reform in a 'Liberal' way and enact their legislation over the veto of the House of Lords in time for the 1915 election. Pease's bill of 1912 consequently sought to create an electorate of $9 1/2$ million males on a one-man-one-vote basis with a six months' residence requirement and an occupation qualification for land or business premises to appease the right wing of the party.[82] It survived second reading intact but 'female' clauses looked inevitable during the committee stage in January 1913 and the government braced itself to accept them if faced with no alternative other than losing the bill altogether. At this moment, however, luck deserted both the government and the women. Bonar Law's complaint to Mr Speaker Lowther, that the tacking on of a female suffrage amendment to the bill would alter its purpose so drastically as to make the bill different in principle from the original one, found a sympathetic auditor. In judging the bill invalid, and thus terminating its progress, the Speaker did not act on Asquith's instructions: had the bill passed, it would have rid the government of one of its irritations. But he ended the only serious attempt made by this administration to effect *political* reform, as opposed to their various essays in social engineering. The terms of Pease's case still bear recollection: that the present system of registration depended on eleven different franchises with at least nineteen variations; that there were still 'about 4,200,000 individuals of twenty-one years of age without votes'.[83]

Some quarrelling in cabinet had arisen from the franchise problem, though less than other issues had caused because franchise did not become the preoccupation that defence or Ireland assumed in these years. Personal animosities occasioned some difficulties even after the McKenna controversy faded into a memory, and Lloyd George and Churchill frequently discovered themselves at the centre of it. The 'progressive' alliance of 1906–10 had lost much of its zest: by 1912 observers saw Lloyd George as closer to Grey than to Churchill while Churchill had moved into a 'defence' frame of mind that cut across the chancellor's determination to reduce military expenditure. Lloyd George's aggression over the estimates reflected the withering away of the radicalism associated with the People's Budget; his economics since then had owed more to convention than inspiration and his celebrated impatience with detail, which so infuriated a new entrant to the cabinet, Sir Charles Hobhouse, took him close to the wind on several occasions and almost turned the 1914 budget into a fiasco. Mistrust of him, always strong, increased markedly in 1913 when public allegations that he had speculated in American Marconi shares and benefited from his ministerial knowledge of contracts gave rise to a major scandal which prompted an offer of resignation from Lloyd George, refused by Asquith, and a revival of wholesome propaganda about land reform to pull attention away from the embarrassment and inject new life into a flagging party.[84] Yet his very encouragement of social-radical enthusiasm stimulated the resistance of those, like the 'Holt cave' of businessmen associated with the Liverpool ship-owner Richard Holt, who believed that property had suffered enough. It also prevented him from supplanting Edward Grey as heir apparent to Asquith in the eyes of most party men. His relations with Churchill deteriorated markedly when he came to consider the estimates for 1913–14 and the first lord dug in his heels against more cuts. That crisis only receded at the beginning of 1914 after Asquith, worried not so much about Churchill's impending resignation as about Grey's, helped smooth the waters and bring the chancellor to a compromise.

One of the arguments used in resisting defence expenditure rested on an improvement in Anglo-German relations. Certainly the tensions of Agadir had long since passed. Haldane had visited Germany in 1912 and spread some goodwill which a voluble section of Liberal backbench opinion constantly amplified. Under the chairmanship of Sir John Brunner, a Liberal foreign policy committee applied considerable pressure on the government to dissociate itself from international moves to 'encircle' Germany while a cross-party Balkan Committee in the House of Commons contained numerous noisy radicals full of anti-Tsarist fervour and consumed by the future of Bosnia-Herzegovina. Indeed, the focus of concern in foreign policy had moved away from Germany and towards her unstable ally. For since 1907 the British government's understanding with, and support for, Tsarist Russia had created much unease in radical circles which expressed itself strongly during the Bosnian crisis of 1908, when the Russians and Austrians saw an opportunity for annexations in the Balkans, and in 1912 when Russian pressure on Persia and the outbreak of war between the Balkan allies (Bulgaria, Serbia, Greece, Montenegro) and Turkey brought chaos to the region that had proved so important a touchstone of party politics in the 1870s. The Balkan wars of 1912 and 1913 achieved a far smaller impact than the Russo-Turkish war of a generation before. But they developed British anxieties over possible Russian involvement and the effect this might have on Anglo-French treaty commitments. In November 1912, for example, Riddell believed he had 'never seen L[loyd] G[eorge] himself so much disturbed' as in these early days of crisis in the Balkans.[85] Such events heightened the atmosphere of insecurity which radicals thought a consequence of secret diplomatic alliances and entanglements; they therefore redoubled criticism of Grey. By 1914 the foreign secretary had come to reflect many of the party's inner tensions. He approved of franchise reform and women's suffrage but worried over the radical offensive against incomes and land. He preferred Churchill's vision of defensive need to Lloyd George's. Also he felt keenly that, whatever the party decided to recommend on Irish devolution, Ulster must be excluded from the prescription.

Avoiding bloodshed in Ireland had completed Churchill's list of requirements for turning the corner after 1912. Since then, however, the government had paid no great attention to Ulster and the resistance to Home Rule that all competent observers of Irish politics expected from the northern counties. Conservatives, on the other hand, had seen a genuine grievance to exploit, one that would help the party to find a single voice as it had manifestly failed to do over tariffs. Leo Amery looked back on the Tory involvement in Ulster in a typically frank letter to Austen Chamberlain's half-brother, Neville, in the summer of 1914. 'We only drifted into it really,' he wrote, 'if we are to be honest with ourselves, because Ulster was the easiest thing to talk about when public opinion was apathetic and because on the face of it it seemed a moderate and reasonable attitude.'[86]

Certainly the Ulstermen received short shrift in the Home Rule bill of 1912–13. The Lords predictably threw the bill out in both sessions but of course the parliament act would now come into play and make the ultimate passage of the bill inevitable. Thwarted inside parliament, the Conservative party elected to fight outside. Lansdowne, their leader in the Lords, still bore the scars inflicted by his moderation over the parliament bill: he wanted no more from Ireland and assumed a more rigid pose than many of the extreme men of Belfast. In picking up the mantle of Ulster in defiance of parliament, however, the Tory party adopted a guise that could only appear unnatural in the party of national cohesion. And when Bonar Law told the vast crowd rallying at Blenheim Palace in July 1912 that he could conceive of no lengths to which the Ulstermen might go in their resistance in which he would not support them, he threatened to turn the Conservative party into a band of guerrillas.

Ulster reached Blenheim before it reached the cabinet: Liberal ministers took cognizance of the Ulster problem when it had become too late effectively to accommodate it. A section of the cabinet including Grey, Lloyd George and Churchill tried to bend the minds of their colleagues towards some mechanism for excluding the Protestant counties of the north from the Home Rule bill. But the Conservative party saw much to be gained from refusing the concessions which the Liberals half-heartedly offered in suggesting merely temporary exclusion; through the spring and summer of 1914 the impasse over Ireland dominated high-political discussion in both major parties with a level of intensity not witnessed at Westminster since 1886. Administrative confusions compounded the plight of the ministers. In March, an absurd failure of communication between the war minister, J. E. B. Seely, the commander-in-chief in Ireland, General Paget, and Brigadier-General Sir Hubert Gough, a fanatical Ulsterman commanding the third cavalry brigade stationed at the Curragh, placed British officers there in the position of deciding whether or not to obey orders, which no one had given, to carry out offensive operations against the militant loyalists of the northern counties. Seely resigned and Asquith took the War Office himself, but the move came too late to reassure Ulster Protestants or, for that matter, King George whose distress over the Irish imbroglio had become the occasion for much comment. Then came the news, just a month later, that a substantial armoury of weapons and ammunition had successfully been landed at Larne, north of Belfast, in contempt of the authorities. There could be no doubt of the direction in which events pointed. When a conference of party leaders meeting at Buckingham Palace in July 1914 failed to make progress on the Ulster question, the assumption became general that open war must soon erupt, not in Morocco, or Persia, or the Balkans, but in Ireland.

These tense months during 1913 and 1914 imply, for some historians, a slide to catastrophe.[87] But whose catastrophe? The prospect of major bloodshed in northern Ireland obviously threatened a human disaster in 1914; it did not of itself herald a political one, despite the anxiety of some ministers. True, the Asquith government had failed to assuage Irish ambitions, but then so had every British government since 1874. All the evidence available to British politicians insisted that Ireland bored the British electorate. If they could show their constituency that they had done their best to act honourably, then little more seemed necessary. Indeed, Liberals could be forgiven for thinking Ireland a Conservative problem. Bonar Law, Smith and Carson had harnessed their party to the fortunes of a country about which the British public knew little and cared less; and through their behaviour since 1912 they had placed themselves outside traditional Conservative judgements about the sanctity of parliament. Other issues, meanwhile, had begun to work in the Liberals' favour. Some backbenchers saw their pressing forward of Welsh disestablishment (not finally accomplished until 1920) as more significant than the Home Rule controversy, for it rallied Nonconformity into a new fighting spirit. 'We are back again in 1906 so far as concerns the Dissenters', one diarist noted in March 1914.[88] Again, the unpopularity attaching to national insurance had weakened with the passage of time and experience of the system. And the impetus given the party by the legislative programme of 1912–13, plus Lloyd George's one-man drive to reclaim radicalism with his land programme (intended to rationalize land management and safeguard tenant farmers against landlords), indicated that a government which had gone through the usual mid-term depression had begun its recovery in plenty of time for its next trial of strength.

Liberal language after 1913 developed an optimistic future tense about the 1915 election. Of course, the mood required qualification. The Labour party had so far refused to renew the Gladstone–MacDonald pact; and since the Osborne judgement had been reversed by the Liberals in 1913, the possibility of Labour's fielding 100, even 150 candidates at the next election called for consideration. Some Conservative resurgence in by-elections also brought its daunting moments but, seen overall, the performance of the government in by-elections since 1910 seemed no worse than one might expect. Besides, unless it wanted to jump back into the hole it had dug for itself over food taxes, the Tory party could talk only about Ireland.

Fighting an election against a background of violence in Ireland would prove unpleasant, no doubt, but the Conservative party would also find itself with an awkward manifesto to write. To foresee in the 1915 election a Liberal victory, followed by a renewed understanding with part or all of the Labour party, seemed neither stupid nor unrealistic. Nor does anything in the historical record make nonsense of the contention.

The election never came. Wherever the corner the Liberals had hoped to turn was, they never reached it. The Archduke Franz Ferdinand's murder at the hands of an unbalanced Bosnian nationalist in June 1914 had aroused few comments among politicians preoccupied by the Irish crisis. At the end of a cabinet meeting on 24 July, called to discuss the latest phase of the Irish discussions, ministers became dully aware that the foreign secretary's 'quiet, grave tones' persisted after others stopped speaking. Edward Grey had begun to read out a document; it was the Austrian ultimatum to Serbia. The escalation no one had taken seriously over the past three weeks seemed suddenly to have begun and, as the imagination strained to picture the mobilization of the armies of most of the Western world, John Redmond and Sir Edward Carson shrank to nothing. Two days later, Herbert Samuel, writing to his mother, could not assimilate the news. 'How infinitely small,' he wrote, 'in the shadow of this awful catastrophe, appear the petty troubles of Ulster and one's own personal concerns cannot be spoken of.'[89] For a week or so it appeared that Britain might resist the magnetism of Europe's alliance system. Lloyd George led a group of ministers hoping to keep Britain out of the coming war but, once it emerged that Asquith had no intention of staying out or resigning office, dissident ministers returned to their posts under cover of the German 'rape' of Belgium that transformed every act of prudence into a carrying of the cross. Only Morley and John Burns actually went: the rest hung together, fortified by a party truce for the duration of the war, to face a trial more terrible than anyone could yet envisage.

There we leave them. For Asquith and his kind, the experience of a lifetime passed overnight a new threshold of irrelevance. Lloyd George, on the other hand, grew as never before in this strange environment and established in December 1916 the greatest war ministry seen in Britain since the days of Pitt the Younger. Faces once noticed at the back of the smoking room or on the more arid committees came to fill the formal ministerial photographs as politics and business merged their men of push and go.[90] Ireland forgotten, until the Dublin rising of Easter 1916 brought a flash on the horizon,

the Conservative party worked its way back to the centre of government through two coalitions, making itself the victor at home ir-
respective of what happened in the trenches. But the Labour party
collapsed in disarray. Ramsay MacDonald and Philip Snowden stood
out against the war, leaving the party to Arthur Henderson and their
own integrity in the hands of Horatio Bottomley and the gutter mind
of a wartime press. The next election came not in 1915 but in the
khaki atmosphere of 1918 with an unknowable new electorate
created by the fourth reform act of that year. Manhood suffrage,
and votes for women over the age of thirty, made 'democracy', the
slogan of the past century, close to a reality. A glance at the list of
successful candidates conveys at once a sense of military background
and the war experience that would mould the consciousness of
political leaders and form the assumptions of a Mosley, an Eden, a
Macmillan. But many names known to the history of the nineteenth
century no longer appear in the roll-call of the twentieth. So many
families, whose continuities have given this book much of its texture,
slid into oblivion in the squalor of Flanders as white hopes went
under the gun. Their parents received the buff envelope, marked 'War
Office', and felt the future slip away. 'He put his hands over his face
and we walked into an empty room and sat down in silence.'[91]
Asquith's despair at the death of his son Raymond on the Somme in
1916 may serve as an emblem for the loss of a generation educated in
the deportment of a governing class. That education, acquired more
than imparted, had prepared them for a task very different from the
one to which their school or college sent them in the false spring of
1915. Rarely has the unfolding of expectation into history seemed so
tragic or laden with importance. In their own awareness, the young
of that special society rode the crest of an open future. In ours, they
stand caught between a past inadequate to their purpose and the
promise of worse to come.

APPENDIX

Some People

This appendix contains a selection of names mentioned *en passant* in the text; it does not include any individuals discussed at length there.

ABERCROMBY, James, 1st Baron Dunfermline (1776–1858). Cab. (master of the mint), 1834; Speaker of Commons, 1835–9. Father a general; educ. for Bar. MP Midhurst and Calne in unreformed parlt and Edinburgh in reformed one after 1832. Prominent part in Scottish business; chief baron of exchequer of Scotland, 1830–32.

ACLAND, Sir Arthur Herbert Dyke, 13th bart (1847–1926). Father 11th bart; friend of Gladstone in youth. Educ. Rugby, Christ Church; 2nd law/ mod. hist. Cab. 1892–5 at education (i.e. vice-pres. of committee of council); opposed 1902 act. Roseberian in 1890s. Withdrew from politics on medical advice, 1898. Early career university teaching and administration. MP Rotherham after 1885. Ordained, 1871; lapsed, 1879. Nickname 'Stumpy'.

ALBERT, Francis Charles Augustus Emmanuel, Prince Consort (1819–61). 2nd son of Ernest, Duke of Saxe-Coburg-Gotha. Educ. Brussels and Bonn; travelled widely with Baron Stockmar. Engaged to Victoria, 1839; married, 1840. Backed Great Exhibition, 1851. Peelite in 1840s. Conciliatory influence during international disputes. Title of Consort, 1857.

ALTHORP, John Charles Spencer, Viscount, 3rd Earl Spencer (1782–1845). Father 2nd Earl; mother d. of 1st Earl Lucan. Harrow with Robinson, Duncannon and Ponsonby; Trinity, Cambridge – removed early. Renegade Tory; Whig MP Northamptonshire, 1806–34. Grey's chancellor of exchequer, 1830–34; 'the tortoise on which the world reposes' (Melbourne).

ARBUTHNOT, Charles (1767–1850). Wellington's chancellor of duchy, 1828–30, but power mainly exercised outside cab. as patronage secretary (1809–23). He and his wife close to Liverpool, Castlereagh, Wellington, Bathurst and Peel. Losing touch with party by mid-1820s: fanatical anti-

Canningite. Suggestions of administrative incompetence and hysteria; 'in himself quite enough to overset any Administration' (H of C Clerk).

ARCH, Joseph (1826–1919). Father a farm worker at Barford, near Warwick. Agricultural labourer at 9; self-educated. Primitive Methodist lay preacher. Contested a seat in 1880 but not elected till 1885 (Lib: Norfolk, North-West). Out, 1886–92; back again, same seat, 1892–5. Autobiography edited by Countess of Warwick. Retired, 1900.

ASHBOURNE, Edward Gibson, baron (1837–1913). Lord chancellor of Ireland in every Cons. govt between 1885 and 1905. Born Dublin; educ. Trinity College Dublin. Irish Bar, 1860. Spent most of his time in Ireland after peerage (1885). Deemed 'soft' on the Catholic question.

ASKWITH, Sir George Ranken (1861–1942). Asquith's trouble-shooter in industrial disputes. Legal background: Marlborough, Brasenose, 1st mod. hist. 1884. Then read law: Bar, 1886. Devilled for Henry James. Counsel for HM Commissioners of Works; assist. sec. railway branch of Board of Trade, 1907.

BATHURST, Henry, 3rd Earl (1762–1834). Liverpool's sec. for war and the colonies. Stayed out of Canning's govt with Wellington: latter's lord pres. of council, 1828–30. Sometimes seen as a possible coalition PM – 'a kind of Portland-like King Log' (C. W. Wynn).

BEACH, Sir Michael Hicks, 9th bart, 1st Earl St Aldwyn (1837–1916). Cab. from 1876 and Salisbury's chancellor of exchequer, 1885–6, 1895–1902. Educ. Eton and Christ Church. Twice married; personality change after first wife died in childbirth in 1860s. Influence in Gloucestershire (seat Williamstrip Park); MP for E. Gloucestershire, 1864–85, and Bristol West, 1885–1906. Posts at Colonies, Ireland and Board of Trade. 'He would make a very good Home Secretary: and would hang everybody' (Salisbury).

BEXLEY, Nicholas Vansittart, 1st baron (1766–1851). Liverpool's chancellor of exchequer, 1812–23. Father governor of Bengal; mother d. of governor of Madras. Educ. Cheam and Christ Church; read for Bar but entered politics early. Closest to Addington in early years. Took weight of blame for post-war depression. 'Mediocre abilities with accommodating and moderate views.'

BRADLAUGH, Charles (1833–91). Father solicitors clerk. Educ. elementary schools near native Hoxton. Variety of clerical jobs; failed coal agent; soldier for a time. Rose to responsible post in solicitor's office. Proprietor *The National Reformer*. Fought Northampton 1868, 1874 (twice). Elected, 1880; re-elected April 1881; expelled Feb. 1882; re-elected March 1882; excluded 1884; elected 1885. Retained seat till death.

BRIGHT, John (1811–89). Son of Rochdale millowner. As a Quaker cut his political teeth on temperance, opposition to church rates and capital punishment. Commons 1843 for Durham; opposed ten hours bill and Maynooth. From 1847 to 1885 MP for Manchester or Birmingham. Opposed Gladstone on Home Rule. Last public speech 1887.

BROUGHAM, Henry Peter, baron Brougham and Vaux (1778–1868). Grey's lord chancellor, 1830–34. Father lord of manor of Brougham, Westmorland. Educ. Edinburgh University: one of founders of *Edinburgh Review*. Bar, 1808; MP after 1810; peerage, 1830. Defended Queen Caroline, 1820. Behind Society for Diffusion of Useful Knowledge (1825). Anti-slaver; opposed repeal of navigation acts. No office after 1834.

BRUCE, Henry Austin, 1st baron Aberdare, (1832–95). Scottish descent but life (and wealth) built on Welsh coal: seat Duffyn, Glam. Gladstone's home sec., 1868–73, and mainly remembered for his licensing bill. No university: educ. St Omer and Swansea grammar. Bar at 22; practised till 1843. 2nd wife d. of Sir William Napier, historian. Commons from 1852 for Merthyr (to 1868) then Renfrewshire. Lord pres. of council after 1873 reshuffle. After 1874 devoted to education (first chancellor Univ. of Wales) and Royal Niger Company. Great clubman.

BUCKINGHAM, R. P. C. T. N. B. C. Grenville, 3rd Duke of B. and Chandos (1823–89). Only son 2nd Duke; Earl Temple to 1839; Marquess of Chandos 1839–61. Cab. in Derby govt 1866–8 (lord pres.; then Colonies). Gov. of Madras 1875–80. Educ. Eton, Christ Church. MP Buckingham 1846–57; lost Oxford to Gladstone in 1859. Paid off most of his father's debts. 'A staunch conservative, but seldom spoke at length on political subjects.' Diabetic.

BURDETT, Sir Francis, bart (1770–1844). Son of 4th bart. Educ. Westminster School and Oxford. In Paris during early days of French revolution. Radical MP after 1796; imprisoned 1810 and 1820. Advocate of Catholic emancipation in 1820s. Disturbed by Reform in 1832 and turned Tory. Tory MP for North Wilts from 1837. 'Above forty thousand a year' in rents from his land in 1830s, according to Wellington.

CAIRNS, Hugh McCalmont, 1st Earl (1819–85). Number two to Disraeli by late 1860s; his lord chancellor in 1868 and again 1874–80. Scots family but his environment Irish; father captain in 47th reg. of foot, County Down. Educ. Belfast Acad. and Trinity College, Dublin. Read for Bar in England. QC 1858. MP Belfast from 1852. Sol. gen. in 1858 min. govt. Opposition leader in Lords 1868–70. Evangelical churchman; Sunday-school teacher. 'If he had any humour... it was assiduously concealed.' Salisbury called him Great Cat.

CARDWELL, Edward, Viscount (1813–86). Father a Liverpool merchant. Educ. Winchester, Balliol: brilliant academic career. MP 1842–74 (Clitheroe; Liverpool; Oxford city). Highly rated by Peel and Gladstone in 1840s. Peelite after 1846. Cab. from 1852 (Board of Trade 1852–5; Ireland 1959–61; Colonies 1864–6; War 1868–74). Bitter, Hamilton says, at his exclusion in 1880.

CARLINGFORD, Chichester Samuel Parkinson-Fortescue, baron (1823–98). Irish gentry with an army flavour in County Louth. Educ. privately and Christ Church. MP Louth 1847–74. Under-sec. for colonies under Palmerston. Chief sec. for Ireland in 1865 but demoted to accommodate Hartington in 1871. Succeeded Argyll as lord privy seal in Gladstone's 1880 govt, but always uneasy and reciprocated prime minister's dislike. Opposed Home Rule; Unionist after 1886. Political leverage derived mainly from formidable and much-married wife, Countess Waldegrave, who died in 1879.

CARNARVON, H. H. Molyneaux Herbert, 4th Earl of (1831–90). Father 3rd Earl; mother a Norfolk Howard. Courtesy title Viscount Porchester. Educ. Eton, Christ Church (pupil of Mansel). Earldom 1859. Land in Notts and Somerset. Devout Anglican given to moods. Known to his intimates as 'Twitters'.

CARSON, Edward Henry, baron (1854–1935). Single-cause politician with a surprising *Dublin* background: father an engineer there. Educ. Portarlington School and Trinity College, Dublin; read for Irish Bar. Junior crown prosecutor; silk 1889. Balfour's sol. gen. for Ireland 1892. MP Dublin Univ. for 26 years from 1892. Ulster his passion even after 1914 – not an administrative success in later years. Donated £10,000 to Ulster Volunteer Force. Took responsibility for Larne gun-running.

CHILDERS, Hugh Culling Eardley (1827–96). Gladstone's chancellor of exchequer, 1882–5. In-married family: great-grandfather on both sides an extinct Irish peer, Lord Eardley (1744–1824). Educ. Cheam School and Wadham, Oxford (left after 2 years) then Trinity, Cambridge. After degree went to Australia till 1858. MP for Pontefract 1860–85 (seat Cantley, nr Doncaster). Palmerstonian Whig in early career; Gladstonian after 1865. Admiralty 1868 but resigned 1871 after son lost at sea. War Office 1880. Unpopular after move to Exchequer. Health failed after 1886; did not stand in 1892.

CLARENDON, George William Frederick, 4th Earl of (1800–70). Foreign Office under Aberdeen, Palmerston, Russell and Gladstone (1853–8, 1865–6, 1868–70). Diplomatic service when 'still little more than a boy': attaché St Petersburg at 20. Many diplomatic assignments. Entered cab. as lord privy seal in 1839. Board of Trade 1846 but Ireland (1847–52) a formative experience. Talk of a Clarendon govt 1852–3. Health suspect in later years.

COBDEN, Richard (1804–65). Yeoman background; father small farmer near Midhurst, Sussex. Educ. in Yorkshire. Warehouse clerk then commercial traveller. After 1828 immersed in calico-printing business at Salden, Lancs. Moved to Manchester 1832 as wealthy man. Political engagement bankrupted him by 1845. £120,000 raised by public subscription for him. MP Stockport 1841–7; West Riding 1847–57; Rochdale 1859. Refused Board of Trade from Palmerston 1859. Negotiated free trade treaty with France 1860.

CRANBROOK, see HARDY

CROKER, John Wilson (1780–1857). Minister outside cab. (first sec. to Admiralty) 1809–30. Devon family but brought up in Ireland where father surveyor-gen. of customs and excise. Educ. at Portarlington and Trinity College, Dublin. Wrote for Murray's *Quarterly Review*; agent and political adviser to disreputable Marquess (Hertford). Close to Wellington and Peel until 1827 when fears developed that Croker had turned Canningite. Satirized as Rigby in Disraeli's *Coningsby*.

CROSS, Richard Assheton, 1st Viscount (1823–1914). Disraeli's home sec. 1874–80. Born Red Scar, near Preston: family connected with court of common pleas which sat there. Educ. Rugby (under Arnold) and Trinity, Cambridge; pres. of union. Bar 1849; northern circuit. MP Preston for short period but left to join Parr, Lyon and Co., bankers. Parlt again after 1868. In later Tory cabinets closest to Smith and Northcote. Queen ran him after death of Beaconsfield. 'Rather fond of talking' (Lucy).

DILKE, Sir Charles Wentworth, 2nd bart (1843–1911). Son of 1st bart (MP Wallingford 1865–8); mother d. of captain in Madras cavalry. Married (2nd) widow of Mark Pattison, 1885. Educ. privately and Trinity Hall, Cambridge; Bar 1866. Radical MP for Chelsea 1868–86; Forest of Dean 1892–1911.

DUDLEY, John William Ward, 1st Earl of (1781–1833). Aristocratic background, educ. privately and at Oxford and Edinburgh. MP for series of seats after 1802; friend of Canning and acted with Tory party. Declined under-sec. at Foreign Office 1822. Foreign Office under Canning 1827, and Wellington 1828. Resigned with Huskisson in 1828 and held no further office. Eccentricity had already turned to madness. Died in an asylum.

DUNCOMBE, Thomas Slingsby (1796–1861). Yorkshire background: estate near Boroughbridge; mother d. of bishop of Peterborough. Harrow and then Coldstream Guards till 1819. Fought seats as a Whig in 1820s; his 5 contests before 1832 reputed to have cost £40,000. MP Finsbury 1834–61. Not consistently radical. Mild sympathy with chartists. Bankrupt in 1830s; snappy dresser; ill for many years before his death.

DURHAM, John George Lambton, 1st Earl of (1792–1840). Father W. H. Lambton, MP for Durham; mother a Villiers. Educ. Eton; then 10th Dragoons, rose to lieutenant. MP for County Durham 1813–28: one of Goderich's resignation peers. Married Grey's daughter Louisa. Supported Canning. Lord privy seal in Grey's cab. 1830–33. Did not serve under Melbourne but missions to St Petersburg and Canada. Collieries alone yielded £50,000 p.a. in 1820s.

ELLENBOROUGH, Edward Law, Earl of (1790–1871). Father chief justice in Liverpool govt. Distantly related to Grey. Married Castlereagh's sister who died in 1819. Frustrated foreign minister: he loathed Canning and felt bitter over Wellington's passing over him to appoint Aberdeen in 1828. Career in fact entirely concerned with India. Pres. of Board of Control in Tory ministry of 1834–5. Peel made him governor-general in 1841. Recalled in disgrace, 1844. At Board of Control when his censure of Clemency Canning brought him down in 1858. Impetuous, self-righteous and ill-tempered.

ESHER, Reginald Balliol Brett, 2nd Viscount (1852–1930). Well connected family: father master of the rolls, mother d. of Belgian minister in London. Eton (with Rosebery) and Trinity, Cambridge. Retained veneration for Hartington after serving as his private sec., 1878–85. MP for only 5 years – Lib: Penryn and Falmouth, 1880–85. Refused political jobs from his lifelong friend Balfour. Power told in court circle at Windsor and through his membership of committees. Fastidious aesthete. Sometimes small-minded but not negligible.

FORSTER, William Edward (1818–86). Dorsetshire origin. Father a Quaker minister, mother a Buxton and sister of Elizabeth Fry. No university, therefore: attended Friends schools. Went into wool – first in Norwich, then with Pease's in Darlington. Bradford partnership with W. Fison dates from 1842. Left Friends, 1850, and married Dr Arnold's daughter. MP Bradford, 1861–86, without a break. Education and Ireland his main policy preoccupations. Nickname 'Buckshot'. Never handsome, if not 'revoltingly hideous' (Dilke).

FRERE, Sir Henry Bartle Edward (1815–84). East Anglian family with deep parliamentary roots. Educ. Bath grammar and Haileybury for Indian civil service. Entered Bombay service in 1834 and rose to become commissioner of Sind: there during mutiny. Gov. of Bombay 1862; returned to England 1867. Cape Town 1877.

GIBSON, Thomas Milner (1806–84). Born Trinidad: father major of 37th Foot. Unitarian school; then Charterhouse and Trinity, Cambridge. Tory MP

Ipswich 1837; resigned on turning Liberal, 1839. Radical MP Manchester, 1841–57; Ashton-under-Lyne, 1857–68. Retired on state pension. Died on his yacht in the Mediterranean. Wife at the centre of a circle of spiritualists.

GORST, Sir John Eldon (1834–1916). Disraeli's organizational expert of 1870s. Modest background in Lancashire. Preston grammar school and St John's, Cambridge. Read for Bar and ultimately became sol. gen. in 1885–6. Ministerial career mostly bound up with education, 1895–1902. MP Chatham 1875–92, Cambridge University 1892–1906.

GOSCHEN, George Joachim (1831–1907). Salisbury's chancellor of exchequer 1886–92. Liberal until 1885. Son of London banker; educ. London, Saxe-Meiningen, Rugby and Oriel College, Oxford (1st; pres. of union) Father's firm in 1850s. MP City of London, 1863–80; St George's (as Unionist), 1887–1900 (Ripon and E. Edinburgh in between). Cab. posts in Lib. govts after 1866. His recalcitrance over Admiralty estimates disrupted cab. in 1873–4. The opposite of 'weak-kneed', *pace* Gladstone. Reverted to Admiralty in Salisbury govt of 1895; retired 1900.

GOULBURN, Henry (1784–1856). Mother d. of 4th Viscount Chetwynd. Educ. Trinity, Cambridge. Succession of seats and junior posts after 1808. Wellington's chancellor of exchequer, 1828–30. MP Cambridge University from 1831 to death in 1856. Home Office in Peel's 100-day ministry; Exchequer again in 1841. No office after 1846. A coming man who never quite came – perhaps because he was 'the most furious Protestant that ever was' (Mrs Arbuthnot).

GRAHAM, Sir James Robert George (1792–1861). Established border family. Educ. Westminster and Christ Church (left early). Uncertain beginning as a Whig MP after 1818: retired to seat at Netherby for much of the 1820s. Many changes of constituency. High office only once – as Peel's home sec., 1841–6. Deepening despondency after 1846; 'like many timid politicians he often rushes headlong into measures which he inwardly disapproves in order to escape from some danger, the magnitude of which he overrates' (Palmerston). Greville calls him 'the Cicero and the Romeo of Yorkshire and Cumberland'.

HALSBURY, Hardinge Stanley Giffard, 1st Earl of (1823–1921). Lord chancellor in all Salisbury's governments. Father, Stanley Lees Giffard, edited the *Standard* and educated his son at home before sending him to Oxford where he took a fourth-class degree. Bar, nevertheless, by 1850. MP Launceston 1877–85 (peerage). Fame began at 80 when he symbolized resistance to the Liberal attack on the House of Lords.

HARCOURT, Lewis, 1st Viscount (1863–1922). Only surviving son of Sir William by his first wife who died at the birth. Brought up by his father from whom he remained inseparable. Educ. Eton but no university; sent abroad. Private sec. to father throughout his career and exercised considerable power through knowing everybody who mattered. Ministerial career of his own (1st commissioner of works) 1907–10 and 1915–16; but influence wider than executive experience. Known throughout Westminster as 'Loulou'. Death 'by misadventure'.

HARDIE, James Keir (1856–1915). Born in Lanarkshire. Father a ship's carpenter; mother a domestic servant. Down the mine at 10; soon sacked and blacklisted as an agitator. Paid his way by journalism while acting as unpaid organizer to miners' union in Lanarkshire and Ayrshire. Commons career began in 1892 (SW Ham). Chairman ILP, 1893. MP Bradford 1896; Merthyr from 1900 to his death.

HARDY, Gathorne, 1st Earl of Cranbrook (1814–1906). Father MP for Bradford (died 1855), a judge and part owner of an ironworks. Educ. Shrewsbury and Oriel, Oxford. Read for Bar. Death of father gave him large income. MP (Cons.) Leominster 1856–65; Oxford University 1865–78 (peerage). Replaced Walpole at Home Office in 1867. War Office and India office under Disraeli. Run by anti-Disraelians as possible alternative leader after 1867. Sat on Salisbury's left in 1886–92 cab. (lord pres.) 'Not a bad fellow but rather dense' (India Office official). Nickname 'Old Granny'.

HARMSWORTH, Alfred Charles William, Viscount Northcliffe (1865–1922). Born near Dublin: father a barrister. Came to England when 2. Stamford grammar school and Hampstead: no university. Responsibility for helping feed 6 brothers and 3 sisters; went into freelance journalism. Ventures included *Daily Mail* (1896), *Daily Mirror* (1903), control of *Observer* (1905–12) and purchase of *Times* in 1908. Greatly disliked in political circles: private influence probably less than he assumed. Lived next door to Rosebery in Berkeley Square. R. A. Hudson married his widow.

HARTSHORN, Vernon (1871–1931). Born Monmouthshire: father a miner. Pit as a boy; then a clerk; then a checkweighman. Agent South Wales Miners' Federation (1905); Executive Council 1911. Did not become MP until after the war though fought Mid-Glamorgan in both elections of 1910. Primitive Methodist. 'Very nice man. Not at all violent. Blind in one eye' (Riddell).

HENLEY, Joseph Warner (1793–1884). Second-generation country gentleman: father London merchant who bought estate in Oxfordshire. Magdalen, Oxford; two years in his father's London office; then into shire politics. MP Oxfordshire 1841–78; married a Fane. Board of Trade in the two Tory govts of the fifties. Declined the Home Office in 1866 (going deaf); opposed disestablishment in 1869. 'Very shrewd and clever, but crotchety and easily offended' (Malmesbury).

HERRIES, John Charles (1778–1855). Father London merchant. Educ. Cheam and Leipzig. Began in civil service (Treasury, then revenue dept); priv. sec. to Vansittart and Portland. Commons for Harwich (Tory) 1823–41. Ministerial career peaked early when he became Goderich's chancellor of exchequer. Thereafter more important in organizational matters, though War Office during 100 days. Protectionist MP (Stamford) after party split. Whig view from Clarendon: 'Herries is old womanish without much character to spare but with ability enough to make him disbelieve 3/4ths of what he himself says.'

HERSCHELL, Farrer, 1st baron (1837–99). Polish Jews on his father's side though father a Dissenting Christian minister. Brought up in Nonconformist atmosphere though later became Anglican. Faith excluded him from English universities; so Bonn and University College London. Bar 1860. MP Durham 1874–85. Loyal to Gladstone over Home Rule. Became his lord chancellor in 1886 and 1892–4 after Henry James deserted with Chamberlain.

HUNT, George Ward (1825–77). Tory minister after 1868. Eldest son of Rev. George Hunt, Winkfield, Berks. Eton; Christ Church; Bar. MP for Northants North from 1857 till death. Disraeli's chancellor of exchequer for a few months in 1868: downhill thereafter. Knew about county affairs and agriculture: introduced cattle plague bill in 1866. But a disaster at Admiralty in 1874. 'Unqualified personal failure' (Lucy). Died of gout.

HUSKISSON, William (1770–1830). Small family estate at Oxley, nr Wolverhampton. Stayed in midlands till 13. Educ. Paris where maternal uncle physician to British Embassy. Acquainted with Franklin and Jefferson; present at fall of Bastille. Priv. sec. to British ambassador till his recall, 1792. Commons 1796 (Morpeth); series of seats culminating Liverpool, 1823–30. Board of Trade 1823–7; Colonies and leader of House 1827–8. Run over by train while opening Manchester–Liverpool railway. 'A wretched speaker with no command of words, with awkward motions, and a most vulgar, uneducated accent.'

JAMES, Henry, Lord (1828–1911). Born in Hereford; father a surgeon. First name on roll of Cheltenham College, 1841. Keen cricketer; pres. MCC 1889. Trained as engineer but left to study law. Bar 1852. Oxford circuit with Henry Matthews. MP Taunton 1869. Legal officer in Gladstone's govts 1873–85. After Home Rule came on, MP for Bury. No cab. appointment in either party until Salisbury made him chancellor of duchy in 1895. But wide social circle (including Prince of Wales) and significant legal patronage. Unmarried. 'He was rarely brief.'

KIMBERLEY, John Wodehouse, 1st Earl of (1826–1902). Never made the Foreign Office which was always the object of his ambition (cf. ELLENBOROUGH). Whig family, Wymondham, Norfolk; father son of 2nd baron. Eton; Christ Church; 1st in classics. Under-sec. foreign affairs 1852–61,

apart from Derby govt of 1858–9. Began cab. career as lord privy seal in
Gladstone's first govt but spent most of time dealing with Ireland or colonies. Gladstonian in 1886 despite marrying d. of 3rd Earl of Clare. 'Not
impressive, although extremely able and efficient' (Bruce).

KING, Hon. Peter John LOCKE- (1811–85). 2nd son of 7th Lord King.
Educ. Harrow; Trinity, Cambridge. MP East Surrey 1847–74. Main preoccupation the lowering of the county franchise to £10.

LANSDOWNE, Henry Petty-Fitzmaurice, 3rd Marquess of (1780–1863).
Son of prime minister Shelburne (1782–3); grandfather of Balfour's foreign
secretary. Westminster school and Edinburgh (supposedly on advice of Bentham). Foxite in early years; chancellor of exchequer in Ministry of All the
Talents but main significance came much later. Joined Canning in 1827.
Played senior statesman to Russell in govts of 1830s and 1840s, opposing
reform and remaining a fixed duty man on corn. 'The father of the Cabinet,
always calm, wise, and absolutely straight' (Argyll).

LOREBURN, Robert Threshie Reid, Earl (1846–1923). Lord chancellor
under Campbell-Bannerman and Asquith. Born Corfu: father chief justice
of Ionian islands. Cheltenham College (cf. JAMES) then Balliol. Double 1st;
kept wicket for 1st eleven; pres. MCC 1911. Devilled for Henry James in
early legal career; and helped by him to become MP Hereford, 1880. Early
promise not fulfilled in legal career. In politics a depressive with a bad
temper and a weak heart. 'Always disgruntled' (Birrell). Heart attack 1912.

LOWE, Robert, 1st Viscount Sherbrooke (1811–92). Father a rector; mother
d. of a rector. Educ. Winchester and University College, Oxford; 1st classics,
2nd mathematics. Fellow of Magdalen, 1835. Australia, 1843–50. Commons from 1852 to 1880 for three constituencies. Gladstone's chancellor
of exchequer, 1868–73. Home Office, 1873–4. Peerage, 1880. Poor executive but formidable critic. Almost blind for much of adult life but greatly
feared for severity of his tongue.

LYNDHURST, John Singleton Copley, Lord (1772–1863). Son of portrait
painter of same name. Trinity College, Cambridge; Bar 1804. Entered parlt
1818. Established himself in 1820s as central law officer in Tory politics.
Canning made him lord chancellor despite his opposition to Catholic emancipation. Remained until 1830. Accepted a legal appointment from Grey
(1830–34) but returned to Woolsack in Peel's two govts. Growing blind by
late 1840s. Refused office from Derby. Disliked for his indestructibility. 'He
is a shabby fellow and always follows *le plus fort* but consequently is a good
political barometer' (Mrs. Arbuthnot).

LYTTON, Edward Robert Bulwer, 1st Earl of (1831–91). Son of novelist
Bulwer-Lytton (colonial sec., 1858–9) and himself a notable poet. Educ.

Harrow and Bonn. String of private and diplomatic appointments. Viceroy of India 1876–80. Paris Embassy 1887–91. Opium eater.

MALMESBURY, James Howard (Fitz)Harris, 3rd Earl of (1807–89). Foreign secretary in the Derby ministries of the fifties and lord privy seal 1866–8 and 1874–6. Educ. Eton and Oriel, Oxford. Almost all of career spent in the House of Lords. Acquaintance of Louis Napoleon. Ladies' man. Father had been Canning's under-sec. at Foreign Office during Napoleonic war. Seat Heron Court, Christchurch, Dorset: experience of and troubled by Swing and Reform riots.

MANN, Tom (1856–1951). Father colliery book-keeper, Foleshill, nr Coventry. Mother died when he was 2. Only three years' schooling: colliery farm at 9; pit at 10. Apprenticed to engineers when father moved to Birmingham; joined ASE (gen. sec. after First World War). SDF 1885; friendship with Engels and Eleanor Marx; met Burns. Phases of Georgeism, Malthusianism, vegetarianism, teetotalism. Quaker sympathies: Sunday-school teacher; considered ordination. 1st pres. dockers' union 1893. New Zealand and Australia 1901–10. Ed. *Industrial Syndicalist* 1910–11. Founder-member Communist Party of Great Britain. Retired 1921.

MANNERS, Lord John James Robert, 7th Duke of Rutland (1818–1906). Brother of 6th Duke. Trinity College, Cambridge. MP Newark 1841–7 (with Gladstone). Congenital Disraelian: features in three of his novels. But supported Maynooth. Protectionist, then Conservative, MP for a series of constituencies between 1847 and 1888 (dukedom). Minor cabinet post in *every* Tory govt between 1852 and 1892. 'Skim-milk manner, always unoffending' (Lucy).

MATTHEWS, Henry, Viscount Llandaff (1826–1913). Born Ceylon: father a judge: Mother a Blount; so brought up as a Roman Catholic and educ. Paris and London. Bar 1850, but private income. Cross-examined Dilke. Won Dungarvon in 1868 for Tories 'at the cost of 800 bottles of whisky'. Lost it 1874, moved to Birmingham East. Home Rule sympathies. Friend of Churchill and shared his tastes. Home Office 1886–92: 1st Catholic to become a cabinet minister. Never married. Parliamentary manner like 'French dancing master'.

MILNER, Alfred, 1st Viscount (1854–1925). Born in Germany and spent much of youth there. Educ. Tübingen gymnasium and King's College, London. Witnessed German attack on France in 1870. Balliol, Oxford, 1872; double 1st; pres. of union. Bar 1881. Only ever fought one seat, Harrow in 1885, and lost. Private sec. to Goschen; helped Harcourt with 1894 budget. Gov. of Cape 1897–1902. High commissioner till 1905, then returned to Britain. Political influence became overt during First World War but important figure behind imperial politics in pre-war years.

MORANT, Sir Robert Laurie (1863–1920). Permanent under-secretary at education department 1903–11; guiding spirit behind Balfour act of 1902. Father decorative artist; mother d. of headmaster of Mill Hill school. Born Hampstead; educ. Winchester and New College, Oxford: 1st in theology. Tutor to crown prince of Siam, 1886–94. Connected with education dept from 1895. Left in 1911 to become chairman of National Insurance Health Commission.

MORLEY, John, Viscount (1838–1923). Born Blackburn, Lancs: father a surgeon from West Riding; mother's family northeastern shipowners. Cheltenham College and Lincoln College, Oxford, but left with pass degree after quarrel with father over JM's loss of religious faith. Freelance journalism in London; picked up by *Saturday Review* and through it met Cranborne and Leslie Stephen. Also friend of Mill. Read law in chambers of the positivist Frederic Harrison but never practised after Bar (1873). Ed. *Fortnightly* for 15 years (1867–82). MP Newcastle 1883–95; Montrose Burghs 1896–1908. Lib. cabs. 1886–1914; India or Ireland apart from last four years as lord pres. Resigned 1914. Hypersensitive with tendency towards depression. 'Offers to his pious opinions all the devotion he withdraws from his Creator' (Munro-Ferguson). Campbell-Bannerman called him 'Priscilla'. Many books, including *Life of Gladstone* (1903).

MULGRAVE, Henry Phipps, Viscount Normanby and 1st Earl of (1755–1831). Yorkshire background: seat near Whitby. Army his spiritual home; one of Pitt's military advisers. Foreign sec. in 1805 and Admiralty under Portland and Perceval. Master of the ordnance 1810–18. 'A high Tory, and complete John Bull' (Haydon).

NAAS, Richard Southwell Bourke, 6th Earl of Mayo (1822–72). Eldest son 5th Earl. Born Dublin; early life spent in Meath. Educ. at home and Trinity College, Dublin (ordinary degree). 'Clever shot.' Chief sec. for Ireland in Derby govts, 1852 and 1858–9. Likewise 1866 but appointed gov. gen. of India before fall of Disraeli. Assassinated while paying official visit to penal settlement on Andaman Islands.

NORTHBROOK, Thomas George Baring, 1st Earl of (1826–1904). Not to be confused with father, Sir Francis Baring, baron Northbrook (chancellor of exchequer 1839–41; Admiralty 1849–52). Educ. privately and Christ Church (2nd). Whig MP after 1857. Wide range of under-secs. in late 1850s and early 1860s. Admiralty in Lib. govts after 1868 until retired from high office in 1886 (also gov. gen. of India after NAAS). Opposed Home Rule, tariff reform and all deviations from Whiggery. 'A safe, strong man' (Granville).

NORTHCOTE, Sir Stafford Henry, 1st Earl of Iddesleigh (1818–87). Northcote baronetcy had long roots (at The Pynes, nr Exeter). Born Portland Place,

London; mother d. of East India Co. employee. Eton; Balliol; barrister. Priv. sec. to Gladstone 1842 and helped him with his Oxford elections until 1853. 8th bart 1851. Board of Trade and India, 1866–7, but major ministerial career begins as chancellor of exchequer to Disraeli, 1874–80, and leader of opposition in Commons, 1880–85. Disaster in latter role. Earldom 1885. Died on the day of his resignation. Despised by Churchill and Fourth party; but even Disraeli had thought him 'a complete Jesuit'.

O'BRIEN, William (1852–1928). Born Mallow, County Cork, son of solicitor's clerk and local shopkeeper's daughter. Parents Catholic; but educ. at Protestant high school and The Queen's College, Cork. Then journalism – Cork *Daily Herald*, Dublin *Freeman's Journal*. Parnell made him editor of Land League's *United Ireland*, 1881. Suppressed by Forster; O'Brien sent to Kilmainham. Returned to editorship after treaty. MP Mallow, 1883. 1887 jail again (6 months) for conspiracy, and again (with Dillon) in 1891. MP NE Cork and later Cork City after 1885. Founder United Irish League 1898. Opposed Redmond over Ulster question before war.

O'BRIEN, William Smith (1803–64). Father Sir Edward O'Brien, bart, of County Clare. Son later inherited estates in Limerick. Harrow; Trinity College, Cambridge. Commons after 1828 (MP Ennis 1828–31; County Limerick 1835–49). Joined Repeal Association 1843 but seceded in 1846 to form Irish confederation. Sentenced to be hanged, drawn and quartered for part in 1848 rising; commuted to transportation for life. Tasmania until pardoned in 1854. Lived thereafter in Brussels. Visited America and Poland.

PALMER, *see* SELBORNE

PANMURE, Fox Maule, 2nd baron, 11th Earl of Dalhousie (1801–74). Not to be confused with father, William Ramsay Maule (1771–1852), 1st baron, Foxite MP for Forfar and dissolute tyrant of Brechin castle. Fox Maule educ. Charterhouse; then army; retired as captain of 79th Highlanders. Lib. MP for Scottish constituencies from 1835 to peerage in 1852. War Office under Palmerston 1855–8. Other interests predominantly Scottish: supported Free Church during Disruption. Scottish power gave him his leverage rather than any executive ability. Granville thought him 'one of the dullest men he ever knew'. Nickname 'Mars'.

PARKES, Joseph (1796–1865). Born Warwick; son of a manufacturer. 'Miseducated' (his word) at Greenwich; then Glasgow University. Articled to London solicitor and entered Bentham circle. Birmingham solicitor, 1822–33, and active in Birmingham politics from 1828. Married Joseph Priestley's eldest daughter. Nervous of BPU and did not join till 1832. Sec. to Municipal Corporations Commission from 1833. Simultaneously a figure in the Grote circle of philosophic radicals. Retired from political work 1847. Back-room figure valued for his knowledge of electoral law and Birmingham sentiment.

PORTAL, Sir Gerald Herbert (1858–94). Son of Melville Portal (1819–1904), cons. MP N. Hants, 1849–57; mother d. of 2nd Earl of Minto. Career entirely spent in diplomacy: Eton, then straight into diplomatic service. Married into Bertie family. Posts at Rome, Cairo, Zanzibar. Uganda mission killed him. Brother died there; he reached London, 1893, but died shortly afterwards of fever.

REDMOND, John Edward (1856–1918). Son of William Archer Redmond, MP for Wexford, who was a Home Ruler and friend of Parnell. Born Ballytrent, Wexford, of long-established Catholic gentry. Educ. by Jesuits. Trinity College, Dublin but left after 2 years. Clerk in Commons, 1880. MP New Ross, County Wexford, 1881. Bar, 1886, but private means. Chief supporter of Parnell in 1890. Chairman of Irish Parliamentary Party from 1900.

REID, Sir Thomas Wemyss (1842–1905). Journalist and author with some political significance. Entered journalism early: provincial papers from 1861. Ed. *Leeds Mercury* 1870–87. Manager of Cassells, 1887–1905. Founded the *Speaker* and edited it 1890–97. Close to Herbert Gladstone. Supported Forster on education and Gladstone on Home Rule. Rosebery man in the 1890s. Wrote lives of Forster, Monckton Milnes and Lyon Playfair.

RICHMOND, Charles Gordon-Lennox, 5th Duke of (1791–1860). Westminster school followed by military career; rose to lieutenant in 13th Light Dragoons. Tory MP Chichester, 1812–19 (peerage). Turned Whig when he believed Tories went soft on the Catholic question. Accepted office under Grey. Fought pitched battle alongside fifty of his tenants against Swing rioters. Left govt for cross-benches over 'appropriation' 1834. Opposed Peel on the corn laws. Declined office from Derby in 1852. 'Prejudiced, narrow-minded, illiterate, and ignorant, good-looking, good-humoured and unaffected, tedious, prolix, unassuming, and a duke' (Greville). Died of dropsy.

RIDLEY, Sir Matthew White, 5th bart and 1st Viscount (1842–1904). Father Cons. MP N. Northumberland 1859–68; mother d. of the Sir James Parke who controversially became baron Wensleydale. Harrow; Balliol (double 1st); fellow of All Souls. Succeeded father in county constituency, 1868. Married daughter of Liberal whip, Marjoribanks. Junior office after 1874. Home secretary under Salisbury, 1895–1900.

ROEBUCK, John Arthur (1801–79). Born Madras; father in Indian Civil Service; mother d. of Sheridan's brother-in-law. England after death of father, but mother took him to Canada when 9. Educ. there. Returned at 21. Bar 1831. MP Bath 1832–7 (radical); then in and out of parliament before moving to Sheffield in 1849 (MP with one break till death). Palmerstonian in foreign policy in 1850s and 1860s. Attracted notoriety in later career for depiction of working men as spendthrifts and wifebeaters.

SANDARS, John Satterfield (1853–1934). Priv. sec. of Balfour, 1892–1905, when he built a considerable reputation as a power behind the throne. Son of Charles Sandars of Mackworth, Derbyshire. Repton; Magdalen College, Oxford. Bar 1877; practised till 1886. Priv. sec. to Henry Matthews at Home Office, 1886–92. Fought Mid-Derbyshire 1892 but never entered House. Lived in Torquay.

SANDON, Dudley Francis Stuart Ryder, Viscount, 3rd Earl of Harrowby (1831–1900). Harrow; Christ Church; tour in the East with Carnarvon whose churchmanship he shared. Married a Cecil. MP Lichfield, 1856–9, as Palmerstonian Whig. Priv. sec. to Labouchere senior at Colonial Office. Out, 1859–68. Cons. MP Liverpool 1868–82 (peerage). Education main preoccupation: supported Forster's bill and extended it with his own in 1876. Lord privy seal in Salisbury's first govt. Chronic invalid in later years.

SELBORNE, Roundell Palmer, 1st Earl of (1812–95). Father rector with private means, Mixbury, Oxon. Two brothers entered church; a third seceded to Rome. Rugby, then Winchester (cont. of Lowe, Cardwell, Trollope) and Christ Church. Brilliant success there in classics. Read for Bar and became an equity lawyer. Peelite MP Plymouth, 1847–52; 1853–7; Richmond, 1861–72 (peerage). Law officer in Liberal governments after 1861. Anglicanism central: supported Disraeli's Public Worship Regulation Act but opposed Welsh disestablishment. Starched sense of principle and propriety. 'Gladstone on stilts' (Gathorne Hardy).

SMITH, Frederick Edwin, 1st Earl of Birkenhead (1872–1930). Father estate agent in (and mayor of) Birkenhead. Educ. Birkenhead and Wadham College, Oxford (cont. of John Simon, C. B. Fry and Francis Hirst). 1st in jurisprudence, 1895. Fellow of Merton. Married d. of Henry Furneaux, fellow of Corpus Christi College and ed. of Tacitus. Bar 1899. Practised in Liverpool where Archibald Salvidge recruited him for Tory candidature. MP Liverpool, Walton, from 1906. Distinguished career in politics, law and the *demi-monde* after 1914.

SMITH, William Henry (1825–91). Father owned impressive news-agency covering the country but based in The Strand. Strict Methodist background; educ. at home; much friction when he wanted to be ordained. Father pressed him into family business: became the Son of W. H. Smith and Son. Tory preference when Whigs rejected him socially; though originally stood (1865) as a 'Liberal-Conservative'. Beat Mill at Westminster 1868. Educational interests brought him close to Sandon and the Liberal Forster. Cab. from 1877 (succeeded Hunt at Admiralty). Number two to Salisbury from 1886 to death. Weak heart. Worth £1 million.

SUTTON, Charles MANNERS- (1780–1845). Son of Archbishop of Canterbury of same name. Took title of Viscount Canterbury in 1835. Speaker of

Commons 1817–35; the escapade of 1832 his only excitement. 'I do not pay much attention to what the Speaker says as he is very apt to take up false notions' (Mrs. Arbuthnot).

TEMPLE, William Francis COWPER-, 1st baron Mount Temple (1811–88). 2nd son of 5th Earl Cowper; mother Melbourne's daughter who married Palmerston as her second husband. Military background: lieutenant in Royal Horse Guards. MP Hertford 1835–68, Hampshire South 1868–80. Minor office in Liberal govts 1846–66. Vocal on behalf of ratepayers and tenant farmers.

TENTERDEN, Charles Stuart Aubrey Abbott, 3rd baron (1834–82). Eton and then Foreign Office. Precis-writer to Lord Stanley, 1866. Assistant under-sec. for foreign affairs 1871–3. Permanent under-sec. 1873–82. Freemason.

THISTLEWOOD, Arthur (1770–1820). Born Tupholme, near Lincoln, illeg. son of well-known stock-breeder. Father intended him to become a land surveyor but he left home for America and revolutionary France. Returned to England, 1794. Rose to lieutenant in 3rd Lincolnshire reg. of militia. Married money (Jane Worsley) in 1804 but family cut him off when she died. Left north for London; joined Spenceans. Visited Paris, 1814. Imprisoned 1818–19 for writing to Sidmouth. Arrested after Cato Street. Hanged and decapitated at Newgate, 1 May 1820. Always carried a swordstick.

TILLETT, Ben (1860–1943). Born Easton, Bristol; father a railway labourer. Ran away and joined the circus. Royal navy at 13, then merchant navy; tea-porter at London docks by his early 20s. Dock strike of 1889 brought him national prominence. Worked thereafter for federation within trade union movement. Two visits to Australia. LCC in 1892; joined SDF and ILP. Fought four seats before 1914 but unsuccessful until he won N. Salford (1917–24; 1929–31). Supported patriotic stance during First World War.

TREVELYAN, Sir George Otto, 2nd bart (1838–1928). Son of Sir Charles Trevelyan, former assist. sec. to Treasury and co-author of Northcote-Trevelyan report on civil service; and himself father of the radical (later Labour) MP C. P. Trevelyan and the historian G. M. Trevelyan. Early life spent in England (Harrow; Trinity, Cambridge); then India when his father became gov. of Madras. Entered House as Palmerstonian for Tynemouth, 1865. Junior office, 1868 but resigned over education bill. Never hit it off with Gladstone. Cab. 1882–6 (Ireland; Duchy; Scottish Office) but Unionist in 1886–7. Scottish Office again 1892–5. Spencer thought him 'extremely excitable' and 'impulsive'.

VANSITTART, see BEXLEY

WOLFF, Sir Henry Drummond (1830–1908). Mother Horatio Walpole's daughter, Georgiana. Father Rev. Joseph Wolff who cofounded the Irvingite church with Henry Drummond. Rugby; then educ. abroad. Entered Foreign Office at 16. Assist. priv. sec. to Malmesbury and Lytton in 2nd Derby govt. Parlt career effectively 1874–85; rest spent abroad in diplomatic work. MP Christchurch and Portsmouth. Bought property at Boscombe, nr Bournemouth, from Malmesbury.

WOOD, Sir Charles, 1st Viscount Halifax (1800–85). Russell's chancellor of exchequer 1846–52. Educ. Eton; Oriel College, Oxford. Commons in 1826 for Great Grimsby (Whig) but main connexion with Halifax where MP between 1832 and 1865. Peerage 1866. Oddly, Exchequer first cab. appointment; thereafter posts at Board of Control, Admiralty and privy seal. Peremptory manner: 'he bullies Ld. John & the Cabt as if he was born a Grey' (Clarendon). Nickname 'Spider'.

WYNN, Charles Watkin Williams (1775–1850). Son of 4th bart of Wynnstay, Denbighshire; mother sister of 1st Marquess of Buckingham. Educ. Westminster and Christ Church (friend of Southey). Bar 1798. Family influence in Montgomeryshire made him MP for county continuously from 1799 to 1850 when he had become father of the Commons. Cab. only for 1822–8 at Board of Control. Canning kept him on and found him 'the worst man of business I ever met'. Wellington would not have him. Fussy, crotchety manner, 'too full of difficulty and *splitting of hairs*' (Fremantle).

Notes

All books are published in London unless described otherwise.

Introduction to the Second Edition

1 Hayden White, *The Content of the Form* (1987); see also 'Meta-history and Topics of Discourse', Paul Ricoeur, *Temps et récit* (3 vols., 1983–5).
2 W. H. Walsh, *Introduction to the Philosophy of History* (1951).

Chapter 1. The Transformation of Party

1 Lord Colchester (ed.), *The Diary and Correspondence of Charles Abbot, Lord Colchester* (3 vols., 1861), iii, 108.
2 See F. C. Mather (ed.), *Chartism and Society: an anthology of documents* (London and New York, 1980), 21, 53–4.
3 A. S. Foord, 'The Waning of the Influence of the Crown', *English Historical Review*, LXII (1947).
4 Lady Gwendolyn Cecil, *Life of Robert, Marquis of Salisbury* (4 vols., 1921–32), i, 2–4.
5 Sir Herbert Maxwell (ed.), *The Creevey Papers: a selection from the letters and diaries of the late Thomas Creevey M.P.* (2 vols., 1903), i, 258.
6 Fraser, thesis, 42; Valerie Cromwell, 'The Losing of the Initiative by the House of Commons, 1780–1914', *Transactions of the Royal Historical Society*, 5s, 18 (1968), 8.
7 Their proportion is estimated at one MP in six between 1790 and 1832: G. P. Judd, *Members of Parliament 1734–1832* (New Haven and London, 1955), 51–2. I rely heavily here on Professor Judd's analysis.
8 Quoted in Fraser, thesis, 97.
9 Louis J. Jennings (ed.), *The Correspondence and Diaries of the late Rt. Hon. John Wilson Croker* (3 vols., 1884), ii, 60.
10 C. D. Yonge, *The Life and Administration of Robert Banks, Second Earl of Liverpool* (3 vols., 1868), iii, 215.

11 Quoted in J. E. Cookson, *Lord Liverpool's Administration: the crucial years, 1815–22* (Edinburgh and London, 1975), 310.

12 Jennings, *Croker*, ii, 60.

13 For a recent analysis of electoral politics in the period, see Frank O'Gorman, *Voters, Patrons and Parties: the unreformed electoral system of Hanoverian England 1714–1832* (Oxford, 1989).

14 Peter Jupp, *British and Irish Elections 1784–1831* (1973), 78.

15 Prochaska, thesis, 14.

16 A. Aspinall and A. E. Smith (eds.), *English Historical Documents*, XI (1959), 244.

17 A. Aspinall (ed.), *The Letters of King George IV* (3 vols., Cambridge, 1938), ii, 310n.

18 W. H. Mallock and Lady Gwendolen Ramsden (eds.), *Letters, Remains and Memoirs of E. A. Seymour, Twelfth Duke of Somerset* (1893), 24.

19 A. Aspinall (ed.), *The Correspondence of Charles Arbuthnot*, Royal Historical Society, Camden Series, 3s LXV (1941), xiv.

20 C. W. New, *The Life of Henry Brougham to 1830* (Oxford, 1961), 167–8; *Colchester*, iii, 608–9; Elizabeth Longford, *Wellington: Pillar of State* (1972), 101.

21 George Pellew, *The Life and Correspondence of the Right Honble. Henry Addington, First Viscount Sidmouth* (3 vols., 1847), iii, 196.

22 Historical Manuscripts Commission, Bathurst, 76 (1923), 388.

23 For the American and Canadian perspectives, see Kenneth Bourne, *Britain and the Balance of Power in North America 1815–1908* (1967), 3–16, and C. J. Bartlett, *Defence and Diplomacy: Britain and the Great Powers 1815–1914* (Manchester, 1993), 13–14.

24 See the petitions presented and Peel's attack on the bill in *Hansard*, 1s XXX (6 March 1815), 23–6 and *infra*.

25 C. S. Parker, *Sir Robert Peel* (3 vols., 1899), i, 168.

26 See in particular the petitions brought on 13 March 1816: *Hansard*, XXXIII, 216ff.

27 Brougham in Maxwell, *Creevey*, i, 248.

28 Pellew, *Sidmouth*, iii, 148.

29 Historical Manuscripts Commission, *Dropmore*, 10 (1927), 435.

30 Horace Twiss, *The Public and Private Life of Lord Chancellor Eldon, with selections from his correspondence* (3 vols., 1844), ii, 342.

31 HMC, *Dropmore*, 10, 418–19.

32 Pellew, *Sidmouth*, iii, 199.

33 *Croker*, i, 108.

34 *Creevey*, i, 272.

35 Quoted in Wasson, thesis, 102.

36 Sumner, thesis; Fraser, thesis; but cf. Greville, in Henry Reeve (ed.), *The Greville Memoirs: a journal of the reigns of King George IV and King William IV* (3 vols., 1875), i, 3–4; and HMC, *Dropmore*, 10, 442.

37 *Letters of George IV*, ii, 290–92; *Parliamentary Debates*, 10 June 1819, XL, 1082–4.

38 Peter Dixon, *Canning: politician and statesman* (1976), 191; I. J. Prothero, *Artisans and Politics in Early Nineteenth-Century London: John Gast and his times* (1979), 114.

39 Cookson, *op. cit.*, 184; Yonge, *Liverpool*, ii, 408–9; Twiss, *Eldon*, 337–8.

40 Francis Place's phrase: see W. E. S. Thomas, *The Philosophic Radicals* (Oxford, 1979), 71.

41 John Stevenson, *Popular Disturbances in England 1700–1870* (1979), 197–8.

42 Duke of Buckingham and Chandos, *Memoirs of the Court of George IV* (2 vols., 1859), i, 73.

43 Lewis Melville (ed.), *The Huskisson Papers* (1931), 113; Wendy Hinde, *Canning* (1973), 298–300.

44 Cookson, *op. cit.*, 288–9.

45 *Ibid.*, 310.

46 Harvey, thesis, 323–89. Cf. the same author's 'The Third Party in British Politics 1818–21', *Bulletin of the Institute of Historical Research*, 51 (1978), 146–59.

47 *Colchester*, iii, 249.

48 F. Bamford and Duke of Wellington (eds.), *The Journal of Mrs. Arbuthnot* (2 vols., 1950), i, 71, 96.

49 Croker, i, 229; John Derry, *Castlereagh* (1976), 227. Cf. H. W. V. Temperley, 'Canning, Wellington and George the Fourth', *English Historical Review*, XXXVIII (1923); and A. Aspinall, 'Canning's Return to Office in September 1822', *ibid.*, LXXVIII (1963).

50 Buckingham, *Memoirs*, i, 194.

51 *Croker*, i, 229.

52 Quoted in Austin Mitchell, *The Whigs in Opposition 1815–30* (Oxford, 1967), 173.

53 *Croker*, i, 231–2; Buckingham, *Memoirs*, i, 494.

54 *Journal of Mrs. Arbuthnot*, i, 286, 336.

55 HMC, *Bathurst*, 76, 571.

56 See English Historical Documents, XI, 101–2.

57 *Hansard* (Lords), 17 May 1825, new series, XIII, 741–3.

58 A. J. B. Hilton, *Cash, Corn, Commerce: the economic policy of the Tory governments* (Oxford, 1977), 215–16.

59 Dr Machin estimates Protestant gains at only sixteen: G. I. T. Machin, *The Catholic Question in English Politics* (Oxford, 1964), 85–6. For a significantly higher estimate, see Simes, thesis, 283.

60 Greville, *Memoirs*, ii, 2.

61 A. Aspinall, 'The Formation of Canning's Ministry, February-August 1827', *Royal Historical Society*, Camden Series, 3s, LIX (1937), *passim*. Cf. E. A. Wasson, 'The Coalitions of 1827 and the Crisis of Whig Leadership', *Historical Journal*, 20 (1977), 587–606.

62 *Colchester*, iii, 463.

63 See W. D. Jones, *Prosperity Robinson* (New York, 1967), 145.

64 *Huskisson Papers*, 277.

65 Buckingham, *Memoirs*, ii, 380; Ellenborough diary in Lord Colchester (ed.), *Lord Ellenborough's Diary 1828–30* (2 vols., 1881), i, 3; *Journal of Mrs. Arbuthnot*, ii, 161.

66 Sefton's judgement: *Creevey*, ii, 144.

67 G. I. T. Machin, 'Resistance to Repeal of the Test and Corporation Acts, 1828', *Historical Journal*, 22 (1979), 115–39.

68 See J. T. Ward, *Sir James Graham* (1967), 79.

69 *Journal of Mrs. Arbuthnot*, ii, 290.

70 Odurkere, thesis, 40–41.

71 Howick's journal, 22 October 1830, quoted in Mitchell, *op. cit.*, 245.

Chapter 2   Renewal and Consolidation

1   Caroline Grosvenor and Charles Beilby (eds.), *The First Lady Wharn-cliffe and Her Family 1779–1856* (2 vols., 1927), ii, 222.

2   Hobhouse's diary, 21 November 1830, in Lord Broughton, *Recollections of a Long Life* (6 vols., 1909–11), iv, 72.

3   Duke of Wellington (ed.), *Despatches, Correspondence, and Memoranda of Field Marshall Arthur Duke of Wellington, K.G.* (8 vols., 1867–80), vii, 332–3.

4   Broughton, *Recollections*, iv, 70.

5   *Greville Memoirs*, ii, 66

6   *Ibid.*, ii, 75; A. Aspinall (ed.), *Three Early Nineteenth Century Diaries* (1952), 47. For the Swing Riots see Eric Hobsbawm and George Rudé, *Captain Swing* (1969).

7   Le Marchant's diary, 1 March 1831, *Three Diaries*, 13.

8   For Wellington, see *Despatches*, vii, 450. For the election see Michael Brock, *The Great Reform Act* (1973), 195–6, and Odurkere, thesis, 136–51. Cf. Newbould, thesis, 125; and B. T. Bradfield, 'Sir Richard Vyvyan and the Country Gentlemen 1830–34', *English Historical Review*, LXXXIII (1968), 734.

9   Memo. by Wellington, 22 September 1831, *Despatches*, vii, 530.

10 Earl of Ilchester (ed.), *Elizabeth Lady Holland to her Son 1821–45* (1946), 115; Broughton, *Recollections*, iv, 140.

11 Sir Denis Le Marchant, *Memoir of John Charles Viscount Althorp, Third Earl Spencer* (1876), 355; Custance, thesis, 63; Holland's diary, 16 November 1831, in Abraham D. Kriegel (ed.), *The Holland House Diaries 1831–40* (London and Boston, Mass., 1977), 79; Parker, *Peel*, ii, 189.

12 J. Hamburger, *James Mill and the Art of Revolution* (1963), 125.

13 Le Marchant's diary, *Three Diaries*, 273.

14 Ward, *Sir James Graham*, 132.

15 *Lady Wharncliffe and Her Family*, ii, 165; Custance, thesis, 150; Newbould, thesis, 170–72.

16 *Parliamentary Debates*, XV, 149 (5 February 1833).

17 *Greville Memoirs*, iii, 17.

18 Ilchester, *Lady Holland to her Son*, 148.

19 Norman Gash, *Politics in the Age of Peel* (1953, revised edition, Hassocks, 1977), 75. Much of this section draws on Professor Gash's definitive analysis.

20 See J. Milton-Smith, 'Earl Grey's Cabinet and the Objects of Parliamentary Reform', *Historical Journal*, 15 (1972), 65.

21 For the 1833 parliament see F. S. Wooley's seminal article, 'The Personnel of the Parliament of 1833', *English Historical Review*, LIII (1938). I have used Professor Cannon's estimate of the size of the electorate: see John Cannon, *Parliamentary Reform 1642–1832* (Cambridge, 1972), 259 n3, 290–92.

22 Historical Manuscripts Commission, *Wellington: political correspondence* (1975), i, 107.

23 Edward Hughes, 'Bishops and Reform 1831–33: some fresh correspondence', *English Historical Review*, LVI (1941), 488.

24 Gross, thesis, 35.

25 Sweeney, thesis, 42–3.

26 For the initial discussion see Oliver MacDonagh, 'The Nineteenth-Century Revolution in Government', *Historical Journal*, I (1958), and Henry Parris, 'The Nineteenth-Century Revolution in Government: a reappraisal reappraised', *Historical Journal*, 3 (1960). The issues are discussed in Valerie Cromwell, *Revolution or Evolution; British government in the nineteenth century* (1977).

27 Quotations from Keith Feiling, *The Second Tory Party 1714–1832* (1951), 345; and William C. Lubenow, *The Politics of Government Growth* (Newton Abbot, 1971), 39.

28 *Greville Memoirs*, iii, 178; Jasper Ridley, *Palmerston* (1970), 114.

29 Wellington, *Despatches*, vii, 444.

30 See Travis L. Crosby, *English Farmers and the Policy of Protection* (Hassocks, 1977), 99–100.

31 Parkes to Durham, 15 December 1834, in Thomas, *The Philosophic Radicals*, 273.

32 Greville's diary, 24 March 1835, *Greville Memoirs*, iii, 235.

33 See Kenneth Bourne (ed.), *The Letters of the third Viscount Palmerston to Laurence and Elizabeth Sulivan 1814–63*, Royal Historical Society, Camden Series, 4s, XXIII (1979), 260–62.

34 Quoted in Newbould, thesis, 267. Cf. *Greville Memoirs*, iii, 313, and Custance, thesis, 174.

35 Newbould, thesis, 270.

36 Close, thesis, 488–9. I am indebted to Dr Close's research for the data in this section.

37 Quoted in Cameron, thesis, 152.

38 Le Marchant quoted in Newbould, thesis, 279.

39 Letter, 2 April 1839, Lady Holland to her Son, 174.

40   For some worries see J. Pope Hennessy, *Monckton Milnes* (2 vols., 1949–51), i, 98–9; and Malmesbury's diary, 7 January 1840, in *3rd Earl of Malmesbury, Memoirs of an ex-Minister* (2 vols., 1884), i, 80.

41   Henry Reeve (ed.), *A Journal of the Reign of Queen Victoria from 1837 to 1852 by the late Charles C. F. Greville* (3 vols., 1885), i, 158; Parker, *Peel*, ii, 378.

42   Quoted in Cameron, thesis, 229; cf. Ebrington, quoted in Newbould, thesis, 340.

43   See John Prest, *Politics in the Age of Cobden* (1977), 64.

44   Newbould, thesis, 380–81.

45   Fisher, thesis, 111.

46   Chamberlain, thesis, 13.

47   Quoted in Ward, *Sir James Graham*, 209.

48   Parker, *Peel*, iii, 37.

49   Lord Monson and G. Leveson Gower (eds.), *Memoirs of George Elers* (1903), 306.

50   Gladstone's diary, 21 January 1842, in M. R. D. Foot and H. C. G. Matthew (eds.), *The Gladstone Diaries* (14 vols., Oxford, 1968–94), iii, 173.

51   Fisher, thesis, 86–7; Crosby, *English Farmers*, 121–4.

52   Memo. by Anson, 29 November 1843, quoted in Eyck, thesis, 37.

53   Parker, *Peel*, iii, 8.

54   Note circulated to cabinet and referred to by Gladstone in his diary, 8–10 June 1843: *The Gladstone Diaries*, iii, 287. For the impact of the Repeal movement generally see Oliver MacDonagh, 'O'Connell and Repeal, 1840–45' in Michael Bentley and John Stevenson (eds.), *High and Low Politics in Modern Britain* (Oxford, 1983), 4–27.

55   Quoted in Fisher, thesis, 143.

56   *Letters of Palmerston to Sulivan*, 276.

57   See Robert Stewart, 'The Ten Hours and Sugar Crises of 1844', *Historical Journal*, 12 (1969), 48. Cf. D. R. Fisher, 'Peel and the Conservative Party: the sugar crisis of 1844 reconsidered', *ibid.*, 18 (1975), 279–302.

58   *Croker*, iii, 30.

59   Ellenborough's diary, 24 January 1829, *Colchester*, i, 320.

60   Quoted in Robert Stewart, *The Politics of Protection: Lord Derby and the Protectionist Party 1841–52* (Cambridge, 1971), 29–30.

61   John Prest, *Lord John Russell* (1972), 213. For the background to Aberdeen's unease, see Chamberlain, thesis, *passim*.

62   Grey's journal, 24 May 1846, quoted in F. A. Dreyer, 'The Whigs and the Political Crisis of 1845', *English Historical Review*, LXXX (1965), 534. For a different view compare Mullen, thesis, 142–3.

63   Fisher, thesis, 417, 462.

64   *Croker*, iii, 60–63; Fitzwilliam to Russell, 30 June 1846, quoted in Mullen, thesis, 395–6.

65   Keith Robbins, *John Bright* (1979), 70.

Chapter 3   The Mechanics of Stability

1   Stanley's diary, 30 April 1850, in J. R. Vincent (ed.), *Disraeli, Derby and the Conservative Party: the political journals of Lord Stanley 1849–69* (Hassocks, 1978), 17. The phrase recurs six times in one column-length of *Hansard*: CX, 1039–40.

2   Stanley to Croker, 7 June 1847, *Croker*, iii, 107.

3   See in particular Peter Mandler, *Aristocratic Government in the Age of Reform: whigs and liberals 1830–52* (Oxford, 1990); Richard Brent, *Liberal Anglican Politics: whiggery, religion and reform* (Oxford, 1987); Jonathan Parry, *The Rise and Fall of Liberal Government in Victorian England* (New Haven, 1994).

4   George Villiers, *A Vanished Victorian* (1938), 160.

5   It was Clarendon who privately commended one Irish MP as 'a very ridiculous but not ill-disposed savage'. See K. Theodore Hoppen, *Elections, Politics and Society in Ireland 1832–1885* (Oxford, 1984), 333–4.

6   Dreyer, thesis, 127.

7   Malmesbury's diary, 6 March 1848, *Memoirs*, 161; Grey to Russell, 7–8 March 1848, in G. P. Gooch (ed.), *The Later Correspondence of Lord John Russell 1840–78* (2 vols., 1925), i, 186–7. Cf. F. W. H. Cavendish, *Society, Politics and Diplomacy 1820–64: passages from the journal of F. W. H. Cavendish* (1913), 144.

8   Gladstone's diary, 10 April 1848, *The Gladstone Diaries*, iv, 23.

9   Bright to Wilson, 18 April 1848, quoted in Dreyer, thesis, 163.

10 Gladstone, quoted in J. B. Conacher, *The Peelites and the Party System* (Newton Abbot, 1972), 9; Cardwell to Lincoln, 15 October 1849, in John Martineau, *Henry Pelham, Fifth Duke of Newcastle* (1908), 89.

11 Benjamin Disraeli, *Lord George Bentinck* (1852), 459.

12 Disraeli to Lady Londonderry, 12 April and 30 September 1849, in Marchioness of Londonderry (ed.), *Letters from Benjamin Disraeli to Frances Anne Marchioness of Londonderry 1837–61* (1938), 67, 75.

13 Palmerston to Russell, 14 April 1849, *Later Correspondence*, i, 194.

14 *Parliamentary Debates* (Lords), 7–8 May 1849. Stanley's diary under 6 May seems to be a misprint for 8 May: cf. *Political Journals*, 7.

15 Dreyer, thesis, 306–7.

16 Quoted in Edward Norman, *The English Catholic Church in the Nineteenth Century* (Oxford, 1984), 104.

17 Stanley's diary, 12 February 1851, *Political Journals*, 39–40.

18 The Ecclesiastical Titles Act attempted to render illegal any attempt to purloin titles appropriate only to Anglican bishops. It was never enforced and quietly repealed in 1871.

19 *Later Correspondence*, i, 181.

20 Disraeli to Derby, ? February 1852, quoted in W. D. Jones, *Lord Derby and Victorian Conservatism* (Oxford, 1956), 159.

21 The complexity of contemporary analyses is helpfully demonstrated by Professor Conacher, *The Peelites*, 116.

22 Cavendish's diary, 5 March 1857, *Society, Politics and Diplomacy*, 305; Stanley's diary, 17 February 1853, *Political Journals*, 99.

23 Cranborne in 1859: see Paul Smith, *Lord Salisbury on Politics* (Cambridge, 1972), 42.

24 Stanley's diary, see *Political Journals*, 96, 110–11, 122.

25 *Morning Advertiser* quoted in Olive Anderson, *A Liberal State at War* (1967), 153.

26 Monckton Milnes' notebook, ? 1848, in Pope Hennessy, *op. cit.*, ii, 274.

27 J. R. Fisher studies these elections in 'Issues and Influence: two by-elections in South Nottinghamshire in the mid-nineteenth century', *Historical Journal*, 24 (1981), 155–66.

28 For an introduction to this complex idea see Eric Hobsbawm, 'The Labour Aristocracy in Nineteenth-Century Britain', in Hobsbawm, *Labouring Men: studies in the history of Labour* (1964), 272–315; and the criticisms of Henry Pelling's essay, 'The Concept of the Labour Aristocracy', in his *Popular Politics and Society in Late-Victorian Britain* (1968), 37–61. Cf. A. E. Musson, 'Class Struggle and the Labour Aristocracy', *Social History* (1976), 335–56.

29 Quoted in Buchanan, thesis, 227–8.

30 Stanley's diary, n.d. (1853), *Political Journals*, 189; Clarendon to Cowley, 14 July 1855, in Sir Herbert Maxwell, *Life and Letters of Sir George William Frederick, Fourth Earl of Clarendon* (2 vols., 1913), ii, 86; Lytton in Commons, 22 March 1859, quoted in Barnett, thesis, 253 (author's emphasis).

31 Aberdeen's word: see Roundell, first Earl of Selborne, *Family and Personal Memorials* (2 vols., 1896), ii, 313; Maxwell, *Clarendon*, ii, 167; and Bright's famous remarks on the theme in *The Times*, 28 October 1858.

32 Quoted in Christopher Kent, 'Higher Journalism and the mid-Victorian Clerisy', *Victorian Studies*, 13 (1969–70), 189.

33 Aberdeen to Gladstone, 2 September 1852, in Conacher, *The Peelites*, 124.

34 Amey, thesis, 51.

35 Gladstone's diary, 13 May 1850, *The Gladstone Diaries*, iv, 210.

36 Stanley's diary, under 1 May 1851, *Political Journals*, 63.

37 For a detailed discussion of legislation during the war years, see Olive Anderson, *A Liberal State at War* (1967), 163–82.

38 Maxwell, *Clarendon*, ii, 144.

39 Cavendish's diary, 20 October 1857, *Society, Politics and Diplomacy*, 313–14.

40 Lincoln to Granville, 18 April 1853, in Lord Edmond Fitzmaurice, *Life of Lord Granville* (2 vols., 1905), i, 79–80; Russell to Panmure, 29 December 1852, in Sir G. Douglas and Sir D. G. Ramsey (eds.), *The Panmure Papers* (2 vols., 1908), i, 36.

41 Stanley's diary, under June 1852, *Political Journals*, 72; Palmerston to Sulivan, 24 December 1852, in Hon. Evelyn Ashley, *The Life of Henry John Temple, Viscount Palmerston* (2 vols., 1876), ii, 4.

42 Palmerston to brother, 3 April 1853, Ashley, *Palmerston*, ii, 2.

43 Palmerston to Aberdeen, 1 November 1853, *ibid.*, i, 45.

44 Palmerston to Russell, 29 January 1854, and 28 October 1862, Prest, *Lord John Russell*, 363, 393.

45 Gladstone's diary, 5 February 1855, *The Gladstone Diaries*, v, 19; Ashley, *Palmerston*, ii, 78.

46 Hawkins, thesis, 89.

47 Clarendon to Granville, 16 September 1855, Maxwell, *Clarendon*, ii, 92.

48 Stanley's diary, 4 June 1857, *Political Journals*, 151.

49 Clarendon to wife, 1 October 1857, Maxwell, *Clarendon*, ii, 153; letter, 31 July 1857, Disraeli to Lady Londonderry, 162. Cf. Argyll's view that Palmerston did not care about the India bill of the autumn: *George Douglas, eighth Duke of Argyll, Autobiography and Memoirs* (ed. Duchess of Argyll, 2 vols., 1906), ii, 86.

50 Gladstone in 1855, quoted in Hawkins, thesis, 70.

51 According to Aberdeen: see Hawkins, *op. cit.*, 161.

52 Lewis to Head, 5 February 1858, in Rev. Sir G. F. Lewis (ed.), *Letters of the Right Hon. Sir George Cornewall Lewis, Bart., to various friends* (1870), 329.

53 Russell to Dean of Bristol, 8 January 1858, quoted in Prest, *Russell*, 380; Lewis to Head, 20 January 1859, in *Letters*, 363; Derby to Malmesbury, 5 March 1860, in Malmesbury, *Memoirs*, 515–16; Gladstone to Russell, 23 May 1860 in *The Gladstone Diaries*, v, 490 n7.

54 In the event, the act established a council of fifteen of whom seven were to be elected by the East India Company and the rest nominated by the Crown.

55 See W. D. Jones, *Lord Derby and Victorian Conservatism*, 243.

56 Lewis to Head, 1 August 1858, *Letters*, 338; Fitzmaurice, *Granville*, i, 320.

57 Disraeli introducing motion of leave to introduce a reform bill, 28 February 1859, *Hansard*, CLII, 968.

58 Dodson on Second Reading, 22 March 1859, *Hansard*, CLIII, 571–2.

59 Disraeli to Derby, 3 April 1859, quoted in Hawkins, thesis, 475. Dr Hawkins finds reform a greater preoccupation than Italy at the election. Cf. D. E. D. Beales, *England and Italy 1859–60* (1961), *passim*.

60 *The Times*, 30 October 1858.

61 Letter, 9 November 1861, Disraeli to Lady Londonderry, 185.

62 See Sheridan Gilley, 'The Garibaldi Riots of 1862', *Historical Journal*, 16 (1973), 697–732.

63 Derby to Malmesbury, 31 October 1862, *Memoirs*, 565–6. Cf. Bruce to brother, 10 November 1862, in *Letters of the Rt. Hon. Henry Austin Bruce G. C. B., Lord Aberdare of Duffryn* (Oxford, private circulation, 2 vols., 1902), i, 196.

64 Gladstone's diary, 7 May 1864, *The Gladstone Diaries*, v, 274. For the Conservatives see Keith Sandiford, *Great Britain and the Schleswig-Holstein Question 1848–64* (Toronto and Buffalo, 1975), 154.

65 Russell to Parker, 10 May 1859, *Later Correspondence*, ii, 230.

66 Stanley's diary, 24 October 1864, *Political Journals*, 225; Malmesbury's diary, 30 April 1865, *Memoirs*, 606.

67 Quoted in James Winter, *Robert Lowe* (Toronto and Buffalo, 1976), 201.

Chapter 4   Occupying the Centre

1 Disraeli to Hardy, 23 April 1868, in A. E. Gathorne Hardy, *Gathorne Hardy, First Earl of Cranbrook* (2 vols., 1910), i, 276.

2 H. A. Bruce to John Bruce, 19 December 1863, in *Letters of H. A. Bruce*, i, 205.

3 Sir Frederic Rogers to Kate Rogers, 25 November 1865, in G. E. Marindin (ed.), *The Letters of Frederic Lord Blachford* (1896), 258.

4 Delane to Bernal Osborne, 1 February 1866, in P. H. Bagenal, *The Life of Ralph Bernal Osborne M.P.* (private circulation, 1884), 223.

5 Stanley's diary, 10 June 1866, *Political Journals*, 252.

6 In conversation with Stanley, 30 April 1866, *Political Journals*, 250.

7 The amendment was carried by 315 to 304: *Hansard*, 18 June 1866, CLXXXIV, 552–3; cf. Gladstone's diary, 19 June, in *The Gladstone Diaries*, vi, 444.

8 Bulwer to Lady Salisbury, 5 October 1866, in Lady Burghclere (ed.), *A Great Lady's Friendships: letters to Mary, Marchioness of Salisbury, Countess of Derby 1862–1890* (1933), 88–9.

9 Stanley's diary, 26 July 1866, *Political Journals*, 261.

10 Quoted in Robert Blake, *Disraeli* (1966), 456.

11 William White, *The Inner Life of the House of Commons* (1898, 1915 edition), 68ff.

12 See Maurice Cowling's difficult but superb study, *1867: Disraeli, Gladstone and Revolution; the passing of the second reform bill* (Cambridge, 1967), especially 217–86.

13 Cf. Royden Harrison, *Before the Socialists: studies in labour and politics* (London and Toronto, 1965), 78–135.

14 Gladstone to Russell, 2 November 1867, *Later Correspondence*, ii, 362–3.

15 Lord Eustace Cecil quoted in Cowling, *op. cit.*, 16.

16 Glyn to Gladstone, 17 September 1868, quoted in A. F. Thompson, 'The Whigs and the General Election of 1868', *English Historical Review*, LXIII (1948), 189.

17 Quoted in Paul Smith, *Disraelian Democracy and Social Reform* (London and Toronto, 1967), 304.

18   Granville to Gladstone, 7 August 1879, in Agatha Ramm (ed.), *The Political Correspondence of Mr. Gladstone and Lord Granville 1876–86* (2 vols., Oxford, 1962), i, 100.

19   I have compiled the table from figures given by Michael Rush in his essay on 'The M.P.s' in Stuart Walkland (ed.), *The House of Commons in the Twentieth Century* (Oxford 1979), 98.

20   Cf. D. C. Moore's chapter on 'Why Poll Books Became Unpublishable' in his *The Politics of Deference* (Hassocks, 1976), 401–15.

21   Bailey, thesis, 112. I rely heavily on Dr Bailey's work here.

22   Granville to Gladstone, 4 September 1877, in Ramm, *op. cit.*, i, 51.

23   On the origins of the 'mandate', see Vernon Bogdanor, *The People and the Party System: the referendum and electoral reform in British politics* (Cambridge, 1981), 17–20.

24   Newcastle and Southwark respectively. The latter led Disraeli to thump the cabinet table in triumph: R. A. Cross, *A Political History* (Eccle Riggs, Lancs., privately printed, 1903), 63. For Buckinghamshire see R. W. Davis, *Political Change and Continuity 1760–1885* (Newton Abbot, 1972), 17; and for Newcastle, T. J. Nossiter, *Influence, Opinion and Political Idioms in Reformed England: case studies from the north-east 1832–74* (Hassocks, 1975), 39.

25   Quoted in Viscount Chilston, *W. H. Smith* (London and Toronto, 1965), 94.

26   Granville to Gladstone, 29 November 1875, in Ramm (ed.), *The Political Correspondence of Mr. Gladstone and Lord Granville 1868–76*, Royal Historical Society, Camden Series, 3s LXXXI–II (2 vols., 1952), ii, 475.

27   Professor H. J. Hanham's magisterial survey, *Elections and Party Management, Politics in the time of Disraeli and Gladstone* (1959, revised edition, Hassocks, 1978) is especially relevant here and informs much of this section.

28   For this and related subjects see E. P. Hennock, *Fit and Proper Persons; ideal and reality in nineteenth-century urban government* (1973).

29   Quoted in Hanham, *op. cit.*, 52 n3.

30   Lady Cowper, *Lord Cowper: a memoir* (private circulation, 1913), 139–40. He was thirty-one at the time. Cf. Harcourt to Bramwell, 12 August 1874, in A. G. Gardiner, *The Life of Sir William Harcourt* (2 vols., 1923), i, 279.

31   These developments are acutely considered in Boyd Hilton, 'Gladstone's Theological Politics' in Bentley and Stevenson (eds.), *High and Low Politics*, 28–57. Cf. Hilton's later work, *The Age of Atonement: the influence of evangelicalism on social and economic thought 1785–1865* (Oxford, 1988).

32   Quoted in H. C. G. Matthew, *The Liberal Imperialists* (Oxford, 1973), vii.

33   For example, Dunne, thesis, 48; cf. E. D. Steele, *Irish Land and British Politics; tenant-right and nationality* (Cambridge, 1973), *passim*.

34 Harcourt to Spencer Butler, n.d. (December 1868), Gardiner, *Harcourt*, i, 189. Harcourt had just won Oxford, the seat lost by Gladstone in 1865.

35 Disraeli at Manchester, 3 April 1872, quoted in Blake, *Disraeli*, 523.

36 Gladstone to Granville, 13 September 1869, *Correspondence 1868–76*, i, 54; Gladstone's diary, 22 September 1869, *The Gladstone Diaries*, vii, 136.

37 On the relationship between Whigs and Protestantism over this issue, see J. P. Parry, *Democracy and Religion: Gladstone and the Liberal Party 1867–75* (Cambridge, 1986).

38 Gladstone to Spencer, 28 March 1869, *The Gladstone Diaries*, vii, 46.

39 Gladstone to Bright, 30 December 1869, *The Gladstone Diaries*, vii, 202. He congratulated Bright for saying nothing at Birmingham: *ibid.*, 219–20.

40 Granville to Gladstone, 25 September 1869, *Correspondence 1868–76*, i, 59; Argyll to Gladstone, 19 November 1869, *Memoirs*, ii, 254; Gladstone to Clarendon, 6 October 1869, *The Gladstone Diaries*, vii, 142; Gladstone to Granville, 22 September 1869, *Correspondence 1868–76*, i, 58.

41 Gladstone's diary, 17 April 1870, *The Gladstone Diaries*, vii, 279.

42 *Hansard*, 16 June 1870, CCII, 266–8. Cf. diary, same date.

43 Granville to Argyll, 5 June 1870, in Fitzmaurice, *Granville*, ii, 25.

44 Gladstone to Halifax, 29 July 1870, *The Gladstone Diaries*, vii, 335ff. The government asked parliament for 20,000 extra men and a grant of £2m: see D. M. Schreuder, 'Gladstone as "Troublemaker": Liberal foreign policy and the German annexation of Alsace-Lorraine 1870–71', *Journal of British Studies*, 17 (1978), 106–35.

45 Kimberley's journal, 25 February 1871, in Ethel Drus (ed.), *A Journal of Events during the Gladstone Ministry 1868–74 by John, First Earl of Kimberley*, Royal Historical Society, Camden Miscellany, XXI (1958), 21. Cf. Gladstone to Granville, 19 November 1870, *Correspondence 1868–76*, i, 161ff.

46 Bright to Granville, 29 May 1871, quoted in Brian Harrison, *Drink and the Victorians* (1971), 267.

47 I have told the story of this odd relationship elsewhere. See Michael Bentley, 'Gladstonian Liberals and Provincial Notables: Whitby Politics, 1868–80', *Historical Research*, 64 (1991).

48 T. W. Heyck, *The Dimensions of British Radicalism: the case of Ireland* (Urbana, 1974), *passim*. Harcourt put radical numbers at 70 in 1875 as against about 150 Whigs. See John P. Rossi, 'The Transformation of the British Liberal Party: a study of the tactics of the Liberal opposition 1874–80', *Transactions of the American Philosophical Society*, 68/8 (1978), 17.

49 Gladstone to Granville, 3 September 1873, *Correspondence 1868–76*, ii, 405; Joseph Chamberlain, 'The Liberal Party and its Leaders', *Fortnightly Review*, 20/14 (September 1873), 291.

50   Cf. Spencer to Hartington, 12 March 1873, in Peter Gordon (ed.), *The Red Earl: the papers of the fifth Earl Spencer 1835–1910* (2 vols., Northampton, 1981–), i, 108. For the Whig contribution to the government's defeat see J. P. Parry, 'Religion and the Collapse of Gladstone's First Government 1870–74', *Historical Journal*, 25 (1982), 71–101.

51   This fear of the drink interest ran back at least as far as the Surrey by-election of 1871: cf. Bruce to wife, 28 August 1871, *Letters*, i, 312.

52   Gladstone to Granville, 8 January 1874, *Correspondence 1868–76*, ii, 438–41. For previous quotations see Kimberley's journal, 5 August 1873, Drus, *op. cit.*, 41; Harcourt to Bright, 8 August 1873, Gardiner, *Harcourt*, i, 257.

53   Cf. Disraeli to Lady Bradford, 27 February 1874, in Marquess of Zetland (ed.), *The Letters of Disraeli to Lady Bradford and Lady Chesterfield* (2 vols., 1929), i, 55. For Forster see Sir Henry Lucy, *The Disraeli Parliament 1874–80* (1885), 17. Joseph Arch did indeed become a Member of Parliament but not until he won North-West Norfolk in 1885, after contesting Wilton in 1880. Except for 1886–92, he sat for that constituency until his retirement in 1900.

54   Hardy's diary, 18 July and 6 August 1874, *Cranbrook*, i, 341–2; Salisbury to Carnarvon, 24 July 1874, in Lady Gwendolyn Cecil, *Life of Robert Marqis of Salisbury by his daughter* (4 vols., 1921–32), ii, 63.

55   Disraeli to Lady Bradford, 16 July 1874, *Letters of Disraeli*, i, 23.

56   Disraeli to Lady Bradford, 29 June 1875, in W. F. Monypenny and G. E. Buckle, *The Life of Benjamin Disraeli, Earl of Beaconsfield* (6 vols., 2-volume edition, 1929), ii, 711; Disraeli to Queen, 17 July 1875, quoted in Dwyer, thesis, 178.

57   *The Times*, 18 October 1875, quoted in Buchanan, thesis, 243.

58   Disraeli to Lady Bradford, 5 May 1874, *Letters of Disraeli*, i, 80–81.

59   Blachford to Church, 8 February 1875, *Letters of Lord Blachford*, 361.

60   Gladstone to Granville, 20 August 1876, *Correspondence 1876–86*, i, 1.

61   Kirkpatrick, thesis, 40ff.

62   Salisbury to Mallet, 14 January 1876, Cecil, *Salisbury*, i, 80.

63   Cairns to Cross, n.d. (1876), in Cross, *Political History*, 38. For the Bulgarian issue generally, see R. T. Shannon, *Gladstone and the Bulgarian Agitation 1876* (1963).

64   Salisbury to Beaconsfield, 23 September 1876, *Salisbury*, ii, 85.

65   Childers to Clarke, 20 September 1876, in Lt. Col. Spencer Childers, *The Life and Correspondence of the Right Hon. Hugh C. E. Childers* (2 vols., 1901), i, 242; Spencer to Hartington, 29 October 1876, *Red Earl*, i, 126; Gladstone to Granville, 2 November 1876, *Correspondence 1868–76*, i, 17.

66   Salisbury to Lady Salisbury, n.d. (November 1876), Cecil, ii, 91.

67   Disraeli to Lady Bradford, ?8 September, 1876 and to the Queen, 27 February 1877, in Monypenny and Buckle, ii, 933, 997; Leveson to Granville, n.d. (March 1877), *Gladstone–Granville Correspondence 1876–86*, i, 33.

68 See Charles Whibley, *Lord John Manners and his Friends* (2 vols., Edinburgh, 1925), ii, 173–4.
69 Beach to Frere, 25 December 1878, in Lady Victoria Hicks Beach, *Life of Sir Michael Hicks Beach* (2 vols., 1932), i, 117–18.
70 Beaconsfield to Lytton, 14 August 1879, Monypenny and Buckle, ii, 1349.
71 Childers to Clarke, 30 October 1879, Childers, i, 264.

Chapter 5   Conservative Ascendancy

1 Spencer to Granville, 10 September 1880, *Red Earl*, i, 161; for a detailed analysis of the election see Trevor Lloyd, *The General Election of 1880* (Oxford, 1968).
2 Cowper quoted in Dunne, thesis, 70.
3 Hamilton's diary, 16 September 1881, in Dudley W. R. Bahlman (ed.), *The Diaries of Edward Walter Hamilton* (2 vols., Oxford, 1972), i, 188.
4 Hamilton's diary, 13 March 1881, *ibid.*, i, 114.
5 For Granville's financial problems see John Vincent (ed.), *The Later Derby Diaries: home rule, Liberal Unionism, and aristocratic life in late Victorian England* (Bristol, 1981), 92–6.
6 Johnson, thesis, *passim*.
7 Gladstone to Granville, 4 May 1880, *Correspondence 1876–86*, i, 124 (emphasis in original).
8 For the by-elections see Hamilton's diary, especially i, 125–6.
9 Gladstone to Granville, 13 April 1882, *Correspondence 1876–86*, i, 360.
10 For tenurial politics in these years see J. R. Fisher, 'The Farmers' Alliance: an agricultural protest movement of the 1880s', *Agricultural History Review*, 26 (1978), 15–25; 'Tenant Right: farmer against landlord in Victorian England 1847–83', *Agricultural History*, 47 (1973); and Avner Offer, *Property and Politics 1870–1914: landownership, law, ideology, and urban development in England* (Cambridge, 1981).
11 See H. J. Hanham, 'The Problem of Highland Discontent 1880–85', *Transactions of the Royal Historical Society*, 5s, 19 (1969); cf. Roy Douglas, *Land, People and Politics: a history of the land question in the United Kingdom 1878–1952* (1976), 60–95.
12 Hamilton's diary, 27 July 1882, *Diaries of Hamilton*, i, 312.
13 See, for example, Gladstone to Granville, 4–5 July 1882, *Correspondence 1876–86*, i, 385.
14 These possibilities are discussed in Andrew Jones, *The Politics of Reform, 1884* (Cambridge, 1972), 23, 30–31.
15 Hartington to Spencer, 18 October 1883, *Red Earl*, i, 253.
16 Two permanent reforms date from this time: the closure or *clôture*, which allowed the Speaker to terminate debates, and the guillotine which authorized, on a majority of three to one, restriction of debate on individual sections of a bill.

17 Quoted in A. B. Cooke and John Vincent, *The Governing Passion: cabinet government and party politics in Britain 1885–6* (Brighton, 1974), 253.

18 A luminous exception is John Vincent's Raleigh Lecture on 'Gladstone and Ireland' printed in *Proceedings of the British Academy*, LXIII (1977), 193–238.

19 Central to recent thinking are Cooke and Vincent, *op. cit.*, and the same authors' 'Ireland and Party Politics 1885–7: an unpublished Conservative memoir', *Irish Historical Studies*, XVI (1969). See also Cooke and Vincent (eds.), *Lord Carlingford's Journal: reflections of a cabinet minister, 1885* (1971).

20 Historical Manuscripts Commission, *The Prime Minister's Papers (2): W. E. Gladstone*, eds. J. Brooke and M. Sorenson (1971).

21 In this connexion one might instance works such as Sir Robert Ensor, *England 1870–1914* (Oxford, 1936); J. L. Hammond, *Gladstone and the Irish Nation* (1938); Sir Philip Magnus, *Gladstone* (1954); Michael Barker, *Gladstone and Radicalism: the reconstruction of Liberal policy in Britain 1885–94* (Brighton, 1975).

22 In conversation with Henry James, 30 January 1886: see Lord Askwith, *Lord James of Hereford* (1930), 164. For his inability to renege on 'what he had said', see Derby's report of a discussion on the previous day in Vincent, *Later Diaries*, 59.

23 Richard Jay, *Joseph Chamberlain: a political study* (Oxford, 1981), 123; Derby's diary, 23 March 1886, for Chamberlain's disturbing Hartington with fears over revolution: *Later Diaries*, 65.

24 C. R. Spencer to Earl Spencer, 4 June 1882, *Red Earl*, i, 204.

25 Cooke and Vincent, *The Governing Passion*, 53.

26 Gladstone to Spencer, 30 June 1885, *Red Earl*, i, 311.

27 Gladstone to Granville, 27 July 1881, *Correspondence 1876–86*, i, 286–7.

28 Neal Blewett, 'The Franchise in the United Kingdom 1885–1918', *Past and Present*, 32 (1965), 27–56. Cf. Peter Clarke, 'Electoral Sociology of Modern Britain', *History*, 57 (1972), 31–55; H. C. G. Matthew, R. McKibbin and J. Kay, 'The Franchise Factor in the Rise of the Labour Party', *English Historical Review*, XCI (1976), 723–52; Duncan Tanner, 'The Parliamentary Electoral System, the "Fourth" Reform Act and the Rise of Labour in England and Wales', *Bulletin of the Institute of Historical Research*, 56 (1983), 205–19. I am very grateful to Dr Tanner for allowing me to see his work before it appeared in print.

29 See James Cornford, 'The Transformation of Conservatism', *Victorian Studies*, 7 (1963–4), 35–66; and Henry Pelling, *A Social Geography of British Elections* (1967), 6–9 and *passim*.

30 Chadwick, thesis, 199–200.

31 For these and other changes in wealth-holding, see W. D. Rubinstein, *Men of Property: the very wealthy in Britain since the Industrial Revolution* (1981), *passim*.

32 *Manchester Guardian*, 26 July 1895, quoted in Clarke, 'Electoral Sociology', 50.

33 Details in Powell, thesis, 71–2, and Chadwick, thesis, 200.

34 See Walter Nimocks, *Milner's Young Men: the 'kindergarten' in Edwardian imperial affairs* (1970), 17–74, and John Turner, *Lloyd George's Secretariat* (Cambridge, 1980) for their afterlife.

35 Esher's journal, 9 January 1893, in M. V. Brett (ed.), *Journals and Letters of Reginald Viscount Esher* (4 vols., 1934–8), i, 170–71.

36 For this quotation and the background to the visit see Paul Kennedy, *The Rise of Anglo-German Antagonism, 1860–1914* (1980), 202. The Liberal response to imperialism generally is discussed in H. C. G. Matthew, *The Liberal Imperialists: the ideas and politics of a post-Gladstonian elite* (Oxford, 1973).

37 Quoted in Brooks, thesis, 15. I follow closely here Dr Brooks' excellent study of Gladstone's fourth ministry.

38 Dilke's diary, 21 April 1883, quoted in Jones, *Politics of Reform*, 38.

39 Cecil, *Salisbury*, iv, 159; cf. R. F. Foster, *Lord Randolph Churchill: a political life* (Oxford, 1981), 240.

40 Ripon to Kimberley, 21 July 1892, quoted in Brooks, thesis, 10; cf. Janet Howarth, 'The Liberal Revival in Northants 1880–95', *Historical Journal*, 12 (1969), especially 116–17.

41 Goschen to Dufferin, 10 October 1886, quoted in Foster, *Churchill*, 278; Goschen to Milner, 14 April 1898, quoted in Thomas J. Spinner, *George Joachim Goschen: the transformation of a Victorian Liberal* (Cambridge, 1973), 213.

42 See Algar Thorold, *The Life of Henry Labouchere* (1913), 238.

43 There is a useful graph of these appointments in Bailey, thesis, appendix, 290.

44 Cunningham, thesis, 15–16. Cf. Alan J. Lee, *The Origins of the Popular Press 1856–1914* (1976), *passim*.

45 Esher's journal, 7 January 1890, *Journals and Letters*, i, 141; Acland to Ellis, 1 January 1891, in Powell, thesis, 54. Cf. José Harris, 'The Transition to High Politics in English Social Policy 1880–1914', in Bentley and Stevenson (eds.), *High and Low Politics*, 58–79.

46 Milner to Goschen, 21 August 1894, quoted in Spinner, *Goschen*, 100.

47 Blachford to Taylor, 20 January 1885, *Letters of Lord Blachford*, 424: Hamilton's diary, 16 August 1892, in Johnson, thesis, 7.

48 Chamberlain to Labouchere, 4 December 1885, in Thorold, *Labouchere*, 245. Cf. Chamberlain to Morley, 21 September 1885, in J. L. Garvin and J. Amery, *The Life of Joseph Chamberlain* (6 vols., 1932–69), i, 96.

49 For the background, see W. L. Arnstein, *The Bradlaugh Case: a study in late-Victorian opinion and politics* (Oxford, 1965).

50 In the House of Commons, 28 May 1883: see Jones, *Politics of Reform*, 68 n2.

51 Balfour to Salisbury, March 1886, quoted in Peter Fraser, 'The Liberal-Unionist Alliance: Chamberlain, Hartington and the Conservatives

1886–1904', *English Historical Review*, LXXVII (1962), 65; memo. by Balfour of conversation with Chamberlain, 13 June 1886, in Davis, thesis, 139.

52 Salisbury to Smith, 5 February 1889, in James Cornford, 'The Parliamentary Foundations of the Hotel Cecil', in R. Robson (ed.), *Ideas and Institutions of Victorian Britain: essays in honour of George Kitson Clark* (1967), 268–311.

53 Frances Balfour to Henry Sidgwick, 31 August 1886, printed in her autobiography *Ne Obliviscaris* (2 vols., n.d.), ii, 70.

54 Akers-Douglas to Salisbury, 18 July 1886, in Fraser, 'Liberal-Unionist Alliance', 58. He counted 43 Hartingtonians and 21 Chamberlainites among the 78 Unionists.

55 Joseph to Austen Chamberlain, 11 June 1887, quoted in Jay, *Chamberlain*, 153; Churchill to Chamberlain, 22 August 1887, Garvin and Amery, ii, 315.

56 Salisbury to Beach, 3 July 1887, Cecil, iv, 149–50; Garvin and Amery, ii, 306ff. Cf. Peter Marsh, *The Discipline of Popular Government: Lord Salisbury's domestic statecraft 1881–1902* (Hassocks, 1978), 120–21.

57 Salisbury to the Queen, 24 January 1887, Cecil, iv, 15; Kennedy, *Antagonism*, 192ff.

58 For backbench feeling on education see George Wyndham to his father, 7 September 1889, in J. W. Mackail and Guy Wyndham, *Life and Letters of George Wyndham* (2 vols., 1924), i, 235–6. The tithe question is commented on by J. A. Bridges in his *Reminiscences of a Country Politician* (1906), 119–20.

59 Balfour to Salisbury (not sent), 23 November 1888, in Davis, thesis, 171.

60 Chamberlain to Mary Endicott, 19 March 1888, Garvin and Amery, ii, 347.

61 For Churchill's later life see Foster, *Churchill*, 348–81.

62 Derby's diary, 20 February 1891, *Later Derby Diaries*; for Harcourt see Arthur Ponsonby, *Henry Ponsonby: his life from his letters* (1943), 272.

63 Quoted in Peter Stansky, *Ambitions and Strategies: the struggle for the leadership of the Liberal party in the 1890s* (Oxford, 1964), 40.

64 Hamilton's diary, 1 December 1890, in Spinner, *Goschen*, 169.

65 Harcourt to Morley, 15 July 1892, Gardiner, *Harcourt*, ii, 179.

66 Brooks, thesis, 45ff and *passim*.

67 Gardiner, *Harcourt*, ii, 171.

68 See diary of Gladstone's secretary, Algy West, 3 and 16 August 1893: Horace B. Hutchinson (ed.), *The Private Diaries of Sir Algernon West* (1922), 93; Chamberlain's diary, 17 August 1893, Garvin and Amery, ii, 579.

69 See C. J. Lowe, *The Reluctant Imperialists* (2 vols., 1967), i, 174; cf. West's diary, 24 July: 'Siam the only interest', *Private Diaries*, 176.

70 Details in Stansky, *Ambitions and Strategies*, 41–78.

71 Harcourt to Rosebery, 4 April 1894, Gardiner, ii, 284–5.

72 1 March 1894, quoted in Stansky, *op. cit.*, 79.

73 For the last days of the government see Robert Rhodes James, *Rosebery* (1963), 381–4.

74 Chamberlain to Devonshire, 19 April 1895, Garvin and Amery, ii, 630.

Chapter 6   Breaking the Mould?

1   Marsh, *Discipline of Popular Government*, 237f; see also his more recent biography of Chamberlain, Peter T. Marsh, *Joseph Chamberlain: entrepreneur in politics* (New Haven, 1994), 349–61. For the peers see G. D. Phillips, 'The Whig Lords and Liberalism', *Historical Journal*, 24 (1981), 167–73.

2   Frances Balfour, *Ne Obliviscaris*, ii, 270–71.

3   Devonshire to Salisbury, 24 March 1897, quoted in J. E. B. Munson, 'The Unionist Coalition and Education 1895–1902', *Historical Journal*, 20 (1977), 622.

4   Hamilton's diary, 29 June 1895, in Dudley W. R. Bahlman (ed.), *The Diary of Sir Edward Walter Hamilton 1885–1906* (Hull, 1993), 307.

5   The Chaplin family is assessed in R. J. Olney, *Lincolnshire Politics* (Oxford, 1973), and the same author's *Rural Society and County Government in Nineteenth-Century Lincolnshire* (Lincoln, 1979).

6   Quoted in Cornford, 'Parliamentary Foundations', 296.

7   Avner Offer, *Property and Politics*, 208ff; cf. Salisbury to Balfour, 6 February 1889, quoted in J. P. D. Dunbabin, 'The Politics of the Establishment of County Councils', *Historical Journal*, 6 (1963), 240.

8   Bernard Malet's diary, n.d., quoted in Max Egremont, *Balfour* (1980), 132.

9   Howard Vincent to *The Times*, 30 March 1898, quoted in Kennedy, *Antagonism*, 234.

10 Esher's journal, 29 January 1898, in *Journals and Letters*, i, 210–11.

11 Chamberlain to Selborne, 29 December 1897, quoted in Jay, *Chamberlain*, 214.

12 Marsh, *Joseph Chamberlain*, 429.

13 A. N. Porter, *The Origins of the South African War; Joseph Chamberlain and the diplomacy of imperialism 1895–9* (Manchester, 1980), 84. The events and evidence are reviewed in Marsh, *Chamberlain*, 372–87.

14 Secret Convention between Great Britain and Germany, 30 August 1898, in M. Hurst (ed.), *Key Treaties for the Great Powers 1814–1914* (2 vols., Newton Abbot, 1972), ii, 691.

15 The relationship between Milner, Chamberlain and Selborne comes out well in Selborne's correspondence, edited by George Boyce: see Boyce (ed.), *The Crisis of British Power: the imperial and naval papers of the second Earl of Selborne 1895–1900* (1990), 19–104.

16 See FitzRoy's conversation with Sandars in April 1901, reported in Sir Almeric FitzRoy, *Memoirs* (2 vols., 1925), i, 50.

17 Chamberlain to Devonshire, 22 September 1902, Jay, 264.

18 See *The Times*, 16 May 1903, for a report of the speech.

19 I follow closely here the analyses of Alfred Gollin, *Balfour's Burden: Arthur Balfour and imperial preference* (1965), and R. A. Rempel, *Unionists Divided: Arthur Balfour, Joseph Chamberlain and the Unionist free traders* (Newton Abbot, 1972).

20 See, for example, *The Times*, 2 and 7 October 1903, for Balfour's Sheffield speech and Chamberlain's at Glasgow.

21 Joseph to Austen Chamberlain, 11 March 1904, quoted in Peter Fraser, *Joseph Chamberlain: radicalism and empire 1868–1914* (1966), 254. Cf. Chamberlain to Northcote, 22 April 1904: 'All my efforts and hopes are directed to the election after next' (emphasis in original). See Garvin and Amery, *op. cit.*, vi, 562.

22 For a development of this point see Kennedy, *Antagonism*, 314–19.

23 There has been much recent and valuable work on the history of British Jews in this period. For the background to the Aliens legislation, see Eugene C. Black, *The Social Politics of Anglo-Jewry 1880–1920* (Oxford, 1988), 302–17; Geoffrey Alderman, *Modern British Jewry* (Oxford, 1992), 190–91; David Feldman, *Englishmen and Jews* (New Haven, 1994), 353–9.

24 Rosebery to Ripon, 13 August 1895, in Stansky, *Ambitions and Strategies*, 180. Cf. Rhodes James, *Rosebery*, 405.

25 Grey to Rosebery, 22 February 1902, quoted in Keith Robbins, *Sir Edward Grey: a biography of Lord Grey of Falloden* (1971), 99; for Webb, see his much-remarked article on 'Lord Rosebery's Escape from Hounsditch', *Nineteenth Century*, L (September 1901), 366–86.

26 The judgement of Sir James Kitson (my emphasis). For the illustrations in this paragraph see Ellins, thesis, 196, 201 and 221–3. I draw on Dr Ellin's research throughout this section.

27 Hamilton's diary, 26 November 1898, in Stansky, *op. cit.*, 259.

28 Robbins, *Grey*, 79, 91.

29 Charles Mallet, *Herbert Gladstone: a memoir* (1932), 162, 182.

30 For the Liberal League see Matthew, *The Liberal Imperialists*, 86ff. The Chesterfield speech is also examined in G. R. Searle, *The Quest for National Efficiency* (Oxford, 1971), 127–36.

31 Campbell-Bannerman to Sidney Buxton, 21 November 1900, quoted in John Wilson, *C. B.: a life of Sir Henry Campbell-Bannerman* (1973), 340; Asquith to Gladstone, 7 October 1900, in Stephen Koss, *Asquith* (1976), 52.

32 This dilemma is highlighted in Matthew, *Liberal Imperialists*, 96–7.

33 Ellins, thesis, 210, 235.

34 Matthew, *op. cit.*, 103: for Lloyd George's view, see John Grigg, *Lloyd George: the people's champion 1902–11* (1978), 82–5.

35 *The Times*, 26 November 1905.

36 See F. Bealey and H. Pelling, *Labour and Politics 1900–1906* (1958), 98–124, and the additional information in Peter Clarke, *Lancashire and the New Liberalism* (Cambridge, 1971), 91–3.

37 Stephen Koss, '1906: revival and revivalism', in A. J. A. Morris (ed.), *Edwardian Radicalism* (1974), 83.

38 H. V. Emy, *Liberals, Radicals and Social Politics 1892–1914* (Cambridge, 1973), 68.

39 Quoted in Peter Clarke, *Liberals and Social Democrats* (Cambridge, 1978), 63. For a detailed analysis of New Liberal doctrine, see Michael Freeden, *The New Liberalism: an ideology of social reform* (Oxford, 1978), *passim*.

40 Bertrand Russell, *My Philosophical Development* (1959), 61.

41 See G. Kitson-Clark, *Churchmen and the Condition of England 1832–85* (1973), especially 227–67.

42 Springhall, thesis, *passim*. Cf. Michael Bentley, 'British Parliamentary Institutions and Political Thought 1865–1914', *Parliaments, Estates and Representation*, 3 (1983), 35–46.

43 Meath in *Windsor* Magazine (December 1909), quoted in Springhall, thesis, 28.

44 A. M. Ludovici, *A Defence of Aristocracy* (1915), ix–x, 4.

45 Lady Monkswell's diary, 12 February 1907, in Hon. E. C. F. Collier, *A Victorian Diarist: later extracts from the journals of Mary, Lady Monkswell 1895–1909* (1946), 171–2.

46 Riddell's diary, 7 December 1911, in Lord Riddell, *More Pages from my Diary* (1934), 31. Lady Sackville was referring to her home, near Sevenoaks in Kent.

47 For an introductory study see G. Crossick (ed.), *The Lower Middle Class in Britain 1870–1914* (1977).

48 For this process and its impact on the class structure, see Gareth Stedman Jones, *Languages of Class: studies in English working class history 1832–1982* (Cambridge, 1983), esp. pp. 179–238.

49 According to Harcourt: diary, 16 March 1912, quoted in Ellins, thesis, 364.

50 Quoted in Philip Ziegler, *Diana Cooper* (1981, Harmondsworth, 1983), 31.

51 Sidney Low, *The Governance of England* (1904), 132; cf. A. L. Lowell, *The Government of England* (2 vols., 1908), ii, 513.

52 Balfour to Esher, 17 January 1906, in *Journals and Letters*, ii, 136. Stanmore to Halifax, 23 June 1909, and Northumberland in the Lords, 16 May 1911, quoted in G. D. Phillips, *The Diehards: aristocratic society and politics in Edwardian England* (Cambridge, Mass., 1979), 126, 129.

53 Collier, *A Victorian Diarist*, 208–9.

54 Sidney to Beatrice Webb, 13 December 1905, in Norman Mackenzie, *The Letters of Sidney and Beatrice Webb* (3 vols., Cambridge and

London, 1978), ii, 222; Churchill to Asquith, 29 December 1908, in Randolph S. Churchill and Martin Gilbert, *Winston S. Churchill* (8 vols., 1966–88), ii, *Companion part II*, 863.

55 Bryce to Campbell-Bannerman, 18 December 1904, quoted in Ellins, thesis, 343.

56 Liberal–Labour relations have attracted much attention from historians but see in particular Henry Pelling, *Popular Politics and Society in Late-Victorian Britain* (1968), 101–20, 130–46; Peter Clarke, 'The Progressive Movement in England', *Transactions of the Royal Historical Society*, 5s, 24 (1974), and 'The Electoral Position of the Liberal and Labour Parties 1910–14', *English Historical Review*, XC (1975); and Ross McKibbin, *The Evolution of the Labour Party* (Oxford, 1974). The electoral perspective offered in these pieces has been revised to some degree in a provocative article, H. C. G. Matthew, R. McKibbin and J. Kay, 'The Franchise Factor in the Rise of the Labour Party', *English Historical Review*, XCI (1976), 723–52 and responses to it. Many of these are summarized and contested in Duncan Tanner's important monograph, *Political Change and the Labour Party* (Cambridge, 1990).

57 Churchill to Clementine Churchill, 24 March 1912, *Churchill*, iii, *Companion part III*, 1529.

58 I follow here Brian Harrison, 'Women's Suffrage at Westminster 1868–1928', in Bentley and Stevenson (eds.), *High and Low Politics*, 80–122, and the same author's *Separate Spheres; the opposition to women's suffrage in Britain* (1978). For the WSPU see Andrew Rosen, *Rise Up Women!* (1974).

59 C. P. Scott's diary, 2 February 1911, in Trevor Wilson (ed.), *The Political Diaries of C. P. Scott 1911–28* (1970), 36–7.

60 G. R. Searle, 'The Edwardian Liberal Party and Business', *English Historical Review*, XCVIII (1983), 28–60.

61 See Michael Rush, 'The M.P.s' in Walkland (ed.), *The House of Commons in the Twentieth Century*, 99–100, 118. Other statistics in Searle, *op. cit.*, W. L. Guttsman, *The British Political Elite* (1965), 104–5, and J. A. Thomas, *The House of Commons 1906–11* (Cardiff, 1958).

62 Riddell's diary, n.d. (August 1911), *More Pages*, 22.

63 For the history of the political press in the period, see Stephen E. Koss, *The Rise and Fall of the Political Press in Britain* (2 vols., 1981–4).

64 Riddell's diary. n.d. (October 1908), *ibid.*, 1.

65 Riddell's diary, early November 1911, *ibid.*, 26.

66 Esher to Fisher, 15 October 1907, *Journals and Letters*, ii, 252. For Fowler see FitzRoy's diary, 13 February 1909, *Memoirs*, i, 374; cf. Sir Alfred Pease, *Elections and Recollections* (1932).

67 Ponsonby's diary, 16 April 1906, in Ellins, thesis, 350; Gladstone to Campbell-Bannerman, 21 January 1906, in José Harris and Cameron Hazlehurst, 'Campbell-Bannerman as Prime Minister', *History*, 55 (1970), 375. Cf. H. V. Emy, *Liberals, Radicals and Social Politics*, 184–8.

68 Scawen Blunt's diary, 31 March 1906, in Wilfred Scawen Blunt, *My Diaries: being a personal narrative of events 1888–1914* (2 vols., 1919–20, one-volume edition, 1932), 548. Asquith to Gladstone, 22 October 1905, Ellins, thesis, 339.

69 Balfour to Lansdowne, 13 April 1906, quoted in Roy Jenkins, *Mr. Balfour's Poodle* (1954), 40.

70 Metternich to Bülow, 13 November 1905, quoted in Kennedy, *Antagonism*, 282; Robbins, *Grey*, 145–9.

71 Esher to Maurice Brett and Duchess of Sutherland, 4 and 7 September 1906, *Journals and Letters*, ii, 180, 183.

72 For discussion of this background see Bruce K. Murray, *The People's Budget 1909–10: Lloyd George and Liberal politics* (Oxford, 1980), 1–51, and H. V. Emy, 'The Impact of Financial Policy on English Party Politics before 1914', *Historical Journal*, 15 (1972), 103–32.

73 Murray, *op. cit.*, 310.

74 Riddell's diary, 24 November 1908, *More Pages*, 10.

75 Grey to Margot Asquith, 5 November 1909, in *The Autobiography of Margot Asquith* (2 vols., 1920), ii, 124.

76 Memo., 17 August 1910, quoted in Peter Rowland, *The Last Liberal Governments* (2 vols., 1968–71), i, 308–9.

77 Ross McKibbin, 'James Ramsay MacDonald and the Problem of the Independence of the Labour Party 1910–14', *Journal of Modern History*, 42 (1970), 216–35.

78 Churchill to Morley, 23 December 1909, *Churchill*, ii, *Companion part III*, 928.

79 Derby's diary, 18 September 1865, in Vincent (ed.), *Disraeli, Derby and the Conservative Party*, 236. For the general phenomenon, see Henry Pelling's essay on 'The Working Class and the Origins of the Welfare State' in his *Popular Politics*, 1–19.

80 Riddell's diary, 17 February 1912, *More Pages*, 38–9; cf. Roy Gregory, *The Miners in British Politics* (Oxford, 1968), *passim*.

81 Churchill to Lloyd George, 21 August 1912, *Churchill*, ii, *Companion part III*, 1636.

82 Further details in Martin Pugh, *Electoral Reform in War and Peace 1906–18* (1978), 36–43.

83 Pease at First Reading, 17 June 1912, *Hansard*, XXXIX, 1326, 1341.

84 John Grigg, *Lloyd George: the people's champion* (1973), reviews the Marconi affair. For the land campaign see H. V. Emy, 'The Land Campaign: Lloyd George as a social reformer 1909–14', in A. J. P. Taylor (ed.), *Lloyd George: twelve essays* (1971), 35–70.

85 Riddell's diary, 9 November 1912, *More Pages*, 98.

86 Amery to Neville Chamberlain, 25 July 1914, in John Barnes and David Nicholson (eds.), *The Leo Amery Diaries* (1980), i, 101.

87 The theme has its origins in George Dangerfield, *The Strange Death of Liberal England* (1936), and has recently been restated, from an Irish point of view, in Patricia Jalland, *The Liberals and Ireland* (Brighton,

1980). For Asquith's failing nerve on the subject see his correspondence with his confidante Venetia Stanley – now printed in Michael and Eleanor Brock (eds.), *H. H. Asquith: letters to Venetia Stanley* (Oxford and New York, 1982), especially 106–28.

88 Riddell's diary, 15 March 1914, *More Pages*, 204.
89 Samuel to his mother, 26 July 1914, Samuel MSS, House of Lords Record Office, A/156/466.
90 See Michael Bentley, *The Liberal Mind 1914–29* (Cambridge, 1977), 9–45.
91 *The Autobiography of Margot Asquith*, ii, 244.

Bibliography

Research theses

This list contains only titles referred to in the notes. All the dissertations are doctoral studies unless otherwise indicated.

Amey, P. M., 'The Nature of the Concern with the Empire of Parliament and Some Leading Journals during Palmerston's Second Ministry' (M.Phil., London, 1971).

Bailey, V., 'The Dangerous Classes: social order and popular disturbance in Victorian England, 1867–1900' (Warwick, 1975).

Barnett, C. A., 'Fears of Revolution: "finality" and the reopening of the question of parliamentary reform in England, 1832–67' (Oxford, 1982).

Brooks, D. R., 'Gladstone's Fourth Ministry, 1892–4: policies and personalities' (Cambridge, 1978).

Buchanan, R. A., 'Trade Unions and Public Opinion, 1850–75' (Cambridge, 1957).

Cameron, R. H., 'Lord Melbourne's Second Administration and the Opposition, 1837–41' (London, 1970).

Chadwick, Mary E. J., 'The Electoral System as Set Up by the Third Reform Act' (London, 1978).

Chamberlain, Muriel E., 'The Character of the Foreign Policy of the Earl of Aberdeen, 1841–6' (Oxford, 1961).

Close, D. H., 'The General Elections of 1835 and 1837 in England and Wales' (Oxford, 1967).

Cunningham, H. St. C., 'British Public Opinion, 1877–8' (Sussex, 1979).

Custance, R. D. H., 'The Political Career of William Lamb, second Viscount Melbourne, to 1841' (Oxford, 1977).

Davis, P. G., 'The Role of the Liberal Unionist Party in British Politics, 1886–95' (London, 1975).

Dreyer, F. R., 'The Russell Administration, 1846–52' (St Andrews, 1962).

Dunne, T. J., 'Ireland, England and Empire, 1868–86: the ideologies of British political leadership' (Cambridge, 1976).

Dwyer, F. J., 'The Rise of Richard Assheton Cross and His Work at the Home Office, 1868–80' (B.Litt., Oxford, 1969).

Ellins, R., 'Aspects of the New Liberalism, 1895–1914' (Sheffield, 1980).

Eyck, U. F. J., 'The Political Influence of the Prince Consort' (B.Litt., Oxford, 1958).

Fisher, D. R., 'The Opposition to Sir Robert Peel in the Conservative Party, 1841–6' (Cambridge, 1970).

Fraser, P., 'The Conduct of Public Business in the House of Commons, 1812–27' (London, 1957).

Gross, I., 'Commons and Empire, 1833–41 . . .' (Oxford, 1975).

Harvey, A. D., 'The Grenville Party, 1801–26' (Cambridge, 1972).

Hawkins, A. B., 'British Parliamentary Party Politics, 1855–9' (London, 1979).

Johnson, Nancy E., 'The Role of the Cabinet in the Making of Foreign Policy, 1885–95, with Special Reference to Lord Salisbury's Second Ministry' (Oxford, 1971).

Kirkpatrick, R. L., 'British Imperial Policy, 1874–80' (Oxford, 1953).

Mullen, R. F., 'The House of Lords and the Repeal of the Corn Laws' (Oxford, 1974).

Newbould, I. D. C., 'The Politics of the Cabinets of Grey and Melbourne and Ministerial Relations with the House of Commons, 1830–41' (Manchester, 1971).

Odurkere, J. N., 'The British General Elections of 1830 and 1831' (B.Litt. Oxford, 1977).

Powell, D., 'The Liberal Party and Labour, 1886–1906' (Oxford, 1982).

Prochaska, Alice, 'Westminster Radicalism, 1807–32' (Oxford, 1975).

Simes, D. G. S., 'The Ultra-Tories in British Politics, 1824–34' (Oxford, 1975).

Springhall, J. O., 'Youth and Empire: a study of the propaganda of imperialism to the young in Edwardian Britain' (Sussex, 1968).

Sumner, L. V., 'The General Election of 1818' (Manchester, 1969).

Sweeney, J. M., 'The House of Lords in British Politics, 1830–41' (Oxford, 1973).

Wasson, E. A., 'The Young Whigs: Lords Althorp, Milton and Tavistock and the Whig party, 1809–30' (Cambridge, 1976).

Primary sources

These titles are restricted to those I have found most directly helpful. I have included biographies of the Life and Letters kind if they print useful contemporary material.

Aspinall, A. (ed.), *The Letters of King George IV* (3 vols., Cambridge, 1938).

Aspinall, A. (ed.), *The Correspondence of Charles Arbuthnot* (Royal Historical Society, Camden series, 3s, LXV, 1941).

Aspinall, A. (ed.), *Three Early Nineteenth Century Diaries* (1952).

Aspinall, A. and Smith, E. A. (eds.), *English Historical Documents*, XI (1959).

Asquith, Margot, *The Autobiography of Margot Asquith* (2 vols., 1920).

Bagenal, P. H., *The Life of Ralph Bernal Osborne M. P.* (private circulation, 1884).

Bahlman, Dudley W. R. (ed.), *The Diaries of Edward Walter Hamilton* (2 vols., Oxford, 1972).

Balfour, Lady Frances, *Ne Obliviscaris* (2 vols., n.d.).

Bamford, F. and Wellington, Duke of (eds.), *The Journal of Mrs. Arbuthnot* (2 vols., 1950).

Barnes, J. and Nicholson, D. (eds.), *The Leo Amery Diaries* (vol. i., 1980).

Beach, Lady Victoria Hicks, *Life of Sir Michael Hicks Beach* (2 vols., 1932).

Blunt, Wilfrid Scawen, *My Diaries: being a personal narrative of events 1888–1914* (2 vols., 1919–20).

Bourne, Kenneth (ed.), *The Letters of the third Viscount Palmerston to Laurence and Elizabeth Sulivan 1814–63* (Royal Historical Society, Camden series, 4s, XXIII, 1979).

Brett, Maurice V. (ed.), *Journal and Letters of Reginald Viscount Esher* (4 vols., 1934–8).

Bridges, J. A., *Reminiscences of a Country Politician* (1906).

Brock, Michael and Eleanor (eds.), *Asquith: letters to Venetia Stanley* (Oxford and New York, 1982).

Broughton, Lord, *Recollections of a Long Life* (6 vols., 1909–11).

Bruce, H. A., *Letters of the Rt. Hon. Henry Austin Bruce G. C. B., Lord Aberdare of Duffryn* (private circulation, 2 vols., Oxford, 1902).

Buckingham and Chandos, Duke of, *Memoirs of the Court of George IV* (2 vols., 1859).

Bulwer, Sir Henry and Ashley, Hon. Evelyn, *The Life of Henry John Temple, Viscount Palmerston, with selections from his diaries and correspondence* (3 vols., 1870–74).

Cavendish, F. W. H., *Society, Politics and Diplomacy 1820–64: passages from the journal of F. W. H. Cavendish* (1913).

Cecil, Lady Gwendolyn, *Life of Robert Marquess of Salisbury by his daughter* (4 vols., 1921–32).

Childers, Lt Col. Spencer, *The Life and Correspondence of the Right Hon. Hugh C. E. Childers* (2 vols., 1901).

Colchester, Lord (ed.), *The Diary and Correspondence of Charles Abbot, Lord Colchester* (3 vols., 1861).

Colchester, Lord (ed.), *Lord Ellenborough's Diary 1828–30* (2 vols., 1881).

Collier, Hon. E. C. F. (ed.), *A Victorian Diarist: later extracts from the journals of Mary, Lady Monkswell 1895–1909* (1946).

Cooke, A. B. and Vincent, J. R. (eds.), *Lord Carlingford's Journal: reflections of a cabinet minister, 1885* (Oxford, 1971).

Cowper, Lady, *Earl Cowper: a memoir* (private circulation, 1913).

David, Edward (ed.), *Inside Asquith's Cabinet: from the diaries of Sir Charles Hobhouse* (1977).

Disraeli, Benjamin, *Lord George Bentinck* (1852).

Douglas, George, eighth Duke of Argyll, *Autobiography and Memoirs* (ed. Duchess of Argyll, 2 vols., 1906).

Douglas, Sir G. and Ramsay, Sir D. G. (eds.), *The Panmure Papers* (2 vols., 1908).

Drus, Ethel (ed.), *A Journal of Events during the Gladstone Ministry 1868–74 by John, First Earl of Kimberley* (Royal Historical Society, Camden Miscellany, XXI, 1958).

Fitzmaurice, Lord Edmond, *Life of Lord Granville 1815–1891* (2 vols., 1905).

FitzRoy, Sir Almeric, *Memoirs* (2 vols., 1925).

Foot, M. R. D. and Matthew, Colin (eds.), *The Gladstone Diaries* (8 vols., and cont., Oxford, 1968–94).

Garvin, J. L. and Amery, J., *The Life of Joseph Chamberlain* (6 vols., 1932–69).

Gooch. G. P. (ed.), *The Later Correspondence of Lord John Russell 1840–78* (2 vols., 1925).

Gordon, Peter (ed.), *The Red Earl: the papers of the fifth Earl Spencer 1835–1910* (vol. i, Northampton, 1981).

Grosvenor, Caroline and Beilby, Charles (eds.), *The First Lady Wharncliffe and Her Family 1779–1856* (2 vols., 1927).

Hardy, A. E. Gathorne, *Gathorne Hardy, First Earl of Cranbrook* (2 vols., 1910).

Historical Manuscripts Commission, *Bathurst*, 76 (1923).

Historical Manuscripts Commission, *Dropmore*, 10 (1927).

Historical Manuscripts Commission, *The Prime Ministers' Papers (2): W. E. Gladstone* (ed. J. Brooke and M. Sorenson, 1971).

Historical Manuscripts Commission, *Wellington: political correspondence* (1975).

Holland, Bernard, *The Life of Spencer Compton Eighth Duke of Devonshire* (2 vols., 1911).

Hutchinson, H. G. (ed.), *Private Diaries of the Rt. Hon. Sir Algernon West G. C. B.* (1922).

Ilchester, Earl of (ed.), *Elizabeth Lady Holland to her Son 1821–45* (1946).

Jennings, Louis J. (ed.), *The Correspondence and Diaries of the late Rt. Hon. John Wilson Croker* (3 vols., 1884).

Kriegel, Abraham D. (ed.), *The Holland House Diaries 1831–40* (Boston, Mass., 1977).

Lang, Andrew, *Life, Letters and Diaries of Sir Stafford Northcote, First Earl of Iddesleigh* (Edinburgh and London, 1891).

Le Marchant, Sir Denis, *Memoir of John Charles Viscount Althorp, Third Earl Spencer* (1876).

Lewis, Rev. Sir. G. F. (ed.), *Letters of the Right Hon. Sir George Cornewall Lewis, Bart., to various friends* (1870).

Londonderry, Marchioness of (ed.), *Letters from Benjamin Disraeli to Frances Anne Marchioness of Londonderry 1837–61* (1938).

Mackail, J. W. and Wyndham, Guy, *Life and Letters of George Wyndham* (2 vols., 1924).

Mackenzie, Norman (ed.), *The Letters of Sidney and Beatrice Webb* (3 vols., Cambridge and London, 1978).

Mallet, Charles, *Herbert Gladstone: a memoir* (1932).

Mallock, W. H., and Ramsden, Lady Gwendolen (eds.), *Letters, Remains and Memoirs of E. A. Seymour, Twelfth Duke of Somerset* (1893).

Malmesbury, Earl of, *Memoirs of an ex-Minister* (2 vols., 1884).

Marindin, G. E. (ed.), *The Letters of Frederic Lord Blachford* (1896).

Martineau, John, *Henry Pelham, Fifth Duke of Newcastle* (1898).

Mather, F. C. (ed.), *Chartism and Society: an anthology of documents* (London and New York, 1980).

Maxwell, Sir Herbert (ed.), *The Creevey Papers: a selection from the letters and diaries of the late Thomas Creevey M.P.* (2 vols., 1903).

Maxwell, Sir Herbert, *Life and Letters of George William Frederick, Fourth Earl of Clarendon* (2 vols., 1913).

Melville, Lewis (ed.), *The Huskisson Papers* (1931).

Monson, Lord and Gower, G. Leveson (eds.), *Memoirs of George Elers* (1903).

Monypenny, W. F. and Buckle, G. E., *The Life of Benjamin Disraeli, Earl of Beaconsfield* (6 vols., 1929).

Parker, C. S., *Sir Robert Peel* (3 vols., 1899).

Pellew, George, *The Life and Correspondence of the Right Honble. Henry Addington, First Viscount Sidmouth* (3 vols., 1847).

Ponsonby, Arthur, *Henry Ponsonby: his life from his letters* (1943).

Ramm, Agatha (ed.), *The Political Correspondence of Mr. Gladstone and Lord Granville 1868–76* (Royal Historical Society, Camden Series, 3s, LXXXI–II, 2 vols., 1952).

Ramm, Agatha (ed.), *The Political Correspondence of Mr. Gladstone and Lord Granville 1876–86* (2 vols., Oxford, 1962).

Reeve, Henry (ed.), *The Greville Memoirs: a journal of the reigns of King George IV and King William IV* (3 vols., 1875).

Reeve, Henry (ed.), *A Journal of the Reign of Queen Victoria from 1837 to 1852 by the late Charles C. F. Greville* (3 vols., 1885).

Reid, Stuart J., *Life and Letters of the First Earl of Durham 1792–1840* (2 vols., 1906).

Riddell, Lord, *More Pages from My Diary* (1934).

Selborne, Roundell, first Earl, *Family and Personal Memorials* (2 vols., 1896).

Thorold, Algar L., *The Life of Henry Labouchere* (1913).

Twiss, Horace, *The Public and Private Life of Lord Chancellor Eldon, with selections from his correspondence* (3 vols., 1844).

Vincent, J. R. (ed.), *Disraeli, Derby and the Conservative Party: the political journals of Lord Stanley 1849–69* (Hassocks, 1978).

Vincent, J. R. (ed.), *The Later Derby Diaries: home rule, Liberal Unionism, and aristocratic life in late Victorian England* (Bristol, 1981).

Wellington, Duke of (ed.), *Despatches, Correspondence and Memoranda of Field Marshal Arthur Duke of Wellington, K. G.* (8 vols., 1867–80).

Whibley, Charles, *Lord John Manners and his Friends* (2 vols., Edinburgh, 1925).

White, William, *The Inner Life of the House of Commons* (1898).

Wilson, Trevor (ed.), *The Political Diaries of C. P. Scott 1911–28* (1970).

Wolf, Lucien, *Life of the First Marquess of Ripon* (2 vols., 1921).

Yonge, C. D., *The Life and Administration of Robert Banks, Second Earl of Liverpool* (3 vols., 1868).

Zetland, Marquess of (ed.), *The Letters of Disraeli to Lady Bradford and Lady Chesterfield* (2 vols., 1929).

FURTHER READING

The notes provide the best indication of the sources used in preparing this book. These following paragraphs mention a few secondary works relevant to each chapter and concentrate on material likely to be available to the general reader or sixth-former using a library. Research articles are not included unless they have become central to the historical argument. For the second edition I have included some recently-published material, not all of which is considered in the text.

General

Much of the flavour of the environment within which politicians worked can be gleaned from such books as F. M. L. Thompson, *English Landed Society in the Nineteenth Century* (1963) and the same author's *The Rise of Respectable Society: a social history of Victorian Britain 1830–1900* (1988); Mark Girouard, *The Victorian Country House* (Oxford, 1970); and Donald Olsen, *The Growth of Victorian London* (1979). The economic structures to which they responded have been effectively surveyed in R. Floud and D. McCloskey, *The Economic History of Great Britain since 1700* (2 vols., Cambridge, 1981). How far those dynamics influenced the growth of empire remains controversial: see, for example, E. J. Hobsbawm, *Industry and Empire* (1968) and compare D. K. Fieldhouse, *Economics and Empire 1830–1914* (1973). More recently historians have become exercised by the concept of 'gentlemanly capitalism' as a key to imperial development, thanks to P. J. Cain and A. G. Hopkins, *British Imperialism* (2 vols., 1993). For an excellent review of some of the issues, see Patrick O'Brien, 'A Cost-Benefit analysis of British Imperialism', *Past and Present* (1988). For foreign policy through the period one can follow the story in the company of D. E. D. Beales, *From Castlereagh to Gladstone 1815–85* (1969) and Kenneth Bourne, *The Foreign Policy of Victorian England 1830–1902* (Oxford, 1970). A particularly helpful analysis of the Gladstone–Disraeli period from this point of view is Marvin Swartz, *The Politics of British Foreign Policy in the era of Disraeli and Gladstone* (Oxford, 1985). The internal elements of British politics have been observed in this book to have two key features in the churches and the press as central 'interests'. For the first, see G. I. T. Machin, *Politics and the Churches in Great Britain 1832–68* (Oxford 1967) and G. Kitson Clark, *Churchmen and the Condition of England 1832–85* (1973). Edward Norman, *Church and Society in England 1770–1970 (1973)* has a prose which makes up for everything else, while a recent study of the evangelical side of British (and other) Protestantism is contained in D. W. Bebbington, M. A. Noll and G. A. Rawlyk (eds.), *Evangelicalism: comparative studies of popular protestantism in North America, the British Isles and beyond 1700–1900* (Oxford, 1994) and David Bebbington's *The Nonconformist Conscience: chapel and politics 1879–1914* (1982). Those going deeper should go at once to an important analysis by Boyd Hilton, *The Age of Atonement: the influence of evangelicalism on social and economic thought 1795–1865* (Oxford, 1988). On the press, a number of studies have underlined the importance of an understudied area. The tragedy of Alan Lee's premature death is recalled by the excellence of his *The Origins of the Popular Press 1855–1914* (1976); likewise the historical world has cause to be grateful that Stephen Koss was given time enough to complete his important two volumes on *The Rise and Fall of the Political Press in Britain* (2 vols., 1981–4). A third constituent of the political structure – that of class – has attracted more work than its frequently reductive and unhelpful result recommends. But all modern accounts of 'democracy' (including this one) owe something to E. P. Thompson's *The Making of the English Working Class* (1963) – if only their disagreement with it. And there have been some very worthwhile case-studies of particular cities or communities such as R. Q. Gray's study of the artisanate in Edinburgh (*The Labour Aristocracy in Victorian Edinburgh* [Oxford, 1976]). Two first-rate examples of thoughtful essays in this part of the subject matter appear in collections by Gareth Stedman Jones, *Languages of Class* (1983) and Ross McKibbin, *The Ideologies of Class* (1990). Quite how short-sighted it is to forget the middle class and the aristocracy is underlined by F. M. L. Thompson's work (see above) and by David Cannadine's racy volumes on *The Decline and Fall of the British Aristocracy* (New Haven, 1990) and *Aspects of Aristocracy* (New Haven, 1994). Surveying the field in a succinct way we now also have Alistair Reid, *Social Classes and Social Relations in Britain 1850–1914* (1992). Constitutional history, meanwhile, has fallen from fashion; but that is no reason for students to know nothing about some of the key moments in convention and legislation affecting how Britain has been ruled. Walter Bagehot's *The English Constitution* (1867) should be required reading as a cultural document at the very least. H. J. Hanham has collected some of the more basic documents in *The Nineteenth Century Constitution* (Cambridge, 1969) and G. H. L. Le May offers interesting glosses in his *The Victorian Constitution* (1969). A constitutional classic of 1915 – Charles Seymour's *Electoral Reform in England and Wales* – has been reprinted with an introduction by Michael Hurst (Newton Abbot, 1970).

1. The Transformation of Party

Interest in the period is reviving after a period of neglect but much of the work remains at the level of the research thesis and learned journal. On the political side, analyses of electoral behaviour have become important: see especially Frank O'Gorman, *Voters, Patrons and Parties* (Oxford, 1989) and John A. Phillips, *Electoral Behaviour in Unreformed England* (Princeton, 1982). On the economic dynamics, A. J. B. Hilton, *Cash, Corn, Commerce: the economic policies of the Tory governments 1815–30* (Oxford, 1977) remains crucial. Less crucial, at least so far as its period is concerned, is J. E. Cookson, *Lord Liverpool's Administration: the crucial years, 1815–22* (1975) which should now be supplemented by Professor Gash's reconsideration of *Lord Liverpool* (1984). An older book by Austin Mitchell, *The Whigs in Opposition, 1815–30* (Oxford, 1967) reproduces helpful primary material, though the Whigs have been brought under a rather different light more recently (see next section). The later chapters of John Cannon's *Parliamentary Reform 1642–1832* (Cambridge, 1973) bring an important theme through from the eighteenth century and place the post-war period in a cool and sensible perspective. Frank O'Gorman's thesis on *The Emergence of the Two-Party System* (1982) takes a different direction from the one observed in this chapter and should be read for a contrasting view. Individual politicians and events have attracted a number of studies which throw light on the period as a whole. James J. Sack on *The Grenvillites* (Illinois, 1979) presents a case in point, as does Donald Read's atmospheric account of *Peterloo: the 'massacre' and its background* (Manchester 1958). On the individuals, see John Derry's numerous studies, especially *Castlereagh* (1976) and *Earl Grey* (Oxford, 1992) or perhaps the lives of *Canning* by J. V. Rollo (1965) and Wendy Hinde (1973). Readers who have access to the Camden Series will find that Arthur Aspinall's *The Formation of Canning's Ministry* (1937) contains a mine of information from the archives.

2. Renewal and Consolidation

No one moves far in this period without encountering Professor Norman Gash; his Ford Lectures, *Reaction and Reconstruction in English Politics 1832–52* (Oxford, 1965) offer a wonderful starting point for those new to the period. Two further books by the same author, his biography of *Sir Robert Peel* (2 vols., 1961, 1972) and *Politics in the Age of Peel* (1953, revised 1966) then come into view. John Prest provides much perspective from the Whig-Liberal viewpoint: see his life of *Lord John Russell* (1972) but also *Politics in the Age of Cobden* (1977) which gives an alternative picture of the Anti-Corn Law League to that offered in Norman McCord's earlier study of it (1958) and contains important remarks on the tactics of registration. D. C. Moore's analysis of *The Politics of Deference* (Hassocks, 1976) has had a difficult time at the hands of critics through the 1980s but should be seen for one reading of what the Reformers of 1832 thought they were doing. Contrast in particular Jonathan Parry, *The Rise and Fall of Liberal Government in Victorian Britain* (New Haven, 1993). A different style of argument will be found among a clutch of studies that deal with

Liberal ideology and religion. See in particular Richard Brent, *Liberal Angli-can Politics* (Oxford, 1987) and Peter Mandler, *Aristocratic Government in the Age of Reform* (Oxford, 1990). Boyd Hilton's account of evangelicalism (see GENERAL) has much to say about these years. Closer to the ground, students will find Michael Brock on *The Great Reform Act* (1973) a helpful narrative, while Patricia Hollis (ed.), *Pressure from Without in Early-Victor-ian England* (1974) offers a number of essays which bear on this chapter's themes and the pressure groups that lay behind much popular politics – for which generally see J. T. Ward (ed.), *Popular Movements 1830–50* (1970). William Thomas's elegant essays on *The Philosophic Radicals* (Oxford, 1979) introduce a not-at-all popular group who exercised considerable influence. Economic protection and the agricultural sector receive attention in Robert Stewart, *The Politics of Protection* (Cambridge, 1971) and Travis L. Crosby, *English Farmers and the Politics of Protection* (Hassocks, 1977). Biography enlivens the latter part of the period particularly. See Monica Charlot, *Victoria: the young Queen* (Oxford, 1991), Philip Ziegler on *Melbourne* (1976), Muriel Chamberlain on *Lord Aberdeen* (1983) or the first volume of Kenneth Bourne's excellent study of *Palmerston* (1982).

3. The Mechanics of Stability

'A black hole', I wrote in the first edition and so, to a degree, it remains. The work of Professor Conacher remains pivotal: *The Peelites and the Party System 1846–52* (Newton Abbot, 1972) and *The Aberdeen Coalition* (Cambridge, 1968). But the parliamentary aspect has been sharpened in John Vincent's paper, 'The Parliamentary Dimension of the Crimean War', *Transactions of the Royal Historical Society*, 31 (1981) and by Angus Hawkins's more general analysis of *Parliament, Party and the Art of Politics in Britain 1855–9* (1987). On the war itself the best source is still Olive Anderson, *A Liberal State at War* (1967). Gladstone is best approached through his diary which we now have for the whole of his parliamentary life – see M. R. D. Foot and H. C. G. Matthew (eds.), *The Gladstone Diaries* (14 vols., Oxford, 1968–94) – though the non-specialist will find these entries quite as daunting in their allusive character as they are oppressive in their bulk. Richard Shannon made good use of them for the first volume of his biography of *Gladstone* (1982) which takes the story to 1865. Palmerston has come into better focus through the 1850s and 60s in E. D. Steele's account of *Palmerston and Liberalism* (Cambridge, 1991) and his view receives some corroboration in Jonathan Parry's overview (see previous section). The foreign policy does not yet have the treatment it merits. It is worth mentioning, however, a recent more general book on foreign policy by an expert: C. J. Bartlett, *Defence and Diplomacy: Britain and the Great Powers 1815–1914* (1987). For one useful study of a particular problem, see Keith Sandiford, *Great Britain and the Schleswig-Holstein Question 1848–64* (Toronto and Buffalo, 1975).

4. Occupying the Centre

F. B. Smith explains *The Making of the Second Reform Act* (Cambridge, 1966) by introducing readers to the context of reform; but those who need to know the ins and outs cannot avoid Maurice Cowling, *1867: Disraeli, Gladstone and Revolution* (Cambridge, 1967) – a very difficult narrative study. The post-reform period is best approached through H. J. Hanham's survey of *Elections and Party Management in the Age of Gladstone and Disraeli* (1959, Hassocks, 1978) which has never been superseded, though there is new and interesting material on the Conservative side in Richard Shannon, *The Age of Disraeli* (1992) and in E. J. Feuchtwanger's older book, *Disraeli, Democracy and the Tory Party* (Oxford, 1968). The politics of the first Gladstone government can be explored in the diary of its prime minister; but James Winter's life of *Robert Lowe* is valuable for this period and an indispensable study for the later years of difficulty is J. P. Parry, *Democracy and Religion: Gladstone and the Liberal Party 1867–75* (Cambridge, 1986). On the Conservative side, see Lord Blake's beautifully controlled account of *Disraeli* (1966), which can now be supplemented by the ever-stimulating John Vincent's short and pungent study (1990). In this period a primary source such as the Derby diaries (see primary sources) becomes not only critical reading but often also delightful in itself, crammed with incident, character, prejudice and occasional insight. Paul Smith's edition of Cranborne's political journalism, *Lord Salisbury on Politics* (Cambridge, 1972) is very helpful on the 1860s though his *Disraelian Democracy and Social Reform* (1967) has been updated to some extent in Shannon's study. Labour history supplies an important perspective on these years: see Royden Harrison, *Before the Socialists* (1965) for an impressive collection of studies and, for the other side of the coin, W. D. Rubinstein, *Men of Property: the very wealthy in Britain since the industrial revolution* (1981). The undertow of pressure-group politics also becomes strong again in the 1870s; it can be sensed in D. A. Hamer's treatment of *The Politics of Electoral Pressure* (Hassocks, 1977) and in Brian Harrison's absorbing study of the temperance interest; see his *Drink and the Victorians*. Foreign affairs also come to centre-stage in this decade. These can be followed in Marvin Swartz's analysis listed above and in the early chapters of Paul Kennedy's massive study, *The Rise of the Anglo-German Antagonism 1860–1914* (1980). Richard Shannon's *Gladstone and the Bulgarian Agitation* (Hassocks, 1975) is far more wide-ranging than its title implies.

5. Conservative Ascendancy

Imperialism, if we define it widely enough, forms the cornerstone of much opinion and party activity in these years. Beginners could enter the complex historiography by way of C. C. Eldridge, *Victorian Imperialism* (1978) which prints helpful booklists at the end of each chapter and then perhaps proceed to Richard Shannon's depiction of the late-nineteenth century in *The Crisis of Imperialism 1865–1915* (1974). But any serious student will need to go to the two recent volumes by Cain and Hopkins on *British Imperialism* (see GENERAL) for a recent and influential analysis. C. J. Lowe, *The Reluctant Imperialists* (2 vols., 1967) devotes one of its volumes to significant documents and one to commentary; it may be used alongside a reference-work such as Michael Hurst, *Key Treaties for the Great Powers* (2 vols., Newton Abbot, 1972). For a more direct study of imperialist politics within the party system, H. C. G. Matthew, *The Liberal Imperialists* (Oxford 1973) remains very important. Gladstone can be followed through the diary (or the introductions both printed with them and separately collected: so far we have Colin Matthew, *Gladstone 1809–74* [Oxford, 1991]) and through the printed correspondence, included in the printed diaries, covering the first government; but the four volumes of *Gladstone–Granville Correspondence* (ed. Agatha Ramm) become very valuable also in this period (see primary sources). Students of high-politics will find much relevant material in monographs such as Andrew Jones, *The Politics of Reform, 1884* (Cambridge, 1972) which repays the effort it requires; and A. B. Cooke and John Vincent, *The Governing Passion* (Brighton, 1974), which says more in its first seven chapters than most of us manage to say in a lifetime. Michael Barker, *Gladstone and Radicalism* (Brighton, 1975) and T. A. Jenkins, *Gladstone, Whiggery and the Liberal Party 1874–86* (Oxford, 1988) say the opposite and should be read for the other side of the case. Michael Hurst's older study of *Joseph Chamberlain and Liberal Reunion* (1967) should now be supplemented by biographies of *Joseph Chamberlain* by Richard Jay (Oxford, 1981) and Peter Marsh (New Haven, 1994). There are insights into the radical wing of Liberal politics in E. F. Biagini and A. J. Reid (eds.), *Currents of Radicalism: popular radicalism, organised labour and party politics in Britain, 1850–1914* (Cambridge, 1991). The Liberals' decade of disaster in the 1890s is narrated in a straightforward way by Peter Stansky, *Ambitions and Strategies: the struggle for the leadership of the Liberal party in the 1890s* (Oxford, 1964), though a new primary printed account of *The Destruction of Lord Rosebery: from the diary of Sir Edward Walter Hamilton 1894 5* (ed. David Brooks) demands attention, as does the third and concluding volume of Hamilton's diary generally (ed. Dudley W. R. Bahlman, [Hull, 1993]). On the Conservative side, Peter Marsh chronicles the Salisbury governments in his *The Discipline of Popular Government* (Hassocks, 1978). Salisbury himself remains elusive, though several studies are currently in train – one of them by the present writer. Foreign policy can be followed in a detailed chronology such as that supplied by J. A. S. Grenville, *Lord Salisbury and Foreign Policy* (1964) and Paul Kennedy's survey mentioned above. Robert Taylor has written a political biography which fleshes out the picture a little; but the best thing on Salisbury to date is a collection of essays edited by Lord Blake and Hugh Cecil, *Lord Salisbury: the man and his policies* (Basingstoke, 1987) which should be read in tandem with Paul Smith's edition of Salisbury's political thought. Work on the social dimension of Tory politics repays attention – Martin Pugh, for example, on *The Tories and the People 1880–1935* (Oxford, 1985), and Matthew Fforde, *Conservatism and Collectivism 1886–1914* (Edinburgh, 1890).

6. Breaking the Mould?

Few periods of British political history have received so intense a scrutiny in recent years and this brief note barely scratches the surface. Liberalism has been given an early morning or late evening light according to taste. The former will be detected in some studies from the 1970s – H. V. Emy, *Liberals, Radicals and Social Politics* (Cambridge, 1973), Michael Freeden, *The New Liberalism* (Oxford, 1977) and Peter Clarke's stimulating studies of Edwardian 'progressivism': *Lancashire and the New Liberalism* (Cambridge, 1971) and *Liberals and Social Democrats* (Cambridge, 1978). Less optimistic prognoses for the Liberal party are offered in Paul Thompson, *Socialists, Liberals and Labour* (1967), Henry Pelling, *Popular Politics and Society in Late-Victorian Britain* (1968) and the same author's *Social Geography of British Elections 1885–1910* (1967). Ross McKibbin's early work, especially *The Evolution of the Labour Party 1910–24* (Oxford, 1974) reinforced this trend, but subsequent studies from both sides of the party spectrum have underlined the complication of the processes involved. Two of these are outstanding: David Howell, *British Workers and the Independent Labour Party* (Manchester, 1983) and Duncan Tanner, *Political Change and the Labour party 1900–1918* (Cambridge, 1990). A persistent theme in Tory politics through the period is that of tariff reform which is reconsidered in a penetrating monograph by Alan Sykes, *Tariff Reform in British Politics 1903–13* (Oxford, 1979), which extends the purview of Alfred Gollin's delightful accounts of the complications of 1903 in his *Balfour's Burden* (1965). The approach of the First World War brings Paul Kennedy's examination of Anglo-German antagonism to its conclusion and reminds one of the importance of the Foreign Office, the subject of Zara Steiner (*The Foreign Office and Foreign Policy* [Cambridge, 1969]; *Britain and the Origins of the First World War* [1977]). The world depicted in George Dangerfield's imaginative but fanciful reconstruction of *The Strange Death of Liberal England* (1936) has received attention from more modern historians such as Andrew Rosen, *Rise Up Women!* for the suffragettes, Bob Holton, *British Syndicalism 1900–1914* for the Great Unrest and Patricia Jalland in her strident view of *The Liberals and Ireland* (Brighton, 1980). Another perspective across party lines is contained in G. R. Searle's account of *Corruption in British Politics* (Oxford, 1987). A vast array of biography supplies detail for all these themes: John Wilson on *C-B: a life of Sir Henry Campbell-Bannerman* (1973), Stephen Koss on *Asquith* (1976), Keith Robbins on *Sir Edward Grey* (1971), Ruddock Mackay on *Balfour* (Oxford, 1985), John Campbell on *F. E. Smith, First Earl of Birkenhead* (1983), John Grigg on *The Young Lloyd George* (1973), *Lloyd George: the People's*

Champion 1902–11 (1978), *Lloyd George: From Peace to War 1912–16* (1985) and Bernard Wasserstein on *Herbert Samuel* (Oxford, 1992) are only some of the more recent ones. Primary sources are rich and often compelling. Sir Charles Hobhouse's diaries, edited by Edward David (*Inside Asquith's Cabinet* [1977]) give some intriguing glimpses of high politics on the eve of war; but for these and more magical moments besides, go also to Michael and Eleanor Brock (eds.), *Asquith: letters to Venetia Stanley* (Oxford, 1982).

Index